Exporting Democracy

Exporting Democracy

THE UNITED STATES AND LATIN AMERICA

Themes and Issues

Edited by Abraham F. Lowenthal

The Johns Hopkins University Press
Baltimore and London

The Johns Hopkins University Press
701 West 40th Street
Baltimore, Maryland 21211
The Johns Hopkins Press Ltd., London

The paper used in this book meets the minimum requirements
of American National Standards for Information Sciences—
Permanence of Paper for Printed Library Materials,
ANSI Z39.48-1984.

Library of Congress Cataloging-in-Publication Data

Exporting democracy : the United States and Latin America.
Themes and issues / edited by Abraham F. Lowenthal.
    p.   cm.
  Includes bibliographical references and index.
  ISBN 0-8018-4132-1 (pbk.)
    1. Latin America—Foreign relations—United States.
2. United States—Foreign relations—Latin America.
3. United States—Foreign relations—20th century.
4. Representative government and representation—Latin
America—History—20th century. 5. Latin America—Politics
and government—20th century.
I. Lowenthal, Abraham F.
F1418.E893   1991
327.7308—dc20   90-24061
                                   CIP

Contents

Preface and Acknowledgments

FROM THE mid-1970s through the late 1980s and into the 1990s, Latin America has moved broadly from authoritarianism of various kinds toward democratic politics, also of varying types. Of all the countries in Central and South America in 1976, elected civilian governments ruled only in Costa Rica, Colombia, Venezuela, and Suriname. By the end of 1989, almost every government in Central and South America was civilian and had been elected under reasonably competitive circumstances. The direct presidential elections in December 1989 in Brazil and Chile—the first such polls since 1962 and 1970, respectively—seemed to culminate this dramatic trend. Then, in February 1990, it was carried one dramatic step further with the electoral victory of the Nicaraguan opposition in the most free and fair national election in that country's history.

Latin America's democratic opening has been uneven and fragile, and summarizing it in the aggregate may obscure as much as it reveals. Elected regimes are not necessarily democratic, for instance; much depends on the extent and the conditions of popular participation and on the protection of basic civil rights. But there can be no denying that the past dozen years have seen a considerable swing toward democratic politics in one Latin American country after another.

Under successive administrations of both political parties, the U.S. government since the mid-1970s has frequently expressed its support for Latin America's democratic transitions. Presidents Carter, Reagan, and Bush have all stated explicitly that the promotion of democracy is a central aim of U.S. policy in the Western Hemisphere. Washington has employed various instruments to push for what U.S. officials have regarded as movement toward democracy in countries as different as Chile and Nicaragua, El Salvador and Paraguay, Haiti and Panama. Although not everyone would assign equal importance to the role of U.S. policy, there is broad bipartisan agreement in Washington today that fostering democracy in Latin America—and elsewhere, for that matter—is a legitimate and significant goal of the U.S. policy and that the United States can be effective in pursuing that aim.

With such widespread agreement on the goal of promoting Latin American democracy, there have been strong pressures to step up such efforts and to expand the resources devoted to them. After a generation of strenuous internal debate in the United States on various foreign policy issues and a decade of particularly bitter divisions over Latin American policy, the idea that the United States should and can export democracy is virtually unchallenged in the Washington policy-making community of the early 1990s.

This is not the first time that democratic opening has occurred in Latin American politics or that the U.S. government has proclaimed its desire for a democratic hemisphere. In fact, U.S. support for Latin American democracy has been frequently expressed since the early nineteenth century, and especially since the time of Woodrow Wilson. Some such expressions have no doubt been merely rhetorical, and there have been notable instances when the United States has actually opposed democratic regimes and contributed to their overthrow, propped up dictators, or promoted democratization for ulterior motives. It is clear, however, that on various occasions and in several countries, long before the 1980s, the United States *has* used its influence to promote what U.S. officials sincerely conceived of as democratic politics. Yet no systematic and comparative study of past U.S. attempts to promote Latin American democracy has ever been published, and the Washington policy community seems remarkably unaware of this long history.

This volume is motivated by the collective amnesia that affects both academia and contemporary Washington regarding prior U.S. attempts to promote Latin American democracy. We believe this is the first book in any language to focus sharply and comparatively on the historic influence of the United States on Latin America's prospects for democracy. The extensive literature on Latin America's transition from authoritarian rule devotes little explicit attention to the U.S. role, or to external influence more generally. Despite the powerful influence of *dependencia* and "hegemony" as major concepts for analyzing United States–Latin American relations, the impact of the United States and of U.S. policy on Latin America's democratic prospects has not been emphasized.

Our project (involving scholars from the United States, Latin America, and the United Kingdom) seeks to help fill that gap by analyzing the sources, concepts, instruments, and impact of the recurrent impulse in the United States to export its national political values and institutions. Our methods and purposes are scholarly, but we also want to derive insights from history that may illuminate contemporary policy choices.

More specifically, we have set out to analyze *when* and *where* the United States has sought to promote Latin American democracy, *why, how,* and *with what consequences.* We have sought to assess the meaning and significance of various declared U.S. attempts to promote democracy, and to discern what motivated the U.S. interest in each case. We have specified the prevailing concepts and main instruments the United States employed, and have evaluated their effects. Where relevant, we have studied what caused the U.S. concern with democracy eventually to wane or be abandoned.

Our project has proceeded on the basis of several shared premises and approaches. We have analyzed primarily those instances in which U.S. officials took an active interest in promoting Latin American democracy, rather than repeatedly document the fact that this oft-expressed concern has frequently been ignored and even contradicted. Without denying that the indirect effects of the United States on Latin America—because of its cultural influence, its role in the world economy, and its hegemonic power—may often be more important than deliberate policies, we have concentrated mostly on purposive U.S. actions, both by governmental and nongovernmental actors. We have sought to disaggregate both "the United States" and "Latin America" by asking what groups, forces, and actors in the United States have been concerned with Latin American democracy and what significant differences have existed among U.S. government agencies and officials, and also by analyzing the variance among U.S. policies toward distinct countries. And we have understood Latin America not as a passive arena simply being acted in or upon, but rather as a region characterized by complex political struggles, in which some groups have often sought, with varying degrees of success, to mobilize U.S. involvement.

Our methodology has been self-consciously eclectic and comparative.

• Four authors—Paul Drake, Leslie Bethell, Tony Smith, and Thomas Carothers—concentrate on specific periods when U.S. efforts to promote Latin American democracy were particularly notable: from World War I to the Great Depression; the years immediately following World War II; the Alliance for Progress interlude; and the Reagan era.

• Five chapters—by Carlos Escudé, Heraldo Muñoz, Jonathan Hartlyn, Lorenzo Meyer, and Joseph Tulchin and Knut Walter—focus on countries in which the declared U.S. interest in promoting democracy has recurred several times over an extended period: Argentina, Chile, the Dominican Republic, Mexico, and Nicaragua. In each of these cases, U.S. efforts to build local democracy have been particularly notable, if not always successful.

• Elizabeth Cobbs and Paul Buchanan analyze the extent to which major U.S. interest groups—business enterprises and organized labor—have been concerned with Latin American democracy, and they evaluate the impact these groups have had, particularly by comparison with governmental efforts.

• John Sheahan corrects our emphasis on political concepts and instruments by asking what effects U.S. economic policies have had on Latin America's prospects for democracy, and whether the political impact of U.S. economic policy could somehow be made more positive.

• Laurence Whitehead and I, in separate chapters, draw conclusions about the U.S. capacity to promote Latin American democracy. Whitehead focuses on three cases in which the U.S. track record is long and the extent of U.S. involvement has been great, and shows that even in these settings the

U.S. ability to impose democracy has usually been sharply circumscribed. My own chapter summarizes the volume's contents and then comments on the implications of this history for U.S. foreign policy choices in the 1990s. By way of anticipation, let me simply say here that this book tells a cautionary tale. Past U.S. attempts to promote Latin American democracy have met with little enduring success. Although the idea that the United States knows how to export democracy is widely accepted today, the historical record strongly suggests reasons for skepticism.

On behalf of all contributors to this symposium, I wish to express our great appreciation to those who made this book possible. For the necessary financial support, we owe thanks to the World Peace Foundation and its director, Ambassador Richard J. Bloomfield; the Social Science Research Council and the American Council of Learned Societies and their Joint Committee on Latin American Studies; the Exxon Educational Foundation; the California Council for the Humanities; and the University of Southern California (USC). Ambassador Bloomfield and the World Peace Foundation provided more than financial backing, and indeed helped us conceptualize the project and convey its first results to the Washington policy community. The Joint Committee's support for a preliminary workshop, drawing in turn on support from the Ford Foundation and the Andrew W. Mellon Foundation, enabled us to plan the volume with some care.

For superb research assistance and project coordination, we are grateful to Phillip Pearson, an advanced graduate student at USC. Stephen Brager of the University of California, San Diego, and Shelly McConnell of Stanford University assisted Mr. Pearson with the rapporteurial chores. Tina Gallop of the School of International Relations at USC handled the project's logistics and finances with skill and grace.

I owe a great deal to my fellow contributors to the volume, who made the task of editing less a chore than a pleasant challenge. Special thanks are also due to a few other persons with whom I have discussed these issues at one time or another: Genaro Arriagada, Harry Barnes, Peter D. Bell, Sergio Bitar, Cole Blasier, Paul Boeker, Jorge G. Castañeda, Edwin Corr, Julio Cotler, John Crimmins, Larry Diamond, Albert Fishlow, Adam Garfinkle, Manuel Antonio Garretón, Carl Gershman, Peter Hakim, Albert O. Hirschman, Michael Hunt, Samuel P. Huntington, Terry Karl, Walter Lafeber, Bolivar Lamounier, Cynthia McClintock, Guillermo O'Donnell, Robert Packenham, Robert Pastor, Paulo Sergio Pinheiro, Steve Ropp, Sally Shelton-Colby, Paul Sigmund, Viron Vaky, Francisco Weffort, Howard Wiarda, and especially Peter Winn. Others who have contributed to my understanding of these issues include the members of the Inter-American Dialogue, and the participants in the Carter Center's 1986 conference on "Reinforcing Democracy in the Americas." Finally, I happily acknowledge the continuing help and inspiration of Jane S. Jaquette.

Part One

Themes and Issues

1 | From Good Men to Good Neighbors: 1912–1932

Paul W. Drake

FROM 1912 to 1932, the United States went through its first cycle of intervening in Latin America to promote its version of democracy.[1] Such behavior was intrinsically contradictory, since international law defines *intervention* as "dictatorial interference in the affairs of another state for the purpose of altering the actual condition of things."[2] Accordingly, the U.S. administrations of Woodrow Wilson, Warren Harding, Calvin Coolidge, and Herbert Hoover were torn between instilling democracy through intervention or behaving democratically through nonintervention. That dilemma bedeviled the rise of coercive democratization under presidents Theodore Roosevelt and William Howard Taft, its peak under Wilson, and its gradual decline under the Republicans in the 1920s, culminating in the "hands off" policy of the Good Neighbor under Franklin Roosevelt.

This chapter examines that historical cycle by surveying the Latin American episodes where the United States claimed to be actively fomenting democracy (Table 1.1). Unlike most studies, this one does not focus on U.S. intervention per se but rather on U.S. promulgation of democracy as defined by the United States. It analyzes the evolution of goals, motivations, methods, and results from administration to administration. Those beliefs and practices set precedents for later behavior.

In the opening decades of the twentieth century, the United States and Latin America went through a painful learning process about political engineering in the name of democracy. From Wilson's administration through Hoover's, the United States intensified, then recast, and finally abandoned its pursuit. The United States failed to instill democracy abroad because it proved very difficult to impose that political system through coercive and erratic external meddling. Instead, democracy normally needed to grow out of internal conditions. Those domestic factors were the main determinants

Table 1.1 The Promotion by the United States of Democracy in Latin America, 1913–1933

Year	Nonrecognition	Discouragement of Loans	Supervision or Observation of Elections	Support for Rebels	Invasion
1913	Mexico, Peru		Dominican Republic	Mexico	
1914			Dominican Republic		Mexico
1915	Haiti		Haiti		Haiti
1916	Dominican Republic		Nicaragua		Dominican Republic
1917	Costa Rica	Costa Rica	Haiti		
1918			Haiti, Panama		
1919					
1920	Mexico, Bolivia		Cuba		
1921					
1922					
1923	Honduras	Honduras			Honduras
1924			Dominican Republic		
1925	Ecuador, Nicaragua	Ecuador			
1926					Nicaragua
1927					
1928			Nicaragua		
1929					
1930	Guatemala, Bolivia, Peru, Argentina, Brazil	Nicaragua			
1931	El Salvador, Peru				
1932	Chile	Chile	Nicaragua		
1933					

of and barriers to democratic progress in Latin America in the era. The U.S. crusade was also unsuccessful because policy makers usually defined democracy as merely elections, which were a necessary but insufficient condition for a democratic system. Although some of these lessons were later forgotten in the United States, they emerged clearly in the first era of proselytizing for democracy.

Goals: Democracy, Republicanism, and Electoralism

The United States intervened in Latin America principally for strategic or economic reasons, but it also purported to be inculcating classic, liberal, representative, political democracies. In the jargon of the era, the United States was mainly trying to foster aristocratic "republics" rather than mass "democracies." In other words, it was willing to settle for limited democracies with a narrow range of participation, contestation, and pluralism. When U.S. policy makers advocated "republican" forms of rule, they had in mind constitutional, legal, orderly governments that were elected in some predictable fashion and were not blatantly authoritarian. This acceptance of elitist democracies reflected the fact that the United States itself denied the franchise to all women and many blacks throughout much of this era. Bossism and corruption permeated U.S. as well as Latin American politics. Above all, Washington believed that modest expectations for the scope of democratization comported with the level of development in Latin America.

Within that broad disposition favorable to republicanism, the U.S. government exhibited the following political preferences, in descending order: (1) a friendly democracy modeled after the U.S. system; (2) an aristocratic republic; (3) a "constitutional" government adhering to predictable legal norms and averting succession crises; (4) a "constituted" authoritarian regime able to maintain order, the less repressive, arbitrary, and corrupt the better; (5) an unstable government; (6) an unfriendly government; or (7) a truly revolutionary government, as in Mexico.

The State Department disapproved of armed rebellions of any kind—often mislabeled "revolutions"—even against dictatorships. In the eyes of Washington, virtually all governments were supposed to be legitimized through elections, preferably held honestly and prior to taking office. The United States expressed these preferences throughout Latin America but mainly in the Caribbean Basin, which was regarded as strategically sensitive.

The United States employed two main tests to determine whether a government was democratic: was it installed democratically and did it govern democratically? Policy makers found the first standard the easiest to apply. They usually operationalized it in terms of electoral ascension to office. The second, less common measure normally referred to regimes trying to perpetuate themselves illegally through postponing or rigging elections rather than to regimes infringing on civil liberties. In practice, both criteria really boiled down to an insistence on "free and fair elections."

Defining democracy as essentially balloting amounted to "electoralism," which is

> the faith (widely held by U.S. policymakers) that merely holding elections will channel political action into peaceful contests among elites and accord public legitimacy to the winners in these contests. Electoralism requires that foreign or domestic elites do some political engineering to produce the most common surface manifestations of a democratic polity—parties, electoral laws, contested campaigns, and the like. Yet this sort of tinkering, however well-intended, cannot by itself produce the consensus . . . which must underlie any enduring democracy.[3]

Within the fundamental U.S. quest for order and security, electoralism served four main purposes: pacification, legitimation, demonstration, and extrication. In many cases, convoking elections served multiple objectives simultaneously. Form was more important than substance, as many of these were mock elections, often uncontested:

1. *Pacification elections* were intended to halt or avert armed rebellions against entrenched governments. Since the United States denied the right to revolution or rebellion, authoritarian regimes could only be removed through demands for elections. These elections were designed to resolve conflicts by arbitrating a settlement between feuding factions, who often requested U.S. intervention. The State Department hoped that these electoral habits would become engrained as a way of settling disputes. If so, that would obviate the need for future interventions, which became increasingly unpopular in the United States and overseas.

2. *Legitimation elections* were held to authenticate existing or incoming governments.

3. *Demonstration elections* were convened in occupied countries to mollify anti-imperialist critics in the United States and abroad. These electoral measures appealed to U.S. values, especially when World War I was hailed as making the world safe for democracy. Washington intended these staged elections to placate domestic liberals, who agonized over their conflicting antipathies toward imperialism and toward dictatorship.[4]

4. *Extrication elections* provided a successor regime to facilitate a graceful, face-saving exit of U.S. troops.

In the era, these manufactured elections seldom served two longer range goals of some U.S. policy makers: liberalization and democratization. *Liberalization elections* were supposed to open up authoritarian regimes to allow for slightly greater competition, participation, and expression of civil and political rights; although this occurred in some cases, gains were usually temporary. *Democratization elections* were intended to carry out a fundamental transition from authoritarian rule to representative democracy; this function of elections remained at best an aspiration. In the first three decades of the twentieth century, neither the instruments employed by the United States nor the conditions within most of Latin America proved conducive to deep and durable democratization.[5]

Within Latin America, four common electoral practices undercut the impact of electoralism. One vitiating tendency was *"continuismo,"* in which officeholders manipulated elections to perpetuate their tenure. A widespread means of manipulation was *fraud* in the preparation, conduct, and counting of the balloting. When the government stacked the voting procedures too much in its favor, the opposition often retaliated with *abstention,* resulting in a noncompetitive election lacking in credibility. Once the government declared victory, its adversaries frequently resorted to *rebellion*. All of these behaviors inhibited the ability of elections to provide order or legitimacy, let alone democracy.

Motivations

Whereas the United States had hoped to foster democracy elsewhere mainly by serving as a shining example in the nineteenth century, it turned to more direct interventions in the twentieth.[6] Fundamentally, that activist policy began as a means to national security ends and then evolved into an end in itself. In the minds of most U.S. policy makers, security, capitalism, and representative government were tightly intertwined. The primary U.S. goals were strategic protection and economic expansion, for which engineering democracy was normally a tool or a subordinate objective.

In the era, the main purpose of insisting upon elections was originally to create stability and thus remove temptations for other great powers to intrude. In addition, orderly political systems provided a better investment climate for U.S. businesses. Corrupt, fraudulent, dictatorial governments frequently aroused violent rebellions that cost lives, wasted money, jeopardized foreign debt payments, endangered their neighbors, and invited foreign intervention. Because strategic motivations were primary, Washington was willing to use force to establish democracy only in the Caribbean Basin. Until the Great Depression toppled numerous regimes, it remained fairly easy to give lip service to democracy promotion in South America, where most governments happened to be constitutional republics managed by civilian elites.[7]

The motivations of ethnocentrism and racism, which accompanied U.S. promotion of electoralism and its version of democracy, were double-edged swords. Those attitudes of superiority convinced the United States it had the right and ability to intervene politically in weaker, darker, poorer countries. Those same beliefs, however, compelled policy makers to shy away from complete absorption of those informal colonies and to lower their expectations for democratization there. Furthermore, the efforts of U.S. officials to induce democracy were hampered by their disdain for local practices and customs.[8]

Another reason (or excuse) for U.S. electoral intervention was requests from Latin American opposition groups. They invited U.S. interference because they thought they might win an even-handed contest under U.S. supervision. They also realized that the mere fact of U.S. intrusion could tip the majority in their favor, particularly in client states like Cuba and Nicaragua. Where the power of the United States was overwhelmingly evident, voters interpreted U.S. electoral interference as an expression of discontent with the government and preference for the opposition. Therefore pragmatic, strategic voters switched their allegiance to the side that seemed to have the best chance of winning the contest and governing with U.S. approval. While some Latin Americans cynically welcomed the U.S. presence as another factor in a domestic struggle for power, others sincerely hoped the United States would help them realize their democratic aspirations. Still others bitterly resented U.S. intervention of any kind.[9]

In contrast with the United States, the other great power active in the hemisphere, England, merely pursued order and economic gains. It had virtually no interest in promoting democracy of any type, to the frustration of Woodrow Wilson and other U.S. crusaders. Wilson's ambassador to London informed him that the British had "no idea of our notion of freeing men." They thought it was insane to try to correct "the moral shortcomings of foreign nations."[10]

Methods

The United States employed an escalating series of instruments to promote electoral democracy. Before direct intervention, it usually resorted first to diplomatic lobbying, representations, and hortatory rhetoric. Such notes and protestations seldom proved effective unless backed up by portents of more forceful action. The United States also denied or allowed arms shipments to governments or rebels. Although reluctant to link political and economic issues, Washington sometimes blocked loans, trade, or customs receipts. A show of force often involved stationing warships off the coast of the subject country.

The most common device, however, was to threaten to withhold recognition from an existing or incoming government, and then to carry out that threat if demands were not met. The nonrecognition policy originated as a Latin American proposal. Where the United States wielded great power over a smaller state, nonrecognition could be a severe blow to a government's internal and external prestige and to its international creditworthiness. That policy proved particularly effective when its application implied that the next step might be armed intervention. Although usually acting unilaterally and not wanting to give other powers any influence, the United States sometimes—for example, in Mexico—intensified the pressure by seeking Latin American and European allies for its nonrecognition stance. Most other countries, however, were reluctant to pass judgments on the internal politics of sovereign nations.[11]

If those external levers did not work, the United States escalated to more direct intervention, especially in the Caribbean Basin. It preferred to intercede under treaty rights but was willing to step in simply as a hegemonic power. One tactic was to dispatch troubleshooting missions as third-party negotiators and enforcers. These arbitrators were often invited—whether voluntarily or under duress—by one or both sides within the subject country; these local groups either favored democracy or at least hoped that U.S. intercession would transfer power to them. Once the U.S. envoys arrived, they used their "good offices" to mediate disputes, arrange truces, forge pacts, and hammer together coalitions. They cut those deals either as a substitute for or, more commonly, as a prerequisite for peaceful elections. Washington also sent in advisers to the local government, political parties, and military. Trainers from the United States tried to create professional armed forces to maintain order and to obey civilian authority.

The United States also wrote electoral laws and constitutions in the belief that institutions held the key to democratization. On numerous occasions, it sent electoral observers to make sure that the rules of the game were obeyed. When that ploy failed to insure compliance, the United States went further by totally supervising and managing elections, usually at the request—however involuntary—of governments of occupied countries. It also encouraged or discouraged particular candidates or parties, seeking those most likely to govern effectively and to serve U.S. interests. To a lesser extent, the United States also advocated respect for civil liberties and human rights. In the most extreme cases in the Caribbean and Central America, the United States invaded, occupied, and governed directly, massively violating sovereignty and civil rights in the process. As it repeatedly discovered that only intensive and costly intervention could produce even the semblance of democratic propriety, Washington cooled its ardor for democracy promotion.[12]

When U.S. frustration with electoralism and constitutionalism mounted, a few policy makers suggested that democratization that could be sustained by indigenous forces might require deeper structural changes of long gestation and duration. For example, a weary Woodrow Wilson conceded that agrarian reform was needed in Mexico. Some disillusioned U.S. administrators in the Caribbean observed that only far-reaching economic growth, education, and social reform would ever make democracy there more than a stage show choreographed by domestic and foreign elites. However sincere or cynical, U.S. advocates of their brand of democracy concluded from the historical record that interventionism was counterproductive.

Antecedents under Roosevelt and Taft

Unlike Wilson, Theodore Roosevelt did not intervene in the name of promoting democracy. With unabashed frankness, he exerted military power in the Caribbean Basin in pursuit of U.S. strategic self-interests. He demanded order in those countries to preempt any temptation for European intrusion. Nevertheless, imposing some features of democracy through electoralism also accompanied "the Big Stick."[13]

Cuba, 1906–1909

Cuba became the first laboratory for such political engineering. Because the United States did not want itself or any other great power to govern the island directly, it had been trying to install orderly republican rule since victory over Spain. Under the Platt Amendment to the Cuban constitution, the United States exerted "the right to intervene for . . . the maintenance of a government adequate for the protection of life, property, and individual liberty."[14]

In 1906, civil strife against an authoritarian regime threatened the property of both North Americans and Europeans, who pressed the U.S. government to impose peace. The contending Cuban factions also encouraged U.S. involvement and vied for its support. Washington felt that it could not stop the civil war by supporting the unpopular but constitutional government of Tomás Estrada Palma, because he had taken office through the blatantly unfair elections of 1905.

Justified by the Platt Amendment, Roosevelt dispatched troops to Cuba along with William Howard Taft as provisional governor. Taft negotiated a truce between the warring parties with a promise to supervise elections. Thus he hoped to restore order without full-scale U.S. military engagement in a civil war. It took until 1909 to carry out the extrication with a democratic veneer because the United States had to oversee the annulment of the 1905 elections, the enactment of new electoral legislation, the conduct of a census to register voters, and the actual balloting. Those reforms were crafted and implemented by mixed commissions of Cubans and North Americans, the former dominating numerically but the latter wielding the real power. The United States also expanded the Cuban army to defend future governments against revolts.

The presidential balloting delivered victory to the Liberal rebel leader who had been counted out in 1905, José Miguel Gómez. His inauguration in 1909 allowed U.S. forces to withdraw. As Roosevelt had said to Taft in

1907, "Our business is to establish peace and order on a satisfactory basis, start the new government, and then leave the Island."[15]

In sum, there were several reasons for the United States to engineer a formally democratic election in Cuba: North American and European property holders wanted a peaceful settlement; Cubans desired a mediator; U.S. public opinion clamored for a legitimate democratic government; Roosevelt and Taft preferred stable self-government by Cubans to deep involvement by U.S. forces; and, after restoring order, the invaders could point to the election as the completion of their mission and thus depart. In many respects, a model had been set for future democracy promotions.

Panama, 1906–1912

Under Roosevelt and Taft, the United States also supervised elections in Panama in 1906, 1908, and 1912, partly justified by obligations in the Hay-Bunau Varilla Treaty of 1903 to maintain "constitutional order." In 1912, at the request of both sides in the contest, U.S. soldiers and Canal Zone employees monitored the registration and voting. That intervention minimized fraud and allowed the opposition party to emerge victorious. Government opponents requested similar supervision in 1916, 1918, and during the 1920s, but the United States preferred to stay out, except for a mild supervisory role in the 1918 elections.

From 1912 on, the United States continued to make diplomatic representations on behalf of respectable elections in Panama, but with scant impact. During the successful revolution in 1931, Hoover abstained from the treaty right of intervention. The paramount goal of the United States in Panama was always stability to protect the canal, not democracy. Electoralism did serve that narrower purpose by dissuading opposition forces from rebellion in hopes that they might win a fair election.[16]

The Washington Conference, 1907

The Washington Conference of 1907 formalized the principle of democratic government in Central America. Stung by anti-imperialist criticisms of its occupation of Cuba, the United States saw the virtue of a multilateral approach to stabilizing the turbulent countries on its perimeter. In the General Treaty of Peace and Amity, the five Central American republics agreed not to war with each other, not to interfere in each other's internal politics, not to support revolutionary movements against each other, and not to recognize Central American governments that took power through rebellions rather than free elections. This statement of democratic aspirations had little immediate effect in a region where competitive and just elections were seldom held, except in Costa Rica. Nevertheless, it established a Latin American precedent for later U.S. policy, which the Central Americans expected to enforce the agreements. In contrast with the democratic sentiments expressed, some Central American rulers mainly expected this antirevolutionary doctrine to help them retain office by contriving elections while denying their opponents the right to rebel.[17]

This nonrecognition principle was called the Tobar Doctrine. It had originated earlier in 1907 with Carlos Tobar, an Ecuadorean diplomat. He had proposed that all the American nations should "refuse recognition to *de facto* governments that had been established by revolutions against the constitutional regime." Like Roosevelt and Taft, his main goal was to stamp out disorder and civil wars, not necessarily to instill democracy.[18]

Nicaragua, 1909

The United States referred to those 1907 accords when, in 1909, it severed relations with the Nicaraguan government of José Santos Zelaya. Washington did so on the grounds that Zelaya had allowed disorder, threatened U.S. citizens and property, fomented conflicts with his neighbors, and imposed a dictatorship. In a rare deviation from its antirevolutionary principles, the State Department encouraged the rebels fighting against the government with the claim that those insurgents really represented the "ideals and will of a majority of the Nicaraguan people." This stance precursed more activist Wilsonian diplomacy.[19]

After the rebels triumphed in 1910, the new Nicaraguan president, Juan J. Estrada, secured U.S. recognition by promising to hold elections. The U.S. special agent sent to Managua, however, concluded that truly free elections would be virtually impossible and undoubtedly disruptive. Therefore he accepted Estrada's unanimous election by a constitutional convention, which also ratified the peace settlement between the warring sides. Estrada, a Liberal, took a Conservative as his vice-president. This kind of broken coalition arrangement became typical in Central America in the era, with U.S. advisers negotiating temporary deals to produce facsimiles of elected, constitutional governments.[20]

In 1912, the State Department summed up its policy in Nicaragua in sweeping terms: "The full measure and extent of our policy is to assist in the maintenance of republican institutions upon this hemisphere, and we are anxious that the experiment of a government of the people, for the people, and by the people shall not fail in any republic on this continent." This more idealistic and hemispheric formulation of the policy presaged the expansion of the Wilson years.[21]

Woodrow Wilson and Missionary Diplomacy, 1912–1920

As under most new administrations, the changes in foreign policy from Taft to Wilson were not as dramatic as they seemed. The key objective remained strategic control of the Caribbean region and especially the Panama Canal.

To rationalize interventions, however, Wilson now stressed much less the threat of foreign penetration and much more the need for constitutional governments. The extremely interventionist implications of such zealous democracy promotion were expressed by the U.S. ambassador to the Dominican Republic: "President Wilson's declaration of principles concerning Latin America reserved the right to enter any Latin American country to see that the people's rights were not lost by force or fraud."[22]

Wilson saw the promotion of democracy in the hemisphere as a moral duty of the dominant power and of "good men" in Latin America. After the upheavals against dictatorship in Mexico, he dreaded revolutions and viewed democracy as the antidote. Discouraging armed rebellions was supposed to render future U.S. interventions unnecessary. Wilson also thought that democracies were less likely to initiate warfare, an ironic belief in a democratic country that repeatedly invaded its weaker neighbors. Wilson wanted to encourage what he believed was a global "drift toward democracy," which would lay the foundation for Pan American unity and then a world union of democratic states. In his view, that process would occur through evolution rather than revolution. He also envisioned similar forms of government increasing Latin American political and economic cooperation with the United States instead of Europe. As Wilson told the U.S. Congress, "We are the friends of constitutional government in America; we are more than its friends, we are its champions," and "I am going to teach the South American republics to elect good men!"[23]

In 1913, he announced the "Wilson Doctrine" of nonrecognition of unconstitutional governments in Latin America. Although that weapon had been used on occasion before, most stable governments had been recognized automatically if they could control their own territories and meet their international obligations. Wilson raised the recognition policy to the level of a moral principle, over the objections of the State Department.[24]

In contrast with Central America, the Caribbean, and Mexico, the policy was applied less consistently in South America. For example in 1913, Wilson briefly denied recognition to the provisional government of Peru because it had been established by force. Then in 1914 he quickly reversed himself on the grounds that that government's installation had forestalled an attempt to impose a dictatorship by armed rebels. It had also observed constitutional requirements and maintained order. When forced to choose between two armed movements, Wilson could justify backing the one dedicated to republican rule and the status quo. Also in 1914 Wilson decided not to quarrel with a violent change of government in Ecuador. Again in 1919, he recognized the government of Augusto B. Leguía in Peru, even though it had taken power through a coup d'etat; Wilson wanted to avoid a stalemate between himself and a dictator too powerful to dislodge, as he had encountered in Costa Rica.[25]

The nonrecognition policy proved problematic throughout the hemisphere. Many offices changed hands in ambiguous ways that mixed authoritarian and democratic practices and rendered application of the Wilson doctrine very dicey. For example, a rigged election by the government and a rebellion by its opponents presented the State Department with two undesirable choices in Cuba in 1916–17. Moreover, by 1920 and especially thereafter, the United States had grown weary of the amount of intervention required to carry out the policy of demanding "constitutionalism" and forestalling "revolutions." Nevertheless, until the 1930s Washington continued officially opposing "any government in Central America which is not brought into power by constitutional methods or retained in power by extra constitutional methods."[26]

Although some Latin Americans thought Wilson's constitutionalist demands bespoke noble motives, many opposed the nonrecognition doctrine from the beginning. They feared that it would lead to U.S. meddling in domestic political conflicts. In the name of nonintervention, critics like former Argentine foreign minister Estanislao S. Zeballos preferred the traditional practice of recognizing de facto governments.[27]

During 1914–16, Wilson tried to multilateralize his doctrine by campaigning for a Pan American treaty in support of republican governments in the hemisphere. Thirteen nations, especially Brazil, expressed some interest in the treaty. That Pan American Liberty Pact, however, ran aground on Latin American fears of U.S. intervention. Particularly disturbed by U.S. incursions into Mexico, Chile and Argentina spearheaded the opposition to the agreement. The United States shelved the proposal when World War I captured its attention.[28]

The other main instrument Wilson used to sow republicanism was convening elections. His paternalistic belief in the inferiority and immaturity of the Latin Americans led Wilson to emphasize constitutionalism and electoralism rather than participatory mass self-government. He promoted democracy *for* the people rather than *by* the people. Wilson realized that electoralism would not usher in full-fledged democracy overnight. Nevertheless, he hoped it would further the education of the Latin Americans in democratic norms, which would gain strength in the long run. Wilson's ambassador to England explained to the British that the United States would intervene in Latin America to "Make 'em vote and live by their decisions." If there were rebellions thereafter, "We'll go in again and make 'em vote again." For the long haul, "The United States will be here for two hundred years and it can continue to shoot men for that little space till they learn to vote and rule themselves."[29]

Another Wilsonian method for promoting democracy was to build up more efficient, presumably nonpartisan military and police forces, notably in Nicaragua, Cuba, Haiti, and the Dominican Republic. The main goal, however, was to create professional organizations to uphold law and order, not to inculcate democratic values. After the departure of U.S.

troops, those domestic forces became the most powerful pillars of authoritarianism.[30]

To a lesser extent, Wilson also used economic instruments to promote his vision of democracy. U.S. policy makers saw poverty as a source of political disorder, and viewed both problems as impediments to growing production and commerce with the United States. The State Department encouraged private foreign loans to further economic growth, fiscal health, and democratic stability, as well as to draw countries from the European into the U.S. orbit. The department also discouraged foreign loans to some governments established by force, believing that would dissuade rebels from trying to seize power so as to capture the treasury.[31]

Mexico, 1913–1920

The Taft administration held up recognition to General Victoriano Huerta after he overthrew the revolutionary government of Francisco I. Madero. This delay applied pressure for settlement of damage claims. Even though Great Britain and other European powers extended de facto recognition to Huerta, President Wilson maintained nonrecognition on the new grounds that Huerta had seized power unconstitutionally: "I will not recognize a government of butchers." Wilson vowed not to accept the Mexican government unless it was formed through an election in which Huerta was not a candidate. Wilson's determination was reinforced by the Mexican revolutionaries' own demands for "effective suffrage and no reelection." However, one of Wilson's emissaries in Mexico cautioned him that "We simply cannot expect elections to be held in the sense they are conducted in the United States. . . . All we can reasonably expect is that homage be decently paid . . . to the forms of democracy . . . and that the laws be observed."[32]

As Huerta refused to bend, Wilson recalled the U.S. ambassador and stepped up the pressure for compliance. He lifted an arms embargo so that weapons could reach Huerta's opponents, secured British cooperation through economic concessions, and invaded Veracruz in 1914. Rarely has the United States gone to such lengths to bring down a dictator in Latin America.[33]

Commenting on the imbroglio, Wilson said that his goal was "an orderly and righteous government in Mexico." He expected the regime to deliver "human liberty and human rights" to "the submerged eighty-five percent of the people." Thus his definition of democracy sometimes included social justice, in this case land redistribution. This was an agonizing position for Wilson, who grudgingly considered the idea that democracy in Latin America might require limited social revolutions, whereas he preferred gradualist, elitist democracies guided by enlightened gentlemen. Although sympathetic to Mexico's social problems, he feared that the revolutionaries were too radical, especially when they threatened foreign property.

Wilson worried that both the revolutionaries and Huerta were bad examples to Central Americans. To ease out of the Mexican entanglement, he later opted for order rather than democracy.[34]

Meanwhile, even Mexican opponents of Huerta spurned Wilson's meddling on nationalistic grounds. Attempts to mediate by the A.B.C. powers (Argentina, Brazil, Chile) foundered on the refusal of Mexicans from both camps to allow international intrusion in domestic politics. Although eager to negotiate a peaceful settlement, the Chileans balked at imposing republicanism on Mexico as a violation of another country's sovereignty. Nevertheless, the combined pressure of the U.S. seizure of customs revenues in Veracruz and of battlefield victories by his enemies forced Huerta to abdicate the presidency in 1914.[35]

Trying to mediate the differences between the United States and Mexico, the A.B.C. powers, along with Uruguay, Bolivia, and Guatemala, urged Washington to recognize the government of Venustiano Carranza in 1915. The State Department acceded to that recommendation to restore order, even though Carranza had not been properly elected. The department granted recognition contingent upon promises to safeguard U.S. citizens and property. It also hoped to keep Mexico away from Germany. Following U.S. recognition, Carranza was elected president constitutionally in 1917.

Wilson also became willing to accept an authoritarian regime led by the revolutionists because he had become convinced that agrarian and other socioeconomic reforms were more pressing needs than electoralism. Wilson told the secretary of state in 1915, "The first and most essential step in settling the affairs of Mexico is not to call general elections. It seems to me necessary that a provisional government essentially revolutionary in character should take action to institute reforms by decree before the full forms of the constitution are resumed."[36]

When General Alvaro Obregón became president of Mexico in 1920, the United States again withheld recognition. This time the State Department acted on the more traditional issue of U.S. economic claims and property rights rather than on the question of a constitutional assumption of power. After settling those economic disputes in 1923, Obregón received U.S. recognition.[37]

The Dominican Republic, 1913–1924

Another early test of the strengthened policy of support for constitutional governments and opposition to rebellions came in 1913 in the Dominican Republic. As in several other countries, the United States wrestled with the problem of how to support a constitutional government that was opposed by the majority of politically active citizens. Washington decided to back the elected government against an insurrection. The State Department offered its "good offices" to help settle the conflict between the rebels and the authorities. It warned the revolutionists that any de facto government would be denied recognition, customs receipts, and loans. It also promised them that, if they laid down their arms, the United States would make sure that the government paid heed to their grievances and held fair elections. Over the objections of the Dominican president José Bordas Valdés, the State Department sent observers to the election for a constituent assembly. Apparently those outsiders helped deter fraud and violence, and the opposition won a majority.

Finally in 1914, heavy pressure from the United States produced a provisional government that Washington could recognize and which promised to hold a presidential election under full U.S. supervision. During the balloting, U.S. warships waited at the ports and U.S. sailors stood at each voting booth to maintain order. When the government candidate won, the opposition cried foul. Although the election had not been spotless, it had been clean enough so that the State Department defended the process and the outcome. Its support for the newly elected president was so strong that it intimidated the congress as well as the rebels from mounting any challenge.[38]

When the political situation disintegrated into bloodshed again in 1916, President Wilson ordered a military occupation. Along with restoring peace, he wanted to preempt elections that threatened to give victory to forces opposed to the United States and partial to the Germans. Engaging in heavy-handed censorship and other police-state tactics, the U.S. military government scarcely taught the Dominicans democratic practices. The United States finally turned control over the executive branch back to the Dominicans through the device of a presidential election in 1924.[39]

Haiti, 1915–1934

In Haiti, democracy had never existed, and elections had merely ratified power holders. Both the congress and the courts were creatures of the president. Rebellions against the government became commonplace. No other way existed to change officeholders, who had access to some of the few lucrative posts in the entire country. In vain, the State Department repeatedly lectured the Haitians about President Wilson's opposition to revolts in Latin America and insistence on stable constitutional governments.[40]

The North Americans had trouble getting the Haitians to hold decent elections because most citizens did not participate in politics, no political parties existed, and the constitution only required the president to be elected by the congress. Normally, the congress just ratified the latest winner in the civil wars. The congress itself was not really elected by the people but rather by soldiers voting repeatedly as ordered. As one U.S. envoy explained to President Wilson, "elections as understood in America do not exist in Haiti. Elections being simply a continuation of military system under which the country is governed."[41]

Racism also dissuaded the United States from demanding as much adherence to democratic formalities in Haiti as in the rest of the Caribbean Basin. Some policy makers believed that poor blacks in a tropical climate were ill-prepared for democratic participation. Nevertheless, Wilson insisted on the existence of a putatively democratic government as a condition for recognition.[42]

Exasperated with the failure of diplomatic efforts to produce a government able to maintain order, the United States escalated to a full-scale occupation. A series of insurrections in 1914–15 prompted that military intervention, urged by the British and French governments to protect lives and property. Once in control, the U.S. forces supervised the election of the next president by the Haitian congress. In late 1915 the congress dutifully selected the candidate preferred by the United States, Philippe Sudre Dartiguenave, although he was probably not the choice of most Haitians. The treaty forced on that government gave the United States the future right to intervene to assure "the maintenance of a government adequate for the protection of life, property, and individual liberty." Some Haitian elites welcomed U.S. guarantees of stability, though others strongly opposed the occupation and the tutelage.[43]

The U.S. occupying forces also tried to assure an honest congressional election in 1917. They had to eliminate phony registrations, repeat voters, and bribery. Lawbreakers were tried by U.S. occupation courts, since Haitian courts would not act.[44]

Under President Wilson, the Haitian government remained dominated by heavy U.S. dictatorial control. In 1917, when the congress seemed about to approve a nationalistic constitution unacceptable to Washington, U.S. authorities dissolved that assembly. The State Department then drafted a constitution, which was approved 98,225 to 768 in 1918 in a farcical plebiscite controlled by the armed forces and involving the participation of less than 5 percent of the population. That constitution promised eventual democratic rights but allowed the current dictator to retain power until 1930.

In Haiti, the United States became an accomplice in the suspension of direct elections and of an elected congress for over a decade. The Wilson administration and its successors became willing to settle for "nominal constitutionalism." Meanwhile, the government evolved into a "dual dictatorship," wherein U.S. forces and the compliant Haitian president jointly ruled the country. Neither sovereignty nor democracy existed.[45]

Nicaragua, 1916–1920

In Nicaragua, Wilson confronted a case of "continuismo" by an increasingly unpopular government friendly to the United States. Since that regime's perpetuation seemed likely to engender rebellions, Washington took preventive action. The Nicaraguan president, Adolfo Díaz, planned to retain U.S. backing by cooking up a fraudulent election to recertify his constitutionality in 1916. The opposition Liberals asked the United States to supervise the balloting and promised to cooperate with Washington if they won. The State Department also hoped to use the free election as an excuse to withdraw the marines, who had arrived in 1912. It was torn, however, between wanting a fair contest and wanting its closest allies, Díaz's Conservatives, to continue in office.

Reluctantly, Díaz caved in to U.S. pressure to extend the period of registration, to suspend the state of siege, to allow political meetings, and to welcome marines as electoral observers. However, this arrangement fell short of total U.S. supervision of the election. It permitted the State Department to impose some guarantees while continuing to promote the Conservative candidate it preferred, Emiliano Chamorro.

The United States convinced the Conservatives to back Chamorro and to get him elected in a defensible process. The State Department warned that otherwise it would not recognize the next government, it would withdraw the marine guard, and it would withhold canal option treaty money. The arrival of two battleships off Nicaraguan shores gave those demands added weight. Although the United States also tried to designate the Liberal candidate, it found that party too anti-American. As U.S. pressure mounted, the Liberal candidate withdrew, and most of his followers abstained from the election. When the ballots were counted, Chamorro received nearly all of them. Through electoral legerdemain bearing little resemblance to a democratic process, the United States removed Díaz, discouraged rebellions, and bestowed a patina of legitimacy on its preferred president.[46]

Such successes were short-lived, because the deep-seated political problems and dilemmas continued. When the United States so blatantly manipulated the system, few Nicaraguans took democracy seriously. Nicaraguan presidents knew that their most important audience resided in Washington. They realized that the United States demanded only the trappings of democracy, embodied in tranquil, well-orchestrated elections. If officeholders could portray their opponents as rebels against constitutional authority, they could retain power with U.S. backing, especially if they could also maintain order at a minimal cost.

Chamorro planned to have himself reelected in 1920, despite the constitutional prohibition against a successive term. The State Department urged Chamorro to obey that legal restriction. It also did not want the Conservatives to hang on to power through another crudely managed election like the travesty of 1916, especially while the U.S. guard prevented any rebellion by the outraged Liberals. Washington feared that another stolen election would spark uprisings that might compel massive U.S. intervention. The State Department proclaimed its desire for free elections and its neutrality toward the candidates. However, Chamorro rebuffed its suggestion of a North American adviser to rewrite the electoral laws.

The U.S. envoy to observe the election discovered that many phantom Conservatives were registered while many Liberals had been denied inscription, intimidated, and arrested. The government rejected his proposals for more ample registration, for electoral boards with members from both parties, and for each voter being stamped with indelible ink. Chamorro did make some lesser concessions to curtail abstention by the Liberals, but then he declared victory for his uncle, Diego Manuel Chamorro, in a clearly stacked election.

Although the United States knew the 1920 election was bogus, it did not want to go so far as to insist on a rerun, withhold recognition of the winner, or withdraw the guard to allow the Liberals to rebel. Further intervention would have caused an uproar in the rest of Latin America. Moreover, maintaining order was more important and achievable than full-fledged democracy. A year after the next election in 1924, the United States brought the marines home.[47]

Cuba, 1916–1921

In similar fashion, Washington acquiesced in a counterfeit reelection in Cuba in 1916–17. The United States was more concerned about sending military assistance to help that government quash a rebellion. The State Department also favored that government because it granted concessions to U.S. business interests and declared war on Germany. Despite those economic and strategic ties, the United States did not want that government provoking another uprising by staging a second electoral farce in 1920. Therefore it coerced Cuba into inviting a North American in 1919 to rewrite the electoral law.

In that 1920 contest, many Cubans urged the United States to get involved even more than it wanted to, not only to safeguard the process but also to indicate candidate preferences. The opposition threatened to abstain unless the United States supervised the balloting. The State Department was unwilling to go that far, because U.S. supervisors or observers could not really guarantee a free election without actually conducting every phase of the process, which would amount to another full-scale occupation. Nevertheless, the department constantly pressured the Cuban president to exhibit fairness and curb abuses. It still exerted influence, because all Cubans knew that no election—or other transfer of power—in the Caribbean Basin would be really consummated until Washington passed judgment.

As irregularities in the preparation of the 1920 election multiplied, the United States dispatched agents to observe, but not to supervise, the balloting in every province. Sending observers was justified under the Platt Amendment. Their presence inhibited some fraud, which was nonetheless widespread. The government's adversaries wanted the State Department to nullify the elections, but the department convinced them to pursue their complaints through the Cuban legal system, which it had helped devise. That lengthy judicial process delayed any recourse to armed rebellion or to U.S. intrusion.

Before the inauguration of the new government, the State Department sent a special emissary again to expedite the electoral litigation in the courts and to convene new elections in the disputed provinces. He warned the Cuban authorities that direct U.S. intervention was the only other alternative. When those new elections in 1921 failed to overturn the government's victory, Washington recognized the duly elected government. It did so despite the flagrant intimidation of the opposition by the armed forces during the balloting. Those transgressions could only have been prevented by full-scale U.S. control of the election, which probably would have discredited the government, tilted the balance to the opposition, and outraged international opinion.[48]

Costa Rica, 1917–1919

In 1917, Wilson refused to recognize the Costa Rican government of Federico Tinoco, established by a coup d'etat. The State Department punished the dictatorship, saying it would only recognize a constitutionally elected government and in no case a government run by Tinoco. The department advised all U.S. citizens, especially bankers, against any business dealings with that government. Cheered on by many Costa Ricans, Wilson maintained this stance even though Tinoco offered to help the United States against the Germans in World War I.

After holding a trumped-up legitimating election, Tinoco refused to step down until 1919, despite the U.S. arm twisting. As State Department official Dana G. Munro pointed out, this standoff left the United States in an awkward situation:

> Non-recognition encouraged the opposition and forced the unrecognized administration to resort to oppressive methods to maintain its authority, but the United States' opposition to revolutions made it more difficult for the opposition to resort to the one method of effecting a change which was likely to be effective. Meanwhile internal dissension and uncertainty about the future were apt to bring on economic difficulties that caused hardship to the people as well as to the government, and which created pressures from American business interests for a change in policy.

The Costa Rican episode stands out because Wilson proved willing to pursue constitutionalism even in conflict with U.S. economic and strategic interests. He needed to demonstrate consistency in the recognition policy, which had taken on a life of its own. U.S. businessmen preferred to deal with the Tinoco government. A Senate resolution favored recognition of Tinoco after he declared war against Germany. Secretary of State Robert Lansing warned Wilson, "our settled policy as to nonrecognition of Tinoco . . . runs directly contrary to our interests in prosecuting the war." However, Wilson's claim to be fighting for democracy in Europe reinforced his determination to demand the same in Costa Rica. When implored by some of his diplomatic and military advisers to recognize Tinoco on practical grounds of national interest, Wilson refused, declaring, "I am following in this matter . . . not a course of policy but a course of principle."[49]

Honduras, 1919

In 1919 in Honduras, an armed rebellion erupted when the president tried to impose his successor. He resigned after the United States threatened to intervene unless free elections were held. When the rebel leader seized power, he concocted the simulacrum of an election to make himself president, which elicited recognition from Washington.[50]

The Wilson Legacy

State Department official Munro concluded that democracy promotion in the first two decades of the twentieth century had little positive effect. At worst, "the support of constituted governments and the discouragement of revolutions meant in practice that one party might stay in power indefinitely." Inevitably, U.S. interference favored one side or the other, as those inviting its intrusion realized. The only way that the United States could really force the kinds of elections it wanted in the Caribbean Basin was through total control of civilian and military authorities as well as the electoral process. Such interventions proved distasteful, embarrassing, costly, and devastating to the credibility of the party in power.

Anti-imperialist criticisms also spread throughout the hemisphere and within the United States. In response to the costs of coping with that hostility at home and abroad, Washington increasingly refrained from full-blown intervention. Even by less obtrusive mechanisms, promotion of democratic forms and rituals repeatedly failed to stifle upheavals or to take root, so subsequent U.S. administrations backed away from the crusade.[51]

Warren G. Harding and Normalcy, 1920–1924

In his presidential campaign, Republican Warren G. Harding criticized the interventions of Wilson's Democratic administration. Referring to Haiti, Harding vowed, "I will not empower an Assistant Secretary of the Navy to draft a constitution for helpless neighbors in the West Indies and to jam it down their throats at the point of bayonets borne by United States marines." Harding's promise of less interventionism appealed to U.S. citizens exhausted by foreign adventures after taking up arms for democracy in World War I. Diminished commitments in Latin America also fit with his desire to reduce the costs and roles of government.[52]

After World War I, the main threat to U.S. hegemony in Latin America was not European competition but Latin American nationalism. As a result, the United States backed away from interventionism. It stressed the concepts of the "Open Door" and the "Good Neighbor," especially from the mid-twenties onward. Whereas Wilson had intervened in the name of democracy, the Republicans increasingly abstained in the name of democracy.[53]

That evolution in policy was gradual, however. Wilson had stressed that democracy would take hold once dictatorships and rebellions were discouraged. The Republicans believed that was naive. They initially hoped that rapid social and economic development could lay the foundation for democratic government. At the Latin American Division in the State Department in the 1920s, some policy makers thought that stability would facilitate economic and fiscal modernization, which would lay the groundwork for more orderly and democratic governments, an early variant of modernization theory. Infrastructural improvements in financial institutions, transportation, education, and even sanitation were expected to nurture the growth of both capitalism and democracy. By the end of the 1920s, however, Washington concluded that such structural changes would take much longer than it was willing to intervene in Latin America. Therefore the crusade for democracy was gradually dismantled.[54]

Cuba, 1921–1924

The irregularities in the provincial follow-up elections of 1921 in Cuba showed the incoming Harding administration how difficult it was to force democratic behavior, even when the United States exerted control by treaty. Not wanting to intervene massively, the State Department ended up in the untenable position of insisting on untarnished elections and then recognizing a government whose hands were soiled. By the time the 1924 presidential election took place, the department was losing interest in actively promoting democracy. So long as the Cuban government did not ask for assistance and there was no revolt during or after the mock election, Washington preferred not to interfere.[55]

Central American Treaties in Washington, 1922–1923

At a conference of the Central American republics in Washington, D.C., in 1922–23, they reaffirmed the 1907 agreements. The Central American leaders included a stronger prohibition against recognizing any government established by force of arms, even if it were consecrated by a subsequent free election. In response, the rest of the Latin American countries reiterated their rejection of this nonrecognition doctrine as interventionist. After trying to enforce this strict rule, the exasperated United States would eventually come to accept stable regimes of whatever stripe.[56]

Honduras, 1923–1924

In accord with the new treaties, the State Department admonished the Honduran president to exercise fairness in the 1923 election. The department also made it clear that it would not recognize any government there created by force of arms. U.S. pressure reportedly made the election somewhat more honest than normal, though many opposition supporters were prevented from voting.

Since no candidate secured a majority, the government tried to force the congress to choose its nominee. When the president sought to prolong himself in power, the United States withdrew recognition. After civil war broke out, Washington mediated a settlement between the two sides. The Hondurans formed a provisional government to preside over new elections for a constitutional president. The State Department insisted that no leaders of the rebellion would be recognized as president even if elected. It imposed an arms embargo and asked American companies to withhold loans. Washington also placed warships off the Honduran coast and a contingent of marines in Tegucigalpa, a sort of "mini-invasion." The government finally called the election in 1924 with only three weeks' notice, so the opposition refused to participate. The government's victorious candidate was then recognized by the United States, which had little choice since it did not want to occupy the country militarily.[57]

Haiti

The State Department believed that an electoral exit for the marines would prove exceptionally difficult to arrange in Haiti. The department feared that the weakness of national integration, of socioeconomic development, of participation, and of political parties would spell a return of "anarchy" even under a freely elected government. The U.S. high commissioner in Haiti explained in his 1923 annual report:

> While it is desired that Haiti should have a duly elected legislative body at as early a date as possible, the actual situation must be given due consideration. Until the American intervention and for over 100 years, Haiti has been nothing more or less than a military oligarchy of the most severe type. Ninety-five per cent of its people were and are illiterate, and a large per cent unmoral. Under such conditions the word "democracy" has but an empty sound.[58]

Racism also restrained U.S. demands for democratization. A high-ranking State Department official explained to the secretary of state in 1921 that all previous Haitian elections had been charades, stage-managed by the tiny upper class, the military, and the authoritarian government. Moreover,

> It is well to distinguish at once between the Dominicans and the Haitians. The former, while in many ways not advanced far enough for the highest type of self-government, yet have a preponderance of white blood and culture. The

Haitians on the other hand are negro for the most part, and, barring a very few highly educated politicians, are almost in a state of savagery and complete ignorance. The two situations thus demand different treatment. In Haiti it is necessary to have as complete a rule within a rule by Americans as possible. This sort of control will be required for a long period of time, until the general average of education and enlightenment is raised. In the Dominican Republic, on the other hand, I believe we should endeavor rather to counsel than control.[59]

U.S. policy makers also found it difficult to cultivate democracy in Haiti because they lacked local allies. Some North Americans saw themselves serving the needs of the oppressed peasants, who were incapable of taking advantage of democratic openings. Other U.S. officials tried to create a middle class out of whole cloth. Meanwhile, the francophile upper class and the U.S. invaders reciprocated mutual disdain, and those aristocrats displayed little affinity for democracy. Haitian elites believed that the occupation itself was undemocratic and undermined democratic possibilities by denying nationals experience at real self-government.[60]

The Haitian president was supposed to be picked by an elected congress, but that body had been dissolved in 1917 by the current dictator, Sudre Dartiguenave. Therefore he arranged to have his chosen successor elected president by the twenty-one-member Council of State, which he had appointed to exercise legislative functions. Under National Guard protection, the council in 1922 picked Louis Borno, who extended his rule throughout the rest of the decade. The U.S. secretary of the navy observed that the election, "while absolutely constitutional was more or less farcical in character."[61]

Reluctantly, the State Department acquiesced in these theatrics as preferable to public elections that, if honest, might produce an anti-United States congress or, if dishonest, might ignite rebellions. For the rest of the 1920s, Haiti maintained a flagrantly undemocratic government supported by the United States.[62] One of the marines commanding the National Guard in 1925 opined: "These people had never heard of democracy and couldn't have comprehended it had they heard. They had always been ruled by despots, and despotism was the only government they could understand."[63]

The Dominican Republic, 1924

The U.S. desire to convoke an election to provide an honorable evacuation for the marines from the Dominican Republic also proved difficult. Many Dominicans refused to participate in elections managed by the authoritarian U.S. military regime. Therefore the United States patched together a provisional Dominican government to convene elections. As violence and partisan wrangling agitated the campaigns, the State Department warned that the evacuation could not take place without an orderly, proper election. U.S. agents became more and more deeply involved in negotiations among the contenders to prepare a peaceful election. They also labored to keep the likely losers from withdrawing from the contest, a classic Latin American technique for delegitimizing elections. Mainly under Dominican control, the election transpired without major disturbances in 1924, and the U.S. occupying forces immediately went home.[64]

After the departure of U.S. troops, Dominican politics went on much as before the occupation. Authoritarianism and corruption continued. The major new feature was the tremendous power of the U.S.-trained National Guard, soon dominated by Rafael Trujillo.[65]

After the withdrawal, Sumner Welles, former chief of the Latin American Division in the State Department and U.S. commissioner to the Dominican Republic from 1922 to 1925, concluded that democracy promotion had been in vain:

> Constitutional government . . . is to the average Dominican but an empty phrase. . . . Instead of being regarded as the sacred charter of the people's liberties, the Constitution has been considered a legitimate source of advantage to the party or to the person in control, and has consequently been modified at frequent intervals . . . solely to satisfy the desires or requirements of those enabled thus to advance them.

Welles believed that only fundamental improvements in prosperity and "civic education" would render constitutional democracy truly functional in the Dominican Republic. In his view, the country also needed stronger electoral guarantees of honesty, an independent judiciary, an apolitical national guard, and institutionalized political parties. Welles further concluded that these failures in the Dominican Republic formed part of the general bankruptcy of attempting to impose governments throughout the Caribbean Basin. He castigated those policies as paternalistic, ethnocentric, and ignorant.[66]

Nicaragua, 1924

The State Department hoped to extract the marines from Nicaragua gracefully by manufacturing a fair election in 1924. As the secretary of state explained:

> The Department considers that the success of the whole plan of withdrawal depends upon the government coming into office as the result of the next elections having the support of the majority of the people in order that it will be in such a strong position that when the Marines are then withdrawn there will be no occasion for political disturbance. To bring this about free and fair elections are essential.[67]

Another part of the withdrawal plan was to train a national constabulary that could take the place of U.S. forces, as already done in the Dominican Republic and Haiti. Those U.S. troops had kept the Conservatives in power for ten years by preventing any rebellions, although the Liberals probably represented a majority of the voters. Now the National Guard would be expected to maintain order and supervise elections.

The State Department sent an "election doctor" to draft a new electoral law and to oversee the registration and voting. However, the department did not want to land a large number of election observers and get too deeply involved, especially since the host government rejected that intrusion. Although the United States kept lobbying for a fair contest, the Nicaraguan authorities committed wholesale fraud to achieve a smashing victory. Unwilling to back up its demands with an armed intervention, Washington recognized the newly elected administration. In return, the new president agreed to organize a professional constabulary and to prepare more foolproof elections for 1928. The marines left in 1925.[68]

One U.S. official concluded that true democracy would only come to Nicaragua after many years of economic development, fueled by North American capital:

> The intelligent leaders in Nicaragua . . . realize that Nicaragua today lacks one of the principal foundations for a democratic government in that she has no well-developed middle class. . . . Such a middle class cannot come into existence until the industries of the country are developed. These industries cannot be developed without capital, and capital can be obtained only by foreign loans.[69]

Calvin Coolidge and Vacillation, 1924–1928

Although Coolidge tried to continue Harding's retreat from intervention on behalf of electoral democracy, the new president got snarled in the old dilemmas.

Ecuador, 1925–1928

Coolidge's first entanglement involved a spillover of the Central American recognition policy into Ecuador. In 1925 a coup d'etat in Quito spawned an authoritarian regime, which the United States refused to recognize until it wrote a new constitution in 1928. The State Department insisted on that nonrecognition despite the contrary opinions of U.S. economic advisers and bankers anxious to arrange loans for Ecuador.[70]

Nicaragua, 1926–1928

Although Coolidge presided over the exit of the marines from Nicaragua in 1925, he soon sent them back. The 1924 electoral solution had failed to insure order. That predominantly Liberal government was quickly overthrown by Conservatives, whom the United States and its Central American neighbors refused to recognize. The State Department felt obliged to deny recognition under the 1907 and 1923 Central American treaties. It also wanted to maintain consistency with its policies in other Central American and Caribbean republics. The department, however, underscored that its nonrecognition did not mean that it would depose that government or back any rebellion. The ensuing civil war was stopped by the return of the marines, who supervised another presidential election. Only by intervening far more formidably than it wanted to could the United States enforce its demand for a stable government legitimized by reasonably untainted elections.

Both sides in the Nicaraguan conflict requested U.S. supervision of the 1928 election. To assuage ill feeling in Latin America, the State Department discussed including observers from the other Central American republics but decided that they were unlikely to be impartial. To control the electoral process, U.S. supervisors had to meddle in numerous local affairs, including actions by the police and courts. To keep both sides in the contest, the United States also had to convince them that it was unbiased, since Nicaraguans had grown accustomed to the United States encouraging or discouraging presidential prospects. Both camps courted U.S. favoritism. Before launching their campaigns, candidates checked with the State Department to see if they would be recognized if elected.

The State Department successfully pressured the Nicaraguan government to adopt a humiliating law that gave a national board of elections total authority over the process and made a U.S. representative chairman of the board. The board worked to keep minor parties off the ballot. It wanted either the Conservatives or Liberals to obtain a majority and be able to found a stable government, much like the U.S. two-party system.

The marines worked closely with the evolving National Guard to shield the election from abuses. Meanwhile guerrilla leader Augusto César Sandino called for the withdrawal of U.S. forces and demanded elections supervised by Latin American instead of U.S. observers. Under the control of U.S. troops, the registration and election went smoothly. U.S. officials took charge of printing, distributing, guarding, and tabulating the ballots. Some of the U.S. supervisory procedures violated provisions of the Nicaraguan constitution. Rather than gaining experience in constitutional self-government, Nicaraguans learned to look to the United States to resolve conflicts.

In the fairest election up to that time in Nicaraguan history, the Liberals won. After some nudging from the United States, the Conservative-dominated congress certified the results. Both sides agreed to have the United States supervise elections for the next four years. The State Department acquiesced, though it took an increasingly dim view of such involvements, which were less and less justifiable on security grounds; as the assistant secretary for Latin America said following the 1928 electoral observance, "I fervently hope we will have no more elections in Latin America to supervise."[71]

Cuba, 1927–1928

Another example of the waning enthusiasm of Washington for democracy promotion occurred in Cuba. President Gerardo Machado planned to extend his term through patently illegal constitutional amendments. The State Department voiced its misgivings but did not reproach him harshly. When protests erupted in 1927 against Machado's continuation, the department ended up in the uncomfortable position of backing an increasingly unpopular regime. He consummated his "continuismo" in a sham election in 1928.[72]

Herbert Hoover and Nonintervention, 1928–1932

Although both Harding and Coolidge had maintained Wilson's nonrecognition policy, they had begun to recede from interventionism. Now Herbert Hoover retreated even further, eventually discarding the Wilson doctrine and, in effect, initiating what later became known as the Good Neighbor Policy. The Great Depression soon made interventionism and electoralism too costly. Moreover, Hoover accelerated policy change because he believed that democracy and intervention were incompatible. As he said during his 1928 South American tour, "True democracy is not and cannot be imperialistic."[73]

Hoover reluctantly retained the nonrecognition policy in Central America, as required by those countries themselves in the 1923 treaty, and in part of the Caribbean. Little by little, however, he shelved the policy elsewhere in favor of nonintervention. With the wave of unconstitutional changes in governments set off by the Great Depression, Hoover would return to the pre-Wilson policy of recognizing any government that was in control and able to meet international responsibilities. During 1930–32, he did not insist on elections before accepting the new regimes established by force in Brazil, Argentina, Peru, Panama, and Bolivia. In those cases, the State Department only briefly and perfunctorily withheld recognition and then normally expressed the hope that elections would be held soon to make the government constitutional.[74]

Hoover did try to support constitutional regimes by prohibiting U.S. arms exports to rebels while supplying established governments. The main purpose of this policy, which had been adopted by Congress in 1922, was to promote political stability rather than democracy. For example, the United States slapped an embargo on the rebellion of Getúlio Vargas against the government of Brazil in 1930, but then became the first great power to recognize Vargas's administration after he seized office.[75]

Honduras, 1928–1932

The presidential candidate elected under U.S. pressure in 1924, Miguel Paz Barahona, maintained peace and held a fair election for his successor in 1928. During that contest, the United States discouraged upheavals by anchoring warships in Honduran waters. The opposition won the balloting, and the State Department's threat of nonrecognition to any rebels helped dissuade government partisans and the army from overturning those results.

In another reasonably honest election in 1932, the government's candidate also lost. The winner, Tiburcio Carías, had to suppress a rebellion on his own, because U.S. policy had switched to nonintervention. The State Department even refrained from issuing the usual warning to insurgents that no government established by force of arms would be recognized. It also refused to sell arms to the newly elected government. After consolidating his authority, Carías ruled as a dictator until 1948. His own ascension through the ballot box had not converted him to democratic principles.[76]

The Dominican Republic, 1928–1930

When President Horacio Vásquez had contemplated extending his term two years beyond the 1928 constitutional limit, the State Department had temporarily persuaded him to drop the idea. It did not object, however, when Vásquez achieved his goal legalistically by having elected a constituent assembly that wrote a new constitution adding two years to his presidency. Then he rigged his own reelection in 1930 through the same device. Few people voted in the contrived elections for the constituent assemblies to rubber-stamp the necessary constitutional provisions. In the 1930 presidential election, the procedures were so stacked in the government's favor that the opposition abstained. Although the State Department complained about these frequent changes in the constitution to enthrone Vásquez, it did not protest officially.

After a bloody rebellion, Gen. Rafael Trujillo had himself elected president fraudulently—with more votes than registered voters—in 1930 and reigned until 1961. Informal U.S. attempts to dissuade Trujillo from taking power failed. Despite his grotesquely unconstitutional takeover, the State Department recognized him. It consoled itself that the Central American treaty of 1923 did not have to be applied to the Caribbean. Above all, Washington accepted Trujillo because it did not want any further involvement in the internal politics of the Dominican Republic, which was harming its relations with the rest of Latin America.[77]

Cuba, 1929–1932

As Machado's dictatorship grew more repressive and economic conditions worsened in 1929–32, the State Department agonized over whether to anger Latin America by intervening or to abandon the nonrecognition principle by doing nothing. Policy makers were also ambivalent because the Platt Amendment gave the United States greater responsibility in Cuba than in most countries. And Cubans had become accustomed to Washington taking sides in most conflicts there and usually determining the winner.

The United States struggled in vain to shape Cuban events without recourse to armed intervention. The State Department disapproved of Machado's extending his presidential term. It prodded him to curtail human rights abuses, such as illegal arrests. The department also tried to negotiate a settlement between the repressive government and the rebellious opposition. Although the United States insisted that nonintervention did not mean support for the unconstitutional government, it could not convince Cubans of its neutrality. Therefore Washington increasingly suffered criticisms for supporting a violent dictator. Henceforth in the Caribbean Basin, U.S. pressures for democracy were muted, and those demands carried less weight because military invasion no longer lurked as a credible threat. The noninterventionist decision vis-à-vis Cuba really sounded the death knell of promotion of democracy, however narrowly defined that political system.[78]

Haiti, 1930–1932

Hoover initiated the removal of troops from Haiti, which was completed under Roosevelt. The State Department's major goal was to shore up a stable government so that the United States could withdraw at least by the time of the treaty of occupation's expiration in 1936. As under Coolidge, however, the Hoover administration did not insist on truly free elections in Haiti. The State Department feared that such contests would not be fully representative or that they would produce an anti–United States majority. The department also believed that a sturdy democracy remained unlikely so long as over 90 percent of the population was illiterate and politically marginalized.

Racial and cultural prejudices still reinforced U.S. policy makers' doubts about the viability of democracy in Haiti. For example, the U.S. chargé in 1930 reported to the State Department on the Haitians' supposed unsuitability for democracy:

> In general, while the Anglo-Saxon has a deep sense of the value of social organization and of the obligation of democratic government to assume a large share of responsibility for the social welfare of the masses, and has in addition a profound conviction of the value of democratic government, the Latin mind, on the contrary, is apt to scorn democracy and neglect activities looking to the health and educational welfare of the masses. . . . The action of the Haitian, in common with the Latin in general, is in the main directed by emotion rather than by reason.[79]

President Hoover's commission on Haiti made its report in 1930:

The commission is not convinced that the foundations for democratic and representative government are now broad enough in Haiti. The educated public opinion and literate minority are so small that any government formed in these circumstances is liable to become an oligarchy. The literate few too often look to public office as a means of livelihood. . . . It has been the aim of the American occupation to try to broaden the base of the articulate proletariat and thus make for a sounder democracy and ultimately provide for a more representative government in Haiti. Hence its work in education, in sanitation, in agencies of communications such as roads, telephones, telegraph lines and regular mail routes. These things naturally are deemed of secondary importance by the elite, who see in the rise of a middle class a threat to the continuation of their own leadership. The failure of the occupation to understand the social problems of Haiti, its brusque attempt to plant democracy there by drill and harrow, its determination to set up a middle class—however wise and necessary it may seem to Americans—all these explain why, in part, the high hopes of our good works in this land have not been realized.[80]

Under intense U.S. pressure in 1930, the Haitian government and the opposition agreed that the long-ruling, widely despised president would step down. Meanwhile the Council of State would choose an independent successor, who would then convene a public election of a congress to name a new president. At the same time, the State Department insisted that it would not supervise the elections or lobby for any particular candidate. It wanted the Haitian National Guard to maintain order and Haitians to take on more responsibility for self-government. When the existing president balked, the department made it clear that it would impose this plan by force if necessary. Without further U.S. intervention, his successor and the guard conducted an orderly congressional election in which few Haitians took part. The nationalist opponents of the U.S. occupation won easily. They chose one of their own leaders, Stenio Vincent, as president. Thus the United States helped ease out a rather iron-fisted ruler and install a constitutional replacement opposed to the U.S. presence.[81]

In the 1932 congressional contests, the United States restrained the authorities from massive arrests of their opponents on election day. Since the government controlled all the registration and voting and since most of the population evidenced little interest in the balloting, however, the president's candidates swept every office. The State Department kept a low profile because it did not want to revive interventionism.

During nearly two decades of occupation, the United States had done very little to prepare Haitians to govern themselves democratically. At the start of the 1930s, the U.S. high commissioner lamented that the Haitians were "little better fitted for self-government than they were in 1915." Finally Haiti and the United States reached an agreement in 1933 for the exit of the marines in 1934, though some fiscal controls continued until 1947.[82]

Nicaragua, 1930–1932

Hoover was also eager to remove the troops from Nicaragua. One reason was the incongruity of opposing the Japanese incursion in China while U.S. forces occupied Nicaragua. Hoover waited to abandon Nicaragua, however, while occupying forces finished training the National Guard and guiding the electoral process.

The United States supervised the congressional election of 1930 and the presidential balloting of 1932. Although that presence made those elections more impartial, the United States thereafter had to dissuade the president from trying to extend his term until 1934. It also had to persuade that government to pay for the electoral mission, which was becoming too costly to the State Department, especially since the U.S. Senate had passed a bill prohibiting the use of naval appropriations for marines supervising Nicaraguan elections. The Nicaraguan Liberals won another credible contest in 1932.

Although successful in 1932, the State Department was convinced that this was the last time it wanted to manage a Nicaraguan election. On the eve of departing, it tried to assure the neutrality of the National Guard by getting the Conservatives and Liberals to sign an agreement to divide the officer positions equally, but this was an admission that politics had already permeated the guard. The marines sailed home in January 1933. Shortly thereafter, Anastasio Somoza and the National Guard murdered Sandino and took power illegally. The resulting dynastical dictatorship lasted until 1979. As with Trujillo in the Dominican Republic, the aftermath of U.S. democracy promotion was order without progress, stability with tyranny.[83]

Guatemala, 1930

In December 1930, an army coup in Guatemala presented the United States with an undeniably unconstitutional government. The State Department expressed its displeasure, though it declined to dispatch a warship requested by the ambassador. In response to U.S. protestations, the leader of the rebellion stepped down, the government went through the motions of respecting legal proprieties, and an election was held in which the only candidate, General Jorge Ubico, won handily. Not wanting to intervene to force more fully democratic procedures, the State Department accorded recognition to Ubico, who ruled as a dictator until the social revolution of 1944.[84]

El Salvador, 1931–1932

Feeling bound by the provisions of the 1923 treaty, the United States also denied recognition to the government of General Maximiliano Martínez in El Salvador. In December 1931, he had taken power through the forceful overthrow of his constitutionally elected predecessor. The nonrecognition policy became untenable, because Martínez refused to abdicate while Washington refused to intervene militarily. The State Department had persuaded the British and other governments to hold off, but then they began extending recognition in late 1932. The other Central American republics stuck with the department's position. They hoped that it would discourage rebellions in their own countries, although they worried about worsening relations with their neighbor. In 1934, the other Central American republics repudiated the 1923 treaty, recognized Martínez, and the United States followed suit. The nonrecognition policy officially ended.[85]

Chile, 1932

In 1932, the short-lived Socialist Republic of Chile seized power through a coup d'etat. The State Department withheld recognition pending guarantees that international obligations would be met. It also added demands for protection of foreign persons and property. According to the department, this action was not an extension of its Central American policy against revolutionary governments but rather a traditional concern about governments able to fulfill their responsibilities. Washington never extended recognition until after the socialists were ousted later that year.[86]

After taking over from Hoover, President Franklin Roosevelt emphasized the United States behaving democratically abroad rather than Latin American governments behaving democratically at home. He replaced Wilson's doctrine of nonrecognition with a commitment to nonintervention. For example, the 1923 Central American treaty was scrapped in 1934. Until the end of World War II, the United States refrained from vigorous democracy promotion in the hemisphere.[87]

Conclusion: The Democracy Dilemma

In Latin America, the dilemma for the United States was how to promote democracy democratically. As a liberal democracy, the United States felt most comfortable at least claiming to be pursuing democratic objectives overseas through democratic means, however much it was mainly behaving like another great power. As an emerging hegemon at the start of the twentieth century, the United States tried to set the rules of the game in the Western Hemisphere. It wanted ideological as well as military and economic hegemony and conformity, without having to pay the price of permanent conquest. It coerced the countries in its sphere of influence, especially those in the Caribbean Basin, to internalize its political as well as economic institutions. Intervening to install those institutions was meant to impede penetration by other foreigners, to maintain order, to assure domination, and to obviate the need for interminable occupation or future interventions.[88]

Although proclaiming that its own brand of democracy was best for all countries, the United States gave security and economic interests much higher priority. In the opening decades of the twentieth century, those strategic, economic, and political objectives seldom clashed. When they did, democracy promotion was usually downplayed. Nevertheless, that policy achieved such a momentum of its own under Wilson that it was sometimes pursued in spite of more practical security and economic considerations. The degree of interventionism required to foment democratic behavior, however, eventually became too costly to U.S. public opinion, to peaceful economic expansion, and to good relations with Latin America, so the Wilson Doctrine was discarded.

Democracy promotion also lost favor because of its meager results. In a few cases, that policy did succeed in making political behavior slightly more democratic and in enhancing stability. Most of the time, however, those gains were very ephemeral. Much more common was the manipulation of U.S. policy by local contestants to take power and then to retain it by counting out their opponents and smearing them as undemocratic rebels. By the end of the era, some of Latin America's most ruthless and tenacious tyrants held office in the very countries where the United States had most insisted on democratization. Although the United States rarely desired or installed those dictators, its strengthening of central governments and national guards paved the way to sturdier authoritarian regimes. Those earlier interventions also set a precedent for blaming the United States for those subsequent dictatorships, which it presumably could have deposed like their predecessors.[89]

This first cycle of democracy promotion by the United States in Latin America ended in failure for four main reasons:

1. The United States tried to impose democracy by undemocratic means. Too often, only extreme coercion proved sufficient to elicit democratic performances. That inherent dilemma undercut the policy at home and abroad. In the United States, anti-imperialists who favored democratization as a goal opposed interventionism as a means. In Latin America, nationalists and progressives also resented U.S. intrusion. U.S. policy makers exhibited a lack of sensitivity to local, indigenous needs, capabilities, institutions, cultures, and histories. Such heavy-handed intervention could not provide a neutral arbiter to construct democratic resolutions of disputes. The elections the United States insisted upon were not really fair competitions, since U.S. preferences weighed heavily on the candidates, voters, and results. Worse, landing the marines and forming dictatorial occupation governments scarcely taught democracy by example.

2. The United States was inconsistent in its support for democracy. It worried more about the democratic creation than the democratic conduct of a government, often accepting a regime that could supply order. Indeed, it frequently promoted elections for ulterior motives, including

pacification, legitimation, demonstration, and extrication. Moreover, its insistence on some aspects of democracy was sporadic and diluted by greater concern for the realpolitik of strategic and economic pursuits.

3. The United States normally settled for form over substance, operationalizing "democracy" as "electoralism" and "constitutionalism." Many in Washington believed that such procedures and institutions were, in themselves, the keys to inculcating democracy, at least among the elites. Oftentimes the elections conjured up in Latin America, however, were charades. Therefore some U.S. policy makers concluded that profound and lasting democratization would have required much deeper political changes, including freedom of expression and assembly, elaboration of participatory political parties, subordination of the military, and negotiation of fundamental social-political agreements on consensual rules of the game. A few observers, even President Wilson at times, suggested that also necessary in many countries were significant, long-run structural changes, such as economic development, agrarian reform, income redistribution, education, and other transformations to bring citizenship and power to the impoverished and excluded majorities.

4. Even if sincere, the United States lacked sufficient allies for democracy promotion within the subject countries. True champions of liberal democracy were few and often enemies of United States imperialism. The United States' best friends within Latin America were those groups unopposed to its interference, willing to grant concessions, and unlikely to adhere to the spirit and letter of democratic politics. Even many of those Latin Americans who called for U.S. support for democracy in their countries were really struggling for power rather than democracy. Time and again, the very groups who took office by demanding free elections thereafter ruled as tyrants.

International crusades for democracy probably had little chance of success until both the United States and Latin America were more fully committed to democratic behavior. Democracy promotion seemed more likely to work well when it did not violate sovereignty, which was possible only if democratic values became universalized. Above all, transnational coalitions in favor of democracy appeared unlikely to be fruitful until the democratic forces within Latin America itself became strong enough to prevail either on their own or with only a modicum of external solidarity.

Notes

I wish to thank Susanne Wagner for her assistance with the research and Elizabeth Cobbs, Michael Desch, John J. Johnson, Abraham Lowenthal, David Mares, Peter H. Smith, and Joseph Tulchin for their comments on the manuscript.

1. In this chapter, *democracy* refers to the standard, electoral, competitive, representative political system to which that term has been applied historically in the United States and

other capitalist countries; it does not refer to any broader notion of political, social, or economic equality. It should also be noted that the focus on instances when the United States claimed to be promoting democracy overseas is not meant to deny that it sometimes undermined democracies and supported dictatorships.

2. C. Neale Ronning, *Intervention in Latin America* (New York: Alfred A. Knopf, 1970), p. 3.

3. Terry Karl, "Imposing Consent? Electoralism vs. Democratization in El Salvador," in Paul W. Drake and Eduardo Silva, eds., *Elections and Democratization in Latin America, 1980–1985* (La Jolla, Calif.: Center for Iberian and Latin American Studies, 1986), pp. 9–36.

4. Edward S. Herman and Frank Brodhead, *Demonstration Elections: U.S.-Staged Elections in the Dominican Republic, Vietnam, and El Salvador* (Boston: South End Press, 1984), pp. 2–5.

5. Paul W. Drake and Eduardo Silva, "Introduction: Elections and Democratization in Latin America, 1980–1985," in Drake and Silva, pp. 1–7.

6. In the United States in the early nineteenth century, "America versus Europe" meant "liberty versus despotism." Arthur P. Whitaker, *The Western Hemisphere Idea: Its Rise and Decline* (Ithaca: Cornell University Press, 1954), p. 30.

7. Theodore Paul Wright, Jr., *American Support of Free Elections Abroad* (Washington, D.C.: Public Affairs Press, 1964). Howard J. Wiarda, "Can Democracy Be Exported? The Quest for Democracy in U.S.–Latin American Policy," in Kevin J. Middlebrook and Carlos Rico, eds., *The United States and Latin America in the 1980s: Contending Perspectives on a Decade of Crisis* (Pittsburgh: University of Pittsburgh Press, 1986), pp. 325–52.

8. Rubin Francis Weston, *Racism in U.S. Imperialism: The Influence of Racial Assumptions on American Foreign Policy, 1893–1946* (Columbia: University of Missouri Press, 1972). John J. Johnson, *Latin America in Caricature* (Austin: University of Texas Press, 1980).

9. Wright, p. 34. For a classic Mexican critique of U.S. interventionism in Latin America up through the Wilson years as "tyrannical acts in the name of liberty," because imperialism and democracy are incompatible, see Isidro Fabela, *Los Estados Unidos contra la libertad* (Barcelona: Talleres Gráficos Lux, 1921), p. 14.

10. Mark T. Gilderhus, *Pan American Visions: Woodrow Wilson in the Western Hemisphere, 1913–1921* (Tucson: University of Arizona Press, 1986), pp. 18–20, 34.

11. Wright, pp. 103–8, 139–41.

12. Ibid., pp. 53, 139–49. Emily S. Rosenberg, *Spreading the American Dream: American Economic and Cultural Expansion, 1890–1945* (New York: Hill & Wang, 1982).

13. John Morton Blum, *The Republican Roosevelt* (New York: Atheneum, 1968).

14. Louis A. Pérez, Jr., *Cuba under the Platt Amendment, 1902–1934* (Pittsburgh: University of Pittsburgh Press, 1986). For this and other interventions, see Whitney T. Perkins, *Constraint of Empire: The United States and Caribbean Interventions* (Westport, Conn.: Greenwood Press, 1981). Also useful is Lester D. Langley, *The Banana Wars: An Inner History of American Empire, 1900–1934* (Lexington: University Press of Kentucky, 1983); and Wright, pp. 4–10.

15. Dana G. Munro, *Intervention and Dollar Diplomacy in the Caribbean, 1900–1921* (Princeton: Princeton University Press, 1964), pp. 130–40. Lester D. Langley, *The United States and the Caribbean in the Twentieth Century* (Athens: University of Georgia Press, 1982), pp. 40–43. Jules Robert Benjamin, *The United States and Cuba: Hegemony and Dependent Development, 1880–1934* (Pittsburgh: University of Pittsburgh Press, 1974), pp. 20–26. Wright, pp. 4–16.

16. Wright, pp. 23–34.

17. Ibid., pp. 35–37. Munro, *Intervention,* pp. 152–53.

18. Ronning, pp. 150–55.

19. Sidney Bell, *Righteous Conquest: Woodrow Wilson and the Evolution of the New Diplomacy* (Port Washington, N.Y.: Kennikat Press, 1972), p. 49.

20. Munro, *Intervention*, pp. 173–90. For general coverage of the long history of U.S. interventions in Central America, see Walter LaFeber, *Inevitable Revolutions: The United States in Central America* (New York: Norton, 1984). Even more useful is the older survey by Samuel Flagg Bemis, *The Latin American Policy of the United States: An Historical Interpretation* (New York: Norton, 1943).

21. Wright, pp. 37–42.

22. Melvin M. Knight, *The Americans in Santo Domingo* (New York: Vanguard Press, 1928), p. 57. Munro, *Intervention*, p. 271.

23. Harley Notter, *The Origins of the Foreign Policy of Woodrow Wilson* (New York: Russell & Russell, 1965), pp. 43–47, 222–31, 460–61. N. Gordon Levin, Jr., *Woodrow Wilson and World Politics: America's Response to War and Revolution* (New York: Oxford University Press, 1968). Munro, *Intervention*, p. 271. Bell, pp. 54–55, 72–75. Gilderhus, *Pan American Visions*, pp. 11–12, 17–18.

24. Notter, pp. 222–31. Munro, *Intervention*, p. 426.

25. Notter, pp. 284, 364–65.

26. Munro, *Intervention*, pp. 448–66, 498. Bemis, pp. 172–76. Wright, p. 101.

27. Gilderhus, *Pan American Visions*, p. 12. Falabella, pp. 176–77. Vicente Saenz, *Norteamericanización de Centro América* (San Jose, Costa Rica: Talleres de La Opinión, 1925). Enrique Gil, *Evolución del panamericanismo: el credo de Wilson y el panamericanismo* (Buenos Aires, 1933). John T. Reid, *Spanish American Images of the United States, 1790–1960* (Gainesville: University of Florida Press, 1977).

28. Gilderhus, *Pan American Visions*, pp. 69–77.

29. Bell, pp. 59, 73–74. Notter, pp. 49–50, 82, 100–101, 111–12, 229.

30. James H. McCrocklin, *Garde D'Haiti, 1915–1934: Twenty Years of Organization and Training by the United States Marine Corps* (Annapolis: United States Naval Institute Press, 1956). Marvin Goldwert, *The Constabulary in the Dominican Republic and Nicaragua: Progeny and Legacy of United States Intervention* (Gainesville: University of Florida Press, 1962). David Healy, *Drive to Hegemony: The United States in the Caribbean, 1898–1917* (Madison: University of Wisconsin Press, 1988), pp. 221–27. Munro, *Intervention*, p. 540.

31. Munro, *Intervention*, pp. 533–35. William A. Williams, *The Tragedy of American Diplomacy*, rev. ed. (New York: Delta, 1962).

32. Wright, pp. 69–76.

33. Mark T. Gilderhus, *Diplomacy and Revolution: U.S.-Mexican Relations under Wilson and Carranza* (Tucson: University of Arizona Press, 1977), pp. 2–14. Alan Knight, *U.S.-Mexican Relations, 1910–1940: An Interpretation* (La Jolla, Calif.: Center for U.S.-Mexican Relations, 1987), pp. 6, 103–30. Friedrich Katz, *The Secret War in Mexico: Europe, the United States and the Mexican Revolution* (Chicago: University of Chicago Press, 1981). Robert E. Quirk, *An Affair of Honor: Woodrow Wilson and the Occupation of Vera Cruz* (New York: Norton, 1962). Wright, pp. 71–76.

34. Knight. Gilderhus, *Pan American Visions*, p. 34. Bell, pp. 78–81, 97–99.

35. Gilderhus, *Pan American Visions*, pp. 12–13, 32–34, 52–53. Federico G. Gil, *Latin American-United States Relations* (New York: Harcourt, Brace, Jovanovich, 1971), pp. 108–10. Kenneth J. Grieb, *The United States and Huerta* (Lincoln: University of Nebraska Press, 1969). Michael C. Meyer, *Huerta, A Political Portrait* (Lincoln: University of Nebraska Press, 1972). Larry D. Hill, *Emissaries to a Revolution: Woodrow Wilson's Executive Agents in Mexico* (Baton Rouge: Louisiana State University Press, 1973).

36. Gilderhus, *Diplomacy*, pp. 30–71. Wright, pp. 76–77. Gil, pp. 110–12. Robert Freeman Smith, *The United States and Revolutionary Nationalism in Mexico, 1916–1932* (Chicago: University of Chicago Press, 1972).

37. Gordon Connell-Smith, *The United States and Latin America: An Historical Analysis of Inter-American Relations* (London: Heinemann Educational Books, 1974), p. 148.

38. Munro, *Intervention*, pp. 277–300.

39. Connell-Smith, pp. 140–41. Bruce J. Calder, *The Impact of Intervention: The Dominican Republic during the U.S. Occupation of 1916–1924* (Austin: University of Texas Press, 1984). Sumner Welles, *Naboth's Vineyard: The Dominican Republic, 1844–1924*, 2 vols. (New York: Payson & Clarke, 1928), vol. 2. Stephen M. Fuller and Graham A. Cosmas, *Marines in the Dominican Republic* (Washington, D.C.: U.S. Marines Corps Press, 1974). Max Henríquez Ureña, *Los yanquis en Santo Domingo* (Madrid: M. Aguilar, 1929). Munro, *Intervention*, pp. 313–25. Langley, *The United States*, pp. 77–85.

40. Munro, *Intervention*, pp. 329–34.

41. Ibid., pp. 342–47.

42. Arthur C. Millspaugh, *Haiti under American Control, 1915–1930* (Boston: World Peace Foundation, 1931), pp. 28–30. Gilderhus, *Pan American Visions*, p. 15.

43. Munro, *Intervention*, pp. 353–59. Millspaugh, pp. 38–41. Bemis, pp. 191–93. Hans Schmidt, *The United States Occupation of Haiti, 1915–1934* (New Brunswick, N.J.: Rutgers University Press, 1971).

44. McCrocklin, pp. 101–2.

45. Millspaugh, pp. 1–2, 12–20, 62. McCrocklin, pp. 77–79. Langley, *The United States*, pp. 68–77. Munro, *Intervention*, pp. 368–71. Schmidt, pp. 97–100. For further details on the Haitian occupation and its undemocratic character, see Ludwell Lee Montague, *Haiti and the United States, 1714–1938* (New York: Russell & Russell, 1966).

46. Munro, *Intervention*, pp. 406–13. Henry L. Stimson, *A Brief History of the Relations between the United States and Nicaragua, 1909–1928* (Washington, D.C., 1928).

47. Munro, *Intervention*, pp. 417–25. Wright, pp. 45–51.

48. Munro, *Intervention*, pp. 498–525. Wright, pp. 16–20. Louis A. Pérez, Jr., *Intervention, Revolution, and Politics in Cuba, 1913–1921* (Pittsburgh: University of Pittsburgh Press, 1978).

49. Munro, *Intervention*, pp. 427–36. George W. Baker, Jr., "Woodrow Wilson's Use of the Nonrecognition Policy in Costa Rica," *The Americas* 22 (July 1965): 3–21. Langley, *The United States*, pp. 89–90. Wright, pp. 97–101.

50. Dana G. Munro, *The United States and the Caribbean Republics, 1921–1933* (Princeton: Princeton University Press, 1974), p. 118. Wright, pp. 102–5.

51. Munro, *Intervention*, pp. 540–43.

52. Munro, *The United States*, pp. 4–5. Calder, p. 202. Kenneth J. Grieb, *The Latin American Policy of Warren G. Harding* (Fort Worth: Texas Christian University Press, 1976), pp. 4–9.

53. Benjamin, p. 49. Tulchin. Williams.

54. Munro, *The United States*, pp. 9–10.

55. Ibid., pp. 16–43.

56. Chandler P. Anderson, "Our Policy of Non-Recognition in Central America," *American Journal of International Law* 25 (1931): 298–301. Wright, pp. 55–57. Munro, *The United States*, pp. 124–26. Connell-Smith, p. 129. Tulchin, pp. 102–3. Gil, pp. 75–76. Langley, *The United States*, pp. 107–8.

57. Munro, *The United States*, pp. 126–42. Wright, pp. 105–10.

58. Millspaugh, p. 109.

59. Calder, p. 249.

60. Schmidt, pp. 145–52. Emily Greene Balch, *Occupied Haiti* (New York: Garland Publishing, 1972).

61. Grieb, *Latin American Policy*, pp. 93–95.

62. Munro, *The United States*, pp. 75–79, 85–115. Balch, pp. 28–33. Montague, pp. 238–43. Millspaugh, pp. 233–35.

63. John Houston Craige, *Black Bagdad* (New York: Minton, Balch & Co., 1933), p. 15.

64. Grieb, *Latin American Policy,* pp. 61–78. Munro, *The United States,* pp. 47, 55, 60–64.

65. Calder, pp. 238–39.

66. Welles, pp. 904–21.

67. Wright, p. 50.

68. Munro, *The United States,* pp. 164–86. Wright, pp. 50–55. Langley, pp. 116–17.

69. Benjamin, p. 67.

70. Paul W. Drake, *The Money Doctor in the Andes: U.S. Advisers, Investors, and Economic Reform during the Kemmerer Missions, 1923–1933* (Durham, N.C.: Duke University Press, 1989), pp. 135–64.

71. William Kamman, *A Search for Stability: United States Diplomacy toward Nicaragua, 1925–1933* (Notre Dame, Ind.: University of Notre Dame Press, 1968). Neill Macauley, *The Sandino Affair* (Chicago: Quadrangle Press, 1967). Raymond Leslie Buell, "American Supervision of Elections in Nicaragua," *Foreign Policy Reports* 6, no. 21 (December 24, 1930): 385–402. Wright, pp. 59–65. Langley, *The United States,* pp. 118–25. Munro, *The United States,* pp. 187–254. Goldwert, pp. 29–43.

72. Munro, *The United States,* pp. 345–49.

73. *Addresses Delivered during the Visit of Herbert Hoover, President-Elect of the United States, to Central and South America, November–December, 1928* (Washington, D.C.: Pan American Union Press, 1929), p. 16. Alexander DeConde, *Herbert Hoover's Latin American Policy* (Stanford, Calif.: Stanford University Press, 1951), pp. 4–5, 59.

74. DeConde, pp. 52–59. Munro, *The United States,* pp. 279–80. Benjamin, pp. 77–79. William Starr Meyers, *The Foreign Policies of Herbert Hoover, 1929–1933* (New York: Garland Publishing, 1979), pp. 45–47.

75. DeConde, pp. 93–94, 98–100.

76. Munro, *The United States,* pp. 290–94.

77. E. R. Curry, *Hoover's Dominican Diplomacy and the Origins of the Good Neighbor Policy* (New York: Garland Publishing, 1979). Munro, *The United States,* pp. 294–301.

78. Munro, *The United States,* pp. 349–82. Benjamin, pp. 67–70.

79. Schmidt, pp. 145–46.

80. Millspaugh, pp. 241–49.

81. Munro, *The United States,* pp. 309–18.

82. Schmidt, pp. 211–19. Munro, *The United States,* pp. 333–41.

83. Kamman, pp. 169–236. Buell. Connell-Smith, pp. 150–52. Munro, *The United States,* pp. 255–79. Goldwert, pp. 32–47.

84. DeConde, pp. 56–57. Munro, *The United States,* pp. 281–82.

85. DeConde, pp. 57–58. Langley, *The United States,* pp. 130–31. Munro, *The United States,* pp. 283–90. LaFeber, pp. 72–74.

86. Paul W. Drake, *Socialism and Populism in Chile, 1932–1952* (Urbana: University of Illinois Press, 1978), pp. 76–81. DeConde, p. 55. Bemis, pp. 222–23.

87. Bryce Wood, *The Making of the Good Neighbor Policy* (New York: Norton, 1967). Irwin F. Gellman, *Good Neighbor Diplomacy: United States Policies in Latin America, 1933–1945* (Baltimore: Johns Hopkins University Press, 1979).

88. Duncan Snidal, "The Limits of Hegemonic Stability," *International Organization* 39, no. 4 (Autumn 1985): 579–614.

89. Connell-Smith, pp. 275–83. Cole Blasier, "The United States and Democracy in Latin America," in James M. Malloy and Mitchell A. Seligson, eds., *Authoritarians and Democrats: Regime Transition in Latin America* (Pittsburgh: University of Pittsburgh Press, 1987), pp. 219–34.

2 | From the Second World War to the Cold War: 1944–1954

Leslie Bethell

THE YEARS 1944 and 1945," wrote a contributor to *Inter-American Affairs 1945,* an annual survey edited by Arthur P. Whitaker, the distinguished U.S. historian of Latin America and of U.S.–Latin American relations, "brought more democratic changes in more Latin American countries than perhaps in any single year since the Wars of Independence."[1] There was indeed a sudden and dramatic advance of democracy throughout Latin America at the end of World War II. It was, however, quickly contained. By 1954 it had for the most part reversed.

To understand the political history of Latin America in the decade after 1944, and in particular the successes and failures of democracy, it is necessary to explore not only the shifting balance of domestic political forces in each country but also the complex interplay between domestic politics and international politics as World War II came to an end and, almost simultaneously, the cold war began. This chapter examines the role of the United States, both direct and indirect, in at first encouraging, and at times promoting, and in later controlling, and in at least one case terminating, democratic openings in Latin America during the period from 1944 to 1954.

I

At the beginning of 1944 it could be argued that Uruguay was the only democracy in Latin America; it alone, for example, had an executive freely and fairly elected on universal suffrage. Chile, however, and to a lesser extent Costa Rica and Colombia, also had some claim to call themselves democratic in the sense that their governments were civilian and had been elected (however limited the suffrage and however restricted the political participation), political competition of some kind was permitted (however weak the party system), and the rule of law obtained and basic civil liberties such as freedom of speech, association, and assembly were at least formally honored (however precariously at times). Argentina had been democratic in the two decades before the revolution of 1930, but during the "infamous decade" of the 1930s Argentine democracy was distinctly flawed and in any event had been overthrown in June 1943 in a nationalist military coup. Revolutionary Mexico was a special case: presidents (Lázaro Cárdenas in 1934, Manuel Avila Camacho in 1940) were elected and were emphatically not eligible for reelection, but elections, though competitive, were firmly controlled by the ruling revolutionary party, the Partido Revolucionario Mexicano (PRM) (renamed the Partido Revolucionario Institucional [PRI] in 1946).

During the final twelve months of World War II and the first twelve months after the war democracy was consolidated in a number of countries where it already existed. In Costa Rica in 1944 President Rafael Angel Calderón Guardía, elected in 1940, handed over power to Teodoro Picado, who had himself been elected (though not without accusations of fraud and intimidation). In Colombia President Alfonso López, a Liberal who had been elected in 1942 (though here, too, the elections had not been without violence and fraud), resigned in July 1945 and was replaced as acting president by his foreign minister, Dr. Alberto Lleras Camargo. The presidential elections of 1946, in which one of the two Liberal candidates, Dr. Jorge Eliézer Gaitán, attempted for the first time to broaden the party's popular base, were won by the Conservative candidate Mariano Ospina Pérez running on a bipartisan National Union ticket, thus bringing to an end—democratically—sixteen years of continuous Liberal rule. In Chile elections in 1946 brought to power Gabriel González Videla, the third Popular Front president elected in succession since 1938.

These two years (mid–1944 to mid–1946) also witnessed significant moves in the direction of democracy in countries less obviously democratic but not outright dictatorships. In Ecuador in May 1944 a popular rebellion in which the Alianza Democrática Ecuatoriana (ADE)—a coalition of Socialists, Communists, Conservatives, and dissident Liberals—played a prominent role led to the military coup that overthrew the fraudulently elected and repressive regime of Carlos Arroyo del Río and brought to power the leading opposition figure José María Velasco Ibarra (in exile at the time). The following year a Constituent Assembly was elected and confirmed Velasco in the presidency. In Cuba, Fulgencio Batista permitted free elections in June 1944, which were won by Ramón Grau San Martín, the heir to the popular revolution of 1933–34 and the candidate of the opposition Partido Revolucionario Cubano-Auténtico (PRC-A); Grau defeated Carlos Saladrigas, Batista's candidate and himself the leader of a coalition that called itself Democratic Socialist. (It was at this time that Blas Roca, the Communist leader, praised Batista as "this magnificent reserve of Cuban democracy.")[2] In Panama in May 1945 a newly elected Constituent Assembly appointed an interim president, Enrique A. Jiménez, who had the support of a coalition of opposition groups led by Don Pancho Arias Paredes's Partido Renovador. Jiménez was to serve until elections (which were, however, delayed until October 1948 following the death of Don Pancho). In Peru free elections were permitted for the first time in June 1945; they were won overwhelmingly by José Luis Bustamante y Rivero of the Frente Democrático Nacional (which had been formed the year before)—with the support of the Alianza Popular Revolucionaria Americana (APRA), Peru's most popular political movement. (APRA, which had been excluded from politics for more than a decade, had been legalized a month before the election and in January 1946 joined Bustamante's cabinet.) In Venezuela, still in the aftermath of the long dictatorship of Juan Vicente Gómez (1908–35), President Isaías Medina Angarita toward the end of the war pursued a policy of gradual liberalization in association with Unión Popular, the legal front of the Venezuelan Communist party, but refused to allow direct presidential elections in 1946. On October 18, 1945, a military coup in the name of democracy backed by Acción Democrática (AD) brought down the Medina administration and led to Venezuela's first experiment with democracy; in three successive elections during the next three years, including presidential elections in December 1947, AD won more than 70 percent of the vote.

Even in Mexico the ruling party in January 1946 introduced primary elections of candidates to posts other than president.[3] Miguel Alemán, the presidential candidate of the PRM (albeit the first civilian—and the first university-educated—candidate) was, however, chosen in the traditional manner and safely elected (also in the traditional manner) in July. Mexican democracy was still largely rhetorical. The revolution itself remained the principal source of political legitimacy.

More significant, the same period witnessed a number of successful transitions from military or military-backed dictatorships of various kinds to democracy broadly defined. In Guatemala a popular uprising led to the downfall of the thirteen-year dictatorship of Jorge Ubico in July 1944 and the election in December of Juan José Arévalo, the "spiritual socialist" schoolteacher returned from exile in Argentina. In Brazil at the beginning of 1945 Getúlio Vargas, who had been in power since 1930, took the first steps toward the liberalization of the Estado Novo (1937–45). On February 28 he announced that within three months a date would be set for presidential and congressional elections, and under the electoral law of May 28 national elections were indeed held on December 2—the first relatively democratic elections in the country's history. In Argentina May and June 1945 saw the reactivation of the liberal opposition to the nationalist military regime of Edelmiro Farrell and Juan Perón which culminated on September 19 in a massive demonstration by several hundred thousand people in Buenos

Aires, "The March for Constitution and Liberty," and the first concrete steps toward democratic elections the following year. Finally, the nationalist military government in Bolivia supported by the Movimiento Revolucionario Nacional (MNR) of Víctor Paz Estenssoro, which had come to power as a result of a coup in December 1943, was brought down in July 1946 by a violent popular revolt in which President Gualberto Villarroel was lynched. The driving force behind the revolt was a newly formed coalition of the Liberal right and the Marxist left, the Frente Democrático Antifascista (FDA), which immediately promised to hold democratic elections in January 1947.

Thus, the end of World War II brought not only consolidation of existing democracies but also a number of transitions, both peaceful and violent, to at least partial democracy throughout Latin America. No single country moved in the opposite direction. Indeed by the middle of 1946 the only Latin American states that could not claim to be in some sense popular and democratic in their origins if not in their practice (Perón, though popularly elected, can hardly be said to have established a democratic system in Argentina) were Paraguay and a handful of republics in Central America and the Caribbean: El Salvador, Honduras, Nicaragua, and the Dominican Republic. And most of these dictatorships that had survived the postwar wave of democratization had been shaken; some had been obliged to make at least token gestures toward political liberalization. In El Salvador in May 1944, a few weeks before the fall of Ubico in Guatemala, a popular uprising had actually overthrown the thirteen-year dictatorship of General Maximiliano Hernández Martínez, but in October an election campaign had been aborted and a dictatorship restored. In Honduras there had also been disturbances in May 1944, but they were relatively minor and failed to dislodge Tiburcio Carías Andino. In Nicaragua demonstrations in June 1944, however, had forced Anastasio Somoza, dictator since 1937, to announce in September—and to reiterate during 1945 and 1946—that he would not seek reelection at the end of his "term" in 1947. He permitted Leonardo Argüello, his opponent in 1936, to win the presidential elections in May 1947. (Argüello was, however, the candidate of Somoza against the Independent Liberals and Conservatives, and he was only to remain in office for one month.) Even Rafael Leónidas Trujillo in the Dominican Republic faced for the first time since his seizure of power in 1930 opposition from both labor and the left (including the Communist left). This let to his engineering a carefully controlled opening at the end of the war and elections in May 1947, which were somewhat freer than earlier elections but which he naturally won. In Paraguay in the summer of 1946 General Higinio Morínigo, "elected" unopposed in 1943, ended press censorship, relaxed prohibitions on political activities, and even included Colorados and Febreristas in a coalition cabinet. He promised to prepare Paraguay for a "return to democracy" but no date was ever set for elections.

Four features of Latin American democratization at the end of World War II are worthy of note in the light of the discussion to follow. First, a number of "progressive" political parties that sought to extend the political participation of the middle class and workers and to promote social reform and national economic development came to power for the first time, or at least to a share of power. These included the Auténticos in Cuba, Rómulo Betancourt's AD in Venezuela (which also built up strong support in the rural areas), Haya de la Torre's APRA in Peru, and the Peronists in Argentina. All of them had been recently formed (some of them only at the end of World War II). Most were strongly personalist and populist. Of course, not all of these parties came to power by democratic means. Some were less than thoroughly committed to democracy. And with the passage of time, even their commitment to social and economic change was considerably reduced.

Second, the Latin American left, and especially the Communist left, made gains, albeit much more limited, in the postwar period. After more than twenty years of weakness, isolation, and for the most part illegality, the Latin American Communist parties suddenly achieved for a brief period a degree of popularity, power, and influence—which would never be recaptured except in Cuba after 1959 and (briefly) in Chile in the early 1970s. After the German invasion of Russia and the break up of the short-lived Nazi-Soviet pact, wartime imperatives brought a return to the tactics of class collaboration and the popular front laid down by the Seventh World Congress of the Comintern (1935). Communists, even where they had no legal status, generally supported national unity and the Allied cause; they were part of the antifascist, democratic front (in wartime government coalitions in Cuba, Costa Rica, and Chile) and therefore participants in and beneficiaries of the democratic advance at the end of the war. They also benefited from the temporary but enormous postwar prestige of the Soviet Union. Meanwhile, the Comintern had effectively ceased to function after 1935 and had finally been dissolved in 1943. During the war and its immediate aftermath, the Latin American Communist parties were largely neglected by Moscow and experienced a growing, though relative, independence of action. What became known as Browderism, the belief that Communists should increasingly act as an integral part of nationally oriented, broad popular movements, even to the extent of voluntary dissolution, made headway in several Latin American countries (Cuba, Mexico, and Venezuela, for example).

At the end of the war Communist parties were legalized or at least tolerated in virtually every country. Total membership, less than 100,000 in 1939, had reached half a million by 1947.[4] Communists had considerable success in elections all over Latin America. In some countries, their gains were especially significant.[5] In Costa Rica, for example, Picado won the elections of 1944 with Communist support. In Chile in September 1946 González Videla, a Radical but regarded as "the Communist candidate," was elected president, and in April 1947 90,000 (17 percent) voted for the PCCh in the municipal elections. In Cuba 130,000 in 1944 and 200,000 in 1946 voted for the Partido Socialista Popular (PSP), the Communists. Finally, in Brazil the PCB secured half a million votes (10 percent) in the presidential and congressional elections of December 1945 and again in the elections for governor and state assembly in January 1947.

Third, it was in the immediate postwar years that organized labor was incorporated into democratic politics in a number of Latin American countries. During the 1930s and World War II the size of the working class had expanded considerably. And its character was being rapidly transformed: besides the already important nuclei of workers in the agricultural and mining export sectors, and workers in transportation and public utilities, white collar workers, many of them state employees, and industrial workers were increasingly important. At the same time, union membership expanded: at the end of the war between 3.5 and 4 million workers were unionized in Latin America as a whole.[6] The Confederación de Trabajadores de América Latina (CTAL), founded by the Mexican Marxist labor leader Vicente Lombardo Toledano in 1938, claimed to represent some 3.3 million members in sixteen countries. During the war real standards of living had generally declined: in the interests of the Allied war effort and the battle for production, wages were held down by social pacts and no-strike pledges; at the same time inflation rose as a result of shortages of imports and strong demand pressure, huge balance-of-payments surpluses from export earnings and accumulated reserves, and overvalued exchange rates. And the labor market was increasingly tight, a fact that improved union bargaining power.

In the new liberal atmosphere at the end of the war pent-up demands were released and Latin America experienced its most intense period of labor militancy since 1917–19, at the end of World War I. A variety of political leaders, movements, and parties sought to expand their influence in the labor movement and harness this militancy politically. Communist parties made important advances within the labor unions throughout Latin America. But they did not have things all their own way. In those countries (such as Chile) where there was a well-established non-Communist Marxist left (the Socialist party), it offered a challenge to the Communists. In other countries relatively new parties like the Auténticos in Cuba and AD in Venezuela or personalistic movements of the kind led by Vargas in Brazil and Perón in Argentina emerged as serious (and often successful) rivals to the Communist parties.

Finally, there was a profound, if dimly perceived, shift in the nature of political discourse and ideology during and after World War II. The emergence of "democracy" as a central symbol with almost universal resonance was specific to this period. Of course, the term was used by different actors to mean quite distinct things. For some it meant simply a commitment to the Allied camp. For others it still meant essentially elections and the rule of law. For many people in Latin America, however, the meaning of the term underwent a considerable expansion. Democracy was now seen to imply a commitment to wider popular and especially urban working-class participation in politics. And it also had its economic and social dimensions. It came increasingly to be identified with national economic development, social justice, and a more equal distribution of wealth.

II

The principal factor behind the political climate and the political changes in Latin America during the years 1944, 1945, and 1946 was the victory of the Allies, especially the United States and Britain but including the Soviet Union and thus the victory of democracy over fascism, in World War II. Despite the strength of Axis, especially German, interests in Latin America and indeed widespread pro-Axis (and profascist) sympathies throughout the region in the late 1930s and early 1940s, in the immediate aftermath of Pearl Harbor all the Latin American states except Chile (temporarily) and Argentina (until March 1945) had lined up with the United States and severed relations with the Axis powers; eventually most, although until 1945 by no means all, had declared war. Formally at least, and in some cases with varying degrees of cynicism and realpolitik, they had chosen the side of Freedom and Democracy. The war itself had strengthened existing ties— military, economic, political, ideological—between Latin America (except, of course, Argentina) and the United States. As it became certain that the Allies would win the war and as the nature of the postwar international political and economic order and the hegemonic position of the United States within it became clear, the dominant groups in Latin America, including the military, recognized the need to make some necessary political and ideological adjustments and concessions.

There was also at the end of World War II considerable internal pressure, from the urban middle class and in the economically more developed countries from the urban working class, for more open, democratic political systems. Wartime and postwar demands for democracy drew upon a strong liberal tradition in Latin American politics and culture. But they were also the product of an extraordinary outpouring of wartime propaganda in favor of U.S. democracy and the American way of (and standard of) life directed at Latin America. This was orchestrated above all by Nelson Rockefeller's Office of the Coordinator of Inter-American Affairs (OCIAA). By the end of the war, it should be remembered, press, radio, and the film industry throughout Latin America had been heavily penetrated by U.S. capital.

Thus *indirectly* the United States clearly played an important role in the democratization of Latin America at the end of World War II. But how did the United States *respond* to political developments in Latin America in the years 1944 and 1945? Did the United States *actively* encourage and *directly* promote democracy—and with what results?

The "hard" or "primary" interests of the United States in Latin America have always been geopolitical and strategic (the defense of the Western Hemisphere against external attack or internal subversion by a foreign enemy of the United States and therefore, it was assumed, of the Latin American states) and economic (the promotion of U.S. trade with, and investment in, Latin America). At the same time it was felt—by public opinion and the media as well as by policy makers—that the United States had an interest, albeit "soft" or "secondary," in the dissemination of U.S. ideas and culture, the U.S. economic model, and U.S. political institutions. It was sometimes argued (not always convincingly) that democracies in Latin America would be more stable, peaceful, and friendly than dictatorships and therefore their promotion was in the long-term strategic and economic interests of the United States. In the short term it might, however, be in the interests of the United States to support, or at least not to oppose, stable, peaceful, and friendly dictatorships. Democracy was in the last analysis disposable. And in any case, where outside Uruguay and Argentina (until 1930) and perhaps Chile, Costa Rica, and Colombia was democracy to be found in Latin America? And how should the United States promote it? When in the past the United States had intervened to *impose* democracy by force—for example, in Nicaragua and the Dominican Republic—not only had the political cost been high in terms of conflict and animosity, which threatened U.S. strategic and economic interests, but the results had been poor, or worse, in terms of the advancement of democracy.

During the 1920s and early 1930s the administrations of Harding, Coolidge, and Hoover had abandoned the Wilsonian crusade for democracy in Latin America. The cornerstone of Franklin D. Roosevelt's Good Neighbor Policy was a policy of nonintervention in the internal political affairs of the other American republics (even for the promotion of democracy). Most (though by no means all) U.S. foreign policy makers preferred democracies to dictatorships but they found it hard to reconcile a desire to promote democracy with respect for the principle of nonintervention. As a result they ended up in effect endorsing a number of unsavory dictators, most notoriously Trujillo in the Dominican Republic and Somoza in Nicaragua. With the onset of World War II the United States was concerned only that the Latin American states should be on the side of the Allies. Washington actively cooperated with *all* stable, cooperative regimes in Latin America, dictatorships and democracies, that opposed the Axis powers. Indeed indirectly through credits, purchases of commodities at prices favorable to producers, and military assistance (through the U.S. Lend-Lease Act), this meant maintaining many dictatorships in power. The United States' closest ally in Latin America—and the recipient of more than 70

percent of all lend-lease to Latin America—was the Brazilian dictator Getúlio Vargas.

Some U.S. officials both in Washington and Latin America were troubled by the inconsistencies and ambiguities in the policy of the United States
toward Latin American dictatorships during the war, which was after all
being fought for democracy. For example, Ambassador Walter Thurston
wrote to the secretary of state from San Salvador in January 1944:

> Our pronouncements such as the Atlantic Charter and the Declaration of the
> Four Freedoms (the latter blazoned by us throughout El Salvador in the form
> of posters) are accepted literally by the Salvadoreans as endorsement of the
> basic democratic principles we desire to have prevail currently and universally.
> . . . It is difficult for them to reconcile these pronouncements with the fact that
> the United States tolerates and apparently is gratified to enter into association
> with governments in America which cannot be described as other than total-
> itarian. . . .
>
> The principal defect of a policy of nonintervention accompanied by prop-
> aganda on behalf of democratic doctrines is that it simultaneously stimulates
> dictatorships and popular opposition to them. Moreover, by according dic-
> tators who seize or retain power unconstitutionally the same consideration
> extended to honestly elected presidents we not only impair our moral lead-
> ership but foment the belief that our democratic professions are empty propa-
> ganda and that we are in fact simply guided by expediency.
>
> It is of course unthinkable that we should revert to the folly of interven-
> tion—but it seems to be evident that our present policy is not satisfactory,
> especially in the Caribbean and Central American areas.[7]

Ambassador Ellis O. Briggs, described by William Krehn of *Time* magazine
as "an impossible young man with a vague resemblance to Groucho Marx
and loathsome democratic convictions,"[8] wrote to the secretary of state
from Ciudad Trujillo in July 1944:

> Although Trujillo's dictatorship represents the negation of many of the princi-
> ples to which the United States subscribes, promotion of his overthrow is not
> the responsibility of the American Government nor would such action be
> consistent with our present commitments with respect to non-intervention.
> Trujillo is primarily a Dominican problem, for solution by the Dominican
> people. . . . However, we should decline to endorse Trujillo's dictatorship, or
> to permit ourselves through misinterpretation of our policies to become identi-
> fied with it. Sooner or later American public opinion will interest itself in the
> kind of governments existing in the other American republics and demand
> that, without interfering in their internal affairs, we nevertheless take cog-
> nizance of conditions and base to a larger degree than heretofore our attitude
> toward them on the conduct of those governments toward their own people.[9]

There was a complex interaction between governments, oppositions,
and U.S. embassies in Central America—and elsewhere in the region—
throughout 1944. But it appears that neither Thurston in El Salvador nor

Ambassador Boaz Long in Guatemala played any significant part in the downfall of the two oldest dictatorships in Central America. Indeed they followed strict instructions not to intervene. And there is no evidence of U.S. involvement in the democratic elections in Cuba in June 1944. In Mexico Ambassador George S. Messersmith, the "diplomat of democracy," for a while favored and actively promoted the candidacy of Foreign Minister Ezequiel Padilla for the presidency in the interests of greater democratic choice, free enterprise, and good relations with the United States.[10] But Padilla was quickly dropped when it became clear in 1945 that Alemán had the nomination sewn up. Washington preferred the maintenance of the status quo in Mexico, Central America, and the Caribbean for the duration of the war.

Nevertheless, with the growth of democratic opposition to the dictatorships as the war came to an end and the overthrow and defeat of many dictators and semidictators, the United States became more aware of the ambiguities inherent in its position. Policy began subtly to shift. In September 1944 John Moors Cabot, the chief of the State Department's Division of Caribbean and Central American Affairs, could write to Norman Armour, the acting director of the Office of American Republic Affairs:

> At the present juncture, I do not think we can afford to show particular friendship for hardboiled dictatorships, even though they have cooperated in the war effort. Quite apart from the fact that these administrations, and notably that of Trujillo, are anything but democratic, *we do not wish to give the appearance of violating our non-intervention policy by favoring the existing regimes.*[11]

And when in October Ubico's successor seemed disinclined to proceed with elections, Armour told Ambassador Long that he and a number of his colleagues were deeply concerned at political developments in Guatemala *and elsewhere in Latin America:*

> This problem of support for democratic processes is not an easy one and was discussed at some length in the staff meeting this morning. The idea was advanced that we might have President Roosevelt or the Secretary include in an early address a statement more or less along the following lines: "We wish to cultivate friendly relations with every government in the world and do not feel ourselves entitled to dictate to any country what form of government best suits its national aspirations. We nevertheless must naturally feel a greater affinity, a deeper sympathy and a warmer friendship for governments which effectively represent the practical application of democratic processes."[12]

Long was instructed that this represented the thinking of the department and he was authorized to say so in Guatemala. Washington positively welcomed Ponce's decision to go and quickly recognized both the revolutionary government (which represented "the establishment of democratic ideals and procedures") and the democratically elected Arévalo administration. In November 1944 Adolf Berle, assistant secretary of state, in a circular to U.S. embassies in Latin America underlined the fact that the United States would feel more favorably disposed toward "governments established on the periodically and freely expressed consent of the governed."[13]

At the Inter-American Conference on the Problems of War and Peace (the Chapultepec Conference) held in Mexico City in February and March 1945, the United States led the Latin American states in declaring a "fervent adherence to democratic principles." And during 1945 Washington began more openly to distance itself from and demonstrate official disapproval of Latin American dictatorships. On May 28 the acting secretary of state, Joseph C. Grew, circulated to all missions in Latin America a document by Spruille Braden, formerly U.S. ambassador in Bogotá and Havana and recently appointed to the embassy in Buenos Aires, entitled "Policy re Dictatorships and Disreputable Governments," that recommended an attitude of "aloof formality" rather than friendly cooperation and, more specifically, an end to financial assistance and military aid.[14] Braden's appointment as assistant secretary of state in charge of Latin American affairs in August 1945 in open recognition of the active role he had played in the democratization of Argentina (to be discussed) was seen as a clear signal that a more positive antidictatorship-prodemocracy stance was to be adopted toward Latin America as a whole.[15]

As the opening shots in the cold war were fired (for example, in the conflict with the Soviet Union over democracy in Eastern Europe at the conference of foreign ministers in London in September 1945), there was a new imperative behind the U.S. desire that its allies in Latin America be seen to be democratic. In November 1945 the secretary of state, James F. Byrnes, surprisingly endorsed a proposal by Eduardo Rodríguez Larreta, the Uruguayan foreign minister, in favor of multilateral *intervention* in support of democratic regimes and against oppressive regimes in Latin America.[16] Its implications were not, however, clear. More practically, in December the State Department rejected a request from the Dominican Republic for export licenses for arms shipments on the grounds that it was "unable to perceive that democratic principles have been observed there in theory or in practice."[17]

It is interesting to note that throughout 1945 (and for that matter 1946 and even the first half of 1947) U.S. officials, in Washington and in Latin America, were not disturbed by the fact that Communists were playing a prominent part in the region's democratization. On the contrary, their participation was positively welcomed in, for example, Brazil, Argentina, Bolivia, Costa Rica, and Chile. For reasons we have seen, Communists were part of the antifascist, democratic front. Fascism, not Communism, was the main "totalitarian" enemy of democracy—and of U.S. interests—in Latin America. Significantly it was in Argentina, Brazil, Bolivia, and Paraguay (the countries to which for different reasons the label "fascist" could most readily, though not necessarily convincingly, be attached) that the United States intervened most *directly*—and with some degree of success—in support of democracy at the end of World War II. (There is no firm evidence that the United States played any significant role in, for example, the decision to hold free elections in Peru in June 1945 or in the military coup that brought Acción Democrática to power in Venezuela in October—although both were warmly welcomed.)

As early as August 1944 the Roosevelt administration had launched a diplomatic offensive aimed at democratizing Paraguay, which was not entirely enthusiastic in its support of the Allied cause. Toward the end of 1944 William Beaulac, the U.S. ambassador in Asunción, with the full support and encouragement of the State Department, began a personal campaign "to encourage democracy . . . and liberal institutions in Paraguay." He bluntly informed President Morínigo that future U.S. aid would depend on the restoration of press freedom, the lifting of the ban on political parties, and the holding of honest elections. Persistent U.S. pressure finally led to the democratization program of June–July 1946 as a result of which in the words of La Tribuna the dictator became, albeit briefly, "the prisoner of a democratic cabinet" and the way was open for a new era of democratic politics in Paraguay.[18]

In Bolivia the U.S. embassy was equally active in forging an alliance between right and left (both supporters of the Allies) against the nationalist (and, therefore, it was presumed, pro-Nazi) MNR military government, which had come to power in December 1943. The Frente Democrático Antifascista that brought down Villarroel in July 1946—and apparently opened the way for democracy in Bolivia, too—was strongly supported from Washington.

Alone among Latin American nations, Argentina had remained neutral (and, therefore, from Washington's point of view pro-Axis) in World War II. A declaration of war on March 21, 1945, in order finally to satisfy U.S. demands and to enable Argentina to participate in the San Francisco Conference, temporarily weakened the U.S. campaign to undermine the nationalist military dictatorship there. Spruille Braden, however, arrived as ambassador at the end of May with the "fixed idea" according to Sir David Kelly, the British ambassador, that he had been elected by Providence to deliver democracy to Argentina.[19] He immediately began a four-month campaign to bring down the government to which he was accredited. In his first press conference Braden declared that the United States, which had successfully fought a war for democracy, "believed in the basic freedoms of speech, press, and assembly, and hoped to see them practiced widely, especially throughout the Americas."[20] He intended to keep up a steady pressure, he told the State Department in July (and the State Department fully approved his actions), "until such time as the Nazi militaristic control of this country has been replaced by a constitutional and cooperating democracy."[21] The "real democrats" in Argentina were the opponents of Perón (on the right and the left), and Braden became virtually the leader of the opposition, eventually securing by the time he left Buenos Aires in September to become assistant secretary of state in Washington the right of political parties to organize, the lifting of the state of siege, a timetable for free elections (February 1946), and a recognition that democracy was Argentina's "historic mandate."[22]

In the meantime, Adolf Berle, who had arrived in Rio de Janeiro as U.S. ambassador to Brazil in January 1945 after serving as assistant secretary of state from 1938 to 1944, and who on a visit to Buenos Aires in February had been assured by Perón that there would be free elections in Argentina by October, had been quietly encouraging the dismantling and democratization of the Estado Novo. Vargas, unlike Perón, had been a close ally of the United States throughout the war and there was in any case no need for more than gentle pressure here since he was apparently willing to relinquish power and was leading Brazil steadily toward the elections scheduled for December 2. The White House, the State Department, and the U.S. embassy in Rio all declared themselves entirely happy with the progress being made.

In mid-September, however, Berle became concerned about a new phenomenon—*queremismo* (popular mobilization in favor of the continuation in power of Vargas, whom Berle accepted was "far and away the most popular individual in the country")—and moves supported by the Brazilian Communist party to elect a Constituent Assembly instead of a president and congress (under the slogan "Constituinte com Getúlio"). Mass demonstrations were planned for October 3, the fifteenth anniversary of the revolution of 1930 which first brought Vargas to power. There was a real danger of either a populist (fascist?) coup by Vargas (hence the appearance of another slogan "Remember '37"—a reference to the coup that aborted the elections due to take place in January 1938) or a military coup to prevent it, both of which would threaten the timetable for democratization. It was in these circumstances that Berle, backed by the State Department, which wished to discourage any moves to postpone the December elections, and stiffened by Braden, who passed through Rio de Janeiro on September 23 on his way to Washington, decided upon a "soft intervention" in favor of democracy. (Braden quoted Berle as having "after much sweating" come to the conclusion that "the only way to have democracy was to have it.")[23] His speech at the Hotel Quitandinha in Petrópolis on September 29 in which he publicly affirmed the U.S. position in favor of democracy and against the "continuance of dictatorship" in Brazil was, in Berle's own words, "the atomic bomb that ended Queremismo."[24] This claim was a little premature. Queremismo persisted and it required a second crisis and a military coup against Vargas (on October 29) as well as more discreet pressure from the U.S. embassy to guarantee the elections of December 2. Berle declared himself "delighted with the democratic spectacle."[25]

Thus two U.S. ambassadors had played an important, perhaps decisive, role in the transition to democracy in Argentina and Brazil. At least they had helped ensure that democratic elections would be held. They had, however, no control over the results. In Brazil in December 1945 Brigadier Eduardo Gomes, the candidate of the União Democrática Nacional (UDN), a broad coalition of right, center, and left forces opposed to the Vargas dictatorship, lost to General Eurico Dutra, Vargas's former minister of war, who was known to have pro-Axis (indeed pro-Nazi) sympathies on the eve of Brazil's entry into the war on the side of the Allies and who was the candidate of the Partido Social Democrático (PSD) and the Partido Trabalhista Brasileiro (PTB), the two parties created by Vargas to carry forward at least the economic and social programs of the Estado Novo. In Argentina in February 1946 José P. Tamborini, the candidate of the Unión Democrática, a broad coalition of Conservatives, Radicals, Socialists, and Communists opposed to the military dictatorship, lost to Perón. Spruille Braden, now assistant secretary of state, had never imagined that Perón might win the elections he (Braden) had done so much to bring about. His eleventh-hour attempt to guarantee a victory for the Unión Democrática by publishing a Blue Book in which the evidence, such as it was, that Perón had been linked to the Nazis was rehearsed had the opposite effect of that intended. Perón was able to offer a choice of "Perón or Braden." The Argentine people overwhelmingly chose Perón.

III

During 1947 and 1948 the postwar advance of democracy and reform throughout Latin America ground to a halt and suffered its first major setbacks. In those few countries where dictatorships had survived—Nicaragua, El Salvador, Honduras, the Dominican Republic, and Paraguay—the (largely token) promises of liberalization that had been made were withdrawn or overturned. Trujillo was to survive in the Dominican Republic until 1961, the Somoza dynasty in Nicaragua until 1979. Morínigo in Paraguay, who under pressure from the United States had gone furthest in the direction of political reform, was replaced in February 1948 by Natalicio González after a five-month civil war, a Colorado "terror," and a one-candidate tightly controlled "election." Six years later the thirty-five-year dictatorship of General Alfredo Stroessner began.

In three countries democratization proved illusory. Argentina under Perón turned out to be an elected dictatorship, and although the revolution that finally brought him down in 1955 called itself the Revolución Libertadora, it led to the first of a series of military governments that held power in Argentina for almost twenty of the following thirty years (until genuine democratization in 1983). In Ecuador Velasco Ibarra, who had himself suspended the constitution as early as March 1946, was overthrown in a military coup in August 1947. In 1948, it is true, Galo Plaza Lasso, a progressive landowner, son of a former Liberal president, and candidate of the Movimiento Cívico Ecuatoriano, was elected to the presidency. But four years later the elections of 1952 were won by Velasco, who soon established a populist dictatorship. In Bolivia in 1947 the Frente Democrático Antifascista broke up and the country gradually evolved not toward democracy but toward a reactionary and repressive military dictatorship, which was finally overthrown by the MNR-led revolution of 1952.

In Uruguay, Chile, Costa Rica, and Colombia where democracy existed at the end of World War II and was consolidated and in Cuba, Panama, Peru, Venezuela, and Brazil where democracy of some kind was established and survived, there was in 1947–48 a marked tendency to restrict or curtail political competition and participation, to contain or repress popular mobilization, and to frustrate reformist aspirations. (Guatemala under the reformist administration of Arévalo was the only exception.) This tendency was most visible, first, in the virtual elimination of the Latin American Communist parties as a viable political force in Latin America and, second, in the assertion (or reassertion) of state control over organized labor. In one country after another—most notably in Brazil in May 1947, in Chile in April 1948, and in Costa Rica in July 1948 following the victory of Figueres and his supporters in the civil war of March–April 1948—Communist parties were declared illegal even though they had played by the rules of the democratic game and, particularly in the case of Chile, had deep roots in politics and society. Elected Communist members were removed from the cabinet and from congress in Chile in August 1947 and from congress (as well as state and municipal assemblies) in Brazil in January 1948. (In Peru where the Communists were weak it was APRA that was forced out of central and local government.) Communist labor leaders found themselves purged from the major unions, even though they had been elected and in many cases were notable for the relatively moderate positions they had adopted on strikes.

The Communist purge was part of a more general crackdown on organized labor. Almost everywhere independent labor leaders suffered repression; labor confederations were intervened, marginalized, or disbanded; and antistrike legislation was reinforced followed by a tough stand against strikes. This was particularly true in Brazil (where the Dutra administration introduced new legislation to bring labor under control as early as March 1946), Chile (where the breaking of the coal strike of October 1947 was the central event), Cuba (first under Grau and more particularly under Carlos Prío Socarrás after the elections of 1948), and Costa Rica (after the civil war of 1948). In Mexico the so called *charrazo* of September–October 1948 represented a decisive defeat for the big, militant unions of rail, mine, and oil workers and their postwar challenge to the control over organized labor exercised by the governing revolutionary party, the PRI. Apart from Guatemala and Venezuela (under AD government until November 1948), Argentina provided the only exception to this antilabor trend in Latin America in 1947 and 1948. Perón's regime was based on organized labor (and Perón owed his election to the working-class vote). But he too established government control over the major unions, purged Communist and independent leftists from union leadership, and generally demobilized the working class.

Between the end of 1948 and the middle of 1954 half a dozen democratic regimes were overthrown by military coups and replaced by military dictatorships. In Peru Bustamante, who had been struggling to stay in office for more than a year, was finally brought down in October 1948. General Manuel Odría, using draconian internal security legislation, immediately set about repressing APRA (Haya de la Torre spent the next five years in the Colombian embassy), the labor unions, and the Communists. One month later, on November 24, 1948, the democratic experiment of the *trienio* in Venezuela came to an end and thus began the ten-year dictatorship of Marcos Pérez Jiménez in which AD, the unions, and (from May 1950) the Communists all suffered repression. In Panama José A. Remón, the chief of the National Police, emerged as the country's strongman in 1949. During the following three years he made and unmade presidents and in 1952 was himself "elected" president. In March 1952 Batista brought eight years of Auténtico government to an end in Cuba and established himself in power in a military dictatorship. Colombian democracy survived the *bogotazo,* the predominantly urban uprising that followed the assassination of Gaitán on April 9, 1948, but a state of siege in November 1949 led to the closure of congress (for ten years). The elections in the same month were uncontested by the Liberals and produced a victory for the authoritarian Conservative Laureano Gómez. In June 1953 Gómez was himself overthrown in a military coup, which brought General Gustavo Rojas Pinilla to power. Finally, in Guatemala, where a reactionary coup attempt by Colonel Francisco Arana had been thwarted in 1949, "ten years of spring" came to an end in June 1954 when Colonel Carlos Castillo Armas overthrew the government of Jacobo Arbenz (freely elected in November 1950 to succeed Arévalo) and began the process of dismantling the political, social, and economic reforms of the period since 1944.

At the end of 1954 only four democracies remained in Latin America: Uruguay, Costa Rica, Chile, and Brazil. And not all these countries could be regarded as democratic without qualification. For example, the suffrage was restricted to literates (less than half the population) in Brazil, and Communist parties were proscribed in Costa Rica, Chile, and Brazil. Nor was it possible in 1954 to be confident about their futures as democracies. Chileans in 1952 had elected as president a personalistic, authoritarian caudillo and former dictator (1927–31), Carlos Ibáñez del Campo. Another former dictator Getúlio Vargas had been elected as president in Brazil in 1950. His suicide in August 1954, under pressure from the military to resign, produced a crisis that threatened to end Brazil's first experiment with democracy after less than a decade. Latin America now had two revolutionary regimes: Mexico and (since 1952) Bolivia. There were no fewer than thirteen dictatorships: Guatemala, El Salvador, Honduras, Nicaragua, Panama, Cuba, the Dominican Republic, Venezuela, Colombia, Ecuador, Peru, Paraguay, and Argentina—more than in 1944.

IV

The failure of the postwar struggle for democracy in Latin America can largely be explained in terms of the strength of the dominant classes, rural and urban, and of the military. They had not been weakened, much less destroyed, by World War II as in so many other parts of the world. They had merely been temporarily forced on to the defensive at the end of the war, and after the war were determined to restore the political and social control that had been threatened by the political mobilization of the "dangerous classes," by labor militancy, by the advance of the left—and perhaps even by democracy itself. The commitment of Latin American elites (and the middle classes) to democracy, insofar as it existed in other than a purely rhetorical form, by no means implied an acceptance of broadly based popular participation in the democratic process, competition for power by parties of the left as well as the right and center, and recognition of organized labor as a major political actor. For their part the parties in favor of political and social change generally lacked deep roots in society and were often internally divided and in conflict with each other. Labor unions, despite their impressive growth and the burst of militancy at the end of the war, were still relatively weak and inexperienced (and they still organized only a very small part of the total working population). Moreover, both parties and labor unions no doubt made strategic mistakes. The weakness of the commitment to democracy most obviously on the Communist left but also on the non-Communist center/left (for example, APRA in Peru) and among some sectors of organized labor was also a factor in its defeat.

At the same time domestic class conflicts, different in each country, were strongly influenced by the international environment in which they were played out—that is to say, by the cold war and the fact that Latin America was firmly situated in the United States' camp. Ambiguous and occasionally contradictory signals may have emanated from Washington in 1945 and even in 1946. But the signals were clear in 1947 and 1948. At the very least the cold war and the international stance adopted by the United States reinforced domestic attitudes and tendencies, providing an ideological justification for the shift to the right and for the counteroffensive against the left and against those sectors of organized labor under the influence of the left, which had in many cases already begun. Popular political mobilization and strike activity, whether or not Communist-led, suddenly became Communist-inspired, Moscow-dictated, and therefore "subversive" (not least of democracy itself).[26]

There was another, wider aspect of the interaction of domestic and international politics: the perception the Latin American ruling groups had of the new international economic order overwhelmingly dominated by the United States. At the end of the war the more economically advanced Latin American nations looked to promote economic development through import-substitution industrialization. For this strategy to work, considerable transfers of capital and technology would be required. It was by no means clear that these would be forthcoming, or on what terms they could be attracted. During the war the United States had provided financial and technical assistance to Latin America, mainly for the increased production of strategic raw materials but also in some cases (in Brazil and Mexico, in particular) for the promotion of industry. At the end of the war many Latin American governments had expectations—or hopes—that the United States would continue and indeed expand this role, providing them with long-term development capital.

The United States, however, repeatedly headed off discussion of the economic problems of Latin America at inter-American conferences (in 1945, 1947, 1948) and at this stage refused to support the creation of an Inter-American Development Bank. There was to be no Marshall Plan for Latin America which, it was true, had suffered less in the war and had emerged in economically better shape than many other regions of the world. In 1950 Latin America was the only area of the world without a U.S. aid program, apart from the meagerly funded Point Four technical assistance program established in 1949. Compared with $19 billion in U.S. foreign aid to Western Europe in the period 1945–50, only $400 million (less than 2 percent of total U.S. aid) went to Latin America. Belgium and Luxembourg alone received more than the whole of Latin America.[27]

Latin America, it was clear, would have to look to *private* capital, domestic and foreign, for its development. If more U.S. capital were to be attracted, the right climate had to be created, various guarantees and assurances, both symbolic and real, given: a commitment to liberal, capitalist development and to an "ideology of production," with nationalism curbed (no more "Mexican stunts"—Bernard Baruch's reference to the Mexican nationalization of oil in 1938), the left marginalized, the working class firmly under control, and unions not necessarily weaker but bureaucratized. Above all, political stability had to be maintained—and not necessarily through the strengthening of democratic institutions. Here was a clear point of coincidence of different imperatives. Domestically, militant unions and an increasingly mobilized working class threatened dominant classes and elites with moves in the direction of social reform and an expanded democracy, which the elites found unacceptable. At the same time, quite apart from the cold war considerations, they had urgent reasons in terms of the links between the domestic economies of Latin America and the U.S. economy, for taming labor and the left and even, if necessary, for replacing democracy with dictatorship.

Thus, just as the United States *indirectly* promoted the democratization of Latin America at the end of World War II, the United States *indirectly* imposed limits on the democratic advance in the postwar years. But did the United States also play a *direct* role in the overall defeat of democracy in Latin America?

It is important to consider in approaching this question the place of Latin America in U.S. official thinking and policy making after World War II. The paramount importance of Latin America to the United States—both strategic and economic—was never seriously questioned. Although the external threat to the security of the Western Hemisphere from the Axis powers was largely eliminated relatively early in the war, the United States continued to plan for the preservation and strengthening of hemispheric solidarity after the war. This is clear from, for example, the Joint Army and Navy Advisory Board's Western Hemisphere Defense Program in December 1943. Nelson Rockefeller, assistant secretary of state for the American republics from December 1944 to August 1945, took the view at the United Nations conference in San Francisco in April 1945 that the United States could not do what it wanted on the world front unless Western Hemispheric solidarity was guaranteed. Not insignificant was the fact that Latin America represented two-fifths of the votes—twenty out of fifty-one—at the United Nations, making it the most important single voting bloc. Moreover, Latin America remained the United States' most important export market and source of imports and, after Canada, the area in which most U.S. capital was invested.

However, the *primacy* of United States relations with Latin America was no longer unquestioned. Whereas, as Assistant Secretary of State Edward R. Miller wrote in December 1950, the Good Neighbor Policy had been "virtually our sole foreign policy" in the 1930s,[28] it was clear even before the end of the war that the United States had become for the first time in its history a world power in military, economic, and ideological terms, with global interests and concerns. That the United States was now to play a world—not just a hemispheric—role was evident as early as February–March 1945 at the Chapultepec Conference of American States and even more apparent at the United Nations Conference in San Francisco in April where growing signs of United States distrust of the Soviet Union, the United States' only rival at the end of the war, first emerged.

U.S. foreign policy at the end of the war and in the immediate postwar years was marked by hesitancy, confusion, and division. It took some time for a unified and coherent approach to develop. One thing, however, is certain: without exception the senior policy makers in Washington—Truman himself, Edward R. Stettinius, Joseph C. Grew, James F. Byrnes, George C. Marshall, Dean Acheson—showed little interest in and for the most part were ignorant of Latin America.[29] After the dismissal of Nelson Rockefeller as assistant secretary of state in August 1945 Adolf Berle commented, "Men [in high office] who know the hemisphere and love it are few, and those who are known by the hemisphere and loved by it are fewer still." In 1949, complaining bitterly about "sheer neglect and ignorance," Berle declared "we have simply forgotten about Latin America."[30]

A conference of American states in Rio de Janeiro to formulate a regional collective security pact against external attack under article 51 of the U.N. Charter was planned for October 1945. But this was never given top priority and in any case continuing problems between the United States and Perón's Argentina were permitted to delay it. The Inter-American Treaty of Reciprocal Assistance (the Rio treaty) was not signed until August 1947. In the meantime, no significant military assistance was offered to Latin America. An Inter-American Military Cooperation bill was drafted in May 1946 but failed to make progress in the U.S. Congress and was finally abandoned in June 1948. The Soviet Union had replaced Germany and Japan as the enemy, real and potential, of the United States. But there was no Soviet threat to Latin America. The Russians had no atomic bomb, no long-range strategic air force, and an ineffective navy. From the point of view of the United States Latin America was safe, whereas the Eurasian land mass— Western Europe and the Near East—were in great danger: the Truman Doctrine (March 1947), the doctrine of containment, was a result of the perceived Soviet threat to Turkey and Greece. And there were limits even to U.S. resources. Just as Latin America's economic needs were given less attention than Europe's, Latin America was given low strategic priority and remained firmly at the periphery of U.S. strategic concerns. The Mutual Defense Assistance Act (1949) allowed for the expenditure of $1.3 billion; not a cent went to Latin America.[31]

Latin America was secure from external aggression and to some extent it was safe for the United States to neglect it in global terms. This is not to say, however, that the United States was unconcerned at the possibilities for *internal* subversion (from Communists rather than fascists now, of course). The Soviet Union had neither the military means nor the economic means to challenge seriously the hegemony of the United States in Latin America. But it did retain political and ideological influence through the region's Communist parties. Whereas at the end of the war U.S. officials had been on the whole unconcerned at the growth of Communist parties, in the immediate postwar period as the cold war developed Communist activities in Latin America were increasingly monitored by legal attachés (almost always FBI agents), military and naval attachés, and labor attachés in the U.S. embassies and by CIA agents. The intelligence apparatus set up during the war for dealing with Nazi subversion was given a new lease of life. A CIA review of

Soviet aims in Latin America in November 1947 contended there was no possibility of a Communist takeover anywhere in the region, but on the eve of the Ninth International Conference of American States meeting in Bogotá (March–April 1948) U.S. hostility to Communism in Latin America was made explicit in State Department Policy Planning Staff document PPS 26 (March 22) and National Security Council document NSC 7 (March 30).[32] Resolution XXXII of the Final Act at the Bogotá conference asserted that the very legal existence of Communist parties in Latin America was a direct threat to the security of the Western Hemisphere.

The United States was especially concerned about Communist penetration of the Latin American labor unions. As in Western Europe (especially France and Italy), and for that matter in the United States itself, organized labor was the major ideological battleground of the cold war. There were also important strategic issues at stake. In the late forties it was far from clear to the protagonists in the cold war that a long period of relatively peaceful coexistence was on the horizon. Were World War III to break out, Communist-controlled unions in Latin America would threaten the interests of the United States, especially in strategically important industries like petroleum (in Mexico, Venezuela, and Peru—virtually all United States petroleum imports at the end of World War II came from Latin America), copper (in Chile and Peru), even sugar (in Cuba), but also in transport and in industry generally. Moreover, as in the United States itself, militant unions, whether Communist-controlled or not, were a potentially destabilizing force hostile to postwar capitalist development.

In most Latin American countries—for example, Brazil and Cuba—it was not necessary for the United States to exert pressure directly, even behind the scenes, to secure the proscription of Communist parties and the purging of Communists and other militants from labor unions. Nevertheless, there was undoubtedly a general awareness of Washington's approval of such measures. It might even be argued that U.S. pressure was anticipated. In Bolivia, however, the U.S. withdrawal of support in 1947 from the coalition that included the Marxist Partido de la Izquierda Revolucionario (PIR) certainly was a major factor in the decline in that party's fortunes and the marked shift to the right in Bolivian politics in the late forties. And on Chile in 1947 the United States brought to bear considerable direct economic pressure, which was perhaps decisive in persuading González Videla to take a firm stand against Communism and the Communists.[33]

In the meantime the American Federation of Labor (AFL) spearheaded the campaign to drive Communist party members out of the ranks of the international trade union movement. Even during the war when the AFL had officially maintained good relations with Lombardo Toledano and the CTAL in the interests of the war effort, the first steps had been taken toward the creation of "free" trade unions on the U.S. model in Latin America. George Meany visited Latin America and two key figures in the postwar struggle for labor—Bernardo Ibáñez, the Chilean Socialist leader, and Juan Arévalo, the secretary of foreign affairs of the Cuban confederation of labor (CTC)—were invited to Washington in July 1943. The appointment of labor attachés in most of the U.S. embassies in Latin America during 1943–44 can be seen as part of the same process. But it was after the war that the major offensive was launched against the CTAL, which was now affiliated with the World Federation of Trade Unions (WFTU), a "communist front" from a cold war perspective. With State Department "informal assistance," AFL roving "ambassadors" like Irving Brown in Europe and Serafino Romualdi in Latin America were sent out to organize support for pro-United States "free" trade unionism. By 1947–48 the anti-Communists had won the often bitter internal struggles for control of organized labor in Latin America. The major national union confederations disaffiliated from the CTAL. In January 1948 a new organization, the Confederación Interamericana de Trabajadores (CIT)—later to become ORIT—was established in Lima. And in December 1949 the non-Communist unions also left the WFTU and formed the International Confederation of Free Trade Unions (ICFTU).

It has been argued that from one perspective measures against Communist parties and Communist-led (and even independently militant) unions, albeit taken by democratic or semidemocratic governments—in Brazil, Chile, Cuba, Costa Rica, Peru, Venezuela, Mexico—represented a narrowing of the concept and practice of democracy in Latin America. In the immediate postwar years, as we have seen, Communists had played an important role in the struggle for democracy, political and social, in Latin America. Edward J. Rowell, labor attaché in the U.S. embassy in Rio de Janeiro from 1944 to 1948, surveying the labor scene in Brazil in February 1947, commented on the "unquestioned participation and influence of communist leaders," but with "a trade union program which is sympathetic to trade union status and activities as recognized by Western democracies."[34] However, from the perspective of Washington (and the dominant groups in Latin America) in 1947 and 1948, the removal of the Communists from the political and labor scenes *strengthened* democracy. Communism was no longer compatible with democracy. Like fascism it was an alien ideology that threatened it. Resolution XXXII of the Act of Bogotá (directed against the legal status of Communist parties) was entitled "The Preservation and Defense of Democracy in America." The Chilean Communist party was outlawed by a "Law for the Permanent Defense of Democracy." A State Department policy statement on Guatemala in May 1951 declared specifically that "the restriction and control of Communists, as a means of self-preservation, is not inconsistent with the ideals, the aims, and the institutions of democracy."[35]

In its public rhetoric the United States continued to support democracy over dictatorship in Latin America. For example, in a speech to the Pan

American Society on September 19, 1949, Secretary of State Dean Acheson referred to "our long-range objectives in the promotion of democracy."[36] But after 1945–46 little was actually done to promote or even defend democratic principles and practices in Latin America (unless support for anti-Communism is seen in this light). On the contrary, from 1947—and perhaps the departure of Braden from the State Department in June 1947 was an early signal of this—there was a marked shift in U.S. attitudes. Dictators received fewer expressions of disapproval, although the government of Somoza's uncle Victor Román y Reyes, who replaced Leonardo Argüello as president within a month of his election in May 1947, was denied U.S. recognition for almost a year. In the middle of 1947 licences for the export of arms, aircraft, and vessels to Trujillo's Dominican Republic were granted after a ban lasting three years. The United States not only refused to support but at times positively opposed the efforts of the so called "Caribbean Legion" of exiled democrats, sponsored by José "Pepe" Figueres, Ramón Grau San Martín, Rómulo Betancourt, and Juan José Arévalo during 1947–49, to overthrow the dictatorships in Nicaragua and the Dominican Republic and the Communist-backed democratic government in Costa Rica—a form of collective intervention in support of democracy in the Caribbean and Central America.[37] In 1947 the Untied States even began to come to terms with Perón's Argentina now that, as James Reston put it in the *New York Times,* "the administration is concentrating not on catching fascists but on stopping communists."[38] And at the end of 1948, despite statements deploring the use of force as an instrument of political change, the United States offered early recognition (and therefore, in the eyes of Latin American democrats, approval) to the military regimes of Odría and Pérez Jiménez after the overthrow of popularly elected, democratic governments in Peru and Venezuela. To have withheld recognition, it was argued, would have been to intervene in the internal affairs of Peru and Venezuela. Nevertheless, as the tide turned against democracy in Latin America, the overwhelming power of the United States was such that a U.S. policy of early (sometimes eager) recognition of dictatorships could in itself constitute a factor undermining democratic institutions.

Thus, in less than three years, the wheel had turned full circle. As in the period before 1944–45 the principles of nonintervention (even for the promotion of democracy) and recognition of de facto governments (including dictatorships) once again formed the cornerstone of U.S. policy toward Latin America. And it is interesting to see the reemergence in the late forties and early fifties of a number of arguments *against* the active promotion of democracy (and, by implication, the more-ready acceptance of dictatorships). In the first place, Latin America was perhaps not ready for democracy. The roots of democratic values and institutions were shallow; the dominant groups were reactionary and fundamentally antidemocratic, the middle classes progressive but weak, the working classes susceptible to nationalism, populism, and Communism; the military was almost nowhere politically neutral and subordinate to elected civilian authority. Second, the differences between democracy and dictatorship were not clear-cut. "We must recognize," wrote George F. Kennan, in his famous memorandum to the secretary of state in March 1950, following his first and only trip to Latin America, "that the difference between the democratic and authoritarian forms of government is everywhere a relative, rather than an absolute one, and that the distinctions between the two concepts are peculiarly vague and illusive against the background of Latin American psychology and tradition."[39] In July 1950 Assistant Secretary of State Edward Miller authorized a famous article in *Foreign Affairs* written by "Y" (Louis Halle) entitled "On a Certain Impatience with Latin America"[40]—impatience over the persistence of dictatorships and the failures of democracy. Democracy, however, the reader was reminded, is achieved "by evolution rather than revolution." It is "not an absolute condition." The Latin American republics cannot be divided into "immaculate democracies" and "black dictatorships." And "no clear line can be drawn, for purposes of policy, between the sheep and the goats." Finally, intervention by the United States to impose democracy in Latin America from outside did not work. When it had been attempted in the past—most notoriously in Argentina in February 1946—the results had been counterproductive. The United States had harmed the democratic groups it wished to help and strengthened the authoritarian regimes it wished to weaken.[41]

In the new conditions of the cold war the struggle against Communism worldwide, including Latin America, and the threat Communism (and behind it the Soviet Union) posed to the strategic and economic interests of the United States inevitably had priority over efforts to promote democracy in Latin America. Democracies might still be preferable to dictatorships in the abstract, but if dictatorships proved more effective at dealing with Communism they might be preferable to democracies. In his memorandum of March 1950 George Kennan (against all the evidence at the time, it must be emphasized) wrote:

> The activities of the communists represent our most serious problem in the area. They have progressed to a point where they must be regarded as an urgent, major problem. . . . The Monroe Doctrine was understood throughout at least a century of our history as barring precisely that which the communists are now attempting to achieve: namely, the introduction into this hemisphere under any guise or pretext whatsoever of a political system hostile to ourselves and designed to make the Latin American countries pawns in the achievement of the power aspirations of regimes beyond the limits of this continent. . . . If this view is correct, then we cannot take an indulgent and complacent view of communist activities in the New World at this juncture without recognizing that this constitutes an historical turning away from traditional United States policy in the hemisphere. . . . We cannot be dogmatic about the

methods by which local communists can be dealt with. . . . Where the concepts and traditions of popular government are too weak to absorb successfully the intensity of the communist attacks, then we must concede that harsh government measures of repression may be the only answer: that these measures may have to proceed from regimes whose origins and methods would not stand the test of American concepts of democratic procedure, and that such regimes and such methods may be preferable alternatives, and indeed the only alternatives, to further communist success.[42]

It was only a short step to the view that circumstances might arise in which it was necessary for the United States to abandon the principle of nonintervention in Latin America in order to overthrow a democratic government that was "soft on Communism" and install a dictatorship. A democratic government in Latin America now lived in the shadow of a vigilant and increasingly ideologically motivated United States. If it were to be "penetrated" by Communists—and in the atmosphere of the cold war evidence for this could be merely the introduction of necessary, far-reaching social reforms or even the toleration of strong independent trade unions and popular political movements of the left—it could be seen to threaten the strategic and economic interests of the United States and could be undermined or even overthrown. Democracy was again disposable—as it had been before 1944–45.[43]

There is little evidence that the United States was *actively* involved in the overthrow of democracy in, for example, Peru in 1948, Cuba in 1952, or Colombia in 1953, although in view of the strength of U.S. economic interests in Peru and Cuba in particular further research would seem to be justified. What, for example, was the role of the Klein mission to Peru in 1948? In Venezuela, however, where the United States had crucial oil interests, where Communists had a good deal of influence over organized labor, and where the AD government, though anti-Communist, had refused to cede to cold war pressures and outlaw the Communist party (and had been lukewarm on the issue of Communism at Bogotá), there is circumstantial evidence at least that the United States was no mere bystander when on November 24, 1948, a military coup brought to an abrupt end the three-year experiment with democracy. Betancourt, it should be pointed out, always denied U.S. involvement in the coup (of which the United States certainly approved), but the role of U.S. embassy officials and especially the U.S. military attaché Col. E. F. Adams deserves more careful research. In contrast, direct U.S. involvement in the overthrow of democracy in Guatemala in 1954 is unquestioned and has been extensively documented.[44]

In January 1953 the incoming Eisenhower administration immediately adopted a tough attitude toward Communism in Latin America. Its preliminary statement on "United States Objectives and Courses of Action with Respect to Latin America" was almost exclusively concerned with cold war considerations of hemispheric solidarity against the Soviet Union externally and against internal Communist subversion. Its first policy document on Latin America (NSC 144/1, March 18, 1953) did not even list the promotion of democracy as an objective of the United States.[45] And John Foster Dulles, the secretary of state, seemed to go out of his way to court dictators as the strongest defense against Communism (and as more likely to be friendly to U.S. companies).

The shift to the left in Guatemala under Arbenz—signaled, in particular, by the Agrarian Reform (June 1952) and the legalization of the Marxist Partido Guatemalteco de Trabajo (December 1952)—had begun to concern Washington even before Eisenhower took office. By 1953–54 Communist influence over the government of Arbenz, undoubtedly exaggerated by Washington, was believed to pose a direct threat to U.S. corporate interests (specifically, the United Fruit Company). It was the most serious threat of this kind since the nationalization of the Mexican oil industry in 1938. Even more important, if in the judgment of the United States Arbenz had become a pawn of the Communists (and in the frequently quoted words of Ambassador John Peurifoy, "if [Arbenz] is not a communist, he will certainly do until one comes along"), Guatemala was a direct threat to the security of the United States. The Bolivian Revolution with its agrarian reform and nationalization of the tin industry could be tolerated: it was anti-Communist; it did not threaten major U.S. economic interests; and, above all, it did not represent a threat to U.S. strategic interests. In any case, by 1954 its radical thrust was being moderated (under U.S. influence). But the government of Guatemala stood accused of establishing a beachhead for Soviet imperialism in the Western Hemisphere and had to be removed. At the Tenth Inter-American Conference held at Caracas in March 1954 Dulles successfully secured the passage of a strongly worded anti-Communist resolution (the Declaration of Caracas), despite the reasonable apprehension of some delegates that it might be used to sanction U.S. intervention in Latin America and specifically in Guatemala. In June the Eisenhower administration authorized CIA support for the invasion of Guatemala from Honduras. It proved decisive in the overthrow of the Arbenz government.

The invasion of Guatemala in 1954 was the first direct U.S. intervention for the purpose of overthrowing a government in Latin America for almost thirty years—and the first for the overthrow of a democratically elected government (albeit perceived by Washington as having fallen into the hands of Communists). "As you know," President Figueres of Costa Rica wrote to Adolf Berle, "reaction throughout Latin America has been bad. Intervention is considered a worse evil than communism, especially since intervention is never applied to foster a democratic cause."[46]

Even now, however, the ambiguities in the relationship between the United States and Latin American democracy had not been—perhaps could not be—resolved. There remained, if only at the level of rhetoric, an ideological preference for democracy over dictatorship. And perhaps democracy (together with economic development and social reform) was in the end the best way to defeat Communism in Latin America. The issue was discussed at a National Security Council meeting in February 1955, six months after the Guatemalan invasion. Secretary of the Treasury George Humphrey urged the president to continue to "back strong men in Latin American governments" ("whenever a dictator was replaced Communists gained"). Eisenhower, however, it seems, finally agreed with his special assistant Nelson Rockefeller who, anticipating the Alliance for Progress, argued that while "in the short run . . . dictators handle communists effectively . . . in the long run the United States must encourage the growth of democracies in Latin America."[47]

Notes

This essay forms part of a research project on Latin America between World War II and the cold war. A forthcoming volume, Leslie Bethell and Ian Roxborough, eds., *Crisis and Containment in Latin America, 1944–48*, will explore the main features of the immediate postwar years, and especially the containment of labor and the left, in ten Latin American countries. In preparing this essay I have benefited greatly from reading drafts of all these country case studies, but especially those on Chile (Andrew Barnard), Guatemala (James Dunkerley), Venezuela (Steve Ellner), Cuba (Harold Sims), and Bolivia (Laurence Whitehead). For a preliminary version of the introduction to the volume and an outline of the thesis that these years constituted a critical conjuncture in the political, social, and economic history of Latin America in the twentieth century, see Leslie Bethell and Ian Roxborough, "Latin America between the Second World War and the Cold War: Some Reflections on the 1945–48 Conjuncture," *Journal of Latin American Studies* 20 (May 1988): 167–89.

Research on the role of the United States in Latin America in the period after World War II was primarily carried out in Washington, D.C., in the spring and summer of 1987 during my period as a Fellow at the Woodrow Wilson International Center for Scholars. I would like to thank Scott Sherman for research assistance in Washington, and Oliver Marshall for additional research assistance in London.

1. William Ebenstein, "Political and Social Thought in Latin America," in Arthur P. Whitaker, ed., *Inter-American Affairs 1945* (New York: Columbia University Press, 1946), p. 137.

2. Quoted in Hugh Thomas, *Cuba or the Pursuit of Freedom* (London: Eyre & Spottiswoode, 1971), p. 736.

3. I owe this information to Blanca Torres.

4. Fernando Claudin, *The Communist Movement: From Comintern to Cominform* (London: Penguin Books, 1975), p. 309.

5. "The phenomenal rise in Communist parties has been the most striking development of the last two years," wrote Arthur M. Schlesinger, Jr., in his article "Good Fences Make Good Neighbors," published in *Fortune,* August 1946.

6. See Bethell and Roxborough, "Latin America between the Second World War and the Cold War," pp. 174–75.

7. Quoted in Patricia Parkman, *Nonviolent Insurrection in El Salvador: The Fall of Maximiliano Hernández Martínez* (Tucson: University of Arizona Press, 1988), pp. 91–92.

8. William Krehn, *Democracies and Tyrannies of the Caribbean* (Westport, Conn.: Lawrence Hill, 1984), p. 191. The volume is based on articles written in the 1940s and first published in Spanish in Mexico in 1957.

9. July 5, 1944, Department of State, *Foreign Relations of the United States* (henceforth *FRUS) 1944,* vol. 7 (Washington, D.C.: U.S. Government Printing Office, 1967), p. 1016.

10. On the career of Messersmith, see Jesse H. Stiller, *George S. Messersmith, Diplomat of Democracy* (Chapel Hill: University of North Carolina Press, 1987).

11. September 12, 1944, *FRUS 1944,* 7:1025–26 (emphasis added).

12. October 3, 1944, *FRUS 1944,* 7:1140.

13. Quoted in D. M. Dozer, *Are We Good Neighbors? Three Decades of Inter-American Relations, 1930–60* (Gainesville: University of Florida Press, 1959), p. 213.

14. Braden's report dated April 5, 1945 was a revision of a memorandum sent to the State Department from Havana in January. See Bryce Wood, *The Dismantling of the Good Neighbor Policy* (Austin: University of Texas Press, 1985), pp. 94–95.

15. Secretary of State James F. Byrnes, in announcing the appointment, wrote that it was "particularly a recognition of his [Braden's] accurate interpretation of the policies of this Government in its relations with . . . Argentina": it would be Braden's duty "to see that the policies which he has so courageously sponsored in the Argentine are continued with unremitting vigor." *Department of State Bulletin* 13, no. 322 (August 1945).

16. *Department of State Bulletin* 13, no. 892 (December 1945).

17. See the section on Trujillo and the post–World War II "democratic period" in the Dominican Republic in Hartlyn's chapter in this volume.

18. See Michael Grow, *The Good Neighbor Policy and Authoritarianism in Paraguay: United States Economic Expansion and Great Power Rivalry in Latin America during World War II* (Lawrence: Regents Press of Kansas, 1981), chap. 8, "The United States and the Restoration of 'Democracy' in Paraguay," pp. 99–111.

19. See Sir David Kelly, *The Ruling Few* (London: Hollis & Carter, 1953), p. 307.

20. Spruille Braden, *Diplomats and Demagogues: The Memoirs of Spruille Braden* (New Rochelle, N.Y.: Arlington House, 1971), p. 322.

21. July 11, 1945. Quoted in Wood, p. 96.

22. U.S.-Argentine relations during and after World War II, especially during Braden's period in Buenos Aires (May–September 1945), have received a great deal of scholarly attention. See, for example, Mario Rapoport, *Gran Bretaña, Estados Unidos y las clases dirigentes argentinas: 1940–1945* (Buenos Aires: Belgrano, 1981), and "Foreign and Domestic Policy in Argentina during the Second World War," in Guido di Tella and D. Cameron Watt, eds., *Argentina between the Great Powers, 1939–46* (London: Macmillan, 1989); Carlos Escudé, *Gran Bretaña, Estados Unidos, y la declinación argentina, 1942–1949* (Buenos Aires: Belgrano, 1983); Callum A. MacDonald, "The Politics of Intervention: The United States and Argentina, 1941–1946," *Journal of Latin American Studies* 12, pt. 2 (November 1980), and "The Braden Campaign and Anglo-American Relations in Argentina, 1945–46," in di Tella and Watt, *Argentina between the Great Powers, 1939–46;* Roger R. Trask, "Spruille Braden versus George Messersmith: World War II, the Cold War, and Argentine Policy, 1945–1947," *Journal of Inter-American Studies and World Affairs* 26 (February 1984); and Albert P. Vannucci, "Elected by Providence: Spruille Braden in Argentina in 1945," in C. Neale Ronning and Albert P. Vannucci, eds., *Ambassadors in Foreign Policy: The Influence of Individuals on US-Latin American Policy* (New York: Praeger, 1987).

23. Quoted in Jordan A. Schwarz, *Liberal: Adolf A. Berle and the Vision of an American Era* (New York: Free Press, 1987), p. 270.

24. Beatrice Bishop Berle and Travis Beal Jacobs, eds., *Navigating the Rapids, 1918–1971: From the Papers of Adolf A. Berle Jr.* (New York: Harcourt, Brace, Jovanovich, 1973), p. 553.

25. Quoted in Schwarz, p. 272. On U.S.-Brazilian relations at the end of World War II, and especially Berle's period in Rio de Janeiro (January 1945–February 1946), besides Berle's own diaries and correspondence published in *Navigating the Rapids* and chap. 8 of

Schwarz's biography, see Frank D. McCann, *The Brazilian-American Alliance 1937–1945* (Princeton: Princeton University Press, 1973), chap. 15; Stanley Hilton, "The Overthrow of Getúlio Vargas in 1945: Diplomatic Intervention, Defense of Democracy or Political Retribution?" *Hispanic American Historical Review* 67, no. 1 (1987), and *O Ditador e o embaixador. Getúlio Vargas, Adolf Berle Jr. e a queda do Estado Novo* (Rio de Janeiro: Editora Record, 1987); Paulo Sergio Pinheiro, "Os EUA agem em 45," *Isto E* (September 27, 1978), pp. 34–41.

26. The Cold War did not, of course, introduce anti-Communism into Latin America; it had been an element in the political culture of the Latin American elites since the Russian Revolution and the creation of the Comintern. Indeed there was probably more anti-Communism in Latin America at the end of World War I than at the end of World War II. The Catholic church, a powerful influence on Latin American politics and society, was a bastion of anti-Communism.

27. Robert A. Pollard, *Economic Security and the Origins of the Cold War* (New York: Columbia University Press, 1985), p. 213; Stephen G. Rabe, "The Elusive Conference. US Economic Relations with Latin America, 1945–52," *Diplomatic History* 2 (1978): 293.

28. *FRUS 1950,* vol. 2 (Washington, D.C., 1976), pp. 625–26.

29. It is interesting to note that in a massive study of six men—Robert Lovell, John McCloy, Averell Harriman, Charles Bohlen, George Kennan, and Dean Acheson—who shaped U.S. foreign policy in the postwar period, Walter Isaacson and Evan Thomas, *The Wise Men: Six Friends and the World They Made* (New York: Simon & Schuster, 1986), there is no reference to Latin America until the Cuban Missile Crisis (1962).

30. Quoted in Schwarz, pp. 268, 312.

31. Chester Joseph Pach, Jr., "The Containment of US Military Aid to Latin America, 1944–1949," *Diplomatic History* 6 (1982): 242.

32. Pollard, p. 201.

33. On the other hand when in 1950 the U.S. embassy in Caracas asked for instructions regarding the possible dissolution of the Venezuelan Communist party by the Pérez Jiménez regime, the following reply was sent: "[State] Dept. considers each Amer Republic is best judge steps needed protect own internal security but does not believe outlawing party necessarily most effective means dealing with Commie problem. Cong has not banned party in U.S. Outlawing felt increase difficulties observation and control while repression in end tends breed Communism. . . . Both Arg and Urug among Amer Republics permitting existence legal Commie parties, while Commies still strong Braz and Chile despite dissolution. Dept appreciates however situation Ven complicated by abolition AD which gives Commies advantage in wooing masses. On other hand outlawing Commies might intensify their cooperation with AD. Suggest Emb avoid making any recommendation and especially any association anti-Commie campaign with desire fin assistance." Telegram May 10, 1950, Secret, *FRUS 1950,* 2:1021.

34. Monthly Labor Report no. 25 (February 1947). April 8, 1947, RG 59 State Department, 850.4, National Archives, Washington, D.C.

35. May 2, 1951, Secret, *FRUS 1951* (Washington, D.C.: U.S. Government Printing Office, 1983), 2:1420.

36. Quoted in Wood, p. 133.

37. On the Caribbean Legion, see Charles Ameringer, *The Democratic Left in Exile: The Antidictatorial Struggle in the Caribbean, 1945–1959* (Coral Gables, Fla.: University of Miami Press, 1974).

38. *New York Times,* April 15, 1947, quoted in Wood, p. 241 n. 82.

39. *FRUS 1950,* 2:616.

40. Y, "On a Certain Impatience with Latin America," *Foreign Affairs* 28, no. 4 (July 1950): 565–79.

41. See, for example, State Department Policy Statement on the Dominican Republic,

Secret, October 9, 1951, *FRUS 1951,* 2:1378. For expressions of this opinion in December 1952 and March 1953, see Wood, pp. 121, 242.

42. *FRUS 1950,* 2:607-8. The full text of Kennan's memorandum can be found in pp. 598-624. See also George F. Kennan, *Memoirs 1925-50* (Boston: Little, Brown & Co., 1967), pp. 476-84. It might be argued, however, that Kennan's views were not typical. Throughout his career he showed a singular disregard for democracy and human rights as important factors in U.S. policy.

43. "American liberal opinion is all for democracy unless the democratic process decides against them [*sic*]," Adolf Berle had written in his diary as early as September 20, 1945, "—in which case they are apt to go imperialistic." Quoted in Schwarz, p. 268.

44. See, in particular, Richard H. Immerman, *The CIA in Guatemala. The Foreign Policy of Intervention* (Austin: University of Texas Press, 1982) and Stephen Schlesinger and Stephen Kinzer, *Bitter Fruit: The Untold Story of the American Coup in Guatemala* (London: Sinclair Browne, 1982). Also the relevant chapters in Jim Handy, *Gift of the Devil: A History of Guatemala* (Boston: Southend Press, 1984), and James Dunkerley, *Power in the Isthmus: A Political History of Modern Central America* (London: Verso, 1988).

45. *FRUS 1952-4,* vol. 4 (Washington, D.C.: U.S. Government Printing Office, 1983), pp. 6ff. See Stephen Rabe, *Eisenhower and Latin America: The Foreign Policy of Anti-Communism* (Chapel Hill: University of North Carolina Press, 1988), pp. 26-33.

46. Quote in Schwarz, p. 317.

47. See Robert A. Pastor, ed., *Democracy in the Americas: Stopping the Pendulum* (New York: Holmes & Meier, 1989), pp. 148-49. I am grateful to Robert Pastor for drawing my attention to the declassified top-secret memorandum that describes the meeting of the National Security Council on February 17, 1955.

3 | The Alliance for Progress: The 1960s

Tony Smith

> We propose to complete the revolution of the Americas, to build a hemisphere where all men can hope for a suitable standard of living, and all can live out their lives in freedom and dignity. To achieve this goal political freedom must accompany material progress. . . . Let us once again transform the American continent into a vast crucible of revolutionary ideas and efforts.—John F. Kennedy, March 13, 1961

The North American Goal

OF ALL THE North American efforts to bring democracy to Latin America none has ever sounded even remotely so ambitious as the Alliance for Progress. Previous attempts by Washington to foster democracy in the region—as in the Philippines—had limited themselves to essentially political matters: mediating among political factions, monitoring free elections, supervising civilian administration (especially in finance), and assisting in the formation of a national constabulary.[1] Domestic economic and social arrangements had for the most part been left to follow their own course. True, by 1914, Woodrow Wilson had come to feel that social and economic reform would be basic to the eventual consolidation of democracy in Mexico (just as he had heard from Felix Frankfurter that the dilemma for American power in the Philippines was to provide a social basis for democracy after the islands' eventual independence).[2] But it was left to the Kennedy administration (1961–63), building on a variety of initiatives proposed by prominent Latin Americans and acted on during the second Eisenhower administration (1957–61), to interrelate explicitly the variety of problems plaguing the region—including, in differing guises, economic poverty, social inequality, and political oppression—and to insist that all needed to be addressed simultaneously. With the full backing of President Kennedy, some of the best minds in Washington outlined the far-reaching terms of the proposal and saw to it that the alliance had its own separate bureaucratic

71

structure closely related to the State Department and the Agency for International Development.[3] Kennedy called for committing $20 billion over a ten-year period; in fact, $22.3 billion was disbursed to Latin America under the program.[4]

Given its heavy dose of idealism and its subsequent failure, it is surprising that today, nearly thirty years after the Charter of Punta del Este formalizing the alliance was finally made public (August 17, 1961), the document and its attendant declarations can still make stirring reading.[5] The secret to its enduring power comes from the way its unabashed moral earnestness was wedded to what at first reading may seem a thoroughgoing, hard-headed review of what needed to be practically accomplished to make the dream a reality, an approach that emphasized the socioeconomic dimension even more forcefully than the political.

The charter's commitment to democracy appears most strongly in its accompanying declaration, which asserts as the first goal of the alliance the need "to improve and strengthen democratic institutions through application of the principle of self-determination by the people." It then affirms as the "basic principle" of the alliance the conviction that "free men working through the institutions of representative democracy can best satisfy man's aspirations, including those for work, home and land, health and schools. No system can guarantee true progress unless it affirms the dignity of the individual which is the foundation of our civilization."

The charter itself focuses solely on social and economic matters. Socially, it looks to improve medical care, housing, and education, with special attention to the needs of the poor. In economic terms, it seeks more equitable income distribution and to promote growth through more balanced, diversified, and industrialized national economic structures based on higher investment, monetary stability, and regional integration.

But of all the social and economic measures proposed, it is the insistence on land reform that makes the charter appear so serious politically, indeed so radical. Never before or again would the United States put itself this squarely on the line with respect to transforming the socioeconomic character of Latin America. Later programs proposed by Washington, such as the Kissinger Commission Report or the related Caribbean Basin Initiative in the 1980s, pale by comparison.[6]

It is true, of course, that land reform alone is no guarantee that democracy will necessarily follow. The experiences of Taiwan and South Korea are evidence of that. Still, if land reform is no guarantee of democracy, it is nonetheless a necessary precondition in most Third World countries, where concentrated ownership of the land typically not only created vast disparities in wealth that feed class conflict, but also provides the basis for a narrow elite of ruling families whose attitudes and practices are usually profoundly antidemocratic. Certainly in Latin America in the early 1960s, the primary focus of an ambition as great as that of overcoming poverty and instituting democracy had to be the land. With due allowance made for variation in the region, over half the population earned its living in the countryside, while some 5 to 10 percent of the population (again, depending on the country) owned 70 to 90 percent of the land.[7] These figures indicate the involvement of a decisive segment of the population in a polarization of wealth often made worse by the way class differences reinforced ethnic divisions. Such acute and widespread class (and usually ethnic) conflict could only make the prospects for democracy dim indeed. Here an apt comparison can be made with the Philippines, where in its nearly half century of rule, the United States successfully introduced the entire panoply of political mechanisms characteristic of democracy, yet left the social and economic structure untouched. Today the major obstacle facing the durable consolidation of democracy in these islands remains the extended patronage systems of large families whose wealth and prestige rest on their large estates, while some 60 percent of the agrarian population (itself at least half the national total) is landless.[8]

Appropriately enough, therefore, the Alliance for Progress insisted that "unjust structures and systems of land tenure and use" had to be replaced by "an equitable system of property" backed by "timely and adequate credit, technical assistance and improved marketing arrangements" such that "the land will become for the man who works it the basis of his economic stability, the foundation of his increasing welfare, and the guarantee of his freedom and dignity." By tackling land reform, the alliance was bravely confronting the heart of the problems of poverty, social conflict, and political oppression in Latin America.

Yet radical as the suggestions for land reform surely were, the startling aspect of the charter was that these socioeconomic changes would be accompanied by the simultaneous introduction of representative democratic government throughout the continent. It is commonly observed that the alliance was a far more ambitious undertaking than the Marshall Plan launched in 1947, which aimed to revive Europe economically without transforming any of the structural features—economic, social, or political—of that area. Difficult and important as rebuilding Europe may have been, the alliance was a more challenging affair, for it sought to alter basically virtually every domain of life in Latin America. Nor does the contemporary civil rights legislation in the United States bear easy comparison with the alliance. Although there had been wholesale discrimination against black North Americans in the years since their emancipation from slavery, their incorporation into mainstream life seemed largely to be a social task; Kennedy did not question the economic order, and the political character of the nation could actually be confirmed in the process.[9]

Yet another case well worth considering is the American sponsorship of socioeconomic reform in Iran, which began at almost exactly the same time as the Alliance for Progress. Here again, the driving concern was the threat of international Communism and the conviction that if the shah of Iran failed to bring about a more just social order, the price would be his throne and the installation of a Leninist regime in Iran. The evidence that the Kennedy administration was seeking a basic change in the political organization of the country is difficult to find, yet certainly the shah feared it, seeing Washington's efforts "as more or less an American coup." He later referred to these years as "the worst period" of American interference, and denounced "your great American 'liberals' wanting to impose their way of 'democracy' on others, thinking their way is wonderful."[10] The vehicle for change was to be the new American-sponsored prime minister, Ali Amini, and the activist agriculture minister, Hassan Arsanjani, both appearing bent on turning Iran in a liberal democratic direction. However, later, when the shah removed these ministers from power in 1962, the United States was reassured when he asserted his commitment to the social and economic reforms underway.

Given the inconclusive and indirect character of United States policy toward Iran, perhaps the best comparison with the ambitions of the alliance is to be found in the United States occupation of Germany and more especially of Japan. Here Washington's first aim was to "democratize" these conquered, warlike countries, a political goal explicitly tied to changes in their socioeconomic order. As a result, the United States not only insisted on the political requirements of democracy—the usual freedoms basic to the establishment of constitutional, representative government and an independent judiciary—but also on decartelizing the economy, excluding certain right-wing elements from power, and promoting social pluralism (as in sponsoring a free trade-union movement).[11]

These various comparisons—with American policy in the Philippines, Iran, and Japan especially—allow us to see in better perspective how great the ambition of the Alliance for Progress in Latin America actually was. Only in countries occupied after World War II had the United States tried anything so bold. Yet the obvious difference between Washington's policy in Japan and Germany and the alliance was that the United States lacked sovereign power in Latin America and had to content itself with working through local forces to secure its objectives. Working with such little leverage, what reason was there to think a program as ambitious as the Alliance for Progress could ever be enacted?

The Reasoning in Washington

The most important reason that members of the Kennedy administration could think their support for fundamental change in Latin America might bear fruit was that there were political movements in Latin America that the Alliance for Progress could consciously adopt as models to be supported: Rómulo Betancourt's Acción Democrática in Venezuela, Fernando Belaunde's Acción Popular in Peru, or Eduardo Frei's Christian Democrats in Chile, for instance, not to speak of democratic governments in Costa Rica or Uruguay. In 1955, a year before he became president of Brazil, Juscelino Kubitschek laid out in some detail an ambitious assistance program for Latin America, and the idea had been seconded by other presidents of the region including Alberto Lleras Camargo of Colombia. In 1959, the Inter-American Development Bank was started as a multilateral effort. The following year the CIA opened the Institute for Political Education in Costa Rica (it later moved to the Dominican Republic) to provide a place to work intellectually on prospects for democracy in the region: Betancourt, José Figueres, and Juan Bosch were among its teachers. And thanks especially to the wide connections in Latin America of Adolf Berle, the men who formulated the alliance in Washington were able to feel that a program such as the charter proposed would meet with an enthusiastic reception in the region from many in the political elite. Given Washington's extensive contacts among the Latin American military and within the trade union movement there, it could seem a "critical mass" had been achieved to bring about basic change.[12]

At the same time there seemed to be no compelling reason to spell out more precisely than by reference to local Latin American movements what the North Americans meant by "democracy." Washington did not want to prejudice the institutional shape governments might assume in the process of becoming democratic. It seemed obvious that democracy entailed such things as a decline in class polarization thanks to a growing middle class, and the incorporation of the working class into politics through an open, competitive electoral process for offices in a governmental system run under sacrosanct constitutional procedures. To try to say more would be to force local events into a mold they surely would break. An additional reason not to trumpet these models too loudly was that they appeared to have far more to do with what Europeans would call "social democracy" (involving state intervention to assure social welfare and income redistribution) than with the "liberal democracy" North Americans were more comfortable with. So as not to alarm Congress, it was better to remain silent on the details.

What might well make the appeal of democracy to Latin American regimes all the more automatic in the early 1960s, so Washington could assume, was the keenly felt sense that time was running out on the traditional elites in Latin America. Their choice was between democracy, however they cared to define it, and Communist revolution. Presumably, enlightened Latin American leaders could be counted on to see the handwriting on the wall. The result was a U.S. policy of "constructive engagement" (a term later used by the Reagan administration with respect to its policy to help end apartheid in South Africa) that was meant to reply to the exigencies of the moment by a vigorous, if necessarily vague, call to democratic arms.

Washington's concern for political stability in Latin America as a way of keeping hostile foreign powers out of the Western Hemisphere was, of course, long-standing. The Monroe Doctrine of 1823 was seen as a way of providing support to fledgling regimes in Latin America in the wake of their independence from Spain. Later the Roosevelt Corollary (1905) had been a way of insuring that foreign powers did not take advantage of financial instability in Latin America and frequent civil conflicts there to establish a direct presence in the hemisphere. The search for a stable political order in Latin America had been the preeminent national security concern of Washington in the region for well over a century before the Alliance for Progress came into being.[13]

The latest chapter in this story was North American concern with international Communism; by 1961, countering its appeal had become a venerable occupation in Washington. In lands as different as Greece, China, the Philippines, and Vietnam, the United States had taken upon itself the task of defeating local Communist insurgencies. The Alliance for Progress was but one part of a global strategy; regionally it aimed to block a repetition of the Cuban Revolution. Yet the course of the Cuban Revolution had presented special problems to the North Americans. Castro's genius had been to present himself as nothing more than an armed nationalist and so to avoid the most obvious trappings of Communism, reliance on a Leninist party vanguard. The result, so the Cubans believed, was that an armed resistance (the *foco*) working through a series of united front organizations, could deceive both the local middle class and Washington as to its real nature. Only after the triumph of the revolution (as again of Nicaragua in 1979), would Cuban-style Communists reveal their true identity.[14]

The North American response to Communist insurgencies was to fight them on two fronts, the military and the social. The military challenge obliged the United States to conduct a new kind of antiguerrilla warfare (parallel to the British efforts in Kenya and Malaya and the French experience in Algeria) focused on mobility and featuring especially the use of the helicopter and small, flexible fighting units such as the Green Berets. During the 1960s, these tactics were disseminated in Latin America, where their most notable success came with the killing of Che Guevara in Bolivia in 1967.[15] An unstated but widely understood first premise of the alliance, therefore, was to accompany the olive branch of reform with a fist of steel.

To insist on Washington's commitment to the use of force is not to suggest that the call for reform was hypocritical, for the social front of the struggle against Communism concerned Washington every bit as much. During the Kennedy years, North Americans talked about "winning the hearts and minds" (or WHAM, as it was sometimes called) of the Vietnamese and so defeating Ho Chi Minh's bid for power. As in Vietnam, so in Latin America, the core idea was that the exclusion of large numbers of lower-class and ethnically oppressed groups provided the social tinder that could be ignited by Communists in revolution. Part of the solution to the problem of Communism's appeal lay in economic expansion that would directly address the needs of the poor (and few knowledgeable North Americans were so naive as to believe that nothing more than "trickle down" from the rich would do the job). However, most North Americans also recognized that economic growth alone was not enough. Communism had to be combated politically as well through the establishment of a national government widely perceived as legitimate and able to buckle together, through its various institutions, the major class and ethnic elements that composed the country. In the late 1950s, thanks to the influence of what Arthur Schlesinger, Jr., has called the "Charles River School" of "action intellectuals," it had become current in academic circles to hold that large-scale socioeconomic reform might well lead to democratic government in the Third World. Through the work of men like Max Millikan, pushing for the creation of the Agency for International Development, and W. W. Rostow, influential in the White House and the State Department, these ideas were to have special influence in the Kennedy administration.[16]

In short, on its surface the enthusiasm of the Kennedy administration for democracy as a way of blocking the appeal of Communism in Latin America seemed to amount to a serious program. Such thinking was part of an established tradition of concern for political stability in the region; and by virtue of its avoidance of direct military intervention and its reliance on a broad, integrated range of reforms, the Alliance for Progress could present itself as moving a clear step beyond the policies of Woodrow Wilson half a century earlier. Reform groups existed in Latin America that might be invigorated by the support of the alliance, while elites there might finally come to recognize that it was in their interest too to reform in order that their main privileges be preserved. A respectable group of North American intellectuals had given their cachet to the undertaking, and the program appealed to the deep-set moralism of the United States that the national interest and doing good for others might be overlapping goals.

Why, then, did the alliance fail?

The Failure of the Democratic Promise

If there is general agreement that the cause of democracy was not noticeably advanced in Latin America in the 1960s thanks to the Alliance for Progress, there are at least two objections to concluding therefrom that the program was a failure. One objection is that the alliance contributed to a certain economic dynamism in the region and that the current upsurge of democracy there draws some of its inspiration from the experience of the 1960s.[17] Contradicting this reading, however, is evidence that on balance the alliance actually strengthened the forces of the right in Latin America. There were nine military coups against constitutional, civilian governments in the first five years of the alliance, for example, and few of the figures on income distribution, land reform, and the like (as opposed to figures of gross economic growth) substantiate the idea that there were structural socioeconomic reforms of any significance. To link current developments to events of the 1960s appears quite unwarranted.

The second criticism of the notion that the alliance was a failure asserts that through the program the United States achieved its primary goal of blocking a recurrence of the Cuban Revolution in the hemisphere (until the Sandinista victory of 1979). From this perspective, democracy had never been more than a means to an end. To focus on its demise is to label the alliance a failure when in fact it fully accomplished its primary mission.[18] Such an argument, however, discounts the complexity of North American imperialism, making it appear a far cruder force than it actually was. Ideas have often played a role of fundamental importance in the making of U.S. foreign policy, including ideas that have been bad guides for policy. A study of the origins, assumptions, contradictions, shortcomings, and legacies of these ideas is key to an understanding of why this country acts as it does. Nowhere were ideas any more in control than in the Alliance for Progress.

An examination of these ideas themselves may help to answer why the alliance failed in its proclaimed goal of promoting democracy in Latin America. For it is difficult to deny that Washington's concept of how democracy related to social reform was so abstract and vague that the actual implementation of the alliance program lacked anything like an adequate theoretical framework from which to proceed. By comparison, the North Americans were quite vocal as to what they expected from economic development, both as to the ends to be achieved and as to the indicators that would be used to evaluate performance. Politically, however, it was never clearly specified just what would be considered steps toward democracy. How did the reforms proposed explicitly relate to democratization? How were they to be attained? What kind of obstacles might they confront and how should these be faced? None of these basic political matters was addressed; nor did waving a magic wand called Betancourt cause them to disappear. It should scarcely come as a surprise that observers then criticized policy implementation as indecisive, self-contradictory, and too cautious. Yet when these criticisms come, as they often do, from members of the Kennedy administration trying to assign responsibility for the alliance's failure to President Johnson, the origins of the problem in the initial conception of the program are effectively obscured.

The roots of this failure to ask what it might mean to institute democracy in the Latin American context lay in the North American presumption that socioeconomic reform would lead naturally to progressive political change. To their credit, the North American leaders who had emerged from the New Deal era understood, as their predecessors in power had not, that the export of democracy entailed much more than the simple transplantation of such political forms as free elections. Their mistake was not to stress the importance of socioeconomic structures to political relations, but instead to assume that reforms in the one sector would easily breed democracy in the other. The success of the reform movement in Venezuela, led by Betancourt and helped by substantial oil revenues, would not be easily duplicated. To the contrary, reforms such as those called for by the alliance were widely perceived by elites in Latin America as a threat to their power.[19] In most cases, they probably were correct.

Given the dynamics of the cold war, it should come as no surprise that leaders in Washington were unwilling to push these Latin American leaders too hard for fear that the crusade for change designed to prevent Communism might engender the very Communist takeover the alliance was designed to forestall. Much the same reasoning had led earlier to the abandonment of calls for similar reforms in the Philippines and China as well. At bottom, the North Americans knew no better than the leaders in the Third World how to organize politically the vast changes that social and economic reforms would unleash. Little wonder, then, that the leadership in Washington drew back when it came time to convert the outlines of their program into actual practice.

In order to analyze this matter in more depth, we should look in some detail at the two issues that most vividly illustrate North America's retreat from the promise of the charter: the failure to push land reform; and the acquiescence in working with military governments that had overthrown constitutional, civilian governments.

In the domain of socioeconomic ambitions, the failure of the Alliance for Progress can be seen most graphically in the fate of land reform. Here was the program best designed to help alleviate the economic problems of the poor while at the same time contribute to the incorporation of the politically excluded masses into the governing structures of the region through the formation of peasant cooperatives and leagues capable of being linked to national political parties. In theory, the result would be a broadening of the political base, an increase in the number of grass-root and regional political organizations, and a growth in the institutional capacities of the state. Yet while perhaps a million peasant families benefited from land reform during this period, another 10 to 14 million families remained untouched. Worse, given the demographic increase, the ranks of the impoverished actually expanded during this period by more than the number provided for by reform.[20] Where was Washington? While North Americans had precise target figures for what they felt should be accomplished in education and housing, there were no such figures for land reform. Although North Americans had been known to hold up aid distribution to influence Latin policies toward monetary stability, they had never invoked the course of land reform as a reason to withhold support.

Why was Washington reluctant to lend its full support to land reform when the alliance had singled it out as a major focus for its efforts? One reason was a debate within the North American camp over the relative merits of land redistribution versus expanded production. The belief was that redistribution might cut agricultural output, whereas emphasis on commercial agriculture would contribute immediately and directly to economic growth. If "a rising tide lifts all ships," then the poor would ultimately benefit from the process too as inflation was checked, exports were promoted, and the economy expanded with new jobs opening in other sectors.[21] Such a belief was buttressed by various North American interests involved in agribusiness, who could point out the foreign exchange benefits they could bring to Latin America while cautioning that radical slogans such as "the land to those who till it" would depress the opportunities for investment in the agricultural sector.

Yet we should not exaggerate explanations of this sort, for more than theoretical concerns or interest groups handicapped Washington's approach to land reform. Although debates in economic theory certainly mattered, the North Americans showed themselves sensitive to political considerations in other regards. Thus they had consistently insisted that tax reform directed at agriculture be a priority in Latin America for the sake of overall economic well-being as well as an instrument of land reform. Yet little was done to promote it despite the universal acceptance of its necessity. Clearly more than the dictates of abstract theory curtailed Washington's enthusiasm. Similarly with North American agribusiness interests. No doubt they played their role arguing against land reform and siphoning off available funds for their own purposes. But it is difficult to believe that a decisive blow was thereby given to the commitment to land reform.

In fact, the most serious impediment to North American support for land reform came not from ideology or interest groups but from political concerns—from a growing fear that the kind of transformations called for in agriculture might well play into the hands of local Communists. Not only were Communists quite able to work clandestinely through united fronts in order to control the management of fledging peasant associations, but the concomitant disruption of the established order in the countryside might well be followed by the increased influence of radical agitators. In short, much as reform could seem in the abstract as an excellent way to block Communist advances, in practice the process of transforming power relations in the countryside seemed as if it might facilitate Communism's very triumph. Nowhere is the contradiction better expressed than in two of the most quoted phrases of the Kennedy presidency. "Those who make peaceful revolution impossible make violent revolution inevitable," John F. Kennedy said promoting the alliance in 1961. But "evolutionary revolution" turned out to be a far easier process to manage in theory than in practice as the late president himself is reported to have admitted in another of his classic remarks, this one on the death of Rafael Trujillo, long-time dictator of the Dominican Republic: "There are three possibilities in descending order of preference: a decent democratic regime, a continuation of the Trujillo regime, or a Castro regime. We ought to aim at the first, but we really can't renounce the second until we are sure we can avoid the third."

An illuminating account of North American contradictions in this respect appears in Riordan Roett's book analyzing U.S. involvement in agrarian reform in Brazil's Northeast under the terms of the alliance. In 1959, the Brazilian congress had created a special agency to promote the economic and social development of this region, dominated by large sugar plantations and cattle ranches, where a third of the country's population lived, most in severe poverty. An increasingly active Church, concerned students, and an independently formed peasant league complemented the agency's efforts, which itself was under the direction of a distinguished Brazilian economist and historian, Celso Furtado. However, in short order, the North Americans began to fear the leftist tendencies of the agency and its collaborators. The United States then opted to work through local state governments, bypassing the institutions that promised fundamental structural change, and in the process, so Roett reports, actually strengthening the dominant, traditional political order.[22] The support for land reform had given way to a concern with more priority: blocking Communism.

As they backtracked in terms of their commitment to land reform, so, despite their explicit commitment to fostering democracy, the North Americans found a way as well to reconcile themselves to military coups against constitutional, civilian governments in the region. To be sure, when the Peruvian military launched a coup against what would presumably have been the Aprista government of Raúl Haya de la Torre in 1962, President Kennedy took it as a direct assault on the principles of the alliance. He ended economic and military aid, recalled the U.S. ambassador, and delayed recognition of the new government. Yet in due course, Washington relented. Other Latin American governments had refused to follow Kennedy's example, which put Washington in the difficult position of actively intervening alone, and the military promised a return to civilian rule (which occurred in June 1963 with the election of Fernando Belaunde).

Thereafter, United States response to military takeovers in Latin America became more temperate: some were opposed (in the Dominican Republic and Honduras in 1963), some were tolerated (in Guatemala and Ecuador in 1963). Then, in June 1964, when the military staged a coup against the Goulart government in Brazil, one was enthusiastically endorsed. Given this chain of events, it should not come as a total surprise that the United States itself finally launched what might be called a military intervention (if not against a constitutional government, then against what might be called a constitutionalist movement) in the Dominican Republic in 1965.

How did it come to pass that an alliance fundamentally dedicated to the promotion of democratic government could find itself not simply tolerating but actually condoning military rule? The answer depends in part on the country in question, but the general pattern is clear. João Goulart's rule in Brazil appeared manifestly inept and dangerously involved with leftists, for example; similar charges of civilian malfeasance could be adduced easily enough for other situations, so justifying a military takeover. The promise of democratic government now could be made to hang on the promise first of having good government, so establishing conditions for the eventual consolidation of democracy. This conclusion was all the easier to reach given Washington's support for a military track to defeat Communist insurgencies and the role in "civic action" that the United States had already entrusted to the Latin American militaries in an effort to given them a grass-roots political role to play.[23]

Although Washington may not have thought so at the time, the result was yet another version of the classic debate about means and ends, where the means are justified by the ends they serve. According to this logic, the successful establishment of democracy presupposes order and institutions— that is, a centralized state organizing the growing participation of the citizenry in politics through a managed increase of interest groups connected to the government by an expanded party system. Obviously, such an undertaking was no easy affair. If a high level of popular participation in independently formed associations preexisted a military takeover, institution building in the image of the Mexican (or the Turkish) model might prove impossible. Alternately, and more modestly, the military might preside over the economic expansion of a country while curtailing the participation of some groups (such as the Communists) and favoring the activities of others (much as the North Americans had done in the occupation territories after World War II) until the time an orderly transfer of power could be arranged. Such a program seemed to be the ambition of the Brazilian military after the coup of 1964. Either way, it could be rationally argued that the military was the necessary means to the end of democracy, even if the alliance had not originally intended to be party to such a process except in a subsidiary fashion through "civic action" programs.

The problem with such logic is familiar enough to the student of arguments about means and ends. More often than not, the means swallow the end they are supposed to serve. What is to be merely provisional becomes permanent; the detour becomes a road in its own right. Had the North Americans forgotten that in the 1920s and 1930s they had built up National Guards in the Dominican Republic and Nicaragua to serve as bulwarks of constitutional, civilian rule in these countries? In short order, the guards themselves had seized power and two of the most infamous careers in the region were launched: those of Somoza and Trujillo. So too in the 1960s, the means subverted the end they were to serve and came to betray the very mission the North Americans had hoped they would insure. For when the military took power, it typically took steps that did far more than simply eliminate the Communists. By imprisoning (and often killing) leftists, censoring the press, repressing the trade union movement, and banning peasant leagues (to list only the most flagrant violations of democratic norms and procedures), the military undermined the preconditions of democratic government as well. Ironically, the one military government that had at least some promise for fulfilling the intentions of the alliance found little favor in Washington. Although the Peruvian military coup of 1968 did aim to create a broad-based state thanks to land reform, education, and industrial reorganization, it nationalized the North American International Petroleum Corporation and sounded in general hostile to the impact of foreign private investment in Peru—positions the United States could not accept. Once again, it might appear, protecting North American private investors had taken priority over laying the foundations for democracy in Latin America.[24]

As so often occurs in dilemmas over means and ends, the North Americans had at first thought they could avoid choices such as were thrust upon them by events in Latin America. As we have seen, the initial idea of the alliance appears to have been to find political organizations analagous to Betancourt's Acción Demócratica in Venezuela. Belaunde's Acción Popular in Peru or Frei's Christian Democrats in Chile might serve as functional equivalents, bringing about the incorporation of peasants, workers, and ethnically marginalized groups through a controlled process of social and economic reform within the framework of democratic institutions. Such was the spirit of Frei's "Revolution in Liberty," which lasted from 1964 to 1970. Had such experiments been successful, the United States could have maintained its opposition to military government and so avoided the usually specious argument that strong-armed authoritarian rule can be the father of democracy.

But the inability of these reformist parties to bring about their programs for change was to seal the failure of the alliance. Here the case of Chile deserves special attention. There was good reason to look for the triumph of the alliance's goals in Chile if it was to have success anywhere. As early as 1833, constitutional government had been established in Chile and a framework established that after 1874 would permit the gradual incorporation of a wider stratum of the citizenry into an increasingly democratic polity. The country had the good fortune to be spared serious ethnic cleavages, and by the turn of the century the problem of church-state relations had been settled in favor of secularism, a parliamentary system was established (at least in name), and middle-class and socialist parties had begun to appear (though the latter only became significant politically in the 1930s).

The constitution of 1925 established the framework for a multiparty, presidential system that endured until 1973. Although the influence of the

Chilean military should not be understated (it had played the leading role in the foundation of constitutional order in the nineteenth century), it was, by Latin American standards, of relatively marginal importance politically with the exception of the period 1924 to 1932. Thereafter, the constitution of 1925 came fully into its own, although the actual exercise of the franchise remained restricted. In 1949, women were enfranchised; a literacy test and landlords' control of rural voting now remained the only obstacles to universal suffrage. In 1958, new legislation ended landowner power in this respect; in 1970, legislation terminated the literacy requirement. In 1961, when the Alliance for Progress was born, Chile was the most long-lived democracy in Latin America. Both the norms and the procedures of democratic government seemed relatively well established; a comparison with France in 1960 would not be inappropriate.[25]

The alignment of political forces in the country had likewise moved in a direction favorable to implementing the goals of the alliance. In 1957, a Christian Democratic party had appeared (though its roots extended back twenty years). Although more leftist than their namesakes in Europe, the Christian Democrats were nourished by their European connections, especially by the Catholic philosopher Jacques Maritain, to whom they owed their notions of "communitarianism." As the extraordinary changes in the Catholic church known as Vatican II were to demonstrate only a few years later, Chilean Christian Democracy was by no means an isolated affair. The party was unequivocal in its commitment to democracy and resolute in its determination to organize politics at the grass roots. Women and youth clubs and neighborhood committees were formed; the party announced its support for peasant cooperatives based on land reform and for workers' participation in management decisions in commerce; it called for the Chileanization of the country's natural resources. Finally, the party had the good fortune to have as its leader Eduardo Frei, a man of character and vision with solid connections throughout Latin America, in France, and in the United States.[26]

In 1964, Frei won the presidency of Chile with a resounding 56 percent of the vote. The next year, his party won a majority in the Chamber of Deputies, the first time this had occurred in a century. Yet despite Frei's successes in bringing about the beginnings of land reform and the extension of national control over Chile's natural resources, the pace was slow, the process incomplete, and the end calamitous. Part of the problem came from the party's early overconfidence, which meant that it did not look to build coalitions. But its more serious obstacles arose as both the Chilean left and right solidified their positions and moved with utmost determination to oppose Frei's policies. Ultimately, although Frei's six years in office accomplished a great deal in terms of promoting growth, equitable distribution, and democracy all in one, his efforts unleashed the fury of the opposition, so that he was unable to bring about the kind of durable changes that the alliance called for even though Chile was perhaps the Latin America country best able to realize them.[27]

What the Chilean experience obliges us to recognize is the depth of opposition to the alliance that existed within Latin America itself. The point deserves emphasis since much of the literature on the alliance concentrates on the shortcomings of Washington in the execution of the provisions of the Charter of Punta del Este. As we have already seen in the accounts of Washington's attitudes on land reform and military governments, there is no reason to minimize Washington's responsibility for the alliance's failure. But as the case of Chile demonstrates, there is no reason to exaggerate it either. For the North Americans were quite supportive of the Frei government (although the invasion of the Dominican Republic, the discovery of Project Camelot, and the suspicion by some U.S. observers around 1970 that the Christian Democrats were moving too far to the left did mar the relationship). Chile was the country where the alliance presumably had the most likelihood of flowering. Its failure there suggests that any study seeking to understand the alliance needs to devote at least as much analysis to Latin America as to Washington.[28]

Conclusion

Near the opening of this essay, I compared the Alliance for Progress with other efforts by Washington to support the expansion of democracy, both at home in the civil rights movement of the 1960s and abroad—for example, in the Philippines from 1898 to 1946, in the occupations of Germany and Japan (through the Marshall Plan), and perhaps in Iran in the early 1960s. What such comparisons immediately suggest is how fundamentally inadequate Washington's power was alone; for the alliance to prevail, it needed the far-reaching support of organized reformist movements in Latin America. If Washington wanted to do more through the alliance than it was doing for blacks at home, if it wanted to achieve more than it had accomplished in nearly half a century of rule in the Philippines, in short, if it wanted to encourage the kinds of changes it had produced in Japan under General MacArthur, but without military intervention and assuming sovereign authority itself, then certainly its hope was altogether illusory if it could not count on a significant reformist element among the Latin Americans themselves. However, as the Chilean case so poignantly illustrates, even where a powerful reformist group existed and Washington's behavior was relatively exemplary, the odds against the alliance remained enormous. If reform failed in Chile, how distant the prospect must always have been in Brazil, Honduras, or the Dominican Republic.

Does the failure of the Alliance for Progress provide yet more evidence that Wilsonianism is a dangerous tendency in U.S. foreign policy? Certainly it should caution North Americans eager to promote democracy abroad to avoid self-congratulation and to be aware of how unlikely the short-term sacrifice of principle is to achieve long-term reformist goals. It should also make North Americans aware of the limits of their power and thus more modest in what they presume to accomplish abroad. In the literature on U.S. relations with Latin America, one frequently finds quoted the words of Secretary of State Richard Olney [1895–97] that "The United States is practically sovereign in the Western Hemisphere, and its fiat is law as to those subjects to which it confines its interposition." A belief such as this is almost sure to come to ruin.[29]

Yet these lessons need not mean that the United States should forsake backing reform abroad simply because Wilsonianism has so often failed to achieve its objectives. Is the alternative better? The Nixon-Kissinger years, with their utter disregard of alliance-type goals in Latin America, paved the way for exactly the kinds of Communist insurgencies that triumphed in Nicaragua and have wrought such havoc in El Salvador.

Dedicated reformist forces committed to many of the goals for which the alliance once stood exist today in Latin America and their prospects may well be enhanced by timely support from Washington. The chief lessons to recall are three. First, the process of democratization requires that much of the old power structure be dissolved while elements of the new regime are created. Such a complex and subtle process cannot be mandated from without unless an array of local factors lends itself fully to the undertaking. Democracy is a complicated affair growing from a network of agreements and procedures that requires committed leadership, the careful exercise of power, and time to bring to fruition. It is easier to wreck a constitutional order than to build one—which makes the damage the United States did to Guatemala by its intervention in 1954 so grievous. Second, there should be a strong presumption that means to support democracy that are manifestly at odds with it (as in the case of military governments) will not work. A censored press, a broken trade-union movement, and a terrorized peasantry are not the material from which a democratic order is easily assembled. Finally, Washington must prepare to deal with the righteous wrath of certain interests that have its ear and will be hurt by democratization. North American business interests, for example, may run afoul of reforms designed to enlarge the popular base of government. The case of the International Petroleum Corporation in Peru in the 1960s is a particularly clear-cut, but by no means isolated, example of this problem. These conditions are not easy to meet. None of them was anticipated by those who organized the Alliance for Progress, however noble their intentions may have been. Can a successor generation learn from these mistakes without discarding the original inspiration?

Notes

The author would like to thank Arthur Schlesinger, Jr., Lucian Pye, Houchang Chehabi, Fran Hagopian, John Sheahan, and Abraham Lowenthal for comments on specific aspects of this essay. A grant from the Twentieth Century Fund made this research possible.

1. For a properly jaundiced view of efforts to promote constitutionalism and electoralism, see Theodore Paul Wright, Jr., *American Support of Free Elections Abroad* (Washington, D.C.: Public Affairs Press, 1964); also the essays by Drake and Meyer in this volume.

2. Wilson went so far as to endorse the land reform proposals of Pancho Villa and Emiliano Zapata. See Arthur S. Link, ed., *The Papers of Woodrow Wilson* (Princeton: Princeton University Press, 1979), vol. 30, *1914*, pp. 39ff. For John Reed's enthusiastic support, see pp. 186ff. On Wilson in the Philippines, see Peter W. Stanley, *A Nation in the Making: The Philippines and the United States, 1899-1921* (Cambridge: Harvard University Press, 1974), pp. 196ff.

3. Jerome Levinson and Juan de Onis, eds., *The Alliance That Lost Its Way* (Chicago: Quadrangle Books, 1970). This book remains the best general survey of the alliance.

4. Figures reprinted in L. Ronald Scheman, ed., *The Alliance for Progress: A Retrospective* (New York: Praeger, 1988), pp. 10–11.

5. The charter and other official pronouncements are reprinted in the United States Department of State *Bulletin,* September 1961.

6. The Kissinger Commission Report spends far more time discussing matters such as education and housing than land reform, which receives only perfunctory mention. The Caribbean Basin Initiative concentrates on stimulating gross economic output and may be read as an encouragement for agribusiness.

7. U.S. Senate, Committee on Foreign Relations, Subcommittee on American Republics Affairs, *Survey of the Alliance for Progress: Labor Policies and Programs,* Document 17, 91st Congress, 1st session (12844-2) (Washington, D.C.: U.S. Governement Printing Office, 1969), p. 181. Interesting testimony is provided herein by William C. Thiesenhusen, Marion R. Brown, T. Lynn Smith, and Peter Dorner.

8. David Wurfel, *Filipino Politics: Development and Decay* (Ithaca: Cornell University Press, 1988), chaps. 3, 6.

9. Of course, the question of the degree to which the struggle against racial discrimination involves the need to reshape economic practices in the United States is an old one. Dr. Martin Luther King was killed when he sought to broaden his campaign and make economic issues central.

10. James Bill, *The Eagle and the Lion: The Tragedy of American-Iranian Relations* (New Haven: Yale University Press, 1988), chap. 4.

11. Robert Montgomery, *Forced To Be Free* (Chicago: University of Chicago Press, 1957).

12. On the role of Berle, see Levinson and Onis, pp. 52ff. In a letter to me dated October 18, 1989, Arthur Schlesinger, Jr., writes, "There is no question that we saw Betancourt's Venezuela as the model for democratic development; the future of Latin America, it seemed to us, lay between the Castro road and the Betancourt road." On the role of various Latin Americans and the Institute for Political Education, see Howard Wiarda, *The Democratic Revolution in Latin America* (forthcoming, 1990), chap. 5. On the extent of North American influence in the Latin America trade union movement, see the chapter by Buchanan in this volume.

13. An excellent account remains Samuel Flagg Bemis, *The Latin American Policy of the United States: An Interpretation* (New York: Harcourt, Brace, Jovanovich, 1943). See also Tony Smith, *The Pattern of Imperialism: The United States, Great Britain, and the Late-Industrializing World Since 1815* (Cambridge: Cambridge University Press, 1981), chap. 4.

14. Tony Smith, *Thinking Like a Communist: State and Legitimacy in the Soviet Union, China, and Cuba* (New York: Norton, 1987), chap. 5.

15. U.S. Senate, Survey of the Alliance, statements by Edwin Lieuwen and David Burks.

16. On the thinking in Washington, see Arthur M. Schlesinger, Jr., *A Thousand Days: John F. Kennedy in the White House* (New York: Fawcett Publications, 1985), pp. 176ff.; also the excellent review by Robert Packenham, *Liberal America and the Third World: Political Development Ideas in Foreign Aid and Social Science* (Princeton: Princeton University Press, 1973), pp. 59ff. In an interview with me on October 18, 1989, Lucian Pye, an active member of the "Charles River School," confirmed the essential argument of Packenham's book, although he placed even more emphasis on the influence these intellectuals came to have in Washington within the State Department and the White House (thanks to W. W. Rostow) and at the Agency for International Development (thanks to Max Millikan). For an example of their thinking, see especially Max F. Millikan and W. W. Rostow, *A Proposal: Key to an Effective Foreign Policy* (New York: Harper & Row, 1957), chap. 10.

17. Such is the general tenor of most contributions to Scheman. See also Richard N. Goodwin, *A Voice from the Sixties* (New York: Little, Brown & Co., 1988), chap. 8 and pp. 244ff.

18. See the challenge issued by Che Guevara at the Punta del Este Conference, "The Alliance for Progress," in *Che: Selected Works of Ernesto Guevara* (Cambridge: MIT Press, 1969), pp. 265ff. For a more extended discussion and references, see Abraham F. Lowenthal, "'Liberal,' 'Radical,' and 'Bureaucratic' Perspectives on US Latin American Policy: The Alliance for Progress," in Julio Cotler and Richard R. Fagen, eds., *Latin America and the United States: The Changing Realities* (Stanford, Calif.: Stanford University Press, 1974), pp. 221ff.

19. See Levinson and Onis, pp. 60ff, 216.

20. The opposition of many Latin American elites to the goals of the alliance is described repeatedly in the U.S. Senate, *Survey of the Alliance;* see especially Holt, Lieuwen, and Halperin.

21. For a nonpartisan account of economic thinking, see Gerald Meier, *Emerging from Poverty: The Economics That Really Matters* (Oxford: Oxford University Press, 1984); for the fate of the alliance at the hands of orthodox classical economists, see, e.g., Levinson and Onis discussing Lincoln Gordon, pp. 200ff. An overall review of what might be called the "mind set" of official Washington can be found in Lars Schoultz, *National Security and United States Policy toward Latin America* (Princeton: Princeton University Press, 1987).

22. Riordan Roett, *The Politics of Foreign Aid in the Brazilian Northeast* (Nashville, Tenn.: Vanderbilt University Press, 1974), esp. chap. 9. Similar, if less pointed, observations are made by the Senate staff of the Committee on Foreign Relations in their study of land reform in Colombia, in the Senate's *Survey of the Alliance.*

23. For a general model of what is to be done, see Samuel P. Huntington, *Political Order in Changing Societies* (New Haven: Yale University Press, 1968), chap. 4. Under the terms of the alliance, Latin American armies were to undertake "civic action" to bring reform to the countryside. See the testimony of Field Haviland in the Senate's *Survey of the Alliance.* For a study that explicitly pits the promise of the alliance against the reality, see Edwin Lieuwen, *Generals vs. Presidents: Neomilitarism in Latin America* (New York: Praeger, 1964). See also Alfred Stepan, "The New Professionalism of Internal Warfare and Military Role Expansion," in Alfred Stepan, ed., *Authoritarian Brazil: Origins, Policies, and Future* (New Haven: Yale University Press, 1973); and Douglas S. Blaufarb, *The Counterinsurgency Era: U.S. Doctrine and Performance* (New York: Free Press, 1977), chap. 9.

24. On Peru, see Levinson and Onis, pp. 80ff., 98ff., 146ff. Also, essays by Julio Cotler, Peter S. Cleaves, and Henry Pease Garcia in Cynthia McClintock and Abraham F. Lowenthal, eds., *The Peruvian Experiment Reconsidered* (Princeton: Princeton University Press, 1983).

25. Arturo Valenzuela, "Chile: Origins, Consolidation and Breakdown of a Democratic Regime," in Larry Diamond, Juan L. Linz, and Seymour Martin Lipsett, eds., *Democracy in Developing Countries* (Boulder, Colo.: Lynne Rienner, 1989); and Brian Loveman, *Chile: The Legacy of Hispanic Capitalism* (Oxford: Oxford University Press, 1979).

26. Ernst Halperin, *Nationalism and Communism in Chile* (Cambridge: MIT Press, 1965), chap. 5; Leonard Gross, *The Last, Best Hope: Eduardo Frei and Chilean Democracy* (New York: Random House, 1967).

27. Paul E. Sigmund, *The Overthrow of Allende and the Politics of Chile, 1964–1976* (Pittsburgh: University of Pittsburgh Press, 1977), chaps. 3, 4; Loveman, chaps. 8, 9; Eduardo Frei Montalva, "The Alliance That Lost Its Way," *Foreign Affairs* 45 (April 1967); Staff Report of the Select Committee to Study Governmental Operations with respect to Intelligence Activities, United States Senate, *Covert Action in Chile, 1963–1973*, 94th Congress, 1st Session, December 18, 1975. See also the Munoz essay in this volume.

28. For insistence on the difficulty of adapting the alliance to Latin America, see Howard J. Wiarda, "Did the Alliance 'Lose Its Way,' or Were Its Assumptions All Wrong from the Beginning and Are Those Assumptions Still with Us?" in Scheman. For an early, pessimistic evaluation of the likelihood that democracy would soon appear in Latin America, see the posthumously published essays of Frank Tannenbaum, edited by Joseph Maier and Richard W. Weatherhead, *The Future of Democracy in Latin America: Essays by Frank Tannenbaum* (New York: Knopf, 1974).

29. The alliance's advocates avoided connecting their ambitions to Wilson. Milton Eisenhower, who first alerted his brother's administration to the depth of the social problems in Latin America, vigorously endorsed the alliance, but roundly condemned Wilson in favor of FDR's Good Neighbor Policy. See his *The Wine Is Bitter: The United States and Latin America* (New York: Doubleday, 1963), pp. 175ff. Robert F. Kennedy also salutes FDR, but neglects Wilson in his introduction to William D. Rogers, *The Twilight Struggle: The Alliance for Progress and the Politics of Development in Latin America* (New York: Random House, 1967). Lincoln Gordon is similarly discreet: *A New Deal for Latin America: The Alliance for Progress* (Cambridge: Harvard University Press, 1963). Nor do the contributors to the Scheman volume, many of whom were architects of the alliance, refer to Wilson.

4 | The Reagan Years: The 1980s

Thomas Carothers

THE 1980s is an especially important period for the study of the relation between U.S. policy toward Latin America and the development of Latin American democracy. In the 1980s, Latin America experienced a sweeping democratic renewal. All across the region, military dictatorships fell and were replaced by elected, civilian governments. By the end of the decade, only a few blatantly nondemocratic governments remained in power, a dramatic change from the previous decade when most Latin Americans lived under authoritarian rule. Although many of the new democratically elected governments represented only partial movements toward democracy and held power only tenuously, the resurgence of democracy in Latin America was a trend of unquestionable significance.

In the same years that this democratic renewal was occurring, the United States government was making the promotion of democracy the primary stated goal of its Latin America policy. With increasing frequency and clarity across the 1980s, the Reagan administration publicly defined U.S. interests in Latin America in terms of the achievement of democracy and unified disparate policies toward almost every country in the region around that stated goal. In a speech summing up the Reagan administration's Latin America policy in January 1989, Elliott Abrams, assistant secretary of state for inter-American affairs, highlighted the democracy theme: "We in the Reagan Administration gave it [the trend toward democracy in Latin America] our full support. No mere spectator in this revolution, we did more than just welcome the trend rhetorically. Democracy became the organizing principle of our policy. It encompassed the divergent interests of this country within a unifying and coherent framework."[1]

The concurrence of the decisive trend toward democracy in Latin America and the at-least-stated emphasis on promoting democracy in U.S.

policy raises an obvious question. Did the United States have a significant role in the resurgence of democracy in Latin America? The Reagan administration was not bashful about taking credit. As democracy spread in Latin America, administration officials habitually associated the United States with the political gains and even described them as the fruits of U.S. policy. Assistant Secretary Abrams stated flatly in 1988 that the administration "has met with extraordinary success in building democracy [in Latin America]."[2] The purpose of this chapter is to evaluate that claim.

Although promoting democracy was the central *stated* goal of U.S. policy toward Latin America in the 1980s, in some areas of policy this commitment to democracy was almost purely rhetorical; in others, however, it was genuine. This chapter also seeks to sort out the rhetorical and substantive elements of the stated prodemocracy policy and to examine what conception of democracy the Reagan administration employed in the areas in which it was actually concerned with promoting democracy.

The chapter is organized in four sections corresponding to four different policies the Reagan administration pursued in Latin America. Each of these policies had promoting democracy as its stated goal and each relied on a different stated means of achieving that goal. In El Salvador, Honduras, and Guatemala, the Reagan administration sought to stop what it saw as Soviet and Cuban penetration of the United States' backyard. In each of these countries the administration combined increased military assistance with attempts to promote the emergence and maintenance of elected, civilian governments. The policy was publicly presented as an effort to promote democracy by fostering centrist transitions. In Nicaragua and Grenada, the administration ousted or tried to oust leftist governments through military force. These anti-Communist military efforts were publicly presented as prodemocracy campaigns under the rubric of a doctrine of promoting democracy in leftist countries by force, known as the Reagan Doctrine. In South America, after an early, unsuccessful attempt to renew U.S. relations with the declining military dictatorships of the region, the Reagan administration pursued a low-key policy with little discernible substance other than the maintenance of amicable relations with the newly emerging democratic governments and some verbal support for democracy. The administration also cast its South America policy in prodemocracy terms; it is labeled here a policy of democracy by applause. In Chile, Paraguay, Panama, and Haiti, the second Reagan administration gravitated toward a policy of using economic and diplomatic pressure to induce the only remaining right-wing dictatorships of the region to cede power and permit elections. This policy was publicly presented as a policy of democracy by economic and diplomatic pressure, and is referred to here as democracy by pressure.

Democracy by Centrist Transition:
El Salvador, Honduras, and Guatemala

When the Reagan administration took office in 1981 it found Central America in a state of revolutionary ferment. Nicaragua had fallen to the leftist Sandinistas in 1979, and El Salvador and Guatemala were under attack by leftist rebels, while Honduras and Costa Rica watched nervously from the sidelines. The early Reagan team, which was preoccupied with worldwide growth of Soviet power, saw Central America as a prime target of Soviet and Cuban expansionism.[3] The administration was determined to oppose the further spread of leftism in the region and formulated a two-part policy response: first, militarily bolstering the governments that were under ongoing or potential attack by leftist rebels—particularly El Salvador, Honduras, and Guatemala; and second, exerting military pressure against the Nicaraguan government to cease whatever support it was giving to rebels in neighboring countries or to give up power altogether.

Both halves of this military-oriented anti-Communist policy came to be presented as efforts to promote democracy. Toward El Salvador, Honduras, and Guatemala the administration described multilayered policies of military, economic, and political assistance as efforts to promote democracy in which military concerns were subordinated to the overall political goal. The Nicaragua policy was characterized in similar terms: the administration said that the primary purpose of military pressure was to induce the Sandinistas to accept democracy. Throughout the Reagan years, administration officials repeatedly joined these two democracy formulations and declared that the United States' overriding goal in Central America was democracy and that all other goals, such as peace and economic development, depended on the achievement of democracy throughout the region.

El Salvador

El Salvador was the Reagan administration's first foreign policy crisis. In the months before President Reagan took office, the Carter administration's policy of shoring up the precarious civil-military regime had nearly come apart. In December 1980, members of the Salvadoran security forces raped and murdered four U.S. churchwomen in El Salvador, provoking a huge outcry in the United States about military aid to El Salvador. In January 1981, the Salvadoran rebel front launched a "final offensive" that fell short of victory but made very clear the gravity of the military conflict. The incoming Reagan administration wasted no time in engaging itself on El Salvador. Administration officials declared that the United States would draw the line on international Communism in El Salvador and scrambled to increase U.S. assistance to the beleaguered Salvadoran military.

From the start, there were two schools of thought within the Reagan administration over El Salvador and the civil conflicts in Central America generally. On the one hand were the hard-liners, high-level political appointees such as U.S. Ambassador Jeane Kirkpatrick, Secretary of State Alexander Haig, CIA Director William Casey, and national security advisers Richard Allen and William Clark who dominated the early Reagan foreign policy team. They saw the Salvadoran conflict as the current flashpoint of a systematic campaign by the Soviet Union, Cuba, and Nicaragua to spread Communism throughout Central America and ultimately destabilize Mexico and South America. As Secretary of State Haig stated in February 1981, "our problem with El Salvador is external intervention in the internal affairs of a sovereign nation in this hemisphere, nothing more, nothing less."[4] They advocated a purely military response—the United States should give massive aid to the Salvadoran armed forces to help them defeat the rebels as quickly as possible.

On the other hand were the moderates, mid-level political appointees in the Latin America bureau of the State Department (who, though conservative, were generally not ideological zealots) and the mid- and lower-level career staff in the State Department and other foreign policy agencies. Most of them shared the hard-liners' conviction that the Salvadoran rebels were getting aid from Cuba and Nicaragua but believed that the Salvadoran conflict was rooted in domestic political and economic injustices and that the external aid to the rebels was only an aggravating factor, not a fundamental cause. They also recognized that a bipartisan consensus was obligatory for any successful policy and that the Democratic-controlled House of Representatives would be unlikely to approve large new amounts of military aid for El Salvador unless there were progress on human rights and a transition to elected, civilian rule. They pushed for a policy that would integrate increased military assistance with efforts to reduce poverty and inequality as well as foster a more representative political system.

For approximately the first three years of the Reagan administration, no resolution of this debate occurred; both groups simultaneously pursued the policies they believed in. The hard-liners focused on getting as much military aid to El Salvador as possible; they succeeded in increasing that aid from $5.9 million in 1980 to $82 million in 1982 and $81.3 million in 1983. The assistance funded both a large-scale training and reorganization effort for the Salvadoran military and a massive infusion of arms and equipment.[5] The administration's relentless pursuit of increased military aid for El Salvador produced sharp conflicts with many Democrats in Congress who were reluctant to approve aid to a military with a record of human rights abuses.[6] The early Reagan administration essentially stonewalled on the human rights issue, refusing to recognize that the Salvadoran military and police were deeply involved in the death-squad killings that racked Salvadoran society and exerting no high-level pressure for change on Salvadoran military leaders.

The moderates supported the military assistance effort but also attempted to strengthen the economic and political components of the overall policy. They pushed through a major economic assistance program for El Salvador; economic aid rose from $58.3 million in 1980 to $114 million in 1981 up to $245.6 million in 1983. The Salvadoran economy was in a terrible state due both to the civil war and the economic recession affecting all of Latin America; the massive influx of U.S. aid was essential just to keep the economy afloat. The administration also gave some support to the set of economic reforms that had been initiated by the civil-military junta in 1980 (with the Carter administration's strong encouragement), most notably the land reform program.

The moderates also developed the political component of the El Salvador policy, which went under the public heading of promoting democracy and consisted of strengthening the political center and fostering an electoral process that would produce a moderate, elected civilian president. The U.S. embassy became deeply involved in the fledgling Salvadoran electoral process from Constituent Assembly elections in 1982, through the victory of a new constitution in 1983 up to presidential elections in 1984. The embassy worked actively with the Salvadoran political parties to insure cooperation with the process, pressed the military to accept a transition to civilian rule, and in conjunction with the Agency for International Development (AID) gave technical assistance aimed at helping the Salvadoran government carry out technically credible elections.[7]

The military component of the El Salvador policy was clearly of dominant importance in the early years of the administration.[8] The hard-liners largely controlled the policy process in Washington and were little interested in the economic and political components. The policy was publicly presented, however, not as a military-oriented, anti-Communist policy or even as a two-part military and political policy but as a democracy policy in which all three operational elements—military, economic, and political assistance—were subordinate to the overriding goal of bringing democracy to El Salvador.[9]

In 1983 the balance between the different approaches began to shift decisively in favor of the moderates. Early in 1983 President Reagan received pessimistic reports on the Salvadoran war from two special envoys and decided to push for large increases in U.S. military aid. That effort ran into serious problems in Congress, however (due in large part to the Salvadoran military's continuing problem with human rights), and it finally became clear to President Reagan that a policy dominated by the hard-line military approach would neither achieve a quick, decisive solution in El Salvador nor get the necessary sustained bipartisan support at home. In late 1983 the Reagan administration finally exerted some significant high-level pressure for human rights improvements (Vice-President Bush stopped in El Salvador in December 1983 to lecture Salvadoran military leaders on human rights) and appointed the National Bipartisan Commission on Central America, popularly known as the Kissinger Commission, to formulate a bipartisan policy approach to Central America, especially for El Salvador. The Kissinger Commission, which was nominally bipartisan but heavily weighted toward moderate conservatives, recommended an El Salvador policy that was essentially the same as the policy the moderates in the administration had been trying to pursue. The commission thus was important not in creating a new policy but in legitimating one side of the policy debate that had been going on within the administration since 1981.

The 1984 presidential elections in El Salvador, held in two rounds in March and May 1984, completed the transition in U.S. policy from the hard-line to the moderate approach. The United States gave large amounts of assistance to the Salvadoran electoral commission to assure technically credible elections and vigorously supported the Christian Democratic candidate José Napoleón Duarte, both through covert financial assistance and by informal politicking within El Salvador.[10] When Duarte emerged victorious, the administration celebrated the election as the achievement of democracy in El Salvador and a great victory for U.S. policy.

During the Duarte years, the Reagan administration still pursued a two-part military and political policy, which it continued to portray as a unified prodemocracy policy, but the military component was no longer dominant. In the second half of 1984 the Salvadoran military finally began to operate effectively against the rebels and drive the rebels back to relatively limited parts of the national territory. Furthermore, Duarte's election removed the objections of the U.S. Congress to military assistance, ensuring a steady flow of very large quantities of such assistance.[11]

The political component of the policy gained in importance as the military component grew less pressing. Duarte enjoyed considerable international credibility and, initially at least, widespread popular support at home. The administration was determined to make sure he survived in power for the duration of his term. "Promoting democracy," translated to mean helping Duarte stay in power, became the central focus of the policy. The U.S. embassy in El Salvador appointed itself the guardian of the Duarte government and involved itself deeply in the local political situation to reduce conflicts between the government and the other major sectors of society, lessen divisions within the Christian Democratic party itself, and assist Duarte in obtaining the aid and support he needed from Washington. The administration also tried to help Duarte consolidate democratic rule by initiating assistance programs designed to strengthen key governmental institutions such as the judiciary, the legislature, and the police.[12]

U.S. economic assistance to El Salvador increased once Duarte was elected, from its already high level to unprecedented levels in the Central American context. From 1985 on, El Salvador received more than $300 million per year and by the late 1980s, U.S. economic aid constituted more than half of the Salvadoran national budget. The aid continued to go both toward trying to pull El Salvador out of its lengthening economic recession and helping repair the war damage. Both efforts were little more than holding actions, despite the enormous quantities of aid.

Throughout the 1980s, the Reagan administration characterized its El Salvador policy as a prodemocracy policy and, once Duarte was in power, as a successful policy that had brought democracy to El Salvador. The policy was in fact an anti-Communist policy in which promoting democracy, interpreted as fostering the emergence and maintenance of an elected, civilian government, constituted one operational component alongside a massive program of military assistance. During the period up to Duarte's election the military component was clearly dominant; afterward the political component gained priority, but even then the underlying reason for the United States' heavy involvement in El Salvador remained the desire to insure that El Salvador remained non-Communist.

As an anti-communist effort, the El Salvador policy was partially successful. The U.S. military assistance helped build the El Salvadoran armed forces into a force large and competent enough at least to prevent the rebels from winning. The rebels were not defeated, however, and the fundamental socioeconomic problems that fed the rebel cause were not solved.

As a prodemocracy policy, the El Salvador policy was largely unsuccessful. The U.S. support for an electoral transition was a significant factor in the success of that transition. But the emergence of an elected government in El Salvador did not constitute the achievement of democracy. The Duarte government exercised only very limited authority. The military remained a powerful sovereign authority that tolerated the civilian government but did not subordinate itself to it. The economic elite, which has traditionally controlled El Salvador, maintained formal and informal networks of power that greatly limited the civilian government's authority. The Duarte government was a democratically elected government (although it must also be kept in mind that the left was excluded from participation in the 1982 and 1984 elections) but it was unable to function as a sovereign, representative government. Furthermore, political participation, another key element of a working democratic society, was substantially curtailed during the Duarte years. Salvadorans got to vote in periodic elections, but more substantial forms of participation—such as openly expressing political opinions, organizing interest groups, and engaging in advocacy work—were frequently met with violent political repression from the security forces or members of those forces operating in informal death squads. Human rights abuses increased across the course of the Duarte years and by 1987 and 1988 had reached high levels.[13]

The prodemocracy element of the Reagan administration policy in El Salvador was marked by several serious flaws. Perhaps the largest was the inherent contradiction between trying to promote democracy while simultaneously financing a huge buildup of what historically at least has been a profoundly antidemocratic military. The administration denied that any contradiction existed, and tried to portray the Salvadoran military as a defender of democracy. Although the military did come around to permitting and defending a civilian government, this support reflected not the military's desire for democracy but its recognition that civilian rule assured a steady flow of U.S. military aid and did not infringe on the military's sovereignty. The Reagan administration's almost unconditional support for the military reinforced its dominant position in Salvadoran society and assured its ability to dictate the limits on civilian political life.[14]

The second shortcoming concerned the conception of democracy that the Reagan administration applied in El Salvador. There were some officials in the U.S. government in the 1980s who genuinely wanted to promote democracy in El Salvador. But they held to the notion that democracy could be achieved through the electoral process. They willfully ignored the fact that the major power structures in Salvadoran society—principally the military and the economic elite—were antidemocratic and that elections would not reduce their power. And they refused to recognize the Salvadoran left as a major political force in the country and to try to incorporate it into a new political system. The central U.S. idea of "building the political center" in El Salvador was a formulaic concept that had no relation to the true distribution of power in El Salvador. The U.S. officials involved in forging the political solution in El Salvador could not conceive of an El Salvador in which the military was not the dominant actor, the economic elite no longer held the national economy in its hands, the left was incorporated into the political system, and all Salvadorans actually had both the formal and substantial possibility of political participation. In short, the U.S. government had no real conception of democracy in El Salvador.

Honduras

The Reagan administration initially had little interest in Honduras since, unlike El Salvador, Guatemala, and Nicaragua, Honduras was neither threatened by significant leftist rebel groups nor under leftist rule. Due to its long border with Nicaragua, its corrupt, malleable military, and relatively benign political tradition (i.e., one not likely to trigger congressional objections in the United States), however, Honduras soon attracted the administration's attention as the most promising base for the military undertakings that were being planned as part of the emerging anti-Sandinista policy. The major undertaking was the aid program for the Nicaraguan contras. U.S. assistance to the contras began in 1981 and quickly became the Reagan administration's dominant preoccupation in Latin America. Although targeted at Nicaragua, the contra program also was of great relevance to U.S.-Honduran relations. As the main operational base for the contras and the conduit of the vast U.S. paramilitary assistance program, Honduras was significantly affected. The Reagan administration was obliged to devote substantial time and attention, as well as economic and military assistance funds, to maintain Honduran toleration of the contras.

A second, related military undertaking in Honduras was the establishment of a semipermanent U.S. military presence, which the Reagan administration justified as necessary to help defend Honduras against possible Nicaraguan attack but which was clearly part of its campaign to intimidate the Sandinistas. Through a series of increasingly large joint military exercises with the Honduran military, the United States usually had more than one thousand U.S. troops in the country.[15]

The United States also provided large quantities of assistance to the Honduran military, close to $400 million in the 1980s, transforming the traditionally small, constabulary Honduran military into a heavily armed force of over fifty thousand men. This assistance was also justified as necessary to help the Honduran military resist attack by the Nicaraguan military; it was widely understood, however, to be a significant part of the explicit or implicit quid pro quo for the Honduran military's toleration of the contras.

Although the Reagan administration's Honduras policy was dominated by anti-Sandinista ventures, the administration always described its involvement in Honduras in terms of promoting democracy. The policy did in fact have a political component, one that was seen at least by the moderates in the administration as prodemocratic. Even more than in El Salvador, this political component was narrowly focused on the electoral process. A transition to civilian rule had been initiated by the Honduran military in the late 1970s and strongly supported by the Carter administration. The transition was well advanced when the Reagan administration took power; Constituent Assembly elections had been held in April 1980 and presidential elections were set for late 1981. After some backsliding by hard-liners in early 1981, the Reagan administration came around to supporting the electoral process, the moderates because they believed civilian rule would be good for Honduras, the hard-liners because they were persuaded that Congress would not approve the administration's ambitious military plans for Honduras unless a transition to civilian rule occurred.

Once the elections were successfully held and an elected civilian government (led by President Roberto Suazo Córdova of the Liberal party) came into power, the political component of the administration's policy settled into the form it maintained through 1988: the administration sought to assure the maintenance of elected civilian rule, no more, no less. The administration exercised its considerable influence on the military and the business sector to insure that the civilian government remained in power. The main threat to the orderly continuation of elected civilian rule came from President Suazo Córdova himself who in 1985 began to maneuver to postpone or even call off the scheduled presidential elections. The U.S. embassy, together with the Honduran military, blocked Suazo Córdova's move and insured that the elections were held and the results respected.[16] Also, AID funded a multimillion dollar electoral assistance program to help the Honduran electoral commission carry out technically credible elections.[17]

A further element of the administration's effort to guarantee the continuance of elected civilian rule was massive economic assistance. The Honduran economy had undergone a sharp downturn in 1981, making economic stability the major challenge facing the newly elected government. U.S. economic assistance increased to between $80 million and $110 million per year from 1982 through 1984, then jumped up to $229 million in 1985. The aid greatly helped both Suazo Córdova and his successor José Azcona Hoyo keep the economy from collapsing altogether. It also constituted another part of the quid pro quo for the Honduran government's toleration of the contras.

The Reagan administration repeatedly claimed that its policy toward Honduras was a prodemocracy policy both in that it helped foster an elected, civilian government and helped the government defend itself against attack by the totalitarian Sandinistas. In fact the administration's Honduras policy was not a Honduras policy but was one part of the anti-Sandinista Nicaragua policy. For the Reagan administration, Honduras was of interest only as a staging ground for military and paramilitary campaigns against Nicaragua. The claim that the various military programs were necessary to help Honduras defend itself against Nicaraguan attack was specious. There is no significant evidence that Nicaragua was ever planning to invade and conquer Honduras and it was obvious to any observer at the time that the United States would respond to any such invasion by intervening militarily to oust the Sandinistas.

The political component of the administration's policy did help insure the continuation of civilian rule in Honduras but did not, as the administration claimed, lead Honduras to being "truly democratic."[18] Despite elected civilian rule, Honduras remained far from democratic in the 1980s. The military maintained its powerful rule as the arbiter of Honduran politics and ceded little of its authority to the civilian government. The business elite also kept its power. Consequently Honduras continued to be run by the same small elite of military officers and businessmen that had dominated the country for generations. The administration's Honduras policy was if anything a negative force for democratization in that it greatly strengthened the antidemocratic military, reified a formal electoral process that did little to change the antidemocratic structural features of the society, and made a mockery of Honduran sovereignty.

Guatemala

The Reagan administration did not get nearly as involved in Guatemala as in El Salvador and Honduras but the policy it pursued there nonetheless shared much the same conception. In 1981, Guatemala was embroiled in a vicious civil war between a highly repressive right-wing military government and a coalition of leftist guerrilla groups. As with El Salvador, hardliners in the administration saw Guatemala as another case of Soviet and Cuban aggression[19] and pushed for renewed military assistance, whereas moderates saw the conflict as a civil war fanned by external actors and prescribed a mixed policy of military, political, and economic assistance. Both groups agreed on the need for military assistance and this became the main goal of U.S. policy.[20] The moderates also formulated a political component, which aimed to encourage the Guatemala military to improve its atrocious human rights record and at least to consider moving toward civilian rule. In 1981 the administration attempted unsuccessfully to get Congress to reestablish military assistance for Guatemala (military assistance had been terminated in 1977 when Guatemala refused to accept human rights conditions on such assistance). Simultaneous U.S. efforts to persuade the Guatemalan military government to move toward a civilian transition fell on deaf ears.[21]

A military coup ousted President Romeo Lucas García in March 1982 and installed a military junta led by General Efraín Ríos Montt. The administration tried hard to sell Ríos Montt to Congress as a reformist leader taking strong measures to reduce human rights abuses.[22] Congress was skeptical, however, and continued to oppose military aid. In 1983, Ríos Montt was overthrown by General Oscar Mejía Víctores, who finally put Guatemala on a definite road to civilian rule and helped lead the Guatemalan military to victory over the rebels. The administration continued its policy of trying to persuade Congress to grant military assistance to Guatemala and to encourage the Guatemalan government to move ahead with the electoral transition. Presidential elections were finally held in 1985 and Vinicio Cerezo Arévalo, the head of Guatemala's Christian Democratic party, was elected president.

After Cerezo assumed the presidency in December 1985, the balance of U.S. policy changed somewhat. The administration continued to press Congress to approve military aid but somewhat less vigorously than before and with a different rationale. The Guatemalan rebels, although not completely eliminated, had been reduced to a minor irritant. The argument that the Guatemalan military could not defeat the rebels without U.S. assistance thus had to be shelved. In its place, the administration contended that military aid was necessary to show the Guatemalan military that concrete benefits would come to it for having accepted civilian rule. Despite this new rationale and the presence of an elected, civilian government, Congress remained wary of aiding the Guatemalan military and approved only small amounts of aid during Cerezo's term.[23]

The political component of the Guatemala policy expanded in the Cerezo years. The administration greeted Cerezo's election warmly and committed itself to helping Guatemala consolidate its "democratic transition," which in practice meant helping Cerezo survive in power. Elements in the Guatemalan military leadership continually questioned Cerezo's rule and, together with the reactionary Guatemalan business elite, plotted constantly against him. The U.S. embassy in Guatemala, backed by the State Department in Washington, was kept busy defusing conflicts between Cerezo and his many opponents and helping head off numerous coup attempts.

The United States also backed the Cerezo government with large quantities of economic aid. After having received small (relative to its neighbors) amounts of economic aid from 1981 to 1985, Guatemala received $116.7 million in 1986, $187.8 million in 1987, and $132.2 million in 1988.[24] The aid helped Cerezo at least stabilize the ailing Guatemalan economy and mitigate somewhat the harsh criticisms of the private sector. Human rights remained a major problem during the Cerezo years. Selective assassinations continued in the capital and the military maintained repressive forms of control in the countryside.[25] The administration, eager to put the best face possible on the Cerezo government, took little action on the human rights issue and lapsed into the by-then-familiar pattern of denial and avoidance.

The Reagan administration's Guatemala policy, like its El Salvador policy, was an anti-Communist policy with a strong military orientation and a secondary political component touted as a prodemocracy policy. Unlike in El Salvador, the United States was not very influential either militarily or politically in Guatemala. Little U.S. military assistance ever materialized— the Guatemalan army fought its own war, and the United States had almost no role in the conflict. And the United States had little role in the transition to civilian rule—that transition was the military's own project. The United States did help Cerezo stay in power once he was elected. Cerezo's rule was an improvement over the predecessor military regimes but did not represent the achievement of democracy in Guatemala. The Guatemalan military and economic elite continued to exert powerful control over Guatemalan society, political participation was severely limited by a continuing high degree of human rights abuses, and Cerezo rapidly became a weak, ineffectual president. In Guatemala, more than anywhere else in Latin America, an elected government did not constitute the achievement of a working democracy.

Democracy by Force: Nicaragua and Grenada

Nicaragua

The Reagan administration expended incalculable amounts of energy and resources trying to oust the left-wing Sandinista government in Nicaragua. The core of this policy was a program of financial and technical assistance to a group of anti-Sandinista rebels, known as the contras, who fought the Sandinista army from bases in Honduras and Costa Rica. The policy also consisted of economic pressure—the Reagan administration slashed Nicaragua's sugar quota, imposed a trade embargo, and blocked loans and credits to Nicaragua from the multilateral development banks. The policy was capped by a campaign of diplomatic pressure, with U.S. officials criticizing and insulting the Nicaraguan government and trying to induce Nicaragua's neighbors to adopt outspoken anti-Sandinista policies.[26]

The Nicaragua policy was always controlled by the hard-liners in the administration, who were convinced that the Sandinistas were Marxist-Leninist totalitarians, that as Marxist-Leninists they would devote themselves to spreading revolution throughout Central America, and that the only way to insure regional security was to oust the Sandinistas. The moderates in the administration believed that the Sandinistas could be induced by means short of ouster to stop assisting leftist rebels in neighboring countries and advocated the pursuit of a negotiated security accord with Nicaragua. Negotiations between the United States and Nicaragua were held off and on throughout the Reagan years, both as a result of initiatives by moderates and because the hard-liners recognized the political necessity of appearing to be amenable to a negotiated solution, but the negotiations achieved little. The hard-liners also took a negative line toward the Contadora multilateral peace process that was pursued by some Latin American countries in the mid-1980s and the Central American regional peace process led by President Oscar Arias of Costa Rica from 1986 on.

The contra policy provoked unending controversy in the United States, and resulted in continual brawls between the administration and Congress over aid votes.[27] The lines of the debate over contra aid were quickly drawn: proponents held that contra aid was essential to prevent Communism from spreading in Central America and that the contras were a genuine, democratic force; opponents criticized contra aid as a form of interventionism, questioned the legitimacy of the contras, and doubted whether the Sandinistas were the danger the Reagan administration said they were. Aid flowed in a stop and go fashion: after several tens of millions of dollars of covert aid went to the contras in the early 1980s, Congress approved $24 million of lethal aid in 1983, refused to permit anything but nonlethal aid in 1984 and 1985, and then, after an all-out lobbying effort by the administration, approved a $100 million aid package in 1986. The administration was very frustrated by the difficulty of securing a regular aid flow and the National Security Council staff and the CIA developed a secret contra supply network drawing upon donations from selected foreign governments and private organizations as well as the proceeds from secret arms sales to Iran.

The U.S. aid to the contras, though intermittent, added up to several hundred million dollars and enabled the contras to transform themselves from a few loosely organized bands in 1981 to a fairly well-trained and well-equipped army of around ten thousand persons by the mid-1980s. They were able to enter Nicaragua at many points along the Honduran border and harass the Sandinista army significantly but were unable to hold territory and never seriously threatened Sandinista rule. The continuing dominant role of ex-Somocista Guardsmen in the contras' military leadership, as well as recurrent incidents of brutality against Nicaraguan civilians and the weakness of the non-Somocista political directorate, all contributed to the contras' failure to gain consistent support in the United States.

The contra policy began to unravel in late 1986 when the secret contra supply network became public as one element of the Iran-contra scandal. Those revelations soured Congress on further military aid to the contras and the scandal as a whole greatly weakened the United States' image and position in Central America. In 1987 the Central American regional peace process gathered strength; in August of that year the five Central American presidents signed a regional peace accord, which led to a ceasefire between the Nicaraguan government and the contras and, ultimately, to the national elections in February 1990 in which the National Opposition Union (UNO) defeated the Sandinistas.

The administration initially cast its contra-oriented Nicaragua policy as an effort to stop the flow of arms from Nicaragua to El Salvador. Once the contras began operating actively, however, it became obvious that they were intent on fighting the Sandinistas, not patrolling the Nicaraguan-Honduran border, and a new rationale was needed. The administration shifted to an emphasis on promoting democracy. The contras were portrayed as a pro-democracy force, "freedom fighters," struggling to bring freedom to Nicaragua. From 1983 on, President Reagan and his top advisers repeatedly declared that promoting democracy was the administration's primary goal in Nicaragua and that only if Nicaragua were democratic would peace be possible in Central America.[28]

The democracy rationale served at least two important purposes. Making democratization (usually defined as holding free and fair elections and restoring all political and civil rights) one of the United States' conditions for a negotiated security accord gave the administration a principled handle for blocking any such accord. The Sandinistas were unwilling to accept a bilateral agreement with the United States that called for a fundamental change in the internal Nicaraguan political order. The moderates in the Reagan administration tried to soft-pedal the democracy condition and focus on the external security guarantees but the hard-liners refused to back down on the democracy condition; every set of negotiations with the Sandinistas broke down over the democracy issue.

Second, the emphasis on democracy proved useful with Congress. Congress was loath to support the overthrow of a foreign government; it was more willing, however, to consider supporting a campaign to pressure a nondemocratic government to become democratic. In the mid-1980s the administration increasingly stressed the democracy theme in its lobbying efforts on contra aid. The administration's extensive public relations campaign vilifying the Sandinistas succeeded in changing the terms of the debate in Congress over contra aid. In the early 1980s the issue had been framed in terms of Should the United States intervene in Nicaragua's internal affairs? By the mid-1980s it had become Should the United States support the contras as a means of pressuring the Sandinistas to accept democracy? What funding the administration was able to get from Congress was due to the willingness of some moderate Democrats who had answered no to the first question to answer yes to the second.[29]

Whether the Reagan administration's policy had a positive or negative effect on the prospect for democracy in Nicaragua has been debated in the United States since the defeat of the Sandinistas in the February 1990 elections. In attempts to formulate an answer to this question, and in any assessment of the Reagan administration's Nicaraguan policy, a wide focus will be imperative. In the first place, the policy had many effects outside Nicaragua and almost all of them were negative: it caused a serious breakdown of working relations between the Reagan administration and Congress, greatly harmed the image of the United States abroad, hurt the tenor of democracy in the United States (through the Iran-contra activities), and damaged the sovereignty and well-being of other Central American countries, such as Honduras and Costa Rica, that the United States pressured to get involved in the contra war.

With respect to effects on Nicaragua itself, the primary impact of the policy was the tremendous human cost it inflicted on Nicaraguans. Over thirty thousand Nicaraguans were killed in the contra war and tens of thousands wounded, which in per capita terms was significantly higher than the number of U.S. persons killed in the U.S. Civil War and all the wars of the twentieth century *combined*. The war also caused extensive economic damage, worsening the living conditions of almost all Nicaraguans. The political effects of the policy are far less clear, and pale beside the terrible human costs of the war. The active civil war gave the Sandinistas a justification to impose martial law and limit political and civil rights. It did keep the Sandinistas from consolidating their hold on power and was a factor leading to the eventual demise of Sandinista rule. It should be noted, however, that the Sandinistas refused to agree to elections while the contras were on the rise; it was only once the contras had lost any significant chance of further U.S. military aid that the Sandinistas made the concessions necessary to pave the way to the 1990 elections.

Grenada

The 1983 invasion of Grenada, like the contra policy in Nicaragua, was an anti-Communist policy publicly portrayed as a policy of promoting democracy. Problems between Grenada and the United States began in 1979 when Maurice Bishop of the leftist New Jewel movement ousted Prime Minister Eric Gairy, established the People's Revolutionary Government of Grenada, and aligned Grenada with the Soviet Union on many foreign policy issues. When the Reagan administration came into office, U.S.-Grenadan relations turned outright hostile. The Reagan administration saw Grenada as another example of the ominous advance of the perceived Soviet and Cuban conspiracy to spread Communism in the Western Hemisphere and criticized Grenada harshly. Bishop reacted defiantly to the growing U.S. pressure and repeatedly accused President Reagan of planning to invade Grenada.

In 1983 Bishop's hold on power was weakened by persistent dissent from hard-liners in the New Jewel movement. In October Bishop was ousted and assassinated by the dissenters; a Revolutionary Military Council dominated by hard-liners proclaimed itself in charge. The Reagan administration perceived the ouster of Bishop as a dangerous turn to the extreme left. Grenada's immediate neighbors were also troubled and sent a request to the United States for assistance in a military action against Grenada. On October 25, less than two weeks after Bishop's ouster, several thousand U.S. troops landed on Grenada and within three days had wiped out all local resistance and secured the island. A year-long U.S. military occupation followed in which the United States directed a political purification aimed at removing all influence of the New Jewel movement and supervised the holding of elections. The CIA spent $675,000 in covert funds on the electoral process to help insure that a moderate, pro-United States candidate emerged victorious.[30] The United States also gave a large quantity of economic assistance ($48 million) in the year following the invasion as part of the reconstruction effort.[31]

The administration initially justified the invasion as a "rescue mission" to protect American students on the island and as a campaign "to restore order and democracy to Grenada."[32] In the weeks after the invasion, administration officials shifted gears somewhat and emphasized the anti-Communist basis of the invasion, portraying Grenada as "a Soviet-Cuban colony being readied as a major military bastion to export terror and undermine democracy."[33] This latter rationale reflected the administration's core motivation. The invasion of Grenada was an attempt by the administration to "roll back" the Soviet empire by toppling a leftist government on its periphery. The safety of the U.S. students on the island was a genuine concern, but was at most a catalyzing factor on top of the basic anti-Communist motive. A full-scale invasion and year-long occupation were obviously not necessary if the goal were simply to evacuate the students. The democracy rationale was largely rhetorical—the United States was not moved to invade Grenada out of a desire to guarantee Grenadans a democratic society. And the approach taken to the political reconstruction after the invasion exemplified both a formalistic as well as cynical view of democracy in which the United States sought to insure that the electoral process produced an appropriately moderate, pro–United States prime minister.

Democracy by Applause: South America

Preoccupied with its anti-Communist endeavors in Central America, the Reagan administration paid relatively little attention to South America. Nonetheless there was a U.S. policy toward South America in the 1980s and it passed through two distinct stages. In the early 1980s the Reagan administration sought to renew U.S. relations with the military governments of the region, particularly those in Brazil, Argentina, and Chile. U.S. relations with many South American countries had deteriorated during the Carter years, primarily as a result of U.S. concerns over human rights abuses in those countries. The early Reagan administration, imbued with the Kirkpatrick doctrine's belief that a choice must be made between supporting right-wing authoritarians or risking the rise of more leftist totalitarians, saw the military dictatorships of Brazil, Argentina, Chile, and elsewhere as loyal anti-Communist allies deserving of U.S. support. High-level administration officials visited South America and invited their counterparts to Washington. The meetings were friendly and U.S. officials declared a fresh start in U.S.–South American relations. The administration replaced the outspoken Carter human rights policy with what was called "quiet diplomacy" on human rights, which in practice consisted of greatly downplaying the issue. Based on a reassessment of the human rights situation in Argentina, Chile, Panama, and Uruguay, the administration decided to cease the Carter policy of opposing or assisting loans to those countries from the multilateral development banks.[34] High-level U.S.–South American military visits increased and the administration lobbied Congress to lift restrictions on arms sales and military aid for various South American countries.

This early policy met with little success. Many Democrats in Congress objected to a renewal of relations with military dictators and blocked the most substantial aspect of the policy (from the South American point of view), the attempt to renew U.S. military assistance. And despite the abundance of enthusiastic declarations by U.S. and South American officials about a new era of friendship, it soon became apparent that the real basis for friendship was narrower than it first appeared. The Reagan administration's outreach to South America was based on the notion of shared anti-Communist concerns. U.S. officials visiting Brazil, Argentina, and Chile, for example, sought to enlist those countries in the Reagan administration's anti-Communist campaign in Central America. The South American governments, however, were little interested in Central America or a region-wide, U.S.-led anti-Communist crusade; their main interest vis-à-vis the

United States was improved economic relations, particularly more favorable trade and financial policies.

The weakness of new policy was dramatically highlighted by the Falklands War of 1982. The Argentine military government thought that it had cemented a special relationship with the Reagan administration in 1981 by agreeing to help train the nascent Nicaraguan contras and attacked the Falklands in the belief that the United States would stay neutral. The U.S. decision to side with Great Britain was seen by the Argentine military as a tremendous betrayal and showed all South American military governments the shallowness of their new friendships with the Reagan administration. Additionally, the Argentine military's reckless military adventure soured the Reagan administration's effort in the United States to portray the South American military governments as moderate, responsible allies.

The disaster of the Falklands War signaled the start of the decline of the policy of renewed relations with the military governments of South America. The decline was advanced by the fact that those governments were themselves disappearing one by one in the tide of democratic change that was sweeping through South America; Bolivia held presidential elections in 1982, Argentina in 1983, Uruguay in 1984, and Brazil moved to civilian rule in 1985. Changes in the administration's own ideological outlook paralleled the spread of democracy in South America. The administration's early embrace of the Kirkpatrick doctrine faded when some of its strongest advocates left the government toward the end of the first Reagan administration and the rise of moderate democratic regimes in the region invalidated the notion that the United States had to support authoritarian regimes for lack of any centrist alternative.

By the start of the second Reagan administration, the early policy toward South America was being replaced by a low-key policy of verbal support for the new democratic governments of the region. The administration gave the new governments diplomatic and political backing—praising them, inviting their leaders to Washington, sending high-level officials to visit them, and generally treating them with genuine respect. The administration also took a clear stand against military coups in South America. Administration officials publicly declared their opposition to coups and, more important, conveyed that same message privately to South American military officials. When military uprisings broke out in Argentina in 1987 and 1988, the United States quickly declared its support for Alfonsin. Similarly, when the Peruvian military contemplated a coup in late 1988, U.S. officials in the Pentagon told Peruvian military officials they opposed it.

The administration's policy of supporting democracy in South America was as notable for what it did not include as for what it did. The greatest challenge facing the new democratic governments of South America was reversing the devastating recession that had struck the region in the early 1980s. Many of the governments had inherited debt-ridden, nearly bankrupt economies from their military predecessors and found their political survival dependent on their ability to bring about economic improvements. The administration's response on the economic front was minimal. The United States gave little economic aid to South America in the 1980s, and what aid it did give was limited to a handful of countries (Ecuador, Peru, Bolivia, and Colombia). Concerning the debt crisis, a problem of tremendous importance for several major South American countries, the administration held to a noninterventionist approach that rejected debt reduction in favor of austerity programs and some additional lending.[35] And in trade policy, the South American governments discovered that the administration's verbal support for South America did not translate into any tangible benefits.

As in other parts of Latin America, the Reagan administration took credit for having played an important role in the resurgence of democracy in South America. In 1985, for example, when asked about the causes of that resurgence, Assistant Secretary Abrams named U.S. policy as one of the two principal causes[36]—a claim that had no basis in fact. In the early 1980s, when most of the democratic transitions in South America took place, the Reagan administration was trying to support the military governments that were on the way out. If anything, the U.S. policy of that period worked against the democratic trend. The resurgence of democracy was the result of a variety of internal factors, including the loss of political and economic credibility of the military governments, the decline of armed leftist movements, and long-term socioeconomic changes resulting from the strong economic growth of the 1960s and 1970s.[37]

The verbal support for the new democratic governments of South America during the second Reagan administration was a change from the earlier policy, but whether it had any significant effects is uncertain. As most U.S. officials who deal with South America readily admit in private, the United States today has little political influence there. The expressions of support by the Reagan administration for the new governments were unlikely to have had any but the most marginal effect on the domestic standing of those governments. And the South American military forces, whose material or psychological dependence on the United States is minimal, were unlikely to have been strongly influenced by the administration's "no coup" policy. As previously noted, the Reagan administration did not go beyond verbal measures to address the economic problems that constituted the most serious threat to democracy in South America in the second half of the 1980s. The administration was happy to see democracy return to South America, quick to applaud it, and even to take credit for it, but was unwilling to devote any significant amounts of time, energy, or money to support or advance the trend.

Democracy by Pressure: Chile, Paraguay, Panama, and Haiti

During the second Reagan administration, an additional policy presented under the label of promoting democracy emerged, a policy of exerting pressure against the remaining right-wing dictatorships of the region—those in Chile, Paraguay, Panama, and Haiti—to cede power and permit transitions to elected rule. This policy of pressure developed somewhat independently in each of the four countries concerned but shared methods, motivations, and goals enough to be considered a single overarching policy.[38] It is of particular interest in that it represents the clear evolution of the Reagan administration away from the Kirkpatrick Doctrine. The policy of pressure entailed the very sort of public criticism and pressure on anti-Communist, pro–United States governments for which the Reagan administration had initially lambasted the Carter administration.

Chile

The early Reagan administration attempted to reestablish friendly ties with the Chilean military dictator, General Augusto Pinochet, as part of its efforts to improve relations with South American military governments. In 1981 and 1982 the Reagan administration lifted the 1979 ban on Export-Import Bank credits to Chile, renewed military and diplomatic contacts, supported the repeal of restrictions on military sales and assistance to Chile, and opposed a U.N. Human Rights Commission resolution criticizing Chile.[39] The bloom went off this policy in 1983 when Pinochet responded harshly to a major outbreak of civil unrest. The State Department delivered a number of messages urging him to continue a political dialogue with the opposition and to respect human rights.[40] Pinochet ignored the messages and continued his repressive policies, gradually alienating the essentially sympathetic (to Pinochet) State Department.

In 1985, personnel changes in the State Department (the replacement of James Theberge by Harry Barnes as U.S. ambassador to Chile and Langhorne Motley by Elliott Abrams as assistant secretary of state for inter-American affairs) opened the way to a policy of tangible economic and political pressure aimed at encouraging Pinochet to carry out the transition process established in the 1980 constitution. From 1985 on, State Department officials spoke out frequently on the importance the United States attached to a democratic transition in Chile;[41] Ambassador Barnes in particular worked visibly and effectively in Chile to promote the transition process. The administration took some minor punitive economic measures to express the administration's dissatisfaction with Pinochet's backsliding, including abolishing trade preferences of certain Chilean goods, ending Overseas Private Investment Corporation (OPIC) insurance for U.S. corporate investment in Chile, and abstaining on some World Bank loans to

Chile. The administration was by no means unified on this policy. The hard-liners, a reduced but still vocal presence, adamantly opposed the policy of pressure as being no more than warmed-over Carterism that would only anger the Chilean military. They fought the State Department tenaciously on Chile policy from 1985 through the all-important plebiscite of 1988, giving the policy something of a stop-start character but not changing its overall direction.

The policy of pressure intensified as the plebiscite drew near. The Agency for International Development and the National Endowment for Democracy funded a number of civic groups in Chile working to insure a fair plebiscite. The National Democratic Institute for International Affairs, a branch of the National Endowment, assisted the opposition coalition with its campaign.[42] In the closing days before the plebiscite, the State Department received information that Pinochet was seriously considering calling off the plebiscite; Deputy Secretary of State John Whitehead called in the Chilean ambassador and emphasized the United States government's strong desire to see the plebiscite held as scheduled.[43] The plebiscite was success-fully held in October 1988. Pinochet lost, setting in motion the 1989 presidential elections.

The policy of pressure reflected several simultaneous motivations, no one of which dominated the policy process. The policy helped the administration claim to be even-handed with respect to promoting democracy in Latin America—it was easier for the administration to ask Congress to support the contras on the grounds of promoting democracy if it was also taking actions to promote democracy in right-wing Chile. The policy also reflected the belief of many U.S. officials that promoting democracy in Chile was simply the right thing to do, that it was an expression of basic U.S. values. And the policy derived in part from the fear of some officials that if Pinochet did not permit a democratic transition, Chile would become even more polarized, increasing the possibility of serious instability in the longer term.

The policy of pressure against Pinochet was widely praised in the United States and probably did contribute to the Chilean government having held a reasonably fair plebiscite. One must be cautious, however, in assessing the significance of the United States' role. The Chilean transition was rooted in decades of Chilean political history, a uniquely democratic history in Latin America. The transition was the culmination of years of activism by the Chilean opposition as well as the reflection of the genuine constitutionalism of major sectors of Chilean society. The United States adopted a positive stance only very late in the day and was at best a minor actor in what was ultimately a thoroughly Chilean process.

Paraguay

The Reagan administration also gradually moved toward a policy of pressure against General Alfredo Stroessner, Paraguay's long-time dictator.

In the early 1980s, the administration had maintained friendly relations with Stroessner.[44] During the second Reagan administration, however, the United States adopted a more critical line, raising human rights issues and urging Paraguay "to join in Latin America's democratic wave,"[45] and opening contacts with Paraguayan opposition parties. This policy of pressure remained a relatively mild one, both because of the low level of U.S. interest in Paraguay and the absence of many obvious forms of pressure, due to the minimal political and economic relations between the United States and Paraguay.[46]

The policy reflected a similar mix of motivations as the Chile policy, although Paraguay did not have the special symbolic value and visibility in the United States that Chile had. The effects of the policy were positive but extremely modest. Stroessner was ousted from power in February 1989 by a former military loyalist, General Andrés Rodríguez, who held elections in May of that year and was elected president. The verbal pressure the administration had exerted on Stroessner was at most a minor factor in a political transition that was primarily the result of domestic political factors.[47]

Panama

After the 1981 death of Panamanian president Omar Torrijos, the Panamanian military consolidated its hold on power and General Manuel Antonio Noriega emerged as de facto leader of the country. A civilian supported by the military, Nicolás Ardito Barletta, gained the presidency in fraudulent elections in 1984 but after losing the confidence of the military was ousted by Noriega in 1985.[48] The Reagan administration tolerated Noriega's increasing grip on power and scarcely blinked either at the election fraud of 1984 or Barletta's ouster. Noriega was a favored friend in Washington—he was a long-time CIA asset who in addition to cooperating on intelligence matters was hospitable to the large U.S. military presence in Panama and helpful on some contra-related issues.[49]

The friendly line toward Noriega began to change only in 1987 when an outbreak of civil unrest occurred in Panama in response to revelations about Noriega's multifaceted corruption; Noriega harshly suppressed the unrest and pro-Noriega demonstrators damaged a U.S. embassy building. The State Department adopted a critical line, calling for a democratic transition and suspending economic aid. The Defense Department and the CIA, however, refused to go along, maintaining their view that Noriega, although flawed, was a useful U.S. ally. A decisive shift toward an anti-Noriega policy finally occurred in early 1988 when two grand juries in Florida indicted Noriega on drug trafficking charges. The indictments were not the work of the administration per se, but they provoked a shift in U.S. policy by making it impossible for the administration to be seen to be friendly with a drug-trafficking dictator.[50] In late February, Panama's civilian president, Eric

Arturo Delvalle (who had until then been a Noriega lackey) tried to fire Noriega but was himself ousted by Noriega. The administration backed Delvalle in his continued claim to the presidency and supported his efforts to impose economic sanctions against the Noriega regime.

The administration opened up a full-scale verbal assault on Noriega while searching for concrete forms of pressure and beginning negotiations with Noriega for an agreement on his departure from Panama. The State Department advocated various drastic measures of pressure including a military invasion. The Defense Department, wary of the use of military force in highly charged political conflicts and still somewhat forgiving of Noriega, opposed military action. In early April the administration settled on some economic sanctions, which although relatively harsh, were far less than the State Department sought.[51] Noriega rode out the immediate economic crisis and successfully resisted the U.S. pressure. The negotiations over his departure collapsed in May. Noriega remained in power.

The administration cast its anti-Noriega policy as an effort to promote democracy in Panama, calling for presidential elections to be held upon Noriega's departure. In fact the policy was just aimed at getting Noriega out; what would happen after his departure was of little concern. The Reagan administration was not trying to change the Panamanian military's long-standing domination of Panamanian political life, it was trying to remove a notorious strongman who had become a serious public relations liability.

The anti-Noriega policy was obviously a failure, one of the most glaring foreign policy failures of the Reagan administration. The administration pursued a goal without employing the means to reach it, making the United States look inept in the eyes of Latin America and the international community. The economic sanctions worsened the lives of many Panamanians, with no political return. The unilateral manner in which the policy was implemented alienated potential Latin partners and angered the internal Panamanian opposition. The real failure, however, was not the frantic, and ultimately pathetic campaign to oust Noriega but the many years of U.S. friendship with Noriega and the toleration of his destruction of the electoral process in the mid-1980s. In those years the administration helped consolidate the very situation in Panama that it later came to grief trying to change.

Haiti

From 1981 to 1985, the Reagan administration maintained cordial relations with Jean-Claude Duvalier, Haiti's "president-for-life" who, though a corrupt, repressive strongman, was valued as a staunchly anti-Communist friend. With little warning, serious civil unrest broke out in Haiti in late 1985, leading to several months of clashes between demonstrators and government security forces and, in February 1986, the hasty departure of Duvalier and his family from Haiti. The U.S. government was caught by surprise by the outbreak of anti-Duvalierist activity and moved very cautiously during the months preceding Duvalier's departure. Only when it had become clear that Duvalier was in serious trouble did the administration cut off economic aid and speak out in favor of a political transition.

An interim government, led by Duvalier's former military chief of staff, Gen. Henri Namphy, quickly formed and announced its intention to develop a "real and functional democracy."[52] The administration embraced the new government and adopted a highly activist policy, primarily implemented by the U.S. embassy in Port-au-Prince, of attempting to keep the precarious transition process on track. The U.S. embassy "jawboned" the interim government constantly, advising, cajoling, demanding, and beseeching it on the transition. Economic assistance to Haiti was increased from $55.6 million in 1985 to $77.7 million in 1986 and $101.1 million in 1987. The aid was used both as a carrot and stick to induce the interim government to proceed with the transition. The Agency for International Development funded an electoral assistance project to provide technical assistance to the government on electoral matters and educate Haitians about elections. The Defense Department carried out a small, but controversial security assistance program aimed at improving the Haitian military's ability to keep order peaceably.[53] Finally, the embassy encouraged some of the major civilian politicians to take part in the electoral process, and to challenge the interim government on issues of electoral procedures.

The U.S. efforts to keep the Haitian electoral process moving ahead met with growing inactivity and even opposition by the interim government. The United States clung desperately to its policy, however, and fell into the role of apologist for the interim government.[54] When the November 1987 elections were violently halted by remnants of Duvalier's old Tonton Macoutes (with the connivance of the military), the U.S. government was caught looking badly out of touch with the reality of the Haitian political situation and overattached to a disreputable transitional government. Presidential elections were finally held in January 1988 but were a mockery of free and fair elections. The president-elect, Leslie Manigat, served only five months before being ousted by Namphy who was in turn ousted in another coup in September 1988.

The administration's decision in early 1986 to cut off support for Duvalier was a reaction to rapidly evolving events, not a premeditated policy. The policy of supporting a democratic transition in the post-Duvalier period was rooted in vague but uncontroversial motivations. The United States had no strong geopolitical or economic interests to guide its Haiti policy. Thus when Duvalier fell, the administration simply extended the democracy orientation that by 1986 had become a general theme of U.S. policy in Latin America and the Caribbean. In the absence of any strong competing motives, it gave direction to what for years had been a rudderless policy toward Haiti.

The administration's policy was not responsible for the failure of the post-Duvalier democratic transition in Haiti. Nonetheless the U.S. policy was seriously flawed. One flaw was the administration's persistent assumption that the interim government was sincere in its desire to steer Haiti to free and fair elections, an assumption maintained despite continuously accumulating evidence to the contrary. A second flaw was that to the extent the administration did harbor doubts about Namphy's intentions, it overestimated its ability to persuade or coerce him to carry out the transition. The administration lapsed into the common error of overestimating both the leverage gained from economic aid and the ability of the United States to assert its will against a stubborn foreign government. Finally, the U.S. policy was based on the familiar equation of elections with democracy. The far more important, and difficult, question of how to change Haiti's deeply entrenched antidemocratic structures of economic and political power, structures that had not been seriously disrupted by Duvalier's departure, was left unaddressed.

Conclusions

The Reagan administration's claim that the United States played an important role in the resurgence of democracy in Latin America in the 1980s is largely unsubstantiated. In Central America the administration's strenuous anti-Communist policies did prevent the rise of further leftist governments but had only limited effects with respect to democracy. The administration contributed to the transitions to elected civilian rule in El Salvador and Honduras and helped the elected governments in those countries survive many challenges to their rule. El Salvador and Honduras did not, however, become democracies; they achieved only a kind of military-dominated civilian rule. The United States was not a major actor in Guatemala's transition to civilian rule although United States political and economic support did help President Vinicio Cerezo stay in office for the duration of his term.

The policy of force against Nicaragua harmed many Nicaraguans but had at best ambiguous political effects. The Sandinistas did eventually hold free and fair elections, but only after the contra program had lost all chance of further military support from Congress. In Grenada, the U.S. invasion succeeded in toppling an antidemocratic leftist regime, which led to the restoration of elected civilian rule.

In South America the Reagan administration's early policy of renewing relations with the military governments of the region went against the democratic trend that was sweeping through South America in those years. The second Reagan administration jettisoned that policy in favor of a policy of verbal support for the emerging democratic governments. This later policy, although prodemocratic, had little real substance; in particular it did little to help the new democratic governments solve the overwhelming economic problems that constituted the greatest threat to the future of democracy in South America.

The second Reagan administration exerted pressure against the remaining right-wing dictators in Latin America to carry out electoral transitions, with greatly varying results. In Chile the administration contributed to the successful holding of the 1988 plebiscite. In Paraguay the United States sided with the forces of change that brought Stroessner down. In Panama the Reagan administration labored mightily to try to oust Noriega but succeeded only in humiliating the United States and damaging the Panamanian economy. And in Haiti the United States had a minor role facilitating the departure of Duvalier but failed in its effort to steer the interim government to a democratic transition.

A second general question addressed in this chapter is the balance between rhetoric and reality in the Reagan administration's use of the promoting democracy theme in its Latin America policy. The answer that emerges from the preceding analysis is twofold: first, a significant evolution occurred across the Reagan years from purely rhetorical policies of promoting democracy to policies in which democracy was a real concern; and second, even though promoting democracy did become a substantive element of various policies in later years, the conception of democracy to which the Reagan administration subscribed remained extremely limited.

The evolution away from purely rhetorical uses of the promoting democracy theme occurred in all different areas of Latin America policy. In El Salvador, Honduras, and Guatemala, the administration adopted the democracy theme early on to give a more appealing face to its military-oriented, anti-Communist policies. Over time, however, the democracy component of the policies (which consisted of the promotion of elected, civilian governments) rose to a position of equal importance alongside the military component, although the root motivation of U.S. involvement remained anti-Communism. In Nicaragua, promoting democracy was adopted as a rhetorical cover for the militaristic policy aimed at ousting the Sandinista government. During the second Reagan administration, however, the prodemocracy theme came to be an article of faith among Reagan officials responsible for Nicaragua policy—many officials genuinely believed that the contra program was aimed at bringing democracy to Nicaragua and was in fact the best way of promoting democracy in Nicaragua. With respect to South America, a significant evolution occurred across the Reagan years from an initial policy of renewing relations with military dictators to a later policy in which democracy was clearly supported over dictatorship, albeit only through verbal measures. The shift away from any lingering support for right-wing dictators was also evidenced by the policy of pressure that was applied by the later Reagan administration to Pinochet in Chile, Stroessner in Paraguay, Noriega in Panama, and Duvalier in Haiti.

This evolution of the role of promoting democracy in the Reagan administration's Latin America policy was the result of several factors. One major factor was the persistent efforts by liberal and moderate Democrats in Congress to oblige the administration to take account of human rights and democracy in its Latin America policy. The administration discovered that it could not get the military assistance or even the economic assistance it wanted for El Salvador, Honduras, and Guatemala unless it responded to Congressional concerns about human rights abuses and military domination of domestic politics. Similarly, the administration learned that the contra program would get support only to the extent it could be sold to moderate Democrats as a prodemocracy policy. Congressional Democrats also blocked most of the administration's early attempts to restart military assistance to the military dictatorships of South America, taking the wind out of the administration's early promilitary policies in that region. And Congress had a role in encouraging the later Reagan administration to promote democratic transitions in Chile, Panama, and Haiti.

Another important factor in the policy evolution was one internal to the administration—the shift in the balance of power between the moderates and hard-liners. Speaking very generally, the moderates tended to believe that promoting democracy (in whatever fashion they understood the term) was a necessary part of an anti-Communist policy in Latin America, whereas the hard-liners tended to focus on military means and discount the importance of democracy concerns. The balance of power within the Latin American policy-making process shifted quite distinctly across the Reagan years from an early situation in which the hard-liners were clearly dominant to a later situation in which the hard-liners maintained control over the Nicaragua policy but had ceded almost all other areas of Latin America policy to the moderates. The shift reflected both the general moderating trend in the Reagan presidency across the two terms as well as the recurrent tendency in the U.S. foreign policy process for career moderates to absorb, blunt, and ultimately reestablish control over foreign policy initiatives undertaken by incoming ideologically oriented administrations.

The evolution of the democracy policy also reflected the general tendency in policy making of rhetoric shaping reality. Throughout the Reagan years the administration would set out democracy as a goal in some part of its Latin America policy, largely for rhetorical purposes, but then find a specific, substantive prodemocracy policy bubbling up from the foreign policy bureaucracy. When the middle and lower levels of the bureaucracy heard the high-level officials loudly proclaiming democracy as a goal, they saw it was an opportunity to undertake substantive prodemocracy policies. And at the same time, having proclaimed the goal, high-level administration officials found themselves being held to it by Congress and the broader U.S.

foreign policy community. Those high-level officials would then begin to take it seriously, if only not to look unresponsive or hypocritical. The tendency of rhetoric to lead reality renders impossible any simple answer to the question of whether the administration's prodemocracy policies in Latin America were rhetoric or substance. Rhetoric and substance interacted constantly, creating a mix of words and deeds that is nearly impossible to separate.

Although the Reagan administration carried out several very different policies under the label of promoting democracy, the conception of democracy that informed these diverse policies was quite uniform: the Reagan administration held that a country is a democracy when it has a government that came to power through reasonably free and fair elections. A corollary of this view was that the process of democratization in a country is the organization and execution of a national electoral process. Promoting democracy was thus primarily conceived of as encouraging or assisting a country to hold national elections and helping whatever government emerged from the elections to maintain and consolidate power.

This elections-oriented conception of democracy falls short of the conventional Western political science definition of pluralist democracy in at least two important ways. It ignores the crucial question of how much real authority a particular elected government has—whether, for example, an elected government's authority is curtailed in practice by the military, the economic elite, or other power sectors. Additionally, it gives drastically short shrift to the issue of the kinds and degree of political participation that exist within the country in question. Although voting is an important form of political participation, a democracy entails a much broader range of participation including the free expression of opinions, day-to-day interaction between the government and the citizenry, the mobilization of interest groups, and so forth.

For some U.S. officials involved in Latin America policy, primarily some of the hard-liners oriented toward militaristic anti-Communist ventures, the adherence to such a narrow conception of democracy reflected a cynical attitude about using democracy as a public relations tool in the policy process. Most officials, however, were sincere when they referred to countries with elected governments as democracies. They were willing to concede that many of the new, elected governments in Latin America had serious shortcomings; but they treated democracy as an on-off switch in which holding presidential elections flipped the switch from off to on. A striking aspect of the administration's view of democracy vis-à-vis Latin America is that it was neither the product nor the subject of any extensive debate among policy makers. It emerged from the policy process as a shared assumption and was a kind of constant in the midst of a great deal of change of personnel and policies.

The formalistic, institution-oriented view of democracy was not a peculiarity of U.S. foreign policy officials of the 1980s. It is a recurring phenomenon in U.S. foreign policy and has its roots in the extension abroad of certain aspects of the U.S. national experience with democracy. The democratic experience of the United States (or at least the mythical conception of that experience in the popular mind) is unusual both in that the United States was from its origins a democratic culture—that is, there was no centuries-long process of transition from feudalism to democracy—and the institutional configuration of the U.S. government has existed without major change since its creation in the eighteenth century. The unusual "democratic from the start" nature of the United States leads U.S. citizens to have little appreciation of the complexity and difficulty in a traditionally nondemocratic country of transforming the myriad habits, beliefs, and customs antithetical to democracy into democratic ones. The remarkable endurance of the institutional configuration of U.S. democracy leads Americans to equate the U.S. version of democracy with the idea of democracy itself and to believe that if a country adopts U.S.-style forms of government it has become a democracy.

The formalistic, institution-oriented conception of democracy employed by the Reagan administration reflected not only broader currents of U.S. thinking about democracy, but also a long-standing U.S. attitude about political change in Latin America. To the extent the United States has supported democratic change in Latin America in this century, it has generally done so as a way of relieving pressure for more radical political and economic change. The impulse to promote democracy thus has a built-in tension: the impulse is to promote democratic change but the underlying objective is to maintain the basic order of what, historically at least, are quite undemocratic societies. The United States mitigates this tension by promoting very limited, top-down forms of democratic change that do not risk snowballing into uncontrollable populist movements. The Reagan administration's policies demonstrated this pattern almost exactly: the administration was drawn to involvement in Latin America out of a fear of the spread of Communism in the region, came to adopt prodemocracy policies as a means of relieving pressure for more radical change, but inevitably sought only limited, top-down forms of democratic change that did not risk upsetting the traditional structures of power with which the United States has long been allied.

Notes

This chapter is based on numerous interviews with U.S. officials who worked on Latin American affairs during the Reagan years in the White House, the Department of State, Department of Defense, Agency for International Development, the United States Information Agency, and the U.S. Congress. Many of the interviews were confidential and so I am unable to attribute material to particular persons.

I worked in the Office of the Legal Adviser of the Department of State from 1985 to 1988 and during that period worked on some Latin American issues. The chapter is not an account of policy decisions that I observed or in which I participated. Nonetheless, the chapter reflects an insider's perspective regarding the ways policy makers were thinking about Latin America and promoting democracy.

I am grateful to Richard Bloomfield, Larry Diamond, Peter Hakim, Abraham Lowenthal, Viron Vaky, Laurence Whitehead, and Alex Wilde for their comments on earlier drafts. I also thank the Council on Foreign Relations for the financial support that made the writing of this essay possible.

All the figures in the text regarding economic and military assistance are drawn from the Agency for International Development's annual Congressional Presentations and the annual publication by AID entitled "U.S. Overseas Loans and Grants." All of the aid years cited in the text are government fiscal years.

1. Speech by Assistant Secretary of State Elliott Abrams at the University of Oklahoma, January 12, 1989.

2. Elliott Abrams, "Latin America in the Time of Reagan," *New York Times,* July 27, 1988.

3. A detailed description of the early Reagan administration's East-West outlook toward Central America is given in Lars Schoultz, *National Security and United States Policy toward Latin America* (Princeton: Princeton University Press, 1987), pp. 48–67.

4. Press Briefing by Secretary of State Alexander Haig, February 27, 1981, *American Foreign Policy Current Documents 1981* (Washington, D.C.: Department of State, 1984), pp. 1274–76.

5. An outstanding analysis of the many shortcomings of the U.S. military assistance program to El Salvador, written by four active-duty U.S. military officers, is found in A. J. Bacevich, James D. Hallums, Richard H. White, and Thomas F. Young, *American Military Policy in Small Wars: The Case of El Salvador* (Washington, D.C.: Pergamon-Brassey's, 1988).

6. See, generally, Cynthia J. Arnson, *Crossroads: Congress, The Reagan Administration, and Central America* (New York: Pantheon, 1989).

7. Unfortunately there exists no adequate account of the remarkably intense U.S. involvement in the Salvadoran political process from 1981 to 1984. The U.S. election assistance is outlined in Marilyn A. Zak, "Assisting Elections in the Third World," *Washington Quarterly* (Autumn 1987): 175–93.

8. More money was devoted to economic assistance than to military assistance, but largely because the administration found that the Democratic-controlled House of Representatives would only approve military aid if approximately two to three times as much economic aid were given at the same time.

9. "El Salvador: The Search for Peace," address by Assistant Secretary of State for Inter-American Affairs Thomas Enders before the World Affairs Council, Washington, D.C., July 16, 1981, *American Foreign Policy Current Documents 1981,* pp. 1326–30.

10. According to the *Washington Post,* the CIA told the House and Senate intelligence committees that it provided funds to Duarte's campaign. *Washington Post,* April 10, 1984, and May 13, 1984. No exact figures for the funding are available; estimates range from under $500,000 to between $1 million and $3 million.

11. Military assistance to El Salvador more than doubled in 1984 from $81.3 million in 1983 to $196.6 million.

12. AID and the State Department initiated a $9.2 million judicial reform project in 1984. A number of police training programs were carried out from 1985 on, including antiterrorism training by the State Department, investigative training by the Justice Department, and operational training by the Defense Department. Small projects to train the national legislature and to strengthen municipal governments were funded by the AID mission in El Salvador.

13. For information on the human rights situation in El Salvador during the Duarte years,

see *El Salvador: 'Death Squads'—A Governmental Strategy* (London: Amnesty International, 1988).

14. Joel Millman, "El Salvador's Army: A Force unto Itself," *New York Times Magazine* (December 10, 1989): 47, 95–97.

15. *Washington Post,* February 18, 1986; *New York Times,* July 14, 1986.

16. Thomas P. Anderson, *Politics in Central America,* rev. ed. (New York: Praeger, 1988), pp. 161–62; *Christian Science Monitor,* November 26, 1985, and November 29, 1985; *Washington Post,* January 26, 1986.

17. Zak, pp. 184–85.

18. "No Delay for Democracy," address by Secretary of State George Shultz before the National Foreign Policy Conference for Young Political Leaders, Washington, D.C., June 13, 1986, U.S. Department of State, Current Policy no. 846.

19. For example, Deputy Assistant Secretary of State for Inter-American Affairs Stephen Bosworth described the Guatemalan rebels as being "heavily supported and influenced by our adversaries." Statement before the Subcommittee on Human Rights and International Organizations and the Subcommittee on Inter-American Affairs of the House Committee on Foreign Affairs, July 30, 1981, *American Foreign Policy Current Documents 1981,* pp. 1332–34.

20. For example in May 1981, Acting Assistant Secretary of State for Inter-American Affairs John Bushnell said, "I think given the extent of the insurgency and the strong communist support worldwide for it, the administration is disposed to support Guatemala." *Washington Post,* May 5, 1981.

21. *New York Times,* December 16, 1981.

22. President Reagan met briefly with Ríos Montt in December 1982 and later described the Guatemalan leader as "totally dedicated to democracy" and said Ríos Montt had been getting "a bum rap" on human rights. Department of State Press Briefing, December 6, 1982, *American Foreign Policy Current Documents 1982* (Washington, D.C.: Department of State, 1985), pp. 1290–97.

23. U.S. military aid to Guatemala from 1986 to 1988 totaled $20.3 million.

24. Between 1981 and 1985 Guatemala received between $15 million and $30 million of U.S. economic assistance per year.

25. *Guatemala: The Human Rights Record* (London: Amnesty International, 1987); *Closing the Space: Human Rights in Guatemala—May 1987–October 1988* (Washington, D.C.: Americas Watch, 1988); *Christian Science Monitor,* December 29, 1987.

26. The massive story of the administration's Nicaragua policy is ably told by Roy Gutman in his book *Banana Diplomacy: The Making of American Policy in Nicaragua 1981–1987* (New York: Simon & Schuster, 1988).

27. Arnson, *Crossroads.*

28. In a national speech on Nicaragua given from the White House on June 24, 1986, President Reagan declared that "internal freedom in Nicaragua and the security of Central America are indivisible." On other occasions, administration officials went even farther and claimed that democracy in other parts of Central America was not possible without democracy in Nicaragua. In 1983, for example, Assistant Secretary of State Enders stated, "Democracy will not prosper in Nicaragua's neighbors unless it is practiced in Nicaragua as well." See statement by Assistant Secretary Enders before the Senate Foreign Relations Committee, April 12, 1983, *American Foreign Policy Current Documents 1983* (Washington, D.C.: Department of State, 1985), pp. 1302–6.

29. Cynthia Arnson argues that Congress approved $100 million of contra aid in 1986 because a majority in Congress came to believe that internal change in the character of the Sandinista regime was a legitimate, even necessary goal for the United States and that democratization would occur in Nicaragua only if external pressure were applied. Cynthia Arnson, "Contadora and the U.S. Congress," in Bruce M. Bagley, ed., *Contadora and the*

Diplomacy of Peace in Central America, vol. 1: The United States, Central America, and Contadora (Boulder, Colo.: Westview Press, 1987), pp. 123–41.

30. Bob Woodward, *Veil: The Secret Wars of the CIA, 1981–1987* (New York: Pocket Books, 1987), p. 337.

31. In 1984 Grenada received $48.4 million of economic aid, the highest per capita rate of U.S. aid in Latin America. That was the first economic aid Grenada had ever received from the United States. The aid declined rapidly; from 1986 to 1988 Grenada received a total of only $200,000 of U.S. aid.

32. President Reagan said in a press conference on November 3, 1983, that the Grenada operation was not an invasion but "a rescue mission." The quote on restoring order and democracy comes from a statement by President Reagan made at a press conference he held jointly in Washington with Prime Minster Eugenia Charles of Dominica the morning of the invasion, October 25, 1983.

33. Address by President Reagan, October 27, 1983, *American Foreign Policy Current Documents 1983*, pp. 1410–12.

34. On July 1, 1981, the Treasury Department notified Congress that after a State Department review of the human rights situation in Argentina, Chile, Paraguay, and Uruguay, the administration had decided to change the earlier policy of abstention or opposition to loans to those countries from the multilateral development banks. "Letter from the Assistant Secretary of the Treasury for Legislative Affairs to the Chairman of the Subcommittee on International Development Institutions and Finance of the Committee on Banking, Finance and Urban Affairs," House of Representatives, July 1, 1981, *American Foreign Policy Current Documents 1981*, pp. 1371–72.

35. Pedro-Pablo Kuczynski, "The Outlook for Latin American Debt," *Foreign Affairs* 66, no. 1 (Fall 1987): 129–49; *Washington Post*, June 24, 1984, and September 20, 1988; *New York Times*, July 1, 1984, and June 26, 1987, and January 4, 1988.

36. Press interview with Assistant Secretary Abrams in La Paz, Bolivia, August 7, 1985, *American Foreign Policy Collected Documents 1985* (Washington, D.C.: Department of State, 1986), pp. 1075–77.

37. The rapidly growing literature on the causes of the reemergence of democracy in South America uniformly emphasizes the importance of internal political and economic factors. None of the studies finds any great role for U.S. policy. See, for example, Philip O'Brien and Paul Cammack, eds., *Generals in Retreat: The Crisis of Military Rule in Latin America* (Manchester: Manchester University Press, 1985); Guillermo O'Donnell, Philippe C. Schmitter, and Laurence Whitehead, eds., *Transitions from Authoritarian Rule: Latin America* (Baltimore: Johns Hopkins University Press, 1986); Larry Diamond, Juan J. Linz, and Seymour Martin Lipset, *Democracy in Developing Countries*, vol. IV: *Latin America* (Boulder, Colo.: Lynne Rienner, 1989); James M. Malloy and Mitchell Seligson, eds., *Authoritarians and Democrats: Regime Transition in Latin America* (Pittsburgh: University of Pittsburgh Press, 1987); George A. Lopez and Michael Stohl, eds., *Liberalization and Redemocratization in Latin America* (Westport, Conn.: Greenwood Press, 1987).

38. In a speech in June 1987, Assistant Secretary Abrams unified the "challenge" to the United States of how to promote democracy in Chile, Paraguay, Haiti, and Panama, "countries with a friendly people with whom we have a record of cooperation and a base of common democratic values on which to build. . . . This challenge creates a genuine dilemma because change in friendly countries may, in the short run, entail some risks—of instability, polarization, and uncertain relations with the United States. We know that. But we also know that the risks will become much larger—unacceptably large, in the long run— if there is no opening toward a democratic political order." "Latin America and the Caribbean: The Paths to Democracy," address before the Washington World Affairs Council, Washington, D.C., June 30, 1987, U.S. Department of State Current Policy no. 982.

39. *Washington Post*, February 21, 1981, and March 6, 1982; *Journal of Commerce*,

March 4, 1981; *New York Times,* May 11, 1982. In written responses to questions from the Senate Foreign Relations Committee, the Department of Defense stated in May 1981: "The Administration desires and has taken initiatives to improve United States–Chilean bilateral relations in support of all U.S. interests. . . . We in DOD believe that there are important security interests which necessitate close military-to-military cooperation with Chile." *American Foreign Policy Current Documents 1981,* pp. 1186–91.

40. *Washington Post,* July 15, 1983; *New York Times,* August 25, 1983. In November 1983, the Chilean foreign minister, Miguel Schweitzer, complained that "fourteen communiques from the State Department about political dialogue seems excessive to me." *Washington Post,* November 24, 1983.

41. In August 1985 Assistant Secretary Abrams broke with the previous policy of caution in statements regarding Pinochet, declaring, "We are coming to the conclusion that the Chilean government is not committed to a transition to democracy in anything like a reasonable amount of time." Press interview with Abrams, August 7, 1985, *American Foreign Policy Collected Documents 1985,* p. 1082.

42. *New York Times,* June 15, 1988, and November 18, 1988.

43. *Washington Post,* October 4, 1988.

44. *New York Times,* August 15, 1983.

45. Address by Assistant Secretary Abrams before the World Affairs Council, Washington, June 30, 1987 (see n. 38).

46. *New York Times,* March 24, 1987.

47. Stroessner's fall was the result of a combination of factors, including the growing split within his Colorado party, the gradual rise of a formal opposition, and his increasing age and personal weakness. Riordan Roett, "Paraguay after Stroessner," *Foreign Affairs* 68 (Spring 1989): 124–42.

48. Thomas J. Bossert, "Panama," in Morris J. Blachman, William M. LeoGrande, and Kenneth Sharpe, eds., *Confronting Revolution: Security through Diplomacy in Central America* (New York: Pantheon, 1986), pp. 183–206.

49. An extremely detailed account of the U.S. government's long relationship with Noriega is given in Frederick Kempe, *Divorcing the Dictator: America's Bungled Affair with Noriega* (New York: G. P. Putnam's Sons, 1990).

50. Reportedly, the indictments of Noriega were "motivated less by foreign policy considerations than by the doggedness of two Florida Federal grand juries. . . . Although certain agencies, including the State Department, the Central Intelligence Agency and the Pentagon raised reservations about indicting the leader of a strategic ally, they did not interfere with the grand jury process. In fact the Federal grand juries in Florida were so independent that the State Department was unable to get the names of other Panamanian officials who were expected to be indicted." *New York Times,* February 6, 1988.

51. President Reagan invoked the International Emergency Economic Powers Act to halt all payments to the Noriega regime by U.S. citizens and U.S. corporations or their subsidiaries in Panama and to block all Panamanian government assets in the United States.

52. *New York Times,* February 11, 1986.

53. *New York Times,* April 4, 1986, April 11, 1986, August 5, 1986, November 9, 1986, September 6, 1987. Military assistance to Haiti in 1986 and 1987 totalled $3.2 million.

54. In the months before the planned November 1987 elections, civil unrest increased and the Haitian military killed dozens of people. According to a report in the *New York Times,* September 6, 1987, a State Department official commented in September of the year: "You've got a problem with that army, but it's still the only institution in Haiti at the present time. . . . Without that army there's no doubt in my mind that there will be no elections. The army is necessary to hold the country together enough to hold elections." The report continued, "U.S. government officials say any cut or delay in aid or any blunt criticism might alienate or further undermine the Government and thus jeopardize the elections."

5 | U.S. Business: Self-interest and Neutrality

Elizabeth A. Cobbs

THE HISTORY of United States relations with Latin America shows a persistent failure on the part of the U.S. government to come to terms not only with what it actually wants from the relationship but also with its own national motives. Does the United States want the challenge of genuinely democratic neighbors or the acquiescence of political pawns, be they nominal democracies or outright dictatorships? Should the nation be guided by clear economic and political self-interest or, as the Puritans' "city on a hill," should the nation place its historic "responsibility" to furthering democracy first, above other motivations?

Going back to its founding during the Enlightenment, the United States has long been at conflict with itself over the competing pulls of its democratic "mission" and economic self-interest.[1] Readers may suggest that this is more of a conflict between Thomas Jefferson and Alexander Hamilton than an issue for modern, materialistic America, yet anyone who has studied the often sorry history of U.S. relations with Latin America might argue differently. At times U.S. policy toward that region seems positively adolescent: characterized by wild mood swings between a grossly calculated desire to use and control, and, as Paul Drake shows elsewhere in this volume, a quixotic, messianic wish to produce democracy on demand—whenever policy makers and the public suddenly feel it essential to find the familiar face of their own political system in the terrain of Latin America, whatever the cost to others in national sovereignty. From the viewpoint of critics, the mood swings sometimes seem to represent a self-perceived Dr. Jekyll and Mr. Hyde complex: when U.S. policy toward that region is guided mainly by economic self-interest, we are being "bad." On those much rarer occasions when the United States idealistically tries to promote democracy, we are being "good." According to both moderate and radical interpretations of U.S.–Latin American relations, business is widely presumed to be at the far end of the self-interested (and therefore "bad") part of the spectrum. And yet, as this chapter argues, in the post–World War II period business has frequently evidenced a stronger commitment to consistent, constructive relations with Latin America than has the U.S. government, and a good measure of self-interest may be precisely the reason why.

Academics have fought battles for years to determine exactly how self-interested or disinterested the Good Neighbor Policy and the Alliance for Progress were, an implicit presumption being that they ended or failed when, alas, self-interest finally won out.[2] The revisionist literature of the 1960s and 1970s gained much of its moral and argumentative force from the successful attempt to show that U.S. policy, while rhetorically idealistic, was in practice self-serving. But even if a disinterested policy were possible, is it best? As is evident from other chapters in this volume, the prodemocracy campaigns of the United States have usually been self-contradictory failures. They are also not as disinterested or idealistic as they may seem: promoting democracy is a policy that builds domestic consensus (it appeals to what North Americans *think* their country should be about), offering an important self-justification for any U.S. administration's other policy goals, however unrelated.[3] U.S. business behavior in Latin America, on the other hand, shows far more evidence of lessons learned over the years than do studies of the behavior of the U.S. government, which is distressingly cyclical in its mistakes and interventionism. Indeed, from the 1950s forward, U.S. business groups, when they have operated at their most organized and coherent, have frequently taken a more neutral stance toward local political decisions than the U.S. government. Although certain individual businesses have gone way beyond the pale in terms of intervention, they may (as I shall discuss later) be more the exception than the rule.

This is not to say that U.S. businesses, on the whole, care whether the countries in which they operate are democratic or dictatorial. Self-interest suggests only two real preconditions for investment: (1) a level of stability that guarantees that the rules of business are not being changed constantly and that possessions are not threatened with expropriation; (2) an orientation toward economic expansion and a market large enough to allow it on the part of the host nation—ruling out politically stable but small nations such as Paraguay, Albania, and Luxembourg. Democracies, right-wing dictatorships, and Communist gerontocracies all have the potential to deliver these conditions. What business does care about is *not* democracy per se, but favorable, untroubled international relations.

One reason for this commitment to consistent, untroubled relations may be that business has an economic stake in Latin America that is far more tangible, immediate, and fragile than the strategic stake of the government. U.S. diplomats from Sumner Welles to Nelson Rockefeller to Cyrus Vance have long fought a losing battle to convince the U.S. government and public that Latin America is important. Yet few political or economic crises south of the Rio Grande have managed to generate sustained attention by North Americans for more than a year or two, especially since 1945. England is important; Russia is important; China, Japan, and Germany are important. Latin America, well, yes, but . . .—*this* has been the persistent attitude of the government and public. They know they should care, but essentially they do not. Indeed, it is precisely this lack of sustained interest in Latin America, combined with the relative weakness of those nations vis-à-vis the United States, that allows each administration to reinvent Latin American policy anew, constrained little by history, by domestic constituencies, or by any threat of effective retaliation from abroad. As Joseph Tulchin once noted about the interwar period, "this insulation from outside forces gives the process of formulating policy [toward Latin America] an academic quality."[4] One might add that insulation tends to give policy a unilateral quality as well.

But for businessmen invested in Latin America the relationship is different in kind. Not only does the topic hold their interest, but the displeasure of foreign governments, local political upsets, debt crises, and hostility toward Americans can have an immediate, direct effect on their economic well-being. For this reason, business has not only a stake in Latin America, but a stake in well-functioning U.S.–Latin American relations. It is precisely this sustained self-interest that has made U.S. business diplomacy in Latin America more pragmatic, attentive, and reciprocal than that of the government.

This chapter considers the evolution of the U.S. business relationship to Latin America in the post–World War II period, with particular attention to its political dimensions. I will not argue that business sought to promote democracy: it did not. But I also do not find a preference for dictatorships. Instead, I find that over this period business has gradually evolved a style of operating that generally offers more concessions to local sovereignty than does the U.S. government. Although concessions to sovereignty, especially in the form of neutrality toward domestic political decisions, do not promote democracy per se, it may be argued that in the long run such a policy is more productive of local self-determination than a policy that oscillates between extravagant demands for democracy and an active support of dictatorships.

Early Twentieth-Century Background:
Interventionism and Omnipotence

It is ironic and revealing that, in the course of the twentieth century, the interest of U.S. business in Latin America has grown as that of the U.S. government has declined. Before 1940, what international power the United

States had was concentrated in one region alone: the Western Hemisphere. And for a time, as world tensions increased in the 1930s and Nazi Germany threatened to overtake and hold all of Europe, it seemed that the U.S. might be closed off permanently to greater influence worldwide. One consequence was a flurry of attention to "Fortress America" and a concerted effort to mend fences with Latin America through the Good Neighbor Policy. This changed with the fortunes of war. By 1944–45, the United States could look forward to an almost unchallenged global power—politically, economically, militarily. Influence in Latin America could henceforth be simply presumed as an adjunct to global preeminence, which in other areas of the world had to be cultivated, paid for, and assiduously maintained. But while regional considerations became less important to government relative to global issues, they became relatively more important to business.

Before World War II, American business was far more likely to stay at home than go abroad. World War I had brought the first opportunities for concerted expansion to the south, as the U.S. government took an active role in seeking to replace British capital and influence with North American. The wartime Wilson administration built merchant ships to take advantage of trade routes neglected by the British during the war and the liquidation of U.S. debts to Europe brought cash with which to make investments in ailing South American enterprises previously controlled by the British and Germans.[5] In the interwar period, the U.S. State Department continued to use its influence to gain for business a dominant position in the strategic areas of Latin American finance, communications, and petroleum.[6] But once this position was gained, State Department interest in coaxing expansion declined, and the core of North American businessmen was not sufficiently motivated toward foreign investment to undertake major new initiatives themselves. Postwar competition from Europe, and especially Germany after 1933, was still stiff, and American manufacturers largely preferred to invest in the domestic economy. U.S. economic activity in Latin America remained concentrated in raw materials, investments such as mining, and tropical agriculture.

Investments in raw materials were more likely to yield "natural monopolies" than investments in manufacturing.[7] Control of a nation's primary export, whether it be oil or bananas, often connected to control of a central transportation and communications network, gave corporations a kind of power and omnipotence not to be matched by investments in products that could be duplicated by other companies in the same country or abroad. As long as U.S. investments remained concentrated in this kind of economic activity, they were likely to yield North Americans an imperious sway over the fortunes of host countries; thus, for example, Commodore Vanderbilt, Minor Keith, and Sam "The Banana Man" Zemurray ran much of Central America for nearly a hundred years. It is notable that the worst examples of political interventionism on the part of U.S. companies in even the late twentieth century have all come from companies in extractive enterprises or other natural monopolies: the United Fruit Company (Guatemala), International Petroleum Corporation (Peru), and International Telephone and Telegraph (Chile).

But this scenario began to change just before and in the aftermath of World War II. Before the war, as part of the Good Neighbor Policy, the U.S. government developed a much more selective policy of intervention than it had previously had. In the late nineteenth and early twentieth centuries, the U.S. had been relatively willing to shell shores or threaten a landing of troops whenever companies or individuals suffered damage at the hands of local governments. This commitment to intervention on behalf of business had been weakening throughout the 1920s,[8] but with the nationalization of Mexican oil in 1938 the U.S. government put business decisively and publicly on notice that it would use force to defend corporate interests only when the executive branch saw fit for broader security reasons—for example, Guatemala in 1954. Since business confidence is predicated on the reliability and predictability of environmental factors over years if not decades, the on-again, off-again interventionism of the government gradually forced most U.S. companies to find their own accommodation with local regimes.

Also, after World War II, U.S. investors entered manufacturing in Latin America in significant numbers for the first time, especially in large-market countries like Brazil. This trend further increased business vulnerability in several ways: production for consumption (import substitution) instead of for export made local perceptions and sensibilities more relevant; investments in manufacturing did not have the advantages of natural monopolies; and the larger the country the less influence any one company was likely to have over policy and direction. In addition, anti-imperialism and increasing nationalism among Third World colonies and nations after the war further heightened the perils to U.S. investors, just as many of them were exploring foreign opportunities for the first time.

The 1950s: Government Inaction and an Emerging
Business Code of Behavior

For U.S. corporations a central challenge of the postwar period thus became how to cope with rising nationalism in Latin America in the face of greater inherent vulnerability and a changed (or at least a less dependable) U.S. policy toward military intervention on behalf of business. The solution that some businessmen would begin to evolve was a code of conduct based on political neutrality and cooperation with local economic development goals. Eventually, autonomous business organizations and foreign relations lobbies such as the Council of the Americas would debate these questions, but in the 1950s most initial discussion of the problems of foreign investment went on in trade journals and ad hoc forums organized by government.

The Business Advisory Council's Committee on Latin America, organized by the U.S. Department of Commerce, was one of the most important conduits of business opinion to the Department of State during this decade. Top representatives of the biggest U.S. companies in Latin America participated actively in the committee: David Rockefeller of Chase National Bank; Leo Welch of Standard Oil of New Jersey; Sam Baggett of United Fruit Company; H. W. Balgooyen of the American and Foreign Power Company; and H. A. Davies of International Harvester, among others. In their individual responses to a memorandum on U.S. foreign policy toward Latin America written by Assistant Secretary of State Edward Miller in 1952, the committee members revealed a common anxiety about the future of the U.S. business relationship to Latin America. Thomas Taylor called the situation a "crossroads," noting that the transition from a policy of military interventionism to a policy of negotiated protection for American interests placed business "in the vulnerable position of being in mid-stream," ultimately necessitating "a great deal closer relationship and understanding with those countries."[9]

Most of the representatives on the Business Advisory Council seemed to accept the fact "that the use of physical force is out," while continuing to argue in favor of some sort of "prompt and positive support from the United States Government when its interests are prejudiced or discriminated against." The techniques most suggested for carrying out such a protective policy were a firm and consistent trade program supported by embassy staffs with more than a passing knowledge of business and economics, and the use of such bargaining "chips" as foreign aid, imports of "essential supplies" from the United States, and access to the U.S. market to induce Latin Americans to respect U.S. property abroad.

Only two members of the council advocated a more aggressive stance: Leo Welch of Standard Oil and Sam Baggett of United Fruit. Although he did not openly call for military intervention, Welch characterized U.S. policy as "supine" and "unduly subservient" toward Latin America, and said he could not share Assistant Secretary Miller's assumption that "the so-called 'toleration' of Mexico's expropriation of U.S. oil companies marked an advance in American relations with Latin America." Baggett said that American propaganda was "too defensive," and pressed detailed suggestions for an intense, daily campaign against Communism and the Soviet Union. But Baggett and Welch are notable partly for a vehemence and aggressiveness that are a counterpoint to the more moderate suggestions of the majority of council members.[10]

Committee members also discussed how business could protect itself through modifications of its own behavior, in response to a question by Miller as to whether it might be possible to arrive at a common standard of conduct for business abroad. Although some answered that it would be "hardly possible to have a common standard of conduct at the level of details," the respondents generally agreed (with the exception of Welch and Baggett, who did not even respond to this question) that U.S. businessmen should adhere to a general set of principles modeled on the practices of "responsible" business in the United States.[11] Not only should companies investing in Latin America "conduct their business on the same high standard of conduct and efficiency as they would at home," as the International Packers' representative phrased it, but they should also, as another executive wrote, "treat labor fairly, train and develop local people into positions of responsibility, [and] refrain strictly from meddling in the foreign country's politics."[12]

Other executives stressed that companies could insure good relations only by "recognizing and respecting legitimate local rights and aspirations and by scrupulously avoiding any political action," and that businessmen should "learn more about Latin America . . . study the languages, comprehend the national aspirations of the people and learn to see the parallel between the development of those countries in this century and our own in the 19th century."[13] In all, four out of the seven council members who submitted written responses specifically called for a "minimum standard of decent behavior" and two specifically pointed out that this should include neutrality in local politics.

It is clear that at least on a conceptual level some businessmen had begun to apply notions of "corporate responsibility," specifically political neutralism, to foreign investments by the early and mid-1950s. Importantly, this is not evidence of increased morality on the part of business, just of an increased awareness of the dangers and requirements of the postwar world—one in which foreign nationalism exposed direct investments to increased risks, and in which the political logic of the cold war could easily supersede the economic logic of specific business interests in terms of government priorities. That is, with its relatively new political and military commitments, the U.S. government no longer looked to economic ties as being the only binds to other nations. Indeed, one could argue that economics served politics in the postwar world, not the reverse, as in previous decades.

Various writers for the *Harvard Business Review* echoed the same conclusions in the early and mid-1950s. Jack Butler wrote in 1952 that "The age is dead when commercial enterprises could shatter opposition with a 'whiff of grapeshot.' . . . businessmen will have to calculate on their own the hazards involved in acquiring assets overseas . . . [and] work out some way of mitigating the possibility of failure." One way of avoiding these hazards, Butler counseled, was "to remain neutral, virtually aloof from the political tides that shift so often in most underdeveloped countries."[14]

But "political responsibility" was only one half of the story: international businessmen of the era also seemed increasingly concerned through the 1950s to demonstrate their "economic responsibility," and especially the role business could play in implementing the postwar U.S. goal of political stability and democratization through "modernizing" economic development. On the surface, this point of view fit perfectly with the policy of the Eisenhower administration. But the rather empty rhetoric about development spouted by Washington failed to meet the needs and expectations of Latin Americans (as Richard Nixon and the world discovered in 1958), and by extension the concerns of at least some businessmen who recognized that for its own protection business could not afford to ignore development questions to the extent that perhaps the U.S. government could.

Dwight D. Eisenhower assumed office in 1953 with a predisposition toward military alliances as the basis for relations with Latin America and a distaste toward aid as a tool of economic development. Secretary of the Treasury George Humphrey had one of the strongest voices in the cabinet, and his unequivocal opposition both to grants and soft loans for Latin America set the tone for the first years of the administration's policy. Humphrey made his stand on the premise that economic development was going to happen through business dealings or not at all, and that there was no way that government was going to subsidize the development of foreign industry that might eventually compete against American.[15] Although on the surface this perspective seemed to favor business generally, in fact it represented the views of nationalist businessmen, not internationalists. The business community had long been divided into those who, producing largely for the home market, favored protective trade and lending policies, and those businessmen who favored a "universalist" world order to facilitate world trade and investment.[16] In his opposition to the Export-Import Bank, Humphrey clearly showed himself to be of the nationalist, isolationist camp—a fact not appreciated by those who supported tax and credit incentives for foreign investment.

Secretary of State John Foster Dulles, with Eisenhower's support, ran a foreign economic policy based on free trade, development through private investment, and minimal government-to-government assistance. In the larger strategic scheme, both Dulles and Eisenhower lacked interest in Latin America and believed, as Eisenhower expressed it in a letter to his brother, that as a region not "directly open to assault" it did not merit grant aid for economic development.[17] Whatever external or internal threat Communism posed in Latin America could be best handled by a strengthening of Latin American police forces, thought Eisenhower, who initiated the first U.S.-sponsored program to do just that, using monies earmarked for economic development projects.[18] Since the economic status quo in Latin America presented no problem for the United States, and it seemed that whatever problems the status quo presented for the poor of Latin America could be handled by their police, relying on business to produce "trickle-down" development was perfectly consistent with the administration's political "realism."

But although the Eisenhower administration publicly pronounced its confidence in the ability of foreign investment to produce economic development, the government consistently ruled out proposals for tax concessions that would encourage such investment and made virtually no attempts to educate businessmen about their supposed responsibilities.[19] During the second half of Eisenhower's term (1955–60), foreign direct investment in Latin American grew less quickly than at any point in the thirty year period from 1940 to 1970. While American investments in Western Europe and Canada increased in the second half of the 1950s by 123 and 65 percent, respectively, investments in Latin America increased by only 24 percent.[20] Eisenhower and his advisors were slow to take Latin American development questions seriously. They focused on nonstatist solutions to development as much to avoid these questions as to affirm the role of the private sector. U.S. corporations, and their Latin American partners, were on their own.

American trade journals occasionally reflected an awareness of the role assigned to business by the administration, with relevant articles tending to fall into one of two categories: those that proclaimed *all* American ventures abroad to be a form of foreign "aid," regardless of how or for what purposes the particular businesses were organized, and those articles (consistent with the ethos of the Business Advisory Council during Edward Miller's tenure) that encouraged a harder look at how American business could fit itself within the postwar environment of developing countries.

One of the best examples of the first type, from *The Magazine of Wall Street* in 1958, called America's total overseas investment "a gigantic Point Four program . . . which eclipses in scope and magnitude the more publicized achievements of U.S. and U.N. projects." As evidence of the "silent revolution in living standards" brought about by these investments, the author noted that from billboards the world over "Colgate dentrifice smiles its bright assurance of sparkling teeth" and "Palmolive soap caresses with cosmopolitan impartiality the complexions of dusky Nubian maidens, porcelain Japanese Geishas and alabaster Swedish beauties."[21] Other articles on the automobile and food refining industries made similar claims to private "Point Four" programs based on little more than the sheer presence of American capital.[22] In spirit, these articles matched the vapid rhetoric of the Eisenhower government, which was equally vague in its assertions about what American investments would actually accomplish in the way of development.

In contrast, articles in the "corporate social responsibility" school of thought tended to raise substantive questions concerning the *ways* in which corporations conducted themselves abroad. Business analyst Clifton Wharton, Jr., argued that companies had to initiate specific programs to bring about development and cited examples of various companies that had started projects to "grapple with the basic problems of health, disease, and hunger." Without these programs, he admitted, foreign countries were frequently justified in charging that American business was irresponsible and oppor-tunistic. Wharton quoted the president of Costa Rica as saying, "We resent the pretense of speculators who assert that their motive in investing money abroad is to foster the development of our countries. . . . The sole objective in most cases is to make money, and our economic development is only a doubtful consequence." Wharton concluded that it was "up to the execu-tives of foreign subsidiaries to show . . . that privately financed aid and assistance are not a new form of colonialism and exploitation."[23]

Writers in the corporate responsibility mode also frequently noted in the 1950s that political development could, and even should, be a conse-quence of economic development. M. C. Conick, a *Harvard Business Re-view* contributor, pointed out that U.S. business could support the develop-ment of a free press in Latin America (and thereby political democracy) by bolstering advertising revenues. Jack Butler, also in *Harvard Business Re-view,* stated that it was not enough for U.S. companies to pay their taxes abroad when such taxes benefited only the ruling class and tended to "pre-serve the status quo beyond its natural life." While remaining politically aloof, companies had a responsibility to foster the conditions under which local rulers would be encouraged to direct national revenue into avenues that would "elevate the economic level of the people as a whole." According to Butler, grass-roots educational programs for women (who were often "denied a fruitful role in society"), enlightened labor policies, and a corpo-rate attitude supportive of "the right of political self-determination" were all a part of fostering local goodwill toward foreign companies and of mitigat-ing the dislocating effects of industrialization.[24]

Two practical pioneers in international "corporate social responsibility" who emerged in the 1950s were Nelson Rockefeller and Henry Kaiser.[25] Both Kaiser and Rockefeller were well known in the U.S. business commu-nity for innovative programs to share the profits from investments with foreign nationals. Kaiser's ventures in Argentina and Brazil, to establish domestic automobile industries based initially on the manufacture of jeeps, were a common topic in journals like *Business Week.*[26] Rockefeller's Inter-national Basic Economy Corporation, which started in agriculture in Brazil and Venezuela and eventually ran companies throughout Latin America, was frequently cited by writers on foreign investment as the foremost model of corporate social responsibility abroad.[27]

The distinguishing trait of the Rockefeller and Kaiser enterprises was their commitment to encouraging local ownership participation. In Brazil in the 1950s, where the Kaiser and Rockefeller activities overlapped, they im-plemented this commitment through measures that had the effect of pro-moting small-investor participation in the local stock market and thereby establishing one of the presumed "building blocks" of democracy, Ameri-can-style: a burgeoning middle class. In the thinking of Kaiser and Rocke-feller, public participation in the stock market had political as well as economic ramifications. A share in a company was a vote in the economy in the way that a vote in a democracy was a share in the political process.

By marketing their companies through public sales of stock (a highly unusual practice for either foreign or local companies in Latin America at the time), Rockefeller and Kaiser evidenced a common assumption about developing nations and their prospects for long-term political and economic stability. At a congressional hearing during World War II, a representative asked Nelson Rockefeller, "What does South America need?" Rockefeller responded, "I think it needs a great middle class of people such as we have in the United States."[28] This assumption was widely shared by American intellectuals and policy makers, who predicated much of their thinking during the development debates of the 1950s on the idea that economic growth and "modernization," including distribution of resources throughout a society, were the prerequisites for political democracy in the American, Jeffersonian mode. The thinking of Rockefeller, Kaiser, and many others in business, government, and academia was based on certain liberal precepts. Among these was the notion that democracy is not a matter of will (laws and formal constitutions) but a matter of money (wealth and industrialization)—that is, that economic development is the *first* building block of a stable, free society. A second, related assumption was that a substantial and growing middle class is a prerequisite for a prosperous, democratic society, both because a large middle class represents the spreading of abundance throughout the social structure, and because the middle class (the bourgeoisie) has historically been the strongest support for liberal, democratic principles.[29]

To businessmen of the era it was undoubtedly gratifying to think that by fostering economic development they automatically strengthened civil society, promoted democracy, and enhanced local goodwill toward their own companies. And yet, as Rockefeller, Kaiser, and other businessmen demonstrated by an increasing commitment to political neutrality in the 1950s, and as Rockefeller reaffirmed in his 1969 *Report on the Americas,* a preference for democracy did not stand in the way of working relationships with military dictators.[30] Although U.S. businessmen may have been confident in the ultimate redemptive power of economic development, promoting democracy was a goal that ranked behind maintaining amicable, productive relations with host governments. The informal code of conduct that began emerging in the 1950s sought to create these relations through political neutrality and a promise to aid in economic development.

The 1960s: The Alliance for Progress and Business

There is evidence that, after the Eisenhower administration's relative neglect of Latin America, many segments of the business community welcomed John Kennedy's new initiatives. The intent of the Alliance for Progress to promote economic development fitted well with business concerns about finding ways of proving to Latin American nationalists (be they civilians or generals) that private investment could be responsible and beneficial. Especially welcome were indications that Kennedy's approach might include new tax incentives for foreign investment—incentives that Eisenhower's economically orthodox advisors had ruled out. U.S. investment in Latin America had slowed considerably under Eisenhower and was showing an even sharper downward trend as the sixties got underway. Meanwhile, foreign criticism of business exploitation was becoming noticeably bitter abroad, especially in the wake of the Cuban Revolution.

Business concern about these trends was evidenced in several ways. First was the increasingly active discussion of the concept and possibility of joint ventures with Latin American businessmen as a way of promoting at least partial local ownership of foreign enterprises and circumventing nationalist criticisms. The Kaiser and Rockefeller ventures were often cited in this connection, and in the third year of the alliance, business executives would support a U.S. government vote in favor of an Economic Commission for Latin America resolution encouraging joint ventures.[31]

Second, executives also continued to discuss appropriate codes of conduct and ways in which businesses could improve their public relations through advertising, more thorough financial disclosures abroad, training and promotion of foreign nationals, and contributions to community improvement activities in host countries. Business groups held conferences on the subject, articles were written, and business and Department of Commerce officials actively discussed how business could build trust with local communities. Related to this, the early 1960s saw the proliferation of private groups and government committees devoted in one way or another to coping with the foreign crisis of confidence in U.S. business, including the Business Council for International Understanding, the Latin American Information Committee, the Latin American Business Committee, and the Business Group for Latin America.

Initially it seemed that the Kennedy administration would actively encourage these new departures. In the first Alliance for Progress planning document composed by Kennedy's advisory group, which met even before the presidential inauguration, conferees agreed that:

> A better understanding of the contribution of private enterprise is needed within the Executive and Legislative branches of the U.S. Government as well as within the governments of Latin America. . . . The obstacles to private investment, some of them created by the U.S. Government, must be reduced. . . . support should be given to developing and implementing an international code of behavior to be applied equally to private investors and host countries.[32]

But few of Kennedy's primary advisors were drawn from business, unlike in the previous administration, and business input into the alliance was minimal at first. Representatives of business were not even invited to the Punta del Este founding conference in August 1961, though executives from the Rockefeller and Kaiser enterprises and four or five other companies attended anyway, in spite of the lack of any official sanction.[33] The State Department did not announce the formation of a business Committee on the Alliance for Progress (COMAP) until April 1962, nearly a year and a half after planning for the alliance had begun.

It seems that the Kennedy administration's initial lack of a commitment to business involvement was due more to the political emphasis of the alliance in its early years than to any determination to exclude the private sector. As one official of the era later noted, private sector participation "was largely an afterthought," in part because the administration believed "that it was governments that could win the hearts and minds of the Latin American population and save them from Castro."[34] Kennedy's program explicitly called for agrarian and tax reform as prerequisites to aid, and sought democratization and social reform through support of moderate-left political parties in Latin America. These were not goals of the business community, and there may have been some presumption that business would not be sympathetic, helpful, or perhaps even relevant in devising plans. The prophecy may have been prescient or simply self-fulfilling. Although there is little evidence that business opposed either democratization or social reform, as time wore on business leaders became increasingly vocal about being excluded from the alliance and also about the alliance's economic program being subverted by its insistence on prior political change.

Peter Nehemkis, Jr., a Whirlpool executive who had been one of the few business people invited to participate in the earliest alliance planning group, was particularly articulate about his discouragement. He noted in one speech that although U.S. companies paid one-fifth of all taxes collected in Latin America, there had been almost no attempt to halt the sharply downward slide of investment in the region by changing U.S. tax laws to facilitate investment abroad or by encouraging business input into the alliance. The Punta del Este Conference had set a goal of significantly increased private investment in Latin America, and yet the reality was that net new U.S. investment had gone from an inflow of $141 million in 1961, to an outflow of $32 million in 1962, and was still declining into 1963. There were many in the business community, Nehemkis argued, who understood that "business as usual" was not enough to overcome "the pervasive social injustice . . . [and] the meager benefits of industrialization for the masses"—and yet those who had most power to bring economic change were being given the least role.[35] Rather than being tapped as an ally, business was placed in the role of an outsider, and eventually became somewhat of a critic.

And allies were in short supply, both in the United States and Latin America. The U.S. Congress had been lukewarm on the Alliance for Progress from the start: conservatives did not want to see U.S. dollars financing expropriations required by agrarian reform, and liberals such as Wayne Morse and Ernest Gruening in the Senate wanted to see cuts in the military dimensions of foreign aid. Kennedy's proposed allocations for the alliance were cut by one-fifth to begin with, tied to a yearly review, and never came even close to the level of commitment he had initially indicated the United States would make. Latin American businessmen and politicians, even some of whom had been identified with the "democratic left," also questioned the political aspects of the program. Former Brazilian President Juscelino Kubitschek wrote one of the earliest and most critical outside evaluations of the alliance for the Organization of American States. He said that while reforms had to be carried out in order to eliminate "institutionalized poverty," by putting reform first the alliance had "created a system that might result in the postponement of large-scale external aid"—aid that was essential if reformers were to have any hope of taking their nations in new directions. It was, he said, "a vicious circle." Among other things, Kubitschek recommended "permitting private enterprise [in both the U.S. and Latin America] to take part in the conduct of the Alliance. . . . the program would thereby win additional support in an important sector of public opinion and other element from which to obtain objective suggestions."[36]

At a conference in New York in early 1963, Latin American businessmen from ten nations (almost all democratic) expressed their reservations in private, with a view to avoiding conflict with their own governments and that of the United States. Nonetheless, they made it clear that they saw the alliance as a good idea theoretically, but one that had been oversold and inappropriately politicized. By focusing on reform rather than growth the alliance had actually brought about capital flight. "The Latins feel that agrarian and tax reform is their problem and should be handled without outside dictation," one U.S. businessman reported, and that by "selling socialism in Latin America . . . [the] Alliance is backing the wrong horse in their opinion."[37] While it may be argued, correctly for some Latin American businessmen and incorrectly for others, that they would have fought reform under any circumstances, their arguments in favor of respect for national sovereignty (local solutions to local problems) made sense to U.S. executives for whom political neutrality was part of an emerging, if informal and still inconsistent, code of conduct.

David Rockefeller echoed these particular Latin American sentiments and those of many people in the U.S. business community at a speech to the Economic Club of Chicago, shortly after the New York meeting. Rockefeller argued implicitly for a gradualist approach to sociopolitical reform along with a "swiftly-paced" approach to economic growth, saying that anything else was unrealistic considering the "inescapably slow and tedious" nature of social change. Rockefeller also raised the issue of sovereignty, noting:

We must not try to force Latin American countries simply to create a society in our image. These countries must adapt their institutions and policies to their own conditions. It is in our interest that they should be both effective in satisfying the aspirations of the people and consonant with democratic processes. Yet our own experience and that of Western Europe have demonstrated . . . that the variety of policies and institutions under which economies can prosper in a free society is a large one.[38]

Whereas Kennedy's advisors may have assumed that, in Robert Packenham's phrase, "all good things go together"—that is, democracy, reform, and economic growth—David Rockefeller, his brother Nelson, and many others in the business community clearly believed that economic growth was the engine that pulled the other cars.

But the most important criticisms of the Alliance for Progress, from the point of view of its long-term survival, came from the conservative U.S. Congress. By 1963, the honeymoon was long over and many of Kennedy's programs were in trouble. In particular, both Republicans and Democrats questioned the proposed allocation for the Agency for International Development (AID), which may be the reason why Kennedy himself, in his 1963 AID message, stressed that increased efforts to promote private investment would be the "major new initiative" of U.S. foreign aid efforts for the future. AID staff and advisors saw this change as being perhaps the only hope for continued high allocations in foreign aid. Franklin D. Roosevelt, Jr., under secretary of commerce, wrote AID chief David Bell that "the central fact is that the Congress is unlikely to continue to support anything like an adequate aid program unless there is some major change in its image and mode of operation." Roosevelt suggested that one way to accomplish this would be through emphasizing the nation-to-nation (rather than government-to-government) approach that Kennedy had announced. Private enterprise was to be the "New Look" of foreign aid.[39]

As part of this, officials from the Department of Commerce actively encouraged a more coherent, stronger business presence in the alliance throughout 1963. Jack Behrman, the commerce official in charge of relations with the alliance, sought to do this by encouraging unification of the many business groups concerned with U.S.–Latin American relations. Before Behrman could engineer such a merger, however, David Rockefeller took the initiative and did it for him, much to the administration's pleasant surprise. In the summer of 1963, Rockefeller wrote to a variety of the most active participants in the Business Council for International Understanding, the Latin American Information Committee, COMAP, and so on, urging the formation of one organization to represent the U.S. business perspective on Latin America. The idea attained support almost immediately from business as well as from the Kennedy administration. While the administration wanted it made clear to the public that the move was entirely at private initiative, "to discourage Latin American speculation that there has been some special relationship newly constructed with the business community with respect to the Alliance for Progress," Kennedy nonetheless agreed to a first official meeting with the new "Business Group for Latin America" on November 21, 1963.[40] The meeting was postponed when Kennedy decided to make a quick political trip to Texas.

Observers would later agree that the Alliance for Progress was in trouble well before Kennedy was shot in Dallas on November 22.[41] The political dimensions of the alliance were not preempted mainly by its later support for private enterprise, or by the conservatism of Thomas Mann, Lyndon Johnson's appointment to the post of assistant secretary of state for Latin America. The prodemocracy, agrarian, and tax reform elements of the alliance lacked solid support against predictable opposition in both the United States and Latin America and were falling of their own weight well before November 1963. Kennedy seems to have realized this reluctantly, as did AID administrators. Undoubtedly, many mistakes were made in the initial design and selling of the Alliance for Progress, which scholarly study has yet to analyze or explain fully. One of them may have been to wait far too long before attempting to woo the support of what conceivably could have been one of the most important sources of support for the program, and what certainly was one of its most interested audiences: business. Ironically, the Kennedy administration failed to heed the successful strategy pursued over a decade earlier by proponents of the Marshall Plan for Europe, which was to engage immediately the support of the internationalist business community—support that, according to historian Michael Hogan, "played an important role in overcoming conservative opposition . . . in Congress."[42] Indeed, while some historical interpretations have suggested that the Alliance for Progress was killed off by its later attention to private enterprise, it may be that this change in focus actually prolonged its life.[43]

A Formal Relationship Evolves: Business Diplomacy
in Latin America in the Late 1960s and 1970s

According to David Rockefeller, one reason for forming the Business Group for Latin America, which eventually expanded and became the Council of the Americas, was to avoid U.S. government dictation. As long as the government organized and sponsored business input into policy (through groups like COMAP), public officials could pick and choose the kind of advice and advisors they got. Business needed its own forum, separate from government.[44] Considering the government's hot-and-cold interest in Latin American issues, a forum independent of executive or congressional whim made even more sense. The Alliance for Progress had shown how fickle the U.S. commitment was to either democracy or development. Once again, as under Eisenhower, the lesson learned was that if business were to construct a strong relationship with Latin America, it would have to do so on its own.

The Council of the Americas was specifically organized as a neutral forum for discussion among U.S. executives and government representatives, North and South. In the decades since its formal founding in 1965, the council has taken a public stand in favor of only *one* issue (ratification of the Panama Canal Treaty), otherwise preferring to operate more as a clearinghouse for business views than as a lobby per se. In fact, all exchanges between council members and Latin American government representatives are strictly off the record. At the same time, it has implicitly supported the status quo by trying to foster good communication between U.S. business and Latin American governments, many of which were dictatorships from the early 1960s through the early 1980s. Although some executives may have felt, as one former staff member of the council later commented to the author, that "Democracy is a comfortable system to work within because you know the rules," in practice the conditions that U.S. companies operating abroad have sought are stability and free-market policies, whether in Communist China, democratic Costa Rica, or authoritarian Chile.[45]

The more active public lobby group on behalf of U.S.–Latin American relations that evolved during the same time was the American Association of Chambers of Commerce of Latin America (AACCLA), founded in 1967 by U.S. chambers operating in five Latin American countries: Argentina, Brazil, Colombia, Mexico, and Venezuela. From the mid-1970s through the early 1980s, AACCLA was probably the most active business lobby intervening directly with Congress and the president with regard to U.S.–Latin American relations. What characterized their stands in this period was not an ideological preference for either democracy or dictatorship, but a paramount concern for bilateral relations that were not conflict prone. What this often produced, interestingly, was a predisposition to "give" on those issues that Latin American governments consider the highest priority (even when they conflicted somewhat with U.S. ideology), and a willingness to act as a conduit for pressure from abroad. That is, as the segment of U.S. society whose material interests are most affected by foreign needs and wants, international business had a stake in communicating these needs and wants to the U.S. government—which otherwise has little vulnerability to or interest in foreign opinion, especially from the non-European, nonsuperpower nations. For example, AACCLA was consistently supportive of lobbying efforts to maintain U.S. foreign economic aid to Latin America during the Carter and Reagan administrations. It is of note that while lobbying on behalf of its own interests, business may also at times be one of the most active, consistent domestic lobbies on behalf of Latin American perspectives—or at least those perspectives expressed by governing groups.

The U.S. chambers of commerce in Latin America originally organized themselves into a coalition largely in response to the example set by U.S. chambers in Europe, which had begun an association a few years earlier. In 1966, members of the U.S. chamber in Venezuela thought that a parallel coalition for Latin America might be useful for providing mutual support, and especially for encouraging businesses abroad to open chambers in more Latin American countries than the five that already had them. By 1988, the presence of U.S. chambers of commerce in twenty countries attested to the successful attainment of that goal—and to the consequent growth in U.S. business influence vis-à-vis both the U.S. Congress and Latin American governments. The fulfillment of this organizational objective also meant that beginning in the mid-1970s the association could focus its attention on its more primary purposes, which included "representing its constituency before major governmental bodies, especially the U.S. Congress and the Administration . . . [and] interpreting Latin American developments to the news media."[46]

As a lobby, AACCLA's emphasis on nonconfrontational bilateral relations and an open trade policy led it to take several stands at odds with the more conservative elements in U.S. society and government. Specifically, in 1975, AACCLA began to evidence support for a greater normalization of hemispheric trade relations with Cuba. In particular, AACCLA reported favorably in its newsletter on the vote taken by the Organization of American States to drop its eleven-year embargo of Cuba and allow each member nation to set its own policy for trade with the island. AACCLA went even further to encourage the U.S. government not to punish foreign affiliates of U.S. companies that wished to trade with Cuba.

This stand was consistent, of course, with the commercial interests of AACCLA's membership: if they could earn money in Cuba, so much the better. But there was also an issue of sovereignty, AACCLA argued. If certain Latin American countries decided to renew trade with Cuba, but U.S. law prohibited North American affiliates organized under the laws of those nations from trading with the island, "such a situation would reinforce allegations that decisions affecting the host country's economy are taken abroad."[47] In other words, if a U.S. corporation built cars on Brazilian soil utilizing mostly Brazilian labor, capital, and raw materials, Brazil should be able to export those cars to Cuba and improve its balance of payments thereby. Although the U.S. Treasury Department only slowly adopted aspects of AACCLA's liberal interpretation, the organization continued to lobby quietly for trade normalization, especially at the beginning of the Carter administration when it seemed that an improvement in relations with Cuba might be possible.

Throughout the 1970s, AACCLA consistently demonstrated a preference for giving way on issues that impinged on sovereignty, with the understanding that such issues had the greatest potential for undermining bilateral relations and thus business relations. Of course, again, this could mean respect for the sovereignty of dictatorships just as much as for democracies, and in light of the political makeup of Latin America at the time it was dictatorships that were more likely to benefit. Two issues that demonstrated the variable outcomes of such a policy were the Panama Canal Treaty and Jimmy Carter's human rights policy.

On the Panama Canal Treaty, AACCLA was the first U.S. business organization to take a favorable, vocal stand. The association began in 1975 by sending telegrams urging Congress to approve the allocations that were necessary for the negotiations to proceed. When the treaty became an electoral issue in the campaign of 1976, AACCLA kept its members informed of the candidates' stands on the treaty, including Ronald Reagan's statement in early 1976 that "We bought it, we paid for it, we built it, and it is ours, and we intend to keep it." When conservative forces in the House threatened again to cut off all funds for negotiation in June 1976, AACCLA sent telegrams to 150 congressmen. The move was overturned, leading the assistant secretary of state to thank AACCLA's president personally for his help with this "crushing defeat for the anti-negotiation forces."[48]

Once the treaty had been formulated, the Carter administration again looked to AACCLA for leadership. On November 1, 1977, the AACCLA board, meeting in Costa Rica, voted to support the treaty as written. After this, the Council of the Americas also came out publicly in favor of the treaty, breaking with its traditional neutrality. AACCLA tried to develop further support for the treaty within the business community by asking the domestic U.S. Chamber of Commerce (its affiliate) to take a stand in favor of the treaty as well. Interestingly, the national chamber could not achieve a consensus on the subject, which within the United States was simply "too divisive," according to AACCLA's executive secretary.

Only those U.S. businesses with direct ties to Latin America saw the treaty as a "must," because of the strong feelings about it throughout the hemisphere. Speaking before Congress during ratification hearings in 1978, AACCLA's president Patrick Hughson emphasized that the standing treaty from 1903 "symbolized a paternalistic and interventionist image of the United States." Ratification of the new agreement would affirm the "American values of justice and national self-determination."[49] Failure to ratify, he hardly needed mention, would produce a serious rupture in relations with a number of countries. Even after the Senate finally approved the treaty, AACCLA representatives continued to follow it through 1979 when, for a fourth time, they met with and sent telegrams to congressmen—this time to ensure that the allocations needed to implement the agreement were made.

AACCLA's lobbying effort with regard to Carter's human rights policy was not nearly as active—nor as concerned with "American values of justice." But it was consistent. Above all, the chambers of commerce showed their preference for nonacrimonious relations with Latin America. In this case, business showed a willingness to look the other way that National Security Council officials normally reserved only for strategic allies such as South Korea or China or for use as a bargaining chip with important enemies. As far as AACCLA was concerned, "the whole human rights issue is becoming the greatest irritant in U.S.–Latin American relations," and this was enough to make it a problem. In 1976 an AACCLA representative and the U.S. chamber president from Argentina met with the assistant secretary of state for inter-American affairs to register concern, and twice during 1978 AACCLA urged the Senate and House "not to impose punitive human rights constraints" on loans made by the Eximbank to Latin America.[50] The ruling militaries of countries in violation of U.S. human rights standards had made the issue into one of sovereignty, and as in the case of the Panama Canal Treaty AACCLA lined up behind them, albeit less energetically than in the case of the canal treaty. As usual, local sovereignty and stability in inter-American relations came first for AACCLA, this time to the detriment of democracy and social justice.

Central America in the 1980s: The Case of Revolutionary Nicaragua

Business groups and individual corporations will never be entirely consistent, however, and AACCLA was no exception as the debates over policy toward Central America in the 1980s demonstrated. When President Carter asked for $75 million in aid for Nicaragua in late 1979, the past president of the American chamber in Nicaragua initially testified before Congress in support. Especially attractive to the chamber was that $60 of the $75 million was to go for the encouragement of private sector enterprise. But within six months the Nicaraguan chamber had changed its position, and in the process departed from the usual policy of nonconfrontational relations. In April 1980, the current president reversed his predecessor's stand, testifying before Congress that the U.S. should do more to insure that the Sandinista government restored democracy and specifically stating that the $75 million aid package was not likely to be used for the benefit of the private sector.[51] One result was that the Nicaraguan government declared the chamber president persona non grata, and the chamber's credibility and position in the country were severely strained. AACCLA itself did not take a position on Nicaragua or on policies toward El Salvador or Guatemala, preferring to allow local chambers to take their own stand on the issues. But organizational sentiment was nonetheless "strongly supportive" of the Reagan approach throughout the 1980s, according to one AACCLA official.[52]

What is most interesting, though, is not the consistency or inconsistency of specific organizations, but rather overall trends; and it is clear that the overall trend among U.S. bankers and direct investors was a cautious neutrality toward Nicaragua in the early 1980s evidenced by "a low profile sympathetic to the Revolution," in the words of business analyst John Purcell. According to Purcell, U.S. business in Central America in this period was notable chiefly for its "reactive and adaptive" nature, leading to cooperation with oligarchs in Guatemala and revolutionaries in Nicaragua on the premise that "business can be done within a broad spectrum of national ideologies." Bankers pursued cautious but nonpunitive loan policies, while companies with large fixed investments continued operating in both Nicaragua and El Salvador. The Council of the Americas sponsored meetings in New York with members of the Sandinista directorate in 1979, and in 1980 organized a trip of U.S. businessmen to Nicaragua and Costa Rica to meet with private sector and government representatives.[53]

The neutral, adaptive posture of business was due less to the ideological predispositions of executives, according to Purcell, than to financial pragmatism (the desire to hang onto investments) and to common organizational characteristics that led senior executives to listen carefully to managers and analysts at the local level. As one middle manager said about top executives in an interview with Purcell: "They may be as right-wing as Attila the Hun but they are extremely pragmatic when it comes to business decisions." A part of this pragmatism, Purcell notes, may have been a recognition of the declining regional hegemony of the United States in recent years and thus the decreased ability of the U.S. government to protect business investments overseas. Of course, as already noted, it may be argued that the ability of business to depend *categorically* on government for protection in Latin America has been in question since at least 1938, and that business neutrality and adaptability has increased perceptibly since that time. The decline in U.S. hegemony may have simply accelerated the process.[54]

United Fruit, International Petroleum, and ITT: Exceptions or Rules?

The most important exceptions to a gradual fifty-year trend toward political neutrality on the part of business can be found in the behavior of the United Fruit Company, the International Petroleum Company (IPC), and International Telephone and Telegraph (ITT) in the 1950s, 1960s, and 1970s, respectively. Their stories of gross interventionism have been repeated often and need not be elaborated here.[55] But there are some aspects to these incidents that may actually confirm, rather than deny, the general hypotheses concerning the unreliability of government intervention and the corresponding reinforcement of business political neutrality.

First, in all three cases, there is considerable (if not definitive) evidence that the U.S. government instigated the interventions for its own ideological and geopolitical reasons, not primarily to protect U.S. business interests. In the case of Guatemala in 1954, historians in recent years have tended to emphasize John Foster Dulles's anti-Communism and Dwight Eisenhower's commitment to containment in Latin America to explain the reasons for the U.S. overthrow of Jacobo Arbenz, rather than the specific complaints of United Fruit. Similarly, the Kennedy and Johnson administrations' intervention on behalf of IPC, to many observers, went far beyond what the company itself asked of the government and corresponded more with what officials thought of as being the proper way to make Latins conform to the etiquette of the Alliance for Progress than with the actual interests of the company—which was eventually expropriated in its entirety.[56] Lastly, it is clear that although ITT pressed actively for intervention against Salvador Allende, this would have been the policy of the Nixon-Kissinger administration in any case, committed as it was to preventing the further spread of socialism within the hemisphere. What all this means is that protection of business was a complementary but decidedly secondary goal of the U.S. government, not the raison d'etre for intervention, and thus not something upon which business could rely with certainty. Secondary goals can always be shelved to fulfill primary ones. Indeed, although these three corporations engaged in the most blatant kinds of intervention, what the general business community may have learned from their experiences was that government aid was conditional, and—even more important—that it could backfire, as in the case of IPC. "American business is realizing that Washington and its embassies are of questionable value in a Latin American scuffle," businessman George Lodge wrote in 1970. Expropriation and other expressions of nationalism, he added, "are teaching United States companies that their survival and prosperity in the changing environment of Latin America depend very much on themselves."[57]

Second, what makes the political improprieties of these companies seem more like exceptions to the general rule of behavior rather than examples of it is the response that these corporate interventions provoked in the business community. Although the actions of United Fruit seem to have elicited few complaints by other businessmen in 1954, by the early 1960s companies increasingly voiced the concern that they were paying for the transgressions of a few in the form of escalating nationalism. One result was the founding of key business organizations such as the Council of the Americas and AACCLA, which spent much of the decade discussing codes of conduct and the ways in which companies could improve their public relations abroad. As one council official later said, formulating guidelines for corporate conduct in Latin America was a council priority for "most of the sixties."[58] When the International Petroleum Company and its parent company, Standard Oil of New Jersey, intervened in Peruvian politics in the mid-1960s, other U.S. companies refused to support their actions precisely because, as Levinson and Onís put it, "of the widespread feeling that IPC had hardly been a model of corporate responsibility."[59]

The case of ITT in Chile is perhaps even clearer. In 1970, ITT president Harold Geneen began a three-year effort to overthrow the government of Salvador Allende, which included offering funds for rival political parties, endorsing positions of the opposition newspaper *El Mercurio,* submitting suggestions for political and economic sabotage to National Security

Advisor Henry Kissinger, maligning U.S. diplomats who took a "soft" line on Chile, and offering to contribute up to $1 million to a CIA fund for Chilean destabilization. ITT also attempted to involve major U.S. companies and banks in a coordinated effort to pressure the U.S. government for stronger intervention through an "Ad Hoc Committee on Chile," which ITT convened in January 1971. But the Ad Hoc Committee met only twice, and with little result. Kennecott Copper withdrew after concluding that the meetings "had no particular value," while the president of Ralston Purina expressed basic opposition to the ITT approach and ordered his subordinates not to attend any future meetings "even if invited."[60] ITT officials working under Geneen had encountered similar reactions earlier when they had first sought to drum up opposition to Allende's imminent election. As one memo to Geneen stated: "Our poll of companies with plants, or activities in Chile continued to show an almost complete lack of interest on their parts."[61] Only Anaconda Copper, of all the companies ITT contacted, was willing to make protestations to Kissinger directly, and none evidenced the level of intervention suggested by Geneen.

As it turned out, once ITT's actions became public knowledge, they provided the occasion for a public purging of the U.S. corporate conscience and a public shaming of Harold Geneen. At the Senate hearings on ITT's involvement in Chile, four of the largest banks in the nation vociferously proclaimed their policies of political neutrality. Although representatives stopped short of condemning ITT's intervention, they made it clear that, as one banker said, "we would not do it."[62] The senior vice-president of First National City Bank stated that a fundamental presumption of the bank's operating policy was that "every country must find its own way, politically and economically"—to which Senator William Fulbright responded that he wished the State Department felt the same way.[63] The Bank of America representative stated emphatically that "the unique dependence of a bank on good relations with the host government . . . makes it unthinkable to run the risk of political involvement." The executive vice-president of Chase Manhattan Bank countered the notion that ITT's activities were typical of corporate behavior with the comment that "not only is it not a pattern but it is just not done." Ralston Purina and IBM underscored the banks' testimony, with the IBM official calling political intervention "totally abhorrent."[64]

But going beyond questions of fair play and good conduct, the business representatives also made it clear that specific economic interests were at stake. The companies were almost all involved in delicate negotiations over expropriations and sales with the Chilean government at the time of the ITT intervention. The Allende government had required the banks to sell off their branches, and the banks were eager to get the best price possible. At stake was not only the outcome of the negotiations (which several banks had reason to think would end in reasonable compensation), but also the repayment of millions of dollars in loans that had been made both before and after Allende was elected. As it turned out, some banks did arrive at satisfactory agreements with Allende and noted that the socialist government had made commendable progress on its loan payments. Manufacturers Hanover Trust, First National City Bank, and Bank of America (as well as Ralston Purina) all testified that political confrontation or the creation of economic chaos in Chile would have been directly counter to their immediate financial interests.[65] Clearly, these corporations were trying to avoid the kind of outcome which IPC's interventionist behavior had produced in Peru, and which ITT's behavior produced in Allende's Chile: uncompensated expropriation. In this case, self-interest may have operated as an important constraint on behavior, leading companies to learn (or repeat) lessons in negotiation and flexibility that were lost on the U.S. government.

Conclusion

Although this investigation suggests that business behavior may be more politically neutral than often thought, it also raises questions beyond the scope of one article. Specifically, surveys and case studies that would utilize the records of individual companies are needed to determine what the *range* of corporate behaviors is, without unduly emphasizing those corporations that have long records of intervention at the expense of those which have equally long records of political neutrality. ITT, for example, had a history of generally offensive behavior throughout Latin America, which had been specifically documented in the case of Puerto Rico, Peru, and Brazil even before its forays into Chilean politics.[66] It might be noted that ITT was also a conspicuous violator of antitrust laws and a secret contributor to political campaigns in the United States. The pattern of interventionist behavior that studies of ITT reveal may have to do more with that particular corporation and management than with the general record of U.S. business either in Chile or other parts of the region. Although interventionist behavior is critical to document and understand, it is the broadest historical patterns that give insight into how U.S.–Latin American relations have evolved and in what directions policy may be shaped for the future.

In addition to a series of case studies that would more accurately reflect the wide range and large number of U.S. companies operating in Latin America than do present "exposés," we also need closer analytical attention to what constitutes appropriate political behavior. Self-interest may act as a constraint on confrontational behavior, but self-interest also dictates that companies do what they can to cut the best deals for themselves and protect their investments. The question, then, is where does lobbying end, and intervention begin?

Of course, this presumes that lobbying is an appropriate form of political behavior—distinct from and preferable to bribery, covert destabilization, and collusion in the overthrow of governments—and that this is the means by which business legitimately interacts with the political process of a nation. This is not a presumption made by everyone, however, as evidenced by some analyses of U.S. business influence. A telling example is Angela Delli Sante's 1979 contribution to *Capitalism and the State in U.S.- Latin American Relations*. Delli Sante correctly states that a goal of the American Chamber of Commerce in Mexico was to promote acceptance of private enterprise and the capitalist system through its own public relations programs and through encouraging member companies to exhibit social responsibility by endowing university chairs, providing health and educational services to workers, sponsoring sports events, and so forth. She concludes that these activities inherently represented "a direct attempt to tell the Mexican people and the Mexican government what to do."[67]

As far as Delli Sante is concerned (and her viewpoint is not uncommon), it is not legitimate for U.S. business to promote its philosophy of private enterprise in other countries in much the same way that it has in the United States since the advent of welfare and consumer capitalism in the Progressive period. And yet, one might ask, what other philosophy is business supposed to promote, and is it realistic to assume that any human endeavor will exhibit ideological neutrality? The private sector will promote private-sector enterprise by its very nature, and it is logical that it will attempt to do so more overtly when it perceives itself under attack. The truly pertinent question is not whether U.S. business promotes the ideology on which it is founded—of course it does—but whether business does so using measures commonly judged legitimate or illegitimate.

By painting all attempts to cultivate legitimacy and influence within a foreign country as a form of interventionism, one risks perpetuating the false dichotomy between self-interest and virtue. It is an analytical trap that hinders attempts to discover exactly what makes international relations better or worse. Again, Delli Sante's article is helpful as an illustration of this familiar problem. By condemning all types of business influence, the author misses an opportunity to deal with the complexities of the one good example of possibly illegitimate business behavior she is able to cite: the participation of U.S. subsidiaries in a four-month advertising boycott of the newspaper *Excelsior* during 1972 because of its sympathetic coverage of socialist experiments in other parts of Latin America and negative editorials on consumerism, capitalist forms of development, and foreign investment. Private Mexican and U.S. companies both participated in the boycott, which was followed by a negative press campaign in the Mexican media concerning *Excelsior*. It is possible that U.S. companies actually instigated the campaign, although the evidence is sketchy: we know only that U.S. groups participated in the decision along with Mexican bankers and industrialists and that Sears Roebuck held out on the boycott even after other U.S. and Mexican companies had returned to advertising with the paper.[68]

In any case, the story raises important questions. Is participation in a public boycott a legitimate or illegitimate way of attempting to wield influence? Would U.S. participation have been more appropriate if the boycott were organized entirely by the Mexican private sector, or not? Do companies have an obligation to give advertising to newspapers with which they disagree? On the other hand, considering that newspapers represent free speech, is any attempt to use financial power vis-à-vis such a publication, especially a foreign one, politically inappropriate? Of course, going beyond even what jurists or scholars might consider legal or appropriate is the question of what the public of the host country will perceive as fair. This kind of pressure is very likely to be seen as interventionism and may in fact constitute it. Indeed, an interesting point is that one of the largest U.S. corporations in Mexico refused to participate in the boycott on precisely those grounds. Clearly, at least some businesses, in their own self-interest, gave careful consideration to the distinction between business influence and political interference. Scholars need to do the same. Further investigation of the U.S. business role in Latin American politics would give an empirical basis to such analytical distinctions.

Nevertheless, it is to be hoped that the present paper does more than simply raise additional questions; it should also suggest what seem to be important trends and propositions. First is that U.S. business in general has learned some lessons about "correct" and "incorrect" ways of participating in the political life of Latin American nations over the past fifty or so years. These years have taught that U.S. military and diplomatic intervention is not a totally reliable or effective bulwark against anti-Americanism or expropriation; that business has to find its own accommodation with foreign regimes, be they democratic or dictatorial; that conspicuous neutrality on political issues is a useful device for avoiding confrontation with host governments; and that bribery and political contributions are dangerous (and, since the 1977 Foreign Corrupt Practices Act, illegal) ways of cultivating influence abroad. These lessons represent a code of conduct formally supported by organizations like the Council of the Americas, and informally adhered to by probably the majority of corporations. This is not to say that the "rules" are not broken. Clearly they are. But at least business has evolved a widely accepted code of conduct concerning interventionism and political neutrality, which is more than can be said of the U.S. government. As Ernest May once noted, "In appraising the American record in Latin America, one ought to judge either by intentions or results. If by the one, the Government comes off well; if by the other, business does."[69]

A final, related, proposition is that self-interest may (perhaps unfortunately) be a more effective way of directing behavior than appeals to American virtue or democratic ideals. Since 1945, the U.S. government has been able to do pretty much whatever it wanted in the Western Hemisphere with little if any consequences for its global power if U.S. policy failed to please Latin Americans. The fundamental goal of policy has been to maintain the essential acquiescence of other nations in the region on economic and foreign policy questions by whatever means necessary, up to and including physical force. One thing that has made this basic stance tolerable to politicians and a public raised on the principles of the Declaration of Independence is a highly sporadic policy of "promoting democracy" in Latin America. "Promoting democracy" thus becomes a way to cleanse periodically the North American conscience of the tarnish of other less high-minded but more persistent motives in international relations. To accomplish this, North Americans do not actually have to promote democracy, they just need to *think* that is what they are doing. Geopolitically, the United States has been able to do what it wants in the hemisphere because of overwhelming economic and military power. Psychologically, the U.S. government has been able to sell its policy and salve the national conscience precisely because of its supposed democratic ideals.

Individual businesses, however, cannot call on such tremendous power nor can they claim to promote democracy. Governments respond to them based on actual behavior. If subsidiaries are expropriated, parent corporations may suffer losses from which recuperation is not possible. Both logic and observation suggest that business is perhaps more likely than not to be neutral on political questions in Latin America, whereas the U.S. government is more likely than not to be interventionist. That is, it is in the self-interest of business to be nonconfrontational, whereas the U.S. government has only marginal need to get along with its weaker neighbors.

What has this to do with democracy? Perhaps not much. Businessmen on the whole do not "care" whether Latin America is democratic, dictatorial, or some place in between—or if they do care it does not usually affect their investment decisions. But is "caring" of the type represented by episodic, psychologically self-serving "democracy-promotion" programs much better, wedded as they seem to be to a related policy of controlling political change in the Western Hemisphere to our advantage? Sovereignty is not democracy, but it is clearly a prerequisite. The private sector may not have the answer for many things, but with respect to political neutrality it may have a better answer than does the U.S. government.

Notes

1. On the conflict between "republican virtues" and self-interest, see Gordon Wood, *Creation of the American Republic, 1776–1787* (New York: Norton, 1969), and Joyce Appleby, "What Is Still American in the Political Philosophy of Thomas Jefferson?" *William and Mary Quarterly* 39 (1982): 287–309.

2. Works written in this spirit include Lloyd Gardner, *The Economic Aspects of New Deal*

Diplomacy (Madison: University of Wisconsin Press, 1964); David Green, *The Containment of Latin America: A History of the Myths and Realities of the Good Neighbor Policy* (Chicago: Quadrangle Books, 1971); and Jerome Levinson and Juan de Onís, *The Alliance That Lost Its Way: A Critical Report on the Alliance for Progress* (Chicago: Quadrangle Books, 1970). For an exposition of the thesis that the Alliance for Progress failed largely because business ultimately had its way, see Abraham Lowenthal, "United States Policy toward Latin America: 'Liberal,' 'Radical,' and 'Bureaucratic' Perspectives," *Latin American Research Review* 8 (Fall 1973): 3–25; and Ruth Leacock, "JFK, Business, and Brazil," *Hispanic American Historical Review* 8, no. 4 (1979): 636–73.

3. See Thomas Carother's article in this volume. Ronald Reagan's Central American policy provides a good example of the appeal, and nearly independent life, of democracy rhetoric.

4. Joseph S. Tulchin, *The Aftermath of War: World War I and United States Policy toward Latin America* (New York: New York University Press, 1971), p. vi.

5. David Kennedy, *Over Here: The First World War and American Society* (New York: Oxford University Press, 1980), pp. 301–30. Also see Tulchin for a comprehensive overview of U.S. government–planned expansion into South America.

6. Tulchin.

7. A natural monopoly in this sense is any kind of economic activity in which there is normally or frequently only one producer or provider—that is, railroads, utilities, or extractive enterprises requiring investments of capital far beyond the reach of any but one or two of the best-equipped and financed corporations.

8. Tulchin, pp. 242–44; also see Joan Hoff Wilson, *American Business and Foreign Policy, 1920–1933* (Lexington: University of Kentucky Press, 1971), pp. 165–66.

9. A. Thomas Taylor to Edward G. Miller, May 19, 1952, p. 1. National Archives (NA), R.G. 59, Lot file 53D26, Office Files of the Assistant Secretary of State for Latin America, 1949–53, box 3, folder: "Business Advisory Council." Citation hereafter referred to as "Business Advisory Council."

10. Leo Welch to Miller, May 28, 1952, and Sam G. Baggett to Miller, June 4, 1952, "Business Advisory Council."

11. Quotation taken from letter of H. A. Davies to Edward Miller, May 12, 1952, p. 4. Also see letter of H. W. Balgooyen, May 20, 1952, p. 6, "Business Advisory Council."

12. Taylor to Miller, May 19, 1952, p. 3, and F. T. Magennis to George Wythe, p. 4, "Business Advisory Council."

13. Quotation, respectively, from Theodore Weiker, Jr., to Miller, May 12, 1952, p. 6, and H. A. Davies to Miller, May 12, 1952, p. 4, "Business Advisory Council."

14. W. Jack Butler, "Public Relations for Industry in Underdeveloped Countries," *Harvard Business Review* 30, no. 5 (September–October 1952): 64 and 69. For other articles calling for a new type of U.S. business presence abroad, see for example (all in *Harvard Business Review*): J. Anthony Panuch, "A Businessman's Philosophy for Foreign Affairs," 35, no. 2 (March–April 1957): 41–53; H. J. Dernburg, "Prospects for Long-Term Foreign Investment," 28, no. 4 (July 1950): 41–51; M. C. Conick, "Stimulating Private Investment," 31, no. 6 (November–December 1953): 104–12; W. Jack Butler, "Fighting Communism Overseas," 34, no. 4 (July–August 1956): 96–104; and Clifton R. Wharton, Jr., "Aiding the Community: A New Philosophy for Foreign Operations," 32, no. 2 (March–April 1954): 64–72. Also see "Foreign Aid without Tax Dollars," *Nation's Business*, July 1957, pp. 82–88.

15. See *Fortune*, November 1953, p. 114, for a summary of Humphrey's views as expressed during the fight over the Eximbank, in which he sought to diminish the bank's lending power and general authority.

16. Michael Hogan, "Corporatism: A Positive Appraisal," *Diplomatic History* X (Fall 1986): 365; Thomas McCormick, "Every System Needs a Center Sometimes," in Lloyd C.

Gardner, ed., *Redefining the Past: Essays in Diplomatic History in Honor of William Appleman Williams* (Corvallis: Oregon State University Press, 1986), pp. 201–6.

17. Dwight Eisenhower to Milton Eisenhower, December 1, 1954, p. 1. Fundação Getúlio Vargas (Rio de Janeiro), Centro de Pesquisa e Documentação, Eisenhower Library Documents, Code 3, 54.12.01.

18. Eisenhower used discretionary technical assistance funds provided by the Mutual Security Act of 1954 to start a "Public Safety Program" for training foreign police forces in order "to maintain internal security and to destroy the effectiveness of the Communist apparatus in the Western Hemisphere." ("U.S. Policy toward Latin America," National Security Council, August 20, 1956, p. 16; found in *Declassified Documents Reference System,* Carrollton Press, 1982, 333-B.) When the National Security Council established a new operating plan with regard to Latin America in 1956 ("NSC 5613"), the Public Safety Program became the core component in the new "Overseas Internal Security Program." Although Congress attempted to undercut the administration's support for repressive regimes by ruling in 1958 that "internal security requirements shall not normally be the basis for military assistance programs to American Republics," Eisenhower could legitimately claim that no *military* funds were being used for such purposes since the necessary funds were being taken from economic programs instead. For an account of Eisenhower's initiative in suggesting the police programs, see A. J. Langguth, *Hidden Terrors* (New York: Pantheon Books, 1978), p. 48. For the Congressional ruling on internal security programs, see the *Mutual Security Act of 1959,* U.S. Senate Committee on Foreign Relations (Washington, D.C.: U.S. Government Printing Office, 1959), p. 708.

19. According to Burton Kaufman, "The fact was that the White House had never been enthusiastic about any of the provisions for encouraging private investment abroad." Burton J. Kaufman, *Trade and Aid: Eisenhower's Foreign Economic Policy* (Baltimore: Johns Hopkins University Press, 1982), p. 158.

20. Percentages based on investment data for 1955 and 1960 in *Historical Statistics of the United States: Colonial Times to 1970* (Washington, D.C.: U.S. Government Printing Office, 1975), part 2, p. 870.

21. A. W. Zanzi, "$32 Billion Overseas Investment—Capital With a Mission," *The Magazine of Wall Street,* January 4, 1958, p. 442.

22. See "Corn Products Refining: Old Line Company in New Growth Phase," *The Magazine of Wall Street,* October 26, 1957, p. 152, and *Automobile Facts,* February–March 1955, p. 8.

23. Wharton, pp. 65, 72. For similar viewpoints, see Butler, Panuch, Dernburg, and Conick, cited previously. Also see Thomas Aitken, Jr., "The Double Image of American Business Abroad," *Harper's,* August 1960, pp. 12–22.

24. Conick, p. 107; Butler, "Public Relations," pp. 64, 69, 71.

25. See the author's dissertation on this subject, "'Good Works at a Profit': Private Development and United States–Brazil Relations, 1945–1960" (Ph.D. dissertation, Stanford University, 1988).

26. The Kaiser Corporation was frequently praised for its decision to invest in Latin America at all and for its role as a recruiter of foreign capital and technical assistance. See *Business Week,* October 9, 1952, p. 164; and June 21, 1958, p. 108. Also see *Washington Post,* October 10, 1954, editorial, and *Harper's,* August 1960, pp. 12–22.

27. See Butler, "Public Relations," p. 66, where he talks about IBEC; Wharton, p. 68, where he calls the Rockefeller's American International Association "the most outstanding project of all in the field of corporate giving abroad"; and Saville Davis et al., "The Struggle for Men's Minds Abroad," *Harvard Business Review* (July–August 1952): 129, in which Nelson Rockefeller is called "the most far-sighted businessman who has gone into Latin America . . . since the war." It is also noteworthy that, in his widely read *Manual of Corporate Giving* (Washington, D.C.: National Planning Association, 1952), editor Beards-

ley Ruml characterized the Rockefeller projects as the best example of "5% programs" abroad, and that the one article in the book on corporate philanthropy abroad focused on the work of the American International Association.

28. Quotation cited by Representative Lawrence H. Smith (Wisconsin) during the testimony of Nelson Rockefeller in Hearings Before the House Committee on Foreign Affairs, *International Cooperation Act of 1949 ("Point IV" Program)* (Washington, D.C.: U.S. Government Printing Office, 1950), p. 91.

29. Robert A. Packenham, *Liberal America and the Third World: Political Development Ideas and Social Science* (Princeton: Princeton University Press, 1973), esp. pp. 4–5, 199–210. For examples from the era of this outlook, see Max Millikan and Walt W. Rostow, *A Proposal: Key to An Effective Foreign Policy* (New York: Harper, 1957); John J. Johnson, *Political Change in Latin America: The Emergence of the Middle Sectors* (Stanford, Calif.: Stanford University Press, 1958); and David M. Potter, *People of Plenty: Economic Abundance and the American Character* (Chicago: University of Chicago Press, 1954).

30. Rockefeller's *Report on the Americas* has often been remembered as being an endorsement of military involvement in Latin American politics. In actuality, however, Rockefeller's report was considerably more philosophical and objective about such regimes than favorable toward them. Writing at the height of military dominance in Latin America, Rockefeller made the traditional argument of a diplomat: that the United States had to be pragmatic about the existence of governments with which it did not agree, should not isolate itself from them, and should look for and try to reinforce whatever reformist tendencies such regimes might exhibit. Rockefeller argued that military governments might have the one redeeming quality of bringing members of the middle and lower classes into power (and with them a greater social consciousness), but he also concluded that military regimes were ideologically less reliable than democratic, civilian governments and often more xenophobic. The report further emphasized, at the beginning and throughout, that the goal of the United States should be to "strengthen the forces of democracy." In any case, Rockefeller's stand was consistent both with the business code of neutrality and with his own predisposition—going as far back as his support for Peronist Argentina's admission to the United Nations in 1945—to place inter-American cooperation above conformity with U.S. ideological expectations. Nelson A. Rockefeller, *The Rockefeller Report on the Americas* (Chicago: Quadrangle Books, 1969), pp. 20, 31–33, 57–59, 144.

31. Edwin Martin to Lincoln Gordon, August 8, 1963, p. 1. John F. Kennedy Library, Jack Behrman Papers (hereafter JFK, Behrman Papers), box 1, file: "AID and Private Investment Correspondence, 9/63–12/63."

32. "Alliance for Progress," Foreign Policy Clearing House, Faculty Club of Harvard University, December 19, 1960, p. 8. JFK, Behrman Papers, box 1, file: "Alliance for Progress, Origins of the. Reports 1960."

33. Report from Rowland Burstan to Luther Hodges, Secretary of Commerce, on the Punta del Este Conference, August 5–20, 1961, p. 5. JFK, Behrman Papers, box 1, file: "Alliance for Progress, Origins of the. Correspondence."

34. Daniel Sharp, "The Private Sector and the Alliance," in L. Ronald Scheman, ed., *The Alliance for Progress: A Retrospective* (New York: Praeger, 1988), pp. 185–90.

35. Peter Nehemkis, Jr., "Private Investment and the Alliance for Progress," March 21, 1962, pp. 1, 9. JFK, Behrman Papers, box 2, file: "COMAP, Correspondence, 1962." Also see Nehemkis's book, *Latin America: Myth and Reality* (New York: Knopf, 1964). For other statements by executives encouraging an active and reformist role for business in the Alliance for Progress, see Jack Behrman's file, "Foreign Aid and Private Enterprise Correspondence, 1961–1962." JFK, Behrman Papers, box 7. For trade statistics cited, see Peter Grace to Jack Behrman, July 1, 1963, p. 9. JFK, Behrman Papers, box 3, file: "COMAP-Correspondence, 7/63–10/63."

36. Juscelino Kubitschek, "Report on the Alliance for Progress," June 1963, pp. 12, 13, 18. JFK, Behrman Papers, box 2, file with same title.

37. Felix Larkin (W. R. Grace and Co.) to Jack Behrman, March 5, 1963, pp. 1–2 of "informal meetings" summary. JFK, Berhman Papers, box 9, file: "Latin American Business Committee Correspondence, 2/6/63–3/15/63."

38. David Rockefeller, Speech to the Economic Club of Chicago, April 23, 1963, pp. 7–9, 12. JFK, Behrman Papers, box 3, file: "COMAP Correspondence, 3/63–5/63."

39. Franklin D. Roosevelt, Jr., to David Bell, December 2, 1963, pp. 1–10. JFK, Behrman Papers, box 1. The papers of David Bell also reveal the extent to which AID fought an increasingly losing battle against Congress in this period. See, in particular, box 23 of the Bell Papers at JFK.

40. JFK, Behrman Papers: Jack Behrman to Luther Hodges, July 2, 1963, p. 1, box 1, file: "AID Correspondence, 7/63–7/63"; and William Dentzer, Jr., to Jack Behrman, November 7, 1963, p. 1, box 3, file: "COMAP Correspondence, 11/63–12/63."

41. JFK, Oral-History Interviews with Roberto Campos (p. 54) and Lincoln Gordon (pp. 29–31 of Van Grasstek interview).

42. Michael J. Hogan, *The Marshall Plan: America, Britain, and the Reconstruction of Western Europe, 1947–1952* (Cambridge: Cambridge University Press, 1987), p. 140. With regard to the alliance's failure to recruit business support, see Sharp, p. 187.

43. See Lowenthal; and Levinson and Onís.

44. Interview with David Rockefeller, New York City, June 14, 1989.

45. Quote from Alice Lentz, Council of the Americas, New York City, June 14, 1989.

46. Memorandum on History of AACCLA (ca. 1975), p. 2. Obtained from AACCLA, Washington Office, file: "History, AACCLA (Misc.)."

47. Ibid., p. 4. Also see *AACCLA's Washington Letter* for August 4, 1975, September 4, 1975, November 26, 1975, December 29, 1975, and February 1977. AACCLA, Washington Office, file: "AACCLA Washington Letter, 1975–1979."

48. Quote from *AACCLA's Washington Letter,* June 25, 1976, p. 3. Also see October 15, 1975, p. 1, and May 21, 1976, p. 6. AACCLA, Washington Office, file: "AACCLA Washington Letter, 1975–1979."

49. *AACCLA Report,* vol. 8, no. 1 (November–April 1977–78): 3. Information on the U.S. Chamber of Commerce from Keith Miceli, Washington, D.C., June 22, 1989.

50. *AACCLA's Washington Letter,* September 3, 1976, p. 2; April–May 1977, p. 2; and September–October 1977, p. 3. AACCLA, Washington Office, file: "AACCLA Washington Letter, 1975–1979."

51. *AACCLA's Washington Letter,* November–December 1980, p. 1, and April 1980, pp. 1–2.

52. Conversation with Keith Miceli.

53. John F. H. Purcell, "The Perceptions and Interests of U.S. Business in Relation to the Political Crisis in Central America," in Richard E. Feinberg, ed., *Central America: International Dimensions of the Crisis* (New York: Holmes & Meier, 1982), pp. 107, 116, 122.

54. Ibid., pp. 110, 117, 122.

55. See, for example, Stephen Schlesinger and Stephen Kinzer, *Bitter Fruit: The Untold Story of the American Coup in Guatemala* (Garden City, N.Y.: Doubleday, 1982); Adalberto J. Pinelo, *The Multinational Corporation as a Force in Latin American Politics: A Case Study of the International Petroleum Company in Peru* (New York: Praeger, 1973); and "Multinational Corporations and United States Foreign Policy, Hearings on the International Telephone and Telegraph Company and Chile, 1970–1971," parts 1 and 2, U.S. Senate Committee on Foreign Relations (Washington, D.C.: U.S. Government Printing Office, 1973), hereafter referred to as Church Hearings.

56. On Guatemala, see Stephen Rabe, *Eisenhower and Latin America: The Foreign Policy of Anti-Communism* (Chapel Hill: University of North Carolina Press, 1988), and Richard

H. Immerman, *The CIA in Guatemala: The Foreign Policy of Intervention* (Austin: University of Texas Press, 1982). With regard to Peru and IPC, see Levinson and Onís, p. 160.

57. George C. Lodge, *Engines of Change: United States Interests and Revolution in Latin America* (New York: Alfred A. Knopf, 1970), pp. 295, 299.

58. Testimony of Enno Hobbing, Church Hearings, part I, p. 382.

59. Levinson and Onís, p. 160.

60. Testimony of Lyle Mercer, Kennecott Copper Corporation, and William Foster, Ralston Purina, Church Hearings, part I, pp. 320, 375.

61. E. J. Gerrity to H. S. Geneen, September 10, 1970, Church Hearings, part II, p. 595.

62. Testimony of James Greene, Manufacturers Hanover Trust, Church Hearings, part I, p. 361.

63. Testimony of George Clark, First National City Bank, Church Hearings, part I, pp. 343, 353.

64. Testimony of William Bolin, Bank of America (p. 385); William Ogden, Chase Manhattan Bank (p. 371); William Foster, Ralston Purina (p. 376); and Miles Cortez, IBM (p. 379). Church Hearings, part I.

65. Church Hearings, part I, pp. 353, 360–61, 376, 388.

66. See, for example, Levinson and Onís on ITT in Brazil (pp. 143–46) and letter from Don (last name not given) to Teodoro Moscoso, January 14, 1962, regarding political pressures exerted on Puerto Rico. JFK, Moscoso Papers, box 5, file: "Correspondence, 1/62–2/62." In Peru, ITT not only used questionable negotiating tactics with the local government, but attempted to cut a deal for itself at the expense of the North American IPC (Church Hearings, part I, pp. 200–201).

67. Angela M. Delli Sante, "The Private Sector, Business Organizations, and International Influence: A Case Study of Mexico," in *Capitalism and the State in U.S.–Latin American Relations,* ed. Richard R. Fagen (Stanford, Calif.: Stanford University Press, 1979), p. 362.

68. Ibid., pp. 370–77.

69. Ernest R. May, "The Alliance for Progress in Historical Perspective," *Foreign Affairs* (July 1963): 768.

6 | The Impact of U.S. Labor

Paul G. Buchanan

THE ROLE played by organized labor in the conduct of U.S. foreign policy has been a controversial aspect of U.S.–Latin American relations. Accused by the left of being imperialist agents dominated by obsessive anti-Communism and antinationalist perspectives that slavishly respond to the ideological, economic, and security concerns of U.S. government and business, North American labor has also been defended by government and labor leaders alike as a promoter of human rights, shop-floor democracy, equitable socioeconomic and political development, and pluralist labor relations throughout the globe. Since the field of labor relations and union politics can be considered an essential element of any democratic regime, and since promotion of democracy is the announced goal of the U.S. government's Latin American policy, U.S. labor's approach to these issues constitutes the crux of the question about its activities in the region.

This chapter explores the role played by U.S. organized labor in the U.S. government's Latin American policy, concentrating on its ideological and economic foundations, the vehicles and instruments utilized to further its ends, and the overall impact these have had on the prospects for democracy in the region.

Historical Background

U.S. labor's interest in Latin America began in the aftermath of the Spanish-American war. Concerned with potential competition from unorganized labor and craft guilds in the Philippines, Cuba, and Puerto Rico, in 1898 the American Federation of Labor (AFL) announced that it would support unionization efforts throughout the Western Hemisphere. AFL president

Samuel Gompers worked hard to promote the rise of AFL-affiliated unions in the former Spanish colonies, often in opposition to emergent unions that were nationalist, anarchist, or classist. This responded to a political view that saw foreign ideologies as threats to U.S. national security, and an economic view that saw Latin America as the preferred sphere of influence for U.S. capitalist expansion. Opposition on economic and political grounds to Latin American unions guided by different ideologies became a foundation of U.S. labor foreign policy, and was projected throughout the region during the next half century.

Following a series of talks between the AFL and the Confederación Regional de Obreros Mexicanos (CROM), the Pan American Federation of Labor (PAFL) was created in 1918 as a response to the regional activities of the Marxist Industrial Workers of the World (IWW). On matters of substance, the PAFL maintained a "policy squarely in harmony with the policies of the American Federation of Labor."[1] U.S. labor's interest in supporting Latin American labor organizations was thus based upon the latter's support for the AFL position on issues of mutual concern. In turn, U.S. labor initiatives in the region were from the beginning linked to U.S. government objectives.[2] According to Gompers, "the fundamental policy . . . pursued in organizing the Pan American Federation of Labor is based upon the spirit of the Monroe Doctrine, to establish and maintain the most friendly relations between the *governments* of the U.S. and Pan American countries."[3]

Gompers's death in 1924 heralded the end of the PAFL. Without the driving force of its main architect, the last PAFL congress, poorly attended, was held in 1930. The onset of the Great Depression forced a retrenchment of the U.S. union movement that shifted attention away from foreign affairs and led to a drop in AFL financial contributions to PAFL. Affiliated Latin American unions were unable to make up the difference created by the loss of U.S. funding, so PAFL languished. This allowed nationalist and classist sentiment to make inroads among Latin American unions during the interwar period. The anarchist Continental Workers Association (CWA) was established in 1928 as a regional branch of the International Workers Association (IWA). That same year the Latinamerican Union Confederation (LUC) was created as part of the Red Union International founded at the Third Communist International (1920). However, internal cleavages prevented either organization from consolidating, and both collapsed by the mid-1930s. Even so, their presence redoubled U.S. labor efforts to establish its presence in the Latin American union system.[4]

Opposition to independent unionism in Latin America took on special urgency for the AFL following the creation of the Congress of Industrial Organizations (CIO) in 1935. Comprised of a coalition of dissident and independent labor unions who challenged the conservative leadership of the AFL under George Meany, the CIO included anarchists and members of the Communist party. The Confederación de Trabajadores de América Latina

(CTAL) was established with CIO support in 1938 to replace the defunct PAFL. Since it affiliated with the IWW and later the Marxist-oriented World Federation of Trade Unions (WFTU), the AFL opposed CTAL as Communist.

At the same time that it struggled with the CIO on the domestic front, the AFL challenged CIO support for regional unions on issues such as the 1938 Mexican oil nationalization decree and solidarity with the labor opposition to the Mendieta dictatorship in Cuba. This weakened the AFL's position in the eyes of Latin American unionists while simultaneously strengthening that of the CIO. The CIO capitalized on its increased stature by creating a standing committee on Latin America in 1939 (the AFL created a Latin American Department in its International Affairs Office after World War II).

The outbreak of World War II renewed U.S. labor and government interest in Latin America, again out of a shared sense of political, security, and economic concerns extending beyond labor issues proper. The need to combat the fascist threat led U.S. labor and the government into a defensive tactical alliance with the socialist camp. The AFL and U.S. government reversed their positions of opposition to the IWW, CTAL, and other socialist or Communist organizations, and extolled their virtues as antifascist allies. The change in strategic outlook was formalized in 1943, with the creation of the Antifascist Latin American Labor Front, which included CTAL and representatives of U.S., British, and Soviet unions, as well as a host of non-CTAL-affiliated Latin American unions.

The need for tactical expediency did not prevent the AFL, with U.S. government support, from engaging in efforts to undermine CTAL at the very same time it was collaborating in the antifascist struggle. During the war years AFL representatives sponsored by the U.S. government traveled to Latin America to establish "back door" contacts with non-CTAL affiliated unionists, who later were included in travel exchanges with U.S. unions. From 1943 through 1947, a network of pro–United States Latin American unionists was cultivated as an alternative to CTAL and its affiliates. These efforts paved the way for an eventual split with CTAL once the antifascist front was victorious. At the same time, U.S. labor participation in the U.S. government foreign policy apparatus was formalized with the creation of labor attaché posts (most originally located in Latin America) and offices in the Departments of Labor and State that addressed issues of international labor policy, and which were often staffed by unionists.[5]

AFL cultivation of pro–United States union support bore fruit in 1948, when the Confederación Interamericana de Trabajadores (CIT) formed as an alternative to CTAL. A year later, the CIT allied itself with the anti-Communist world labor federation backed by the AFL known as the International Confederation of Free Trade Unions (ICFTU). After a brief dalliance with the WFTU (to which CTAL belonged), the CIO defected and joined the AFL at the creation of the ICFTU in 1949. This followed the purge of Marxists from the CIO begun in 1946 and carried out through the early 1950s, which preceded its unification with the AFL in 1955. Following the ICFTU mandate to promote regional organizations, CIT was reincorporated in 1951 as the Organización Regional Interamericana de Trabajadores (ORIT), becoming the ICFTU regional affiliate in Latin America. As was the case with the PAFL, ORIT was more an instrument of the AFL than a regional labor confederation, and in that capacity responded closely to the directives of the AFL's international affairs office.

Another postwar creation that helped promote U.S. labor interests abroad is the network of Free Trade Secretariats (FTS), world groupings of industrial unions arrayed by industrial sector or functional activity that act as international sounding boards for national union grievances. Headquartered in Europe and linked to the ICFTU, the FTS (later known as International Trade Secretariats or ITS) established Latin American offices in the mid-1950s. As with the ICFTU, the FTS/ITS network relied heavily on AFL-CIO affiliates for funding, making them very responsive to U.S. labor's economic and political interests in the region. Where ORIT focused on the national confederational level, the FTS's emphasis was at the level of sectoral or industry federations, complementing the broader thrust of ORIT policy. Their utility as a political instrument was underscored by U.S. Labor Department official George C. Lodge, who noted that "ITS flexibility, inner cohesion, and conviction make the Secretariats especially effective anti-Communist organizations in the so-called neutralist areas, and thus extremely important to U.S. objectives."[6]

Even so, in the 1960s U.S. government officials and labor leaders saw the need to create a purely North American–operated labor vehicle in order to combat more effectively Castroite infiltration of the Latin American labor movement. Concerned that Latin American representation within ORIT and the different FTSs created divisions over matters of policy that would hinder the formulation of an effective anti-Communist regional labor program, in 1962 the AFL-CIO founded the American Institute for Free Labor Development (AIFLD). On political and economic grounds AIFLD was held to reflect "the unique pluralism and consensus in American society: Labor-Government-Business."[7] Beyond institutionally promoting class collaboration, AIFLD was projected as the U.S. labor counterpart to ORIT and the FTSs, in which the North American approach to labor relations could be directly transmitted to Latin America through AIFLD field offices, educational programs, social projects, and extension facilities.

AIFLD's role grew throughout the 1960s. Superseding the activities of ORIT and the FTS/ITS network, "AIFLD became the principal instrument of the U.S. government for supplying technical assistance—education and training and social projects—to Latin American trade unions."[8] The extension of AIFLD's presence responded to the requirements of the Alliance for

Progress, which along with the export of counterinsurgency tactics and military assistance packages included labor-oriented projects as part of its socioeconomic development program. AFL-CIO president George Meany was appointed chairman of the Labor Advisory Committee (LAC) to the Alliance for Progress, which shaped the content of AIFLD's programmatic thrust in the region. Following LAC guidelines, AIFLD projects were implemented throughout the hemisphere in conjunction with U.S. government developmental programs administered by the Agency for International Development (AID), the Peace Corps, the International Development Bank, and other agencies involved in the Alliance for Progress.[9]

Although AIFLD influence among Latin American unions increased considerably throughout the 1960s, opposition to it also grew. In the United States, foreign policy divisions originated in the AFL-CIO over the issue of support for the Vietnam War. Walter Reuther, head of the Union of Autoworkers (UAW), publicly disagreed with George Meany's support for the war, and after withholding dues in protest, the UAW was suspended from the AFL-CIO in 1968.[10] In Latin America, AFL-CIO, AIFLD, and ORIT collaboration with the CIA in destabilizing labor-based elected regimes and supporting antilabor authoritarian regimes fostered serious opposition within Latin American union ranks. Reuther used revelations about these connections to challenge the foundation of the AFL-CIO's foreign policy, its bureaucratic and elitist orientation,[11] and Meany's leadership. The result was an erosion of regional support for ORIT and AIFLD activities beginning in the late 1960s, which coincided with a more general reappraisal of the U.S. role in world affairs in the age of superpower détente.

From the late 1960s through the 1970s, a series of developments outside of Latin America set the stage for a major shift in the AFL-CIO approach toward the region. In 1969 the AFL-CIO Board of Directors voted to withdraw from the ICFTU because of its alleged reapproachment with Communist unions and, more pointedly, because the ICFTU was considering the application for admittance of the dissident UAW. Since the ICFTU would not submit to the AFL-CIO's demands to harden its line on Communism and dismiss the UAW petition, the AFL-CIO eventually withdrew from the ICFTU. The AFL-CIO did not rejoin the ICFTU until 1982, and during the interim major changes occurred with the ICFTU that had a decided impact on ORIT.

The withdrawal of the AFL-CIO from both organizations removed their major sources of funding and ideological influence. In its absence, the ICFTU increasingly came under the influence of European Social and Christian Democratic thought, as these views gained credence in Europe and Latin America as a middle ground between Stalinism and reflexive U.S. anti-Communism. The emergence of this ideological middle road found echo in the political platforms of the Acción Democrática (AD) and Social Christian (Comite Organizativa Para Elecciones Independientes or COPEI) governments of Venezuela and the major Venezuelan labor confederation, the Confederación de Trabajadores Venezolanos (CTV), as well in the positions of various party and labor currents in and out of office in Costa Rica, Colombia, Ecuador, Peru, and Mexico.[12]

At the same time, AIFLD was forced to downscale many country programs in the face of charges that it was a CIA front. AIFLD's prestige was especially tarnished by congressional findings and press revelations that it was involved in the 1973 *golpe* that ousted Salvador Allende in Chile, following on earlier interventionist activities in the region.[13] Placed under the light of suspicion, AIFLD diminished its regional presence during the course of the 1970s, a process eased by the appearance of repressive military authoritarianism in many Latin American countries.

In the mid 1970s, in the wake of these critiques and confronted by a liberal Democratic administration, the AFL-CIO switched to a position of support for individual and collective freedoms, especially rights of association and judicial due process for persecuted labor unionists. The AFL-CIO endorsed the Carter administration's human rights policy, and AIFLD worked with the State Department to support the cause of imprisoned labor leaders in the Southern Cone and Central America. By the late 1970s and early 1980s the AFL-CIO advocated boycotts of Argentine, Chilean, and Uruguayan products, and lobbied hard for restrictions on military and economic assistance to these countries as well as the Central American autocracies.

The shift in AFL-CIO foreign policy perspective followed the traditional pattern of taking the lead from the U.S. government on issues of regional policy for reasons of tactical expediency, rather than as a result of a policy shift of a substantive nature. Even so, when a wave of (re)democratization swept the region in the 1980s, U.S. labor was in a position to reassert its ties to Latin American unions, even if ideological and practical reasons prevented it from doing so in the measure seen previously.

For one thing, the domestic position of U.S. labor had changed. With the advent of the Reagan administration, labor no longer enjoyed the political favor of the U.S. government. Economically, the recession of the late 1970s and early 1980s seriously weakened U.S. labor's structural power. In Latin America, the history of AFL-CIO regional involvement had clarified the nature of U.S. labor's economic and political objectives. These factors mitigated against the AFL-CIO reassuming a major role in hemispheric labor affairs in the reopened political climates of the 1980s. Even today, AIFLD influence is most strongly felt in the later-developing union movements of Central America, and least felt among the mature industrial unions of South America.

Because of the shifts in the U.S. political and economic landscape, there are signs of more durable change in U.S. labor's Latin American policy. AFL-CIO efforts to improve working conditions in Central America have assisted the rise of procedural democracies in the region during the past two decades. Cooperative programs, land reform and educational projects, sanitary assistance and training, plus other efforts coordinated by AIFLD, AID, and the Peace Corps, have promoted limited worker empowerment and some forms of economic and political emancipation in these countries. This was tragically underscored by the murder of two U.S. AIFLD land reform advisors by a right-wing death squad in San Salvador in 1981, a fact that shows that not only the left has reason to oppose AIFLD.[14]

As of the late 1970s, U.S. labor's influence on the U.S. government's Latin American policy and on regional labor organizations waned at the same time that it was forced to abandon its traditional foreign policy stance and adopt less interventionist and manipulative approaches toward labor relations and political issues in the region. The shifting international labor market and ideological climate at home, as well as political and economic realignments abroad, forced the AFL-CIO to reevaluate the ideological foundations of its foreign policy. With the decline of U.S. regional hegemony and the end of the cold war, the AFL-CIO has found it necessary to reconstruct a more flexible international vision in order to better serve its economic and political interests.

Ideological Bases of U.S. Labor's Latin American Policy

The ideological foundations of U.S. labor's Latin American policy can be disaggregated into two distinct perspectives. Although intertwined and reinforcing, U.S. labor's political and economic perspectives are examined separately before being reincorporated into a single ideological framework.

Political Perspective

The political basis for U.S. labor's foreign policy approach toward Latin America has its origins in the strategic posture outlined in the Monroe Doctrine.[15] U.S. labor traditionally viewed Latin America as part of the preferred sphere of influence of the United States, where U.S. economic, military, and political interests would take precedence. This view held that extrahemispheric attempts to make political and economic inroads in Latin America were dangerous to U.S. security. In that light, U.S. labor had a role to play in preventing external threats from finding root in the region's working classes. U.S. labor's political approach toward Latin America was therefore founded on a defensive premise: resistance to extrahemispheric political influences, specifically those of a "totalitarian" nature. This policy of opposition to extrahemispheric forces took on special importance during World War I, and was a major impetus for the creation of the PAFL. To the defensive, "antitotalitarian" political base was added concrete military security concerns about threats from the south instigated from abroad, an emphasis that continued uninterrupted for the next sixty years.

What shifted over time was U.S. labor's perception of the totalitarian threat. This paralleled U.S. government assessments of the global political-military balance, which lent to government-union political cooperation in the field of foreign policy in general, and issues of Latin American policy in particular. During World War I, the emphasis was on the threat of the Axis powers and the Bolsheviks; during the interwar years the focus was on Soviet Communism and its international expansion; from 1939 to 1945 the emphasis moved toward fighting European and Japanese fascism; and from 1946 to the present the thrust has been opposition to international Marxism-Leninism. On a secondary plane, U.S. labor and government have reacted equally adversely to nationalist-populist movements such as Peronism in Argentina, Vargism in Brazil, and, more recently, Noriega's military populist alliance in Panama.

Following its historical line, the AFL remained closely aligned with the foreign policy of the U.S. government throughout the interwar period, particularly during the Roosevelt administration. The CIO was divided between three ideological tendencies with different foreign policies. The right-wing faction adopted a political perspective much like that of the AFL. The left-wing current, comprised of Communist party members, adhered to the Soviet party line on matters of international affairs. The isolationist wing, headed by John L. Lewis, advocated a retreat from European affairs and a consolidation of U.S. ties with Latin America in the interests of securing a steady source of raw materials and a stable market for U.S. industry.[16]

Events on the continent in 1939 forced a shift in U.S. union strategic perspectives. That year the U.S.S.R. and Germany signed a nonaggression pact. The CIO left wing retreated from its previous position of support for a united front against fascism (which had included advocating a quarantine of Germany, Italy, and Japan), and moved to a position of isolationism and neutrality. This aligned the left wing with Lewis's isolationist bloc in the CIO, which lasted until mid-1941. During the course of 1939 and 1940, the increasing threat posed by Nazi aggression in Europe and Japanese militarism in Asia consolidated the alliance of the AFL and CIO right wing in support of the Roosevelt administration's antifascist efforts, with both groups steadily gaining membership support at the expense of the left-wing/isolationist bloc.

In 1940 the CIO right wing defeated Lewis and his supporters in elections for the CIO national leadership. In June 1941 Germany attacked the U.S.S.R., and the CIO left wing abandoned its policy of neutrality and isolationism in order to join the CIO right wing and AFL in calling for total support for war against the fascist powers. With the December 7, 1941, Japanese attack on Pearl Harbor, the last vestiges of isolationist sentiment were swept aside, and the three CIO currents joined with the AFL in support for the U.S. government's move to a war economy. This was done to preserve labor peace at home while fighting on the antifascist front abroad.[17]

After the war, the anti-Communist foundation of the AFL's Latin American policy was reaffirmed. The report of the Committee on International Relations at the 1946 National Convention warned that "we cannot exaggerate the vehemence and vigor with which the communists in Latin America have been conducting their campaign of vilification against the democratic ideals and the champions of the democratic way of life."[18] By "champions of the democratic way of life" the AFL was presumably referring to the U.S. government and labor, since at the time democratic regimes in the region were few and far between. AFL regional activities were consequently directed toward promoting divisions within CTAL so that there would emerge an anti-Communist consensus in support of the "eventual organization of an inter-American labor body composed of free, independent, democratic unions."[19]

Support for democracy and "free" trade unionism was in this fashion introduced as a labor foreign policy objective, but remained tied to a defensive, anti-Communist perspective that saw the eradication of the Marxist threat as the foremost foreign goal of the United States, something especially important on the international labor front. With the purge of Marxists from the CIO and its merger with the AFL, U.S. labor foreign policy coalesced around the anti-Communist objective.

The Truman administration responded strongly to labor's calls for anti-Communist action in Latin America. In 1946 the U.S. government proposed the establishment of military training and exchange programs involving U.S. and Latin American armed forces, an act that paved the way for the establishment of the Inter-American Defense Treaty of 1949. This followed an AFL vilification campaign that accused State Department officials of Communist sympathies, and which resulted in a reorganization in the State Department so as to better align its Latin American and labor branches with the thrust of AFL policy.[20]

In addition to Communism, ideologies such as national populism greatly concerned U.S. policy makers of the time. John Foster Dulles was quoted as saying that "nationalism is the doorway to communism,"[21] a view reaffirmed in the 1960s by AIFLD, which claimed that Communists used "so-called 'national liberation' in a way such that social revindications give way to anti-U.S. action."[22] This view reflected good insight into the thrust of postwar Marxist revolutionary strategy (since both Marxist-Leninist and Maoist thought held that the best form of making a revolution was via a nationalist, anti-imperialist war that could later open the doors to socialist control), but failed to understand the precise nature of nationalist sentiment in many Latin American countries, which was anything but Marxist-inspired. Moreover, it subordinated support for democratic institutions to the lesser evil and relativist dictates of the "antitotalitarian" logic. Anti-Marxist and antinationalist views, not an interest in democracy per se, thus converged to form a "prodemocratic" or "free" U.S. labor foreign policy perspective that was oriented toward steering the Latin American masses away from totalitarian beliefs, indigenous and foreign.

The Cuban Revolution magnified U.S. fears that Marxism was gaining ground in Latin America. AIFLD official William Doherty voiced this alarm in 1966, testifying that "in Latin America, the key question of our times is the future road of their revolution: Toward Communist totalitarianism or toward democracy. For the American labor movement this is one of the paramount, pivotal issues; all other questions . . . must remain secondary. This is the direct challenge confronting free trade unionists."[23] Given the ideological consensus on the part of the U.S. labor leadership, business groups, and the federal government, it was easy for them jointly to advocate international programs that would include anti-Communist union promotion as part of "democratization" efforts.

The conservative political thrust of the AFL-CIO's Latin American policy continued until the mid-1970s. At that time, shaken by the compound effects of Watergate, the Vietnam War, revelations of AFL-CIO involvement in CIA activities in Latin America and elsewhere, and the sequels to the Meany-Reuther clashes over foreign policy, many affiliate unions began to question the legitimacy and utility of the traditional position.[24] Changes in the U.S. economy, particularly in the composition of the unionized work force via the growth of service unions and entrance of women and minorities into the labor market, gave added voice to the foreign policy debate within the AFL-CIO. These differences came to a head after a wave of military-bureaucratic authoritarianism swept South America in the 1960s and 1970s, where AIFLD complicity in their rise was not rewarded with the establishment of "free" and "democratic" unions, but with the wholesale repression of unions in general, regardless of ideological identification (a situation that many U.S. firms took advantage of, having favorably assessed the investment opportunities provided by such "docile" labor climates).

Differences over foreign policy within the AFL-CIO were recently seen with regard to U.S. Central American policy, and were openly voiced during the 1985 and 1987 AFL-CIO conventions. The 1985 debate was the first public floor discussion of a foreign policy issue at an AFL-CIO convention, and in 1987 over 50 percent of the membership opposed the federation's Central American policy platform. Bureaucratic rationales underpinning the foreign policy agenda of the AFL-CIO must now be defended before a more heterogeneous and independent membership, which in turn has forced the AFL-CIO foreign policy hierarchy to open up to new sources of rank-and-file input and compromise on several issues.[25]

Confronted by internal and external pressures for change, in the 1980s U.S. labor began to adopt a more flexible political approach toward Latin American labor relations, recognizing that ideological diversity in the union movement was a major source of sustenance for many of the new democratic regimes. This was particularly the case with Christian Democratic and Social Democratic ORIT affiliates associated with parties in government or in majority opposition. U.S. labor Latin American policy now downplays anti-Communism in favor of a more explicit prodemocratic position centered on support for the institutionalization of International Labor Organization (ILO) sponsored labor relations frameworks that recognize union ideological pluralism as a political good. This has led to the renewal of AFL-CIO involvement in ORIT; direct collaboration with leftist unions on matters of common interest, such as the Chilean plebescite of 1988; and a shift in emphasis within AIFLD toward projects that promote democratization of national labor relations systems.

> The outlook and purpose of the American labor movement's international work . . . rest on the belief that workers must have the right to organize for a measure of control over the conditions of their work. This means they must have the right to strike, and that they must have the right to express themselves politically, for what is won in bargaining can be taken away by the state. For labor there is only one standard for human rights. All people must have the freedom to create, organize, and control their own organizations and institutions independent of the state.[26]

The restatement of labor's vision of the world carries with it a renunciation of the isolationist stance that periodically is resurrected within the rank and file, as well as of the relativist or lesser-evil approaches of the past. According to the AFL-CIO, the achievement of a stable U.S. foreign policy based on the principles mentioned remains in doubt so long as the anti-totalitarian mentality dominates Washington. "Regretfully, such a foreign policy remains only an aspiration. Too often American foreign policy swings widely from reactive interventionism and paralyzing isolationism, between grandiose rhetoric and feeble performance. This disarray in purpose and execution has been all too apparent in the Reagan Administration."[27]

The labor critique extended to U.S. domestic affairs.

> The struggle for democracy abroad is not served by undermining democracy at home. The AFL-CIO is alarmed and repelled by the actions of some officials in the Reagan administration to circumvent the law and lie to Congress while attempting to fund the Nicaraguan contras. . . . We urge the Reagan administration to pursue in good faith a diplomatic rather than military solution to the conflict [in Central America] within the framework of the Guatemala Plan [signed by the five Central American presidents on August 7, 1987], that will provide for guarantees of democratic freedoms along with a halt to outside aid to all armed opposition groups.[28]

The altered AFL-CIO position on Latin America, particularly its reapproachment with leftist and nationalist unions around the issue of democratic institutionalization, for the first time in the postwar era placed it seriously at odds with the political orientation of the official U.S. foreign policy apparatus.[29]

After years of allowing myopic and reflexive antitotalitarianism to dictate its political approach toward labor developments in Latin America, U.S. labor has recently shifted toward a more neutral and flexible prodemocratic stance. The promotion and guarantee of freedom of association and political representation is the announced center of U.S. labor's Latin American policy, following the more general shift of the U.S. government foreign policy position on democratization.

Economic Perspective

The structural features of U.S. trade unionism are summarized by Robert F. Hoxie:

> The dominant philosophy of the American labor movement has been business unionism . . . a trade union movement which is essentially trade conscious, rather than class conscious. That is to say, it expresses the viewpoint and interests of the workers in a craft or industry rather than those of the working class as a whole. It aims chiefly at more, here and now, for the organized workers of the craft or industry, in terms mainly of higher wages, shorter hours, and better working conditions, regardless for the most part of the welfare of workers outside the particular organic group, and regardless in general of political and social considerations, except insofar as they bear directly upon its own economic ends. It is conservative in the sense that it professes belief in natural rights and accepts as inevitable, if not as just, the existing capitalistic organization and the wage system, as well as existing property rights and the binding force of the contract. It regards unionism mainly as a bargaining institution and seeks its ends chiefly through collective bargaining.[30]

Business unionism is oriented toward class collaboration rather than class conflict, the latter serving as the philosophical base for "revolutionary," "militant," or "classist" syndicalism tied to Marxist ideologies. Unlike its radical counterparts, business unionism adopts a cooperative rather than confrontational premise that views capitalism as a public good rather than a social cost. The objectives here are to lower the level of exploitation and increase the material bases of working-class consent, not to question the private ownership of the means of production.

The apolitical nature of U.S. business unionism was quite transparent in the area of foreign relations, given its antitotalitarian focus. Beyond this political orientation lie the material interests that underride U.S. labor's ideological perspective on foreign policy. U.S. labor interest in promoting North American-style business unionism in Latin America stems from the economic interest in securing raw materials and expanding markets for U.S. goods. A modern means of expanding markets for U.S. goods is through "trickle-down" increases in working-class wages in importing countries. The promotion of business unionism involving procapitalist labor agents in foreign extractive industries and component manufacturers also ensures a steady supply of the raw materials and parts required for the production of U.S. finished goods. As consumers of U.S. goods, both North American labor and organized workers of U.S. trading partners have a vested interest in insuring the uninterrupted flow of foreign inputs to the United States. This helps maintain high levels of union employment and wages in domestic manufacturing industries, U.S. labor's historic bastion.

Labor leaders, government officials, and the corporate community see extension of the U.S. export market as essential for domestic prosperity and political stability. Controlled promotion of business rather than classist unionism was traditionally viewed as a means for incrementally increasing working-class wages and consumption within capitalist frameworks both in Europe and Latin America, opening input and output markets dependent on U.S. prosperity.[31] According to Walter Reuther, "It is in our self-interest in terms of providing a market for finished goods from American industries, a market for goods manufactured by American workers, to see the living standards of others raised—to see their own indigenous economies developed and strengthened."[32] The 1946 AFL convention anticipated this view.

> Production and prosperity in the U.S. depend to a very large extent on our ability to secure, through fair and square international trade and commerce with our Latin American neighbors, certain vital raw materials. Similarly the improvement of the working and living conditions of the Latin American peoples are, in large measure, dependent upon their ability and readiness to supply us with these materials and at the same time to develop their own countries' modern industrial techniques and skills.[33]

After World War II, an additional strategic concern was added to this structural perspective. "We must also remember that many raw materials come from the underdeveloped countries of the world, areas threatened by the Soviet sphere of influence. If they were under Soviet control, our industries would be hard pressed to continue full production at all."[34] The preoccupation echoed concerns voiced earlier. In 1939, John L. Lewis remarked that "Central and South America are capable of absorbing all of our excess and surplus commodities. . . . Obviously, increased trade volume with the Latin American countries would lead to improved political and cultural relationships and make for increased security for the United States when the day comes that some imperialistic foreign power challenges the Monroe Doctrine."[35]

Beyond its view of the proper role of unions, U.S. labor's economic perspective on Latin America was based on unequivocal support for capitalism in general, and for U.S. business investment abroad in particular. Regional development was to be exclusively pursued within capitalist market frameworks, using U.S. private investment and U.S. government economic assistance as the preferred vehicles for promoting economic change. This perspective came to be known as Wall Street internationalism.

No alternate form of economic structure, be it socialist (even democratic socialist), or endogenously controlled state capitalism, satisfied the requirements of this vision. Both jeopardized the repatriation of business profits in the United States, and therefore threatened the material interests of organized U.S. workers. The structural dependence of organized labor on U.S. capital gave it a vested stake in the private pursuit of profit abroad. Material interest dictated that U.S. labor adopt antisocialist and antinationalist postures in Latin America on economic as well as ideological grounds, since limitations on U.S.-dominated capitalist development abroad diminished labor rewards at home.

Traditionally, the primary Latin American policy objective of U.S. labor was to help promote stable investment climates in which U.S. business profitability was protected. Despite rhetorical championing, political preoccupation with promoting democratic institutions was subordinated to this structural logic. The promotion of anti-Communist business unionism was consequently seen as a means of insuring that working-class demands remained within the confines of "bread and butter" issues resolvable by U.S.-dominated capitalist development, since the attendant logics of labor collective action would not threaten the profitability of U.S. investors upon which U.S. union wages depended.

As with its political perspective, the AFL-CIO economic perspective has changed. The realities of economic competition in the late twentieth century forced a reappraisal of the basic tenets of Wall Street internationalism. U.S. foreign investment no longer necessarily brings with it domestic prosperity. To the contrary, it has spurred capital flight leading to "runaway jobs," a process by which U.S. factories shut down, unionized employees are dismissed, and employers move abroad in search of cheaper labor costs and less restrictive employment climates (in terms of occupational safety, worker benefits, and employment stability). In addition, foreign countries with repressive labor policies, where standard rights of association, petition, and grievance are curtailed along with wage rates, social services, and other public goods, pose an increasing threat to U.S. workers in the form of competition in trade waged on the backs of exploited foreign workers. With this in mind, U.S. labor has sought to include "trade with justice" and "social" clauses in U.S. trade legislation and international trade standards.[36]

The AFL-CIO opposes U.S. business investment that it considers exploitative and constrictive of labor rights abroad. Two examples of phenomena that U.S. labor opposes are the *maquiladora* assembly plants on the northern Mexico border and employer-created "company" unions known as *solidarismo* associations in Central America. In the maquiladora program, U.S.-based firms have established labor-intensive assembly operations in Mexican border towns, importing U.S.-made components from parts warehouses on the U.S. side, exporting the finished product back to the United States. Low transportation rates, coupled with dramatically reduced labor costs of a predominantly female labor force unorganized and subject to high turnover rates in an environment of pervasive unemployment, make the "twin plant" phenomenon an attractive option for labor intensive manufacturers.

The AFL-CIO is pledged to resist the export of jobs to the maquiladoras. According to a 1987 AFL-CIO policy statement,

> A sincere, long-term strategy for making the jobs of American workers more secure does not include racing to a foreign country to take advantage of cheap labor. There can be no shortcuts to "competitiveness" by employing low-wage workers in Mexico in jobs that perpetuate rather than relieve their poverty because of pitifully low wages. Production for export in Mexico does nothing to increase the goods available to Mexican workers that would allow them to raise their living standards.[37]

Company-created "workers associations" and "alternative unions" pose another threat. The principle of these solidarismo associations is simple: workers give up the right to strike over pay and working conditions in exchange for company-determined representation and employer-provided benefits. For U.S. labor, such "yellow" or "company" unions are extremely dangerous not only to working-class interests, but to democracy in the region as a whole. Hence the AFL-CIO had added its opposition to this type of employee association to its long-standing opposition to government-controlled unions.[38]

Promotion of autonomous trade unionism abroad is now seen by the AFL-CIO as an essential step toward evening out gross imbalances in the global labor market otherwise encouraged by such capitalist practices, thereby preserving union employment and wages at home. This places the AFL-CIO at odds with sectors of the U.S. government foreign policy establishment and business community who see the solidarismo movement in a positive light because of its docile anti-Communist, probusiness nature.[39]

The AFL-CIO has also begun to promote the regional use of Employee Stock Option Plans (ESOPs). Making workers co-owners (even if a minority) of the firms in which they are employed is believed to increase their stake in the company's success, as it makes a more direct link between individual worker productivity and overall profitability. It also gives the worker a voice in management decisions, which reinforces individual involvement in the productive process. The concept of joint worker ownership through stock options has gained credence in the United States, although not without some labor skepticism. That is because in many instances ESOPs have been used to break unions rather than strengthen their stake in the productive process. On the other hand, under certain guidelines (specifically, union control of ESOPs), organized labor has found ESOPs to be a beneficial way of maintaining employment, practicing wage restraint, increasing productivity, and expanding worker benefits.

AIFLD proposals outlining the use of ESOPs in Central America include a maximum of 60 percent employee ownership in order to encourage private business collaboration, the use of private management as sources for expertise, the need for worker education as part of the process, the solicitation of government support, the separation of union functions from board of director or management functions, and other labor participatory resources.[40] AID has supported these efforts by issuing a directive to its field offices to encourage broadening of the ownership stake of workers in national economic development.[41] The promotion of ESOPs in Latin America by the AIFLD thus responds to a logic Elizabeth Cobb, elsewhere in this volume, ascribes to progressive U.S. business interests when promoting joint ventures with Latin American investors: a share in the company is the economic equivalent of a vote in the political process, enfranchising the worker at the point of production in a fashion comparable with voter registration in electoral systems.[42]

This is a far cry from the days when the unqualified probusiness mentality pervaded U.S. labor's economic thought. The lessons of the past and the economic challenges of the present and future have forced the AFL-CIO to rephrase its foreign economic policy. Although this economic perspective is ultimately grounded in the defense of worker material interests at home, its reorientation has permitted U.S. labor to play a more productive role promoting the institutionalization of democratic labor relations systems in Latin America.

The Integrated Perspective

Schematically, the traditional perspective underriding U.S. labor's Latin American policy can be represented in the following series: from capitalism, to business unionism, to antitotalitarianism, to a pro–United States position. This progression helps explain why U.S. labor activities in Latin America have seldom advanced the cause of union or political democracy, although they sometimes did improve the material well-being of cooperative unionists. The conflict between U.S. labor material interests and the normative concern with democracy was resolved in favor of support for capitalism over democracy because U.S. labor's material interests were guaranteed by the former, not the latter. Anything that opposed U.S.-led capitalist expansion in Latin America was consequently regarded by U.S. labor, capital, and the government alike as a threat to the welfare and security of the United States.

The foreign policy perspective of U.S. labor should not be surprising. The incorporation of organized labor as a subordinate partner in the U.S. foreign policy establishment fulfills a condition for the maintenance of democratic capitalist hegemony in the United States. The postwar experience has shown that under conditions of advanced monopoly capitalism, organized labor is incorporated, via material and political concessions and inducements, in an alliance with the state and capital in order to guarantee the economic stability needed for consensual political reproduction.[43] The bases of working-class consent to this incorporation are material and ideological: higher standards of living measured in wages, benefits, and the like, in increasing measure derived from corporate profits made abroad, exchanged for class collaboration (and subordination) on foreign policy approaches that deny the material and political interests of workers abroad. In this sense, U.S. labor has been a conservative foreign policy actor. It has sought to conserve its organizational privileges and prerogatives at home at the expense of workers elsewhere.[44]

AFL-CIO president George Meany well understood the basic point: "You can't dictate to a country from any angle at all unless you control the means of production. If you don't control the means of production, you can't dictate. Whether you control them through ideological methods or control them through brute force, you must control them."[45] This is the ideological foundation of the imperialist labor aristocracy criticized in the Marxist literature.[46]

During the last fifteen years U.S. labor has been forced to modify this perspective in light of changed international and domestic realities. Sobered by the results of previous forms of intervention and the changed political and economic conditions of the international system, U.S. labor tempered its strategy and broadened its ideological perspective on Latin America. The AFL-CIO now accepts the notion that working-class consent is essential for successful capitalist reproduction both at home *and* abroad, regardless of stage of development or specific location in the global network.

This shift finds its economic foundation in the worsening condition of organized labor in the United States during the past decade. The reorganization of the U.S. productive apparatus undertaken in the 1980s resulted in the structural weakening of organized labor, paralleling the harsher antilabor measures associated with the implementation of monetarist economic policies throughout Latin America in the 1970s. Strategic weakening gave material foundation to the decrease in political influence U.S. labor was able to wield in the area of domestic and foreign policy. The neoclassical tenets underpinning the Reagan administration's structural transformation project were complemented by a political approach that was overtly antilabor in nature (again, paralleling the exclusionary labor policies of modern Latin American authoritarians).

The reassertion of U.S. government's procapital stance and the shift in the U.S. economic nucleus from heavy industry to high technology and services responded to the competitive exigencies of the evolving international market. The move was facilitated by enforcement of legislation that authorized firing of strikers and "right to work" (no closed shop) statutes at the state level, and which eased bankruptcy reorganization schemes that permitted union busting at the federal level. The political dimension of the Reagan administration's antilabor campaign exploited public antipathy toward the hierarchical, bureaucratic, inefficient, and uncompetitive traits of the U.S. labor movement, and was evident in the composition and rulings of the National Labor Relations Board during the 1980s.

At the level of production, elimination of Taylorist and Fordist productive schemes was countered by cutbacks in employer-provided benefits, real wages, and an increasing recomposition of the work force within a general picture of union membership decline and loss of jobs in traditional industries. Shifts in union membership toward service industries with large female, black, and Hispanic memberships, coupled with the gradual appreciation of class-based solidarity on the part of North American workers placed on the defensive and increasingly forced to shoulder the burden of sacrifice imposed by the structural transformation of U.S. capitalism, helped to force a general reevaluation of U.S. labor's economic and political platforms.

In the 1980s belief in U.S. labor benefit through foreign trade fell hard in the face of an increasingly complex and interdependent international division of labor, with U.S. unions forced to wage a defensive struggle for the preservation of wages and jobs at home. As a result of adverse labor market conditions and the antilabor domestic political climate of the 1980s, U.S. labor began to accept the legitimacy of certain types of nonbusiness unionism and the need for constraints on U.S. investment in Latin America. It did so not because it believed in national self-determination or the autonomous political role of the labor movement in dependent capitalism, but because it believes that increased unionization and class militancy, coupled with union political activity under democratic frameworks, can deter firms from investing abroad or force them to operate under conditions similar to those of the United States, thereby balancing the international labor market equation. Material self-interest in a changing world economy, not altruism, prompted U.S. labor to shift its Latin American policy toward selectively working with nationalist or socialist unions on projects of democratic institution building in the areas of labor relations and national political participation. This has added flexibility to U.S. labor's posture in the region after years of reactive anti-Communist orthodoxy, although its self-interest remains apparent.

Vehicles and Instruments of U.S. Labor's Latin American Policy

U.S. labor has used several vehicles and instruments to promote its Latin American policy objectives. These include union to union bilateral exchanges, regional organizations such as the PAFL, ORIT, and the Free Trade Secretariats; quasi-public agencies such as AIFLD, public agencies such as AID, the International Relations Division of the U.S. Department of Labor, and the Office of International Labor Affairs of the U.S. Department of State (to which are attached labor attachés stationed abroad), and the CIA; regional organizations such as the Organization of American States and the Inter-American Development Bank (IDB); international organizations such as the International Labor Office and its Latin American regional affiliate, the Confederación Interamericana de Administratión de Trabajo (CIAT); and nongovernmental agencies such as human rights organizations, solidarity groups, and religious organizations. The instruments used by these vehicles have incorporated material and nonmaterial resources including educational, welfare, and housing programs; organizational assistance; legal and technical advice; loan, grant, credit, and other financial aid packages; union salary allowance support; and direct payouts in the form of bloc allocations of a discretionary or covert nature. This section highlights some of the more salient vehicles utilized by U.S. labor in pursuit of its Latin American foreign policy objectives.

ORIT

ORIT was created as the ICFTU-affiliated, anti-Communist regional labor confederation through which anti-Communist business unionism could be promoted in Latin America. As the ICFTU regional affiliate, ORIT nominally receives its policy guidance and funding from that organization. However, the AFL-CIO presence in ORIT was very strong from the beginning, and despite having Latin Americans in many leadership positions, ORIT remains largely dependent upon the AFL-CIO for both direction and financial sustenance. Half of ORIT's 25 million affiliates belong to the AFL-CIO.[47] Since delegate representation is proportional, with 16 million members the AFL-CIO continues to hold a majority position in ORIT executive committees. With under 3 million affiliates, the next largest delegations from Mexico, Canada, and Argentina lag far behind in representation in the ORIT hierarchy.

In 1980 ORIT included twenty-four national labor confederations and 38 percent of the unionized work force in Latin America, compared with thirteen confederations and 20 percent for the Christian Democratic, Confederación Latino Americano de Sindicalistas Cristianos–Confederación Latino Americano de Trabajadores (CLASC-CLAT), ten confederations and 16 percent for the Cuban-sponsored Comite Para la Unificación Sindical de Trabajadores Latino Americanos (CPUSTAL), and seventeen independent confederations covering 26 percent of the organized proletariat. The biggest labor confederations in Latin America, the Mexican Confederación de Trabajadores Mexicanos (CTM) and the Argentine Confederación General de Trabajo (CGT), are ORIT affiliates, as are the AFL-CIO, Canadian Labor Confederation (CLC), and numerous other labor federations.[48]

ORIT's primary source of funding is the ICFTU, although over half of the ICFTU funds in turn comes from the AFL-CIO and several non-union sources, including U.S. government agencies and international organizations.[49] Direct AFL-CIO grants to ORIT continue to be sizable. In 1985 and 1986 the AFL-CIO provided over $100,000 directly to ORIT. Even now, with a downscaled AFL-CIO presence in the ORIT directorate, it still contributes nearly two-thirds of the ORIT budget through direct or indirect grants, with the remainder largely derived from the Canadian CTC, the Venezuelan CTV, and the Mexican CTM.

The creation of AIFLD undermined AFL-CIO support for the ORIT mission. Where in the 1950s it received the bulk of AFL-CIO funds directed toward Latin America, funding for ORIT after 1961 was reduced while that of AIFLD rose.[50] Disagreements with ICFTU comptroller regulations led to additional AFL-CIO cutbacks to the ICFTU in the latter half of the 1960s, increasing ORIT's financial dependence on the AFL-CIO at the same time the overall scope of its activities were being reduced or subordinated to those of AIFLD.

Originally headquartered in Havana, ORIT moved to Mexico City after the 1959 Cuban Revolution. Its major activities are oriented toward union education programs. In 1951 it began a trade union school at the University of Puerto Rico, and in 1962 it founded a trade union institute in Cuernavaca, Mexico. When the CTM assumed control of the Cuernavaca Institute for its own "superior syndical education school" in the 1970s, ORIT's training facilities were moved to Guatemala and Costa Rica, where they remain. It runs courses and seminars on the role and function of "free" unions, the organizational necessities of peasants and women, and collective bargaining. In this it has collaborated with outside agencies such as the Alliance for Progress and UNESCO. Yet here again the creation of AIFLD seriously curtailed ORIT activities, as AIFLD educational programs duplicated and eventually replaced many of those initially offered by ORIT.

In the 1950s and 1960s, ORIT drew heavily upon the AFL-CIO and AIFLD for its leadership.[51] The interchange between AIFLD and ORIT positions was commonplace, with individuals moving smoothly from one agency to the other without having to redefine objectives or mission. As a result, ORIT had no independent voice in the formulation and implementation of regional labor projects, but was used instead by the U.S. foreign policy apparatus as a semiautonomous implementary agency. According to a U.S. Senate study, this was a major cause of its diminished prestige in the 1960s.

> More fundamental, perhaps, has been the tendency of ORIT to support U.S. Government policy in Latin America. ORIT endorsed the overthrow of the Arbenz regime in Guatemala and of the Goulart regime in Brazil. It supported Burnham over Cheddi Jagan in Guyana, and it approved the U.S. intervention in the Dominican Republic. To many Latin Americans, this looks like ORIT is an instrument of the U.S. State Department.[52]

In the 1970s, with the infusion of social democratic thought and funding, ORIT began to establish an autonomous identity as a regional labor group. It redefined its mission as prodemocratic and political rather than apolitical and anti-Communist. At its tenth congress in 1981 the ORIT directorate revised its charter to reflect this new orientation, putting distance between its activities and those of AIFLD, the AFL-CIO, and the U.S. government. This helped restore ORIT's credibility in the eyes of Latin American labor while decreasing its utility as a U.S. labor instrument, although ideological battles between Social Democratic "reformers" and pro-AFL-CIO "traditionalists" continue within it to this day.

AIFLD

AIFLD was founded in August 1961 as a private, nonprofit corporation. Its formal objectives were listed as "assisting in the development of free, democratic trade union structures in Latin America through labor leader training centers and social development programs in such fields as housing, worker's banks, credit unions, consumer and producer cooperatives and related socio-economic activities."[53] The probusiness orientation of AIFLD was explicit from the start. According to a member of its original board of directors, "AIFLD urges cooperation between labor and management and an end to class struggle. It teaches workers to help increase their company's business and to improve productivity so that they can gain more from an expanding business. It also demonstrates in a very concrete fashion that workers can have better living conditions within the framework of a free, democratic, and capitalist society."[54] Testifying in 1967 on AIFLD's relationship with the U.S. firms operating in the region, William Doherty (current AIFLD executive director) stated that "we are collaborating with the Council on Latin America, which is made up of the primary U.S. business institutions that have activities in that area. Our collaboration takes the form of trying to make the investment climate more attractive and more inviting to them."[55]

AIFLD recently redefined its mission so that it includes strengthening democratic trade unionism in Latin America, fostering self-reliant and independent hemispheric unions, and thus making trade unionism a powerful force for democratic development and social change. It affirms that strong and democratic unions are necessary to give voice to legitimate demands of workers in Latin America and the Caribbean, as they are believed to contribute to the sectoral pluralism AIFLD maintains is essential for the full development of democracy. According to this view, where workers are denied voice through their unions in the political, social, and economic decisions that affect their lives, democracy itself is at risk. Promotion of democratic labor relations institutions, rather than procapitalist anti-Communism, is now AIFLD's announced foreign policy objective.[56]

In line with its collaborative nature, AIFLD's first board of trustees reflected a tripartite character, with twenty-one labor representatives (including the AFL-CIO president, who doubles as AIFLD president, and eleven Latin American union leaders), four business representatives, and five members drawn from various professions. Business representation on the board was taken from U.S. corporations represented in the Council on Latin America, including W. R. Grace, United Fruit, Pan American World Airways, Anaconda, Kennecott Copper, Bristol Myers, Johnson and Johnson, Monsanto, Union Carbide, Gulf Oil, Mobil Oil, ITT, IBM, several banks, and various Rockefeller family holdings. In 1980, after much criticism of the business presence in AIFLD, coupled with increased differences between the business and labor representatives over the direction of AIFLD policy, employer representatives abandoned the board. AIFLD is now a bipartite labor-government venture in foreign policy implementation, with an increased Latin American unionist presence on its twenty-five-member board of trustees. This helped ease Latin American fears that AIFLD was merely a U.S. business front.

Headquartered in Washington, D.C., in space provided by the Communications Workers of America (CWA), AIFLD has at one time or another established offices in virtually every Latin American country. From time to time AIFLD has been forced to close its field offices, either because it was expelled by the local government (Peru, 1971; El Salvador, 1973; Nicaragua, 1980; Panama, 1988) or because conditions become too hazardous to operate effectively (Argentina, 1974; Colombia, 1987). Today it is represented in every Latin American nation save Cuba, Nicaragua (where an office was re-established after the 1990 Sandinista electoral defeat), Suriname, Panama (where an office was re-established after Noriega's ouster), and Colombia.

AIFLD publishes a broad array of educational periodicals in English, Spanish, French, and Portuguese. AIFLD Reports, along with the more episodic literature, constitute yet another ideological tool in the AIFLD repertoire. Educational programs vary from country to country, depending on the organizational and educational levels of the work force, and the ideological climate of the government and unions in question. Courses last from one week to three months, and are also taught in each of the respective national offices. Outstanding graduates are sent to the United States to receive advanced leadership training in these subjects.[57]

Since 1962 AIFLD has operated labor training institutes in the United States, first at the Front Royal Institute in Virginia, Georgetown University, Trinity College, and Mt. Vernon College in Washington, D.C.; Loyola University in New Orleans; and then, as of 1979, at the George Meany Center for Labor Studies in Silver Springs, Maryland. AIFLD has offered courses in labor economics, collective bargaining, "democracy versus totalitarianism," comparative labor organization, productivity, industrial organization, social security, labor legislation, workplace safety, human relations, union education and financing, organizing tactics, and grievance procedures, both in the United States and through its field offices. In 1965, when AIFLD recognized that the needs of urban and rural workers differed considerably, an Agrarian Union Development Service was launched.

Upon completing their U.S. coursework, AIFLD graduates were sent home under a nine-month salaried internship program in order to disseminate new skills and knowledge among their *compañeros*. The current norm is for graduates to return to their unions without AIFLD financial support. The graduate reenters the local union bureaucracy as a technical expert specialized in aspects of the labor process and relations of production, and also engages in ideological dissemination functions, promoting anticorporatist views of labor relations. In some cases, such as during the tenure of military-bureaucratic regimes in the Southern Cone and Central America in the 1970s, unionists were invited to attend AIFLD courses in the United States as a means of freeing them from the oppressive labor climate at home, and, more important, in order for them to set the foundations for eventual reorganization of their unions once the dictators departed.[58]

In the late 1970s, at the behest of the Latin American members of their board of trustees, AIFLD formally recognized its political role in supporting "free" trade unionism, and now devotes half of its efforts to political activities. The shift to an overt political role was one of the reasons cited for the withdrawal of business representatives from the board. The shift responded to several factors. The conservative anti-Communist language and apolitical probusiness facade needed to survive in the U.S. political climate of the cold war era was replaced by a moderated ideological tone and more overt political role once AIFLD's position within the foreign policy apparatus was consolidated. Second, the postdétente world, particularly the evolving posture of the Socialist International, the failure of Marxist revolutionary movements in Latin America, and the upheaval in the authoritarian socialist world, allowed AIFLD to establish bases for dialogue with Democratic Socialist and Christian Democratic union currents. In this regard, while it continues to employ divide-and-conquer tactics against anticapitalist unions in countries such as El Salvador and Nicaragua, AIFLD has shifted its general posture in the face of changing global and regional political realities.

AIFLD receives the majority of its funding from the U.S. government, an uncommon situation for a private, nonprofit corporation. In 1967 92 percent of the AIFLD budget came from the U.S. government, a total of $4.8 million. Of the $17.4 million allocated to AIFLD from 1962 to that year, 89 percent ($15.4 million) was channeled through AID. This amounted to 67 percent of the total allocated for labor programs under the Alliance for Progress. By 1971 AIFLD was the fifteenth largest recipient of AID contracts worldwide.[59] The majority of appropriated funds go to AIFLD educational activities. The entire Social Projects division of AIFLD (with jurisdiction over all noneducational programs) is also funded by AID. In 1987, over 90 percent of the $14.8 million AIFLD budget came from AID, with the remainder donated by the AFL-CIO (1.5 percent) and the conservative-dominated National Endowment for Democracy (8.9 percent).[60]

Reliance on AID funding has posed a problem for AIFLD, for it limits the freedom of action AIFLD is allowed to exercise when using those funds. Disputes over funding priorities and comptroller responsibilities plagued the AID-AIFLD relationship for years, although today AIFLD has greater control over in-country administration of AID contracts. Much of AIFLD's funding was originally channeled into ORIT and ITSs in order to support educational and social projects. As of the late 1960s, AIFLD increasingly assumed direct control of these projects.

CIA funding of AIFLD activities has been extensively documented in the press and in congressional hearings. Covert funds were directed toward securing the cooperation of key labor leaders, promoting some organizations and destabilizing others, and generally lubricating the means of access to influential government bureaucracies and political personalities. CIA funding for AIFLD was channeled through fronts such as the Gotham, Andrew Hamilton, and J. M. Kaplan foundations, through cooperative ITSs, and through agencies such as the Institute of International Labor Studies and other labor educational facilities installed throughout the region.[61] Revelations of AIFLD-CIA connections led to cutbacks in covert funding in the 1970s, but links between the two agencies remain. The CIA continues to place agents in AIFLD country offices and as labor attachés, since the AIFLD cover provides a convenient means of gathering intelligence on Marxist union factions, individual leaders, dissidents, and anti–United States foci, and generally keeps agency headquarters appraised directly of developments in the labor field.

Beyond these activities, AIFLD's efforts center on various social projects, including housing construction, loan and credit programs, literacy, vocational, health, and sanitation training, and so-called Impact Projects that involve material donations to needy unions.[62] Through its loan and credit programs and Impact Projects, AIFLD has funded consumer cooperatives, credit unions, and worker-operated enterprises.[63] By 1988 a Regional Revolving Loan Fund underwritten by AID grants and administered by AIFLD had 114 projects throughout the region. In addition, a Special Projects Fund established in 1976 for purposes of emergency relief had disbursed $257,000 on 73 projects by 1988.

By the 1970s AIFLD had assumed control of the AFL-CIO's Latin American policy, replacing the Latin American department in the International Relations Office. Today it is virtually autonomous from the AFL-CIO Department of International Affairs with regard to issues of Latin American labor policy input and implementation. More important, although both agencies continue to be guided by the general tenets of the AFL-CIO's foreign policy, they no longer respond instrumentally to U.S. government directives. This distancing was most evident in the 1980s, with AIFLD and the AFL-CIO opposing the Reagan administration on a number of political and economic issues both at home and abroad, and where the thrust of AIFLD approaches toward political and economic questions in Latin America ran counter to many of the policies advocated by the departments of defense and state. At a time when the military commanders of the region were signing a hemispheric security agreement against precisely such groups (the November 1987 Pact of Hemispheric Security signed in Mar del Plata, Argentina, which identifies such groups "as Marxist fronts and infiltrators"), AIFLD was openly working with many democratic socialist unions to stabilize the nascent democratic regimes of the region.

Despite protest by senior AIFLD officials and claims by many critics that it has not changed its orientation over the years,[64] it is clear that the contrary is true. Although it remains a major foreign policy vehicle of the AFL-CIO, AIFLD has moved from a reflexive anti-Communist, probusiness posture toward a flexible prodemocratic, proworker stance when addressing Latin American labor and political issues. It has reemphasized bread-and-butter labor education along with political participation and ideological pluralism within union ranks. No less important, from covertly interventionist it has become openly participatory in the political life of the nations to the south.

Labor Attachés

The responsibility for formulating U.S. government labor policy belongs to the State Department, where the coordinator for international labor affairs, in conjunction with AID's Office of Labor Affairs, communicates policy directives to the labor attachés stationed in U.S. embassies abroad.[65] The Office of Inter-American Affairs for Policy and Coordination oversees labor policy application in Latin America. There is no overarching labor policy in the State Department beyond support for ILO standards on labor rights. There is no discrete labor policy for individual countries either. State Department labor policy in Latin America is postoriented and reactive, taking its lead from both events on the domestic labor front and AIFLD initiatives in-country. Only when labor issues become especially sensitive do policy formulation and approval shift to headquarters in Washington.

Labor attachés serve as official U.S. government liaisons with national labor administrations (labor ministries), ORIT, the ICFTU, and labor unions in their host countries. They also serve as AIFLD contract monitors when AID funds are used for AIFLD projects and, more generally, are classified as technical and political supervisors of both AIFLD and union-to-union activities. This has caused problems of coordination and turf battles with AIFLD administrators, who prefer to operate as independently as possible from embassy scrutiny.[66]

Labor attachés are traditionally drawn from four sources: the AFL-CIO, the State Department, the Labor Department, and the CIA. More often than not, personnel from the first three organizations are recruited from their Department of International Affairs (in the case of the AFL-CIO), or from the International Labor Offices of the respective public bureaucracies. Assigned to embassies as political officers, labor attachés serve a function analogous to that of military attachés—that is, official liaisons and intelligence gatherers who serve as primary points of contact between the U.S. government and local unions. Where trade relationships are important (such as East Asia and Western Europe), many labor attachés come from the Labor Department; where the relationship between the United States and the particular country is of less strategic importance, the position is most often filled by a foreign service officer; where local union relations with the AFL-CIO are particularly good, the position is often filled by a unionist; and where Marxist influence in the local labor movement is strong, the job frequently goes to a CIA officer. In countries with particularly large, politically active, or well-organized labor movements, more than one specialist is assigned to the labor attaché's office. The specifics of each case depend on the precise combination of these factors, mixed in with geopolitical and ideological considerations of a multilateral and bilateral nature.

Even if considerable at times, organized labor's representation in U.S. foreign policy agencies has not been of a uniformly high quality. For every individual of high caliber sent, U.S. labor has sent many more into government service as labor attachés and labor advisors without the proper qualifications, either as a form of reward for their activities in the union movement, as a form of patronage, or in order to remove them from positions of influence in the AFL-CIO hierarchy when they were no longer useful.[67] Most recently, U.S. unionists have not been interested in becoming labor attachés, subordinated to ambassadors with Republican connections. Nor are most ambassadors keen on having non-foreign-service officers in that position, particularly given the current ideological differences between the Republican administration and the AFL-CIO. As a result, unionist presence in the current corps of labor attachés in Latin America is very low. Of the sixteen labor attachés currently stationed in Latin America and the Caribbean, only two—in Jamaica and Argentina—have union-related backgrounds.

Union-to-Union Contacts

One of the more effective ways of promoting U.S. labor foreign policy objectives in Latin America has been through direct contacts between U.S. and Latin American unions. This practice began early in the century, with the AFL-CROM discussion of U.S.-Mexican labor issues, and continued during World War II with exchanges between AFL affiliates and non-Marxist Latin American unions. Whether by travel exchanges between individual labor leaders, formal correspondence between union directorates, the establishment of cooperative programs, educational tours, or financial interchanges, support for boycotts or calls for political pressure to be applied on both the U.S. and foreign governments, U.S. unions have found direct contact with their Latin American counterparts to be an efficient means of promoting their economic and political perspective on the region.

A productive form of exchange has been for Latin American unions to request assistance from their U.S. peers when confronting U.S.-based transnational corporations on bread-and-butter issues. In 1953 the AFL pressured the United Fruit Company and the U.S. State Department to accept a negotiated settlement with agricultural workers for the first time in the history of United Fruit's Honduran affiliates.[68] AFL-CIO and ITS pressure on the U.S.-based parent company was critical for the success of unionization efforts in Guatemalan Coca-Cola plants in the late 1970s and early 1980s.[69] More recently, workers at a Union Carbide plant in Brazil successfully appealed to the AFL-CIO for support when contract talks with the company stalled.[70]

Direct U.S. union support for Latin unions is not limited to organizational and economic demands. Direct contacts on political issues have been made as well. Defense of Latin American unionists confronted by political repression has been one area where U.S. unions have been particularly effective. Unlike the 1950s and 1960s when silence was the norm, the AFL-CIO and a host of affiliate unions regularly protested the violations of unionists' rights under the military-bureaucratic regimes of Argentina, Brazil, Bolivia, Chile, Uruguay, Peru, and Central America in the 1970s and 1980s. U.S. unions have also been quick to denounce human rights violations under the socialist authoritarian regimes of Cuba, Suriname, and Nicaragua. This represents another shift. Criticism of conservative authoritarian regimes historically was not as consistently given as that directed toward the socialist camp. Only as of the mid-1970s, when human rights became a central issue in U.S. foreign policy, did U.S. unions take a more critical position on AFL-CIO foreign activities and adopt a consistent stand against labor repression in Latin America.[71]

During the last two decades there has been a trend toward more direct union intervention on behalf of Latin American labor groups on issues of specific concern. This stems not only from the rise of dissenting voices within the U.S. labor movement and a concern with imposing some ethical content on U.S. labor's Latin American policy, but also out of the past failures of the AFL-CIO and umbrella organizations such as ORIT and AIFLD to address many of the immediate concerns of Latin American unionists. With the need to protect U.S. union jobs in light of the international economic realities of the late 1980s, U.S. unions have been quicker to support directly the demands of their Latin American brethren, if for no other reason than out of a finely honed sense of self-preservation.

Conclusion

This essay is not intended as an attack on U.S. labor and its foreign policy objectives in Latin America during the course of this century. Nor does the absence of an assessment of their policies in the region imply ignorance of Marxist-Leninist attempts to gain control of Latin American labor, which had much to do with shaping the thrust of the U.S. labor approach in the region. What the chapter has endeavored to demonstrate is the contradictory nature of U.S. labor's Latin America policy. It has done so by arguing that the promotion of "free" trade unionism in Latin America has both helped and hindered the cause of democracy in the region.

Such promotion helped by providing Latin American workers with a series of educational programs and other forms of assistance that are designed to empower them in the workplace and community and to improve their general standard of living. However it also has, to a far greater extent, hindered the cause of democracy in Latin America by adopting a doctrinaire antitotalitarian line behind the facade of apolitical business unionism, which left it blind to the realities of class struggle in Latin America and the non-Soviet nature of many Marxist and nationalist union movements in the region. For a half century U.S. labor unquestioningly accepted a developmental logic that saw U.S.-promoted capitalist expansion as the panacea for all social ills, to which democratic advocacy was subordinated. Anything that ran counter to this view brought about a reflexive, reactive response from the North American labor hierarchy, paralleling the U.S. government response, that often served to undermine the cause of democratization in Latin America.

The greater the regional hegemony of the United States and depth of the cold war, the more doctrinaire and rigid was the U.S. labor response to labor developments in Latin America. The less the regional hegemony and U.S. influence over a given Latin American country, the more flexible and progressive U.S. labor's approach, particularly during periods of improved superpower relations. Until very recently, U.S. labor strongly supported U.S. government foreign policy in Latin America. Even if in opposition now, it continues to take its lead from the administration, following time-honored practice.

The AFL-CIO's reversed posture has a structural root. The changing international division of labor, and the shifting U.S. position within it, has forced organized labor to reassess its former position of unqualified support for U.S. capitalist international expansion. The quest for profit abroad no longer brings with it benefits for organized workers at home, but instead has resulted in an increasing tide of "runaway jobs" and unfair competition in trade.

As the U.S. economy adjusts to an era of increased international competition, U.S. labor has assumed a defensive position, protecting rank-and-file wages and employment through opposition to further U.S. corporate investment abroad. This prompted U.S. labor to accept political, classist, and militant unions in Latin America, because it believes that the latter will deter or constrain U.S. investors, equalize labor climates worldwide, promote "fair" trading practices, and thereby protect rank-and-file material interests at home. To that end, organizational tactics and other forms of educational projects oriented toward strengthening working class participation in the political arena and the productive process have been emphasized by agencies such as AIFLD without as much concern over the ideology of the unions involved.

Despite its changed strategic outlook, the AFL-CIO remains guided by one fundamental logic: the logic of material and organizational self-preservation. If it has not entirely abandoned manipulation and intrigue as foreign policy tools, the economic and political circumstances of the international moment require that the AFL-CIO foreign policy apparatus adopt a more flexible approach to Latin American labor and political issues. The rationale behind this approach holds that it is both foolish and counterproductive to play the role of labor foils for a U.S. foreign policy elite seemingly unconcerned with the material and political foundations of domestic union consent to its activities overseas. Instead, the logic of organizational survival compels U.S. labor to become a reluctant agent for the promotion of democracy in Latin America and elsewhere, fulfilling the democratic mantle that it has long claimed but seldom seen fit to wear.

Notes

This chapter is a revised version of a paper prepared for presentation at the conference on "The United States and Latin American Democracy," University of Southern California, April 6–9, 1989. Portions of this chapter were written during the author's tenure as a Visiting Faculty Fellow at the Kellogg Institute, University of Notre Dame. Additional logistical assistance was provided by Paul Chase, whose support is gratefully acknowledged. I am indebted to William Bollinger and other conference participants for their comments. A longer version appears as Kellogg Institute *Working Paper* no. 136 (1990) under the title, "'Useful Fools' as Diplomatic Tools: Organized Labor as an Instrument of U.S. Foreign Policy in Latin America."

1. Santiago Iglesias, former leader of the PAFL, quoted in George C. Lodge, *Spearheads*

of Democracy: Labor in Developing Countries (New York: Council on Foreign Relations, 1962), p. 23.

2. See R. Radosh, *Labor and United States Foreign Policy* (New York: Random House, 1969); and J. Scott, *Yankee Unions Go Home! How the AFL Helped the U.S. Build an Empire in Latin America* (Vancouver: New Star Books, 1978).

3. S. Gompers, *Seventy Years of Life and Labour* (New York: Dutton, 1948), cited in Scott, p. 176.

4. Proceedings of the 1934 AFL Annual Convention, cited in Scott, p. 177, and Radosh, p. 354.

5. On the formalization of U.S. labor and government ties during this period, see Serafino Romualdi, *Presidents and Peons: Recollections of a Labor Ambassador in Latin America* (New York: Funk & Wagnalls, 1967), pp. 72–73; H. Spaulding, "U.S. and Latin American Labor: The Dynamics of Imperialist Control," *Latin American Perspectives* 3, no. 1 (Winter 1976): 48; and U.S. Senate, Committee on Foreign Relations, Subcommittee on American Republics Affairs, *Survey of the Alliance for Progress: Labor Policies and Programs,* Document 17, 91st Congress, 1st Session (12844-2) (Washington, D.C.: U.S. Government Printing Office, 1969) (hereafter referred to as Senate Document 17-91).

6. Lodge, pp. 73–74.

7. American Institute for Free Labor Development, "Progress Report to the President's Labor Advisory Committee on Foreign Assistance," March 1967. Cited in Senate Document 17-91, p. 582.

8. Ibid., p. 581.

9. A summary of these is offered in Senate Document 17-91, pp. 601–55.

10. On this, see A. O. Hero and E. Starr, *The Reuther-Meany Foreign Policy Dispute: Union Leaders and Members View World Affairs* (Dobbs Ferry, N.Y.: Oceana Publications, 1970).

11. A problem shared by many collective agents, particularly labor organizations and political parties. See R. Michels, *Political Parties: A Sociological Study of the Oligarchical Tendencies of Modern Democracy* (New York: Free Press, 1966).

12. J. Godio, *Historia del Movimiento Obero Latinoamericano* (Caracas: Editorial Nueva Sociedad, 1985), 3: 260–70.

13. For recounts of these activities, see among others, H. A. Spaulding, Jr., *Organized Labor in Latin America* (New York: New York University Press, 1977); Spaulding, "U.S. and Latin American Labor"; H. W. Berger, "Union Diplomacy: American Labor's Foreign Policy in Latin America, 1932–1955" (Ph.D. dissertation, University of Wisconsin, 1966); G. C. Ross, *El Neocolonialismo Sindical* (Buenos Aires: Editorial La Linea, 1974); D. Torrence, "American Imperialism and Latin American Labor, 1959–1970: A Study of the Role of the Organización Regional Interamericana de Trabajadores in the Latin American Policy of the United States" (Ph.D. dissertation, Northern Illinois University, 1975); J. Steinsleger, *Imperialismo y Sindicatos en America Latina* (Puebla, Mexico: Universidad Autonoma de Puebla, 1976); F. Hirsch, *An Analysis of Our AFL-CIO Role in Latin America, or Under the Covers with the CIA* (San Jose, Calif.: n.p., 1974); K. P. Erickson and P. V. Peppe, "Dependent Capitalist Development, U.S. Foreign Policy, and Repression of the Working Class in Chile and Brazil," *Latin American Perspectives* 1, no. 1 (Winter 1976): 19–44. A recent summary is offered in H. A. Spaulding, Jr., "Solidarity Forever? Latin American Unions and the International Labor Network," *Latin American Research Review* 25, no. 1 (Summer 1989): 253–65.

14. For a discussion of the AFL-CIO/AIFLD role in El Salvador, see W. Bollinger, "El Salvador," in G. M. Greenfield and S. L. Maram, eds., *Latin American Labor Organizations* (Westpoint, Conn.: Greenwood Press, 1987).

15. Samuel Gompers stated that the PAFL represented a means of safeguarding Latin America's "autonomous independence" from the "insidious attempts of autocratic forms of

government located outside the hemisphere," which if successful in their efforts would ensure that the "Monroe Doctrine and all that it implies (would) be destroyed and thrown to the four winds," S. Snow, "Samuel Gompers and the Pan-American Federation of Labor" (Ph.D. dissertation, University of Virginia, 1960), cited in Radosh, p. 352. Also see the proceedings of the 1913 AFL Annual Convention, cited in Scott, p. 173, and Spaulding, *Organized Labor,* p. 253.

16. Scott, pp. 193–96.

17. Ibid.

18. Memorandum from S. Romualdi to M. Woll, FTUC Chairman, December 18, 1943, cited in Romualdi, p. 8.

19. Proceedings of the 1946 Annual Convention, cited in Scott, p. 213.

20. Romualdi, pp. 71–73.

21. Quoted in Godio, 3: 114.

22. AIFLD, "Educación Sindical. El Movimiento Obrero en las Américas," vol. 1 (Mexico, D.F., n.d.), p. 74, cited in Ross, *El Neocolonialismo Sindical,* p. 74.

23. "Town Hall Speech," *AIFLD Report,* June 1966, quoted in Senate Document 17-91, p. 585.

24. See Hero and Starr.

25. See the discussion in Spaulding, "Solidarity Forever?" esp. pp. 255–57.

26. AFL-CIO, *The AFL-CIO Abroad: Perspectives on Labor and the World,* AFL-CIO Publication no. 182 (Washington, D.C., August 1987), pp. 3–4.

27. Ibid., p. 251.

28. AFL-CIO, *Policy Resolutions Adopted October 1987 by the Seventeenth Constitutional Convention,* AFL-CIO Publication no. 3 (Washington, D.C., January 1988), p. 113.

29. AFL-CIO, *AFL-CIO: Twenty Five Years of Solidarity with Latin American Workers* (Washington, D.C.: AIFLD, 1987), p. 5.

30. Senate Document 17-91, p. 578.

31. Radosh, p. 359; Scott, p. 197.

32. Scott, p. 197.

33. Proceedings of the 1946 AFL Annual Convention, cited in Scott, p. 208.

34. Scott, p. 197.

35. *United Mine Workers Journal,* September 15, 1939.

36. On the AFL-CIO position on the Generalized System of Preferences (GSP), GATT, and the issue of workers' rights, see the June 1, 1987, letter and attachments from AFL-CIO Director of International Affairs Tom Kahn to David P. Stark, chairman of the GSP Subcommittee of the Office of the United States Trade Representative; the *American Federationist* 93, no. 7 (November 8, 1986); and the AFL-CIO *Bulletin of the Department of International Affairs* 3, no. 1 (January 1988): 2.

37. AFL-CIO, *Policy Resolutions, 1987,* pp. 45–46.

38. Ibid., p. 106.

39. See the testimony of John T. Joyce, president, International Union of Bricklayers and Allied Craftsmen, AFL-CIO, before the Subcommittee on International Economic Policy and Trade of the Committee on Foreign Affairs, U.S. House of Representatives, on the formation of the Central American Development Organization (CADO), April 13, 1988, especially appendixes IV (ICFTU Resolution), V, and VI (memorandum and telegrams from USIA officials in Washington, and San José, Costa Rica, proposing invited visitor status for solidarismo leaders with attendant justifications).

40. See the November 23, 1988, letters written by AIFLD official John J. Heberle to two Salvadoran unions, in which he outlines the general program, offers the suggestions cited, and includes literature prepared by and for the AFL-CIO on the subject of ESOPs.

41. Memorandum from Alan Woods, Administrator of AID, to AID Mission Directors and Overseas Offices, May 6, 1988.

42. "The Role of U.S. Business," at the end of her discussion of business activities in the 1950s.

43. This in turn depends on the ideological stance of government incumbents, the extent of state intervention in the economy, the political orientation and strength of working-class organizations, the conditions of the labor market, and the overall state of the economy, using either corporatist or pluralist mechanisms of interest representation of varying degrees of comprehensiveness.

44. On the role of trade unions in advanced capitalism, see L. Panitch, "Trade Unions and the Capitalist State," *New Left Review* 125 (1981): 21–41. For a critique of the view that the AFL-CIO is somehow "conservative" on both domestic and foreign affairs, see D. C. Heldman, *American Labor Unions: Political Values and Financial Structure* (Washington, D.C.: Council on American Affairs, 1977), esp. pp. 14, 38–40.

45. House of Representatives, Committee on Foreign Affairs, Subcommittee on International Organizations and Movements, *Winning the Cold War: The U.S. Ideological Offensive,* 88th Congress, 1st Session, part II, April 30, 1963 (Washington, D.C.: U.S. Government Printing Office, 1963), p. 134.

46. On this, see I. Katznelson and K. Prewitt, "Constitutionalism, Class, and the Limits of Choice in U.S. Foreign Policy," in R. R. Fagen, ed., *Capitalism and the State in U.S.-Latin American Relations* (Stanford, Calif.: Stanford University Press, 1979), p. 35; M. Nicolaus, "Theory of the Labor Aristocracy," *Monthly Review* 21, no. 11 (April 1970): 97; and *Argentina in the Hours of the Furnaces* (New York: NACLA, 1975), pp. 56–77.

47. Torrence, chap. 2.

48. Godio, 3: 284–85.

49. Spaulding, *Organized Labor,* p. 257.

50. Senate Document 17-91, pp. 584, 658.

51. Torrence, chap. 2.

52. Senate Document 17-91, p. 581.

53. Radosh, p. 416.

54. Speech given by J. Peter Grace at Houston's International Trade Fair, September 16, 1965, cited in Romualdi, p. 418, Scott, p. 225, and reprinted in amended form as an AIFLD Pamphlet, September 1965.

55. U.S. Senate, Committee on Foreign Relations, *Foreign Assistance Act of 1967,* 90th Congress, 1st Session (Washington, D.C.: U.S. Government Printing Office, 1967), p. 1096. Also see Ross, pp. 117–49.

56. AIFLD, *Annual Progress Report, 1962–1988: 26 Years of Partnership for Progress* (Washington, D.C.: AIFLD, 1988), pp. 1–2.

57. AIFLD, *The Advanced Labor Studies Program of the American Institute for Free Labor Development* (Washington, D.C.: AIFLD, 1988), pp. 14–20.

58. Interview with Dr. Hugo Belloni, program coordinator, AIFLD Argentina, June 28, 1988. From 1962 to 1988, AIFLD trained 602,484 unionists in Latin America, the Caribbean, and the United States: 597,445 were trained in-country, 4,834 graduated from advanced courses at Front Royal Institute or the George Meany Center for Labor Studies, and 205 were trained as labor economists at the participating U.S. universities. The largest number of students came from Colombia (71,839), followed by Brazil (67,361), the Dominican Republic (63,500), Ecuador (62,291), Peru (56,880), Honduras (41,044), Bolivia (36,437), Guatemala (33,941), Chile (27,952), the Caribbean (23,450), and Uruguay (22,164). The remaining countries, save Suriname and Cuba which do not have any AIFLD graduates, have had AIFLD student enrollments of less than 20,000 but more than 1,000. Most recently (1987), Guatemala had the largest number of students enrolled in AIFLD programs (11,856), followed by the Dominican Republic (9,524), Brazil (3,096), and Argentina, Chile, Costa Rica, Ecuador, El Salvador, and Peru with between 2,000 to 3,000 students each. AIFLD, *Annual Progress Report, 1962–1988,* pp. 1–2.

59. Senate Document 17-91, pp. 582–83; Spaulding, *Organized Labor,* p. 260.

60. AFL-CIO, *The AFL-CIO Abroad,* p. 12.

61. Spaulding, *Organized Labor,* p. 260.

62. Ibid., p. 262; Radosh, pp. 430–31; AIFLD, *Annual Progress Report, 1962-1988,* p. 3.

63. Spaulding, *Organized Labor,* p. 262.

64. In an interview with AIFLD Executive Director William C. Doherty, Jr., on February 7, 1989, this writer was told that global realities, not AIFLD's posture, were what had changed over time. When it was pointed out that the present definition of AIFLD's mission clearly contradicts the stated mission it had in the 1960s, Doherty continued to maintain that this was mere tactical expediency rather than a shift in its fundamental antitotalitarian emphasis.

65. Senate Document 17-91, p. 577.

66. Ibid., pp. 616–17.

67. J. P. Windmuller, "Labor: A Partner in American Foreign Policy?" *Annals of the American Academy of Political and Social Science* 350 (November 1963): 113.

68. P. Taft, *Defending Freedom: American Labor and Foreign Affairs* (Los Angeles: Nash Publishing, 1973), pp. 184–85; Romualdi, pp. 268–69 (FF 17).

69. See Spaulding, "Solidarity Forever?" pp. 262–64.

70. *People's Daily World,* September 29, 1988, p. 7-A. Given that this periodical is a mouthpiece for the U.S. Communist party, the approving tone of the coverage is all the more remarkable.

71. See Hirsch, and the sources cited in Spaulding, "Solidarity Forever?"

Part Two

Conclusions

7 | Economic Forces and U.S. Policies

John Sheahan

THE SURVIVAL of democracies in Latin American countries depends above all on their own internal relationships and actions, but the economic policies of the United States can change the odds either favorably or unfavorably. Such policies gain power by acting on two levels at once. The more immediately visible is the level on which policies implemented by the United States act to change the availability and costs of international financing, the strength of world markets, the terms of import restrictions and acceptable export promotion, and in general the conditions of the external economic environment. The less visible, but at least equally important, is the level on which the United States either directly through its own actions, or indirectly through its leading rule in the international financing and development institutions, exerts pressures to shape the economic strategies of the Latin American countries themselves.

On the first level, it is clearly possible to foster relatively favorable conditions by helping to reduce debt burdens, to promote expansion of international financing, to support growth of world demand, and to allow open access to U.S. markets for Latin American exports. Many questions need to be considered even on this level: hardly any positive move comes without some offsetting problem. But the tougher questions may apply to the second level, that of the goals and methods involved in trying to reshape the economic strategies of the Latin American countries.

Something of the difficulty of being sure exactly what kinds of economic strategy help and what do not is suggested by the radically different orientation of changes sought by the United States in the two periods of most active attempts to influence Latin American economic policies, in the 1960s with the Alliance for Progress and in the 1980s. In the 1960s the objectives included support for government programs to promote industrialization, for economic planning, for land reform and other social programs, and for more effective tax systems intended to support high levels of government economic activity. In the 1980s the main objectives were to get Latin American governments out of intervention in the economy, to reduce taxation in order to favor the private sector, to promote trade liberalization and privatization, and to discourage government spending on social programs and subsidies in the names of efficiency and fiscal responsibility. Each of these contradictory general directions probably included some helpful and some unhelpful components. Which are which, for what countries under what conditions?

The central theme of this discussion is that questions of the effects of U.S. policies on the survival of democracy require directing particular attention to the *character* of economic growth in Latin America, and in particular to the degree to which the gains of growth are widely shared, as distinct from concern with effects on efficiency and the rate of growth of national income. The underlying hypothesis is that a democratic system must include the majority of the country in the gains of growth if the system is to maintain public acceptance. If practically all the gains of growth go to a minority, if major groups in the society are left out, the chances of sustainable democracy are squeezed down to a narrow path between two opposing tensions: between efforts of the upper-income minority to protect their advantages, and efforts of the left-out groups (and of those sympathetic with them) to overturn the inequitable system. The economic side of Latin American difficulties with maintaining democracy is rooted in the fact that structural characteristics of many of these economies make normal market forces work in exceptionally unequal ways. Economic policies that are desirable from the viewpoint of economic efficiency and growth, and in the interests of upper-income groups, become instruments of aggravated inequality and therefore adverse for democracy.

The first section in this chapter explains the basic thesis that common structural characteristics of Latin American economies systematically weaken the chances for democracy, by turning normal market forces in directions adverse for wide participation in the gains of growth. These structural conditions set up direct conflicts between the chances for democracy and the free-market economic strategy that the United States is promoting as a requirement for external financial assistance. In the next two sections, this thesis is applied to some historical examples of U.S. economic policies affecting these countries from the 1940s to the 1970s, and then in the 1980s. A concluding section considers what the United States might be able to do now to foster economic conditions likely to improve the prospects for democracy in Latin America.

Relationships between Economic Structures and Political Outcomes

In the northern industrialized countries, it is a reasonable expectation that free markets and political freedom serve in many respects to reinforce each other. In most of Latin America, to varying degrees in different countries, it is not. The central reason why it is not is that structural factors common in Latin American conditions make the operation of market forces exceptionally adverse for equality. When the preferences of the majority can be expressed in any effective way, they understandably favor intervention to block the operation of market forces or to change property rights. Such intervention could strengthen democracy if it is well directed and the costs are kept down, but if the costs become too high in terms of instability and blocked growth, or of threats to property rights, the middle and upper classes turn against democracy to protect themselves. Sustained support for democracy requires that both the poor and the nonpoor can see it working in their interests. If either side has good grounds for the belief that it does not, democracy will be widely regarded at best as a readily disposable value and at worst as a threat.

Efforts by the United States to improve the chances of democracy in Latin America are more likely to be successful if they are guided by concern for the specific difficulties of the Latin American economies, and less likely to be successful if they are dominated by the objective of promoting reliance on private enterprise and free markets. The themes of liberalization and privatization emphasized in the Baker and Brady plans of the 1980s, and by the International Monetary Fund and the World Bank, include both potentially helpful and potentially damaging possibilities.[1] Many Latin American governments have hurt their own economies and unnecessarily aggravated strains on democracy through ill-directed intervention or lack of concern for macroeconomic consistency, and some aspects of the policy changes sought by the United States could help lessen such damage. The problem is that an uncompromising insistence on accepting market forces in the name of efficiency and growth is highly likely to aggravate existing degrees of inequality and tear down support for any democratic system identified with this result.

The basic economic characteristics that have worked against equality in many Latin American countries have been high concentrations of property ownership, and of access to capital and to skills, in the context of relatively abundant unskilled labor and a rapidly growing labor force. Rapid growth of the labor force relative to land and to opportunities for productive employment exerts downward pressure on earnings of the majority of workers, with high shares of income going to owners of property and to the minority with specialized skills. Concentration of ownership itself then further accentuates the inequality related in the first place to the balance among factors of production.[2] Structures of production and trade can further worsen inequality by favoring export earnings of those who own land and other natural resources and by holding down the growth of the industrial sector through the competition of lower cost imports.

All these economic characteristics are matters of degree and are subject to change. Some changes in the last few decades have been very much for the better. Following the acceleration of rates of growth of population in the first half of the twentieth century, they began to slow down markedly in the 1960s.[3] Historically weak support for public education, except in Costa Rica and the Southern Cone, began to change for the better at about the same time. The secondary-school enrollment ratio for the region—a good index of the share of the population that has some chance of getting valuable skills—was only 14 percent in 1960. By 1981 it had risen to 39 percent, a striking improvement but one that still left out the majority.[4]

Although studies of land ownership patterns have consistently shown extraordinarily high concentrations of ownership for most of the countries in the region, land reforms have made significant changes in this pattern in Mexico in the 1930s, Bolivia in the 1950s, Cuba and Nicaragua following their revolutions, and Peru at the end of the 1960s.[5] Concentration of land ownership would not necessarily have any great effects on inequality if rural labor were scarce, and especially if opportunities for productive employment outside of agriculture made it readily possible to move to alternative work. If the number of workers depending on agriculture were decreasing this would be a fairly good sign of positive alternative opportunities. But the long-term trend from 1960 to 1984 showed that only one of the countries with more than 50 percent of the labor force in agriculture in 1960, Colombia, actually reduced the total by 1984. Percentage increases, suggesting worsening pressures on rural incomes, were particularly high in El Salvador and Guatemala (62 percent in each), Honduras (82 percent), and Paraguay (79 percent).[6]

Given such structural conditions, the pattern of international trade when it was relatively uncontrolled, up to the 1930s, probably worsened income distribution. Exports were dominated by primary products generating high returns for owners of land and of minerals. In the twentieth century, rapid growth of the rural labor force aggravated rural poverty, while imports of manufactures held down the potential growth of industrial employment. The first clear exercise of independent Latin American economic strategy, import-substituting industrialization, was aimed at exactly this set of issues. That strategy was highly understandable but not favorable either for equality or for sustained growth. It favored capital-and skill-intensive structures of production, dependent on imported supplies for production and equipment for investment, accomplishing little to raise employment opportunities. By discouraging exports this strategy increased dependence on borrowing and worsened the region's repeated foreign exchange crisis.

Under the strategy of import substitution, management of exchange rates raised exceptionally intense political conflicts because of their joint effects on production and on the distribution of income. Governments responsive to popular preferences, or more specifically to the preferences of urban workers and industrialists, persistently favored low prices of foreign exchange, and resisted use of devaluation as a means of correcting external deficits, in order to keep down the prices of primary commodities relative to urban wages, and the costs of imported inputs for the industrial sector. But the effect of low-cost foreign exchange is invariably to encourage imports and discourage exports, generating trade deficits that keep rising until they lead to foreign exchange crises.[7] For democratic governments, a corrective response by devaluation and fiscal restraint is always difficult to implement because they run against the immediate interests of protected industrialists and urban labor. For the side of society more concerned with resumption of economic growth, the repeated impasse aggravates impatience with democracy itself, and builds up support for military intervention.

Since the strategy of import substitution under state-led development proved in practice to add to the strains on democracy, the case for a contrary emphasis on liberalization and free markets can have a strong appeal. It must in some respects be better. The problem is that in some respects it may also be worse: conditions of high inequality were built into these economies before the industrialization strategy started, so merely reversing course can hardly be a promising answer. What alternative strategies might work better? That question cannot be answered in the same general terms for all countries: the likely answers depend on the structural characteristics of the economy and the particular dimension of market opening under consideration. Three key dimensions are considered briefly here: trade liberalization, intervention in labor markets, and the use of subsidies to change structures of output or consumption.

To allow the pattern of trade to be determined by comparative advantage in an open economy can be either helpful or harmful for equality, depending mainly on the structural conditions of the particular country. A thorough econometric study by François Bourguignon and Christian Morrisson makes clear that exports have more favorable effects on income distribution for those countries in which skills are well diffused (as measured by high ratios of secondary-school attendance), in which comparative advantage is on the side of labor-intensive industrial exports rather than traditional primary products, and in which land ownership is widely diffused rather than concentrated (as measured by the share of small and medium-sized producers in export crops).[8] On all these counts, Latin American conditions have been adverse: trade liberalization with existing lines of comparative advantage is likely to aggravate inequality.

Adverse structural conditions need not stay that way forever. Latin America's potential for a more favorable export structure has been improving on the score of access to education and skills. For a growing number of countries, selective export promotion has been changing trade structures toward higher shares of industrial products in total exports. Selective export help has also stimulated new nontraditional primary products (such as fruit, vegetables, and seafood) that are often more favorable for labor and less land-intensive than traditional primary products. The chances of using trade policy in ways favorable for equality are increasing. The most promising path in the 1990s would surely be to continue or to intensify promotion of the newer kinds of exports, even when the means have to include intervention going beyond normal market incentives. Concern for employment and income distribution would also argue in favor of maintaining enough protection to make sure that the industrial sector does not get demolished in the meantime, rather than to opt for anything like complete reliance on open markets.

In labor markets, intervention is in general adverse for both efficiency and employment. But the importance of the adverse effects and the consequences for equality and for the survival of democracy may differ greatly according to the context of the economy and the particular forms of intervention. Intervention to raise relative wages of better-organized workers in the formal sector is bound to have adverse effects on marginal workers with lower incomes: it hurts the poor as well as the economy as a whole. But when the economy is characterized by persistent downward pressure on wages of unskilled workers, with rising ratios of labor to land and a rapidly growing labor force, to leave the course of wages up to determination by markets may imply indefinitely increasing poverty even when the economy as a whole is growing. It is difficult to believe that a democratic society could long survive in a context juxtaposing rising incomes at the high end with worsening conditions for a substantial minority, or even the majority. To combine criteria of efficiency and of achieving wide participation in the gains of growth involves difficult issues of balancing goals that may for a long period run contrary to each other. Without going into all these issues here, a goal of achieving more participatory growth argues for intervention in labor markets to raise the incomes of lower-income workers by at least the rate at which national income per capita is increasing, if normal market forces are not by themselves achieving such a result.[9]

A more efficient way to seek the same goal—to raise real earnings in line with national income—could be to use extramarket redistribution as distinct from action on wage rates. Extramarket redistribution could take the form of progressive taxation to finance general social programs directed toward reduction of poverty, or more specific forms of subsidies to small farmers to increase production of basic foods consumed mainly by low-income groups, and to low-income consumers on the buying side.[10] Such methods can lessen poverty without any necessity of raising wage costs, and therefore should be more favorable both for employment and for the possibility of generating labor-intensive exports. But subsidies require offsetting taxation to protect macroeconomic balance: the main obstacle in practice may well be the political resistance of the upper-income groups to progressive taxation. If that resistance could be at least partially overcome through competition for votes within a democratic system, there would be little or no case for intervention in wage setting; if it cannot, then such intervention could become a positive component of policies to support democracy.

What does all this mean in terms of U.S. pressures to alter Latin American economic strategies? In general terms, it means that the kinds of changes that would be desirable to support democracy do not line up in any neat way with questions of favoring or opposing liberalization and reliance on free-market forces. Promotion of labor-intensive export industries, and a shift of investment away from highly capital-intensive industries that can survive only with high rates of protection, should help improve employment opportunities and reduce inequality. But that pattern is not the one likely to emerge under anything like all-out trade liberalization because existing comparative advantages in most Latin American countries go in different directions, toward patterns of trade adverse for equality. Similarly, it should be helpful to break away from the kinds of intervention in labor markets that help raise relative earnings of higher-wage workers, but it could hurt badly to leave wages completely up to market forces when the latter act to block any gains in earnings of low-income workers. Subsidies to change incentives and the structure of output can go badly wrong, but it may very well be helpful to provide selective subsidies for output and consumption of foods basic for the poor. Generalized pressure for liberalization and privatization can include some advantages, but may include even more significant disadvantages if the intent is not just to favor growth but, perhaps more important for the sake of helping democracy survive, to favor more participatory societies.

Conflicts in U.S. Policies: From the 1940s to the 1970s

At the start of the postwar period the orientation of U.S. international economic policies provided basically favorable conditions for growth and change in Latin America but at the same time embodied several characteristics that threatened trouble. The favorable conditions were firm support for the new international economic institutions created to help stabilize the world economy, provision of aid for Western European recovery followed by more limited aid for developing countries, and promotion of reductions in trade barriers by the industrialized countries. Two of the problematic factors at the time, and since, were a consistent goal of promoting U.S.-style free-market economic systems no matter what the public preferences or the structural characteristics of other countries, and a growing determination to stamp out any signs of Communist influence, however marginal the influence in the particular case.[11]

For the Truman administration, and for a high proportion of subsequent decision makers, Latin American economic development was a desirable goal both in its own right and as a means to favor more stable societies, less drawn toward the radical left. But the goals that looked jointly reinforcing often proved to be contradictory.[12] The dominant goal of blocking Communism ran against an otherwise promising wish to promote structural reforms, in particular land reform. A growing emphasis on military aid, focused on curbing the radical left (or anyone else who might be mistaken for part of the radical left), reinforced the conservative side within all these countries. It almost surely lessened the willingness of those with all the privileges to negotiate changes toward more participatory societies. On the one hand, the United States offered help to countries wanting to implement changes intended to lessen inequality; on the other hand, it provided powerful support for those within the societies determined to prevent exactly such changes.

The U.S. preference for promoting private enterprise and free markets played a less important role in this period than it was to play in the 1980s. It was manifested in strong support for U.S. investors in any conflicts with host governments, and clearly reduced the scope for national choice in such matters, but it was not extended to a dogmatic position requiring generalized liberalization and privatization as conditions of external credit. The more fundamental problem, of which this was simply a particular manifestation, proved to be the basic conflict between provision of long-term aid and the hope for more independent societies with a sense of capacity to control their own destinies.

Conflict between cold war concerns and support of either structural reforms or democracy in Latin America proved particularly destructive in the first major postwar confrontation, in Guatemala in the 1950s. The newly established democracy in that country started off with a wide range of structural reforms, including land reform. But the interests of a U.S. corporation as the largest landowner in the country, and the fears of the Eisenhower administration about the possible influence of Marxists in the land reform agency, led the United States to put together an invasion by dissident Guatemalan military, a precursor of more such methods to come. The invasion overturned the government, ended democracy in Guatemala, and insured the reversal of land reform.[13] It also insured more than three decades of violent repression in Guatemala, and weakened whatever chances may have existed for nonviolent reform in Central America.

Subsequent efforts through the U.S. aid program to promote agricultural development in Guatemala, and throughout Latin America, have often raised the question of whether advisors working on the basis of U.S. education and experience can provide effective help. That question is given a bitterly negative answer by William and Elizabeth Paddock in a book based on their personal experience in Guatemala: *We Don't Know How.*[14] The

negative answer includes widely applicable issues, but the underlying problem in the particular case may have been less a matter of the technical character of aid and more a matter of having eliminated the kind of government
interested in the welfare of the Guatemalan people.

Conflicts between the dominant theme of blocking Communist influence and the secondary goals of promoting structural reform and more
participatory societies worsened in the early years of the Alliance for Progress. The much more activist U.S. presence in the 1960s blended increasing
military and intelligence operations with increased economic aid. "The
number of U.S. government personnel assigned to Latin America jumped,
crowding the suburbs of various Latin American capitals with embassy
offices, technicians, and cultural and military advisers, and dotting the
countryside with Peace Corps volunteers and military special forces."[15] The
new activism included sending U.S. Marines to the Dominican Republic to
protect the more reactionary side of the military, our side, against a popular
uprising and that part of the military trying to restore a democratically
elected reformist president. It also included sending U.S. naval forces to
Brazil in 1964, just in time to provide possible backup for a military uprising that overturned democracy there.

Whether the economic side of the Alliance for Progress had any potential to strengthen democracy in Latin America can seem an almost irrelevant
question, given the accompanying military-strategic interventions counter
to democracy. But the Brazilian case helps bring out a general question
about the role of economic aid in its own right, a question that applies to
many specific issues. This is the possibility that the very existence of a
significant aid program, subject to unilateral change or interruption by the
United States, can work against the survival of democratic governments.

The context in Brazil immediately preceding the overturn of democracy
provides a good illustration of the points discussed in the first section. In the
1950s the country was a fairly spectacular success story in terms of economic growth, and a notable example of the kind of growth that fosters
rising inequality. It had a large reserve of unskilled and very low-income
labor in agriculture, and did little to provide rural education even at the
primary level. The abundance of unskilled labor, backed up in the rural
sector with low productivity and earnings, helped hold down wages despite
rapid growth. As the hypothesis presented earlier suggests, this inequality-
enhancing system was rejected in the first election, that of 1960, in which a
populist leader could run on a platform promising radical change. The new
government introduced proposals for land reform and tax reforms, went
out of its way to support organization of rural labor, and changed the treatment of foreign investors by restricting withdrawal of profits. It also increased social welfare spending despite rising inflation. Foreign investment
slowed down greatly. The U.S. aid program, which had been helping to fuel
the prior process of unequal growth, was stopped as a protest against eco-

nomic mismanagement. With many other factors in the picture, including anti–United States statements on foreign policy by the populist government, an uprising by the Brazilian military in 1964 swept the democratic government off the scene in a manner scarcely more dignified than that of Guatemala.[16] To make the message clear, the new military government was warmly welcomed by the economist serving as U.S. ambassador to Brazil, and the aid program was immediately reactivated to serve this more responsible client.

To cut off economic aid to a bungling democratic government may be meant to force that government to adopt more coherent economic policies, but it can be heard as a statement that the government itself should be removed. To restore aid promptly and enthusiastically to a repressive military government that understands the statement in the latter sense could easily be seen as something of an invitation to the military forces of the Southern Cone in the following decade.

When an aid program has been helping to maintain a process of economic growth that is highly valued by private investors, and the program is then shut down as an expression of U.S. disapproval, it is hard to avoid fostering a conviction among private investors, and property owners generally, that they have a strong interest in changing the government. By the same token, the existence of an aid program that may be stopped can serve as a restraint on the ability of democratic governments to respond to popular preferences This was notably true in this period for the sensitive issue of policies toward foreign investment. Two notable cases in the 1960s were the failure of President Belaunde in Peru to take promised action to change the privileges of the International Petroleum Company, and the failure of President Frei in Chile to respond to popular pressures for nationalization of the U.S.-owned copper companies.[17] In Peru, when Belaunde backed away from promised action he was swiftly deposed by a populist military government that nationalized the company in question. In Chile Frei's refusal to act cost his Christian Democratic party considerable popular support, making it easier for Allende to win the next election and gain wide approval by nationalizing the companies anyway. Belaunde and Frei might have refused to follow popular pressures even if they had not faced the probability that action against the companies could mean the end of external aid. But if there is any substantial aid program going on, and it can be stopped immediately by the offended donor, the freedom of democratic government to respond to popular pressures is almost necessarily restricted.

It seems evident that aid programs can and often do aggravate dependency, restricting the choices and weakening the legitimacy of democratic governments. But this is only one aspect of a complex set of possibilities. They can conceivably strengthen democratic governments by helping them to solve specific problems and to correct some of the structural factors that make for inequitable growth. Their effects on public support for existing democracy can be positive in the right conditions, just as they can be negative in the wrong conditions. If the government is trying to carry out changes that work to favor more equitable growth, external aid can serve both as evidence of external support and as direct financial assistance. This is a context totally different from the connotation of subservience when the threat of reduced aid is used to force governments away from desired changes. Some of the mixture of positive and negative possibilities may be illuminated by conflicting strands in the experiences of Colombia in this period.

In the first years of the Alliance for Progress Colombia was a newly restored democracy, under the National Front coalition government. The main objective of the first two presidents under this agreement was to stabilize a political system torn apart by violence in the preceding two decades, rather than to implement any major changes in the economy. But land reform was a particularly live issue. The country's political leadership had long been divided between those who saw it as a way to incorporate peasant support in a more participatory political system, and those who saw it instead as an attack on the elite's traditional base of wealth and political power. U.S. support for such reform in the 1960s provided the extra push needed to tilt the balance toward adoption of a land reform program.[18] Actual results were very limited at first, under the conservative administration in office from 1962 to 1966. A U.S. review of progress in the first years of the Alliance for Progress brought out a dismal picture: the economy was drifting, little or nothing had changed, inequality had probably increased, and the effects of the aid program looked pitiful.[19]

Just at the time that this evaluation of the aid program was prepared, a new Colombian president, Carlos Lleras Restrepo, began to make significant changes in the country's economic strategy. He gave more emphasis to implementation of land reform, revised economic policies toward promotion of employment and new exports, began a shift away from protection as the means of promoting industrialization, and adopted a new exchange rate system to restructure incentives in support of these goals. Economic growth and industrialization speeded up, employment increased even more rapidly, and incomes of the previously left-out rural poor began to gain relative to the rest of the society.[20] The new economic strategy was very much helped in the first instance by the country's favorable treatment under the aid program, and that help did not preclude effective action by the national government. In fact, improvement of export earnings and the growing strength of the economy raised national self-confidence to the point that Colombia took the highly unusual step of deciding in 1975 to renounce any further reliance on economic aid.

The happier side of this experience in terms of reducing poverty and strengthening national autonomy was unfortunately followed by a halt to land reform under the president following Lleras Restrepo. The immediate cause was a problem common to almost any major break in economic and social relationships: a promised change beginning to take place stimulated pressures for faster and more complete reform. The radical side of the peasant movement began to seize land directly, landowners and the police responded violently, and the national political leadership caved in to the fear that revolutionary forces were becoming explosive. The leaders of the two traditional parties agreed to bury any further action under the land reform program and to apply repression to get rid of radical leadership in the peasant movement.[21] It was not the United States that turned off the land reform; it was the nation's political leaders. Still, it might have been relevant that the United States was by then no longer in the business of providing support for land reform but was more than ever in the business of providing military support. The military side became the main Colombian answer to demands for land reform. That change coincided with a sharp upturn of violence, a turn that has not since been reversed.

These experiences in Colombia support a two-sided view of the effects of a reform-oriented aid program: such a program will not be much help, if any, under a government that does not particularly want reform, and may even weaken pressures to take positive measures, but it can reinforce the efforts of governments that want to accomplish changes toward lessened inequality. The balance may have been on the negative side in the 1960s, but it need not be that way for an aid program more specifically designed to help implement programs of governments that are genuinely trying to create more equitable economic systems. And even in the conflict-ridden 1960s, it is possible that U.S. aid improved the chances for more equitable growth. This was the key decade for the long-delayed demographic transition toward family planning and lower fertility rates, promising eventually better conditions in labor markets throughout the region. It was also a key decade in terms of greatly increased efforts to widen access to education, and thereby to increase the share of the labor force likely to be able to enter fields requiring higher skills and paying higher wages. It seems at least likely that U.S. financial and technical support made the changes easier to implement, spread their effects more quickly, and in these respects contributed positively to the chances of greater equity.

The decade of the Alliance for Progress turned out to be one in which the share of the Latin American population living in conditions of poverty was considerably reduced. For the nine countries covered in a research study by the Economic Commission for Latin America, the percentage of people below the commission's specified poverty line fell from 51 percent in 1960 to 40 percent by 1970. Using an alternative measure of people below a much more stringent line of "destitution," the percentage fell from 26 percent in 1960 to 19 percent in 1970.[22] These reductions could be considered too slow to make any great difference in acceptability of existing political systems but at least they go in the right direction. Relatively generous aid in this period must have helped in some degree to make living conditions less awful for many people.

The contradictory effects of the Alliance for Progress do not suggest either that a reform-oriented aid program is useless or that it can be counted on to have strong positive effects on equity and the chances of democracy. The observed shift toward authoritarian governments in so many countries during and after the alliance seems much more closely associated with the cold war, with the military side of U.S. policies toward the region, than with the economic aid program. But it is also true that an aid program has a major potential for harm, by strengthening the conservative side of the society receiving aid and by enabling weak governments to postpone efforts for change. At the same time, it had the positive potential of supporting a considerable range of changes favorable for lower-income groups, and some of that potential was actually realized. The experience does not argue for any return to a regionwide program providing large-scale assistance for all countries that want it, regardless of whether their governments are reformist, reactionary, or simply inactive. But it does argue for something of the generosity of the economic side of the alliance, and for willingness to help with specific reforms that can change economic structures in ways favorable for more participatory growth.

Influences on Latin America of U.S. Economic Policies in the 1980s

The severely deflationary policies of the United States from 1978 to 1982 (and of England at the same time) hit Latin American economies hard by worsening their export markets, driving down prices of primary commodities, and driving up interest rates on their external debts. When the debt crisis broke out in 1982 and new private credit was almost completely cut off, that forced the region into contraction with falling investment, deteriorating public services, and accelerating inflation.[23] If the countries had not borrowed too much when external credit was cheap and plentiful in the 1970s, they need not have been hit this hard; if the United States had pursued more stable monetary policies, and especially if its own fiscal deficit had been reduced sharply when the economy recovered after 1982, the strains on Latin America could also have been much less than they were. It took both sides to make things go as badly wrong as they did.

When the United States and the other industrialized countries use contractionary policies to counteract inflationary trends, they certainly affect the developing countries but the effects are not necessarily negative. If such policies help stabilize the world economy, without creating recession, they could be positive for all sides. It was exactly this issue of maintaining overall balance in the world economy that led to the creation of the International Monetary Fund (IMF) in the first place, to provide credit to countries hit by falling external demand in order to prevent cumulative contraction. In line with this objective, most of the industrialized countries supported a major increase in lending facilities for the IMF and the World Bank at the start of the 1980s, to enable them to help the developing countries deal with recessionary world conditions. But that movement ran counter to the U.S. administration's ideological preference to leave the world economy up to private market forces. The administration fought to hold down any increases in lending power for the international financial institutions, and at the same time used its position within them to exert pressure to tighten up conditions for any new loans. The choice was to use the financial crisis to force a particular set of preferences on debtor countries.

For better or worse, the United States rarely speaks with a single voice. While the administration was resisting proposals for positive steps to deal with the strains on the world economy, the Federal Reserve responded swiftly to the Mexican government's announcement, in August 1982, that it could not maintain scheduled payments on its debts. The Federal Reserve took a leading role in negotiations for emergency credit, and quickly changed the direction of U.S. monetary policy to relieve tightness in world financial markets. The change helped considerably to reduce interest costs for Latin American debtors, but the Federal Reserve's room to move in the direction of monetary expansion and lower interest rates was simultaneously restricted by the administration's macroeconomic policies, or more specifically by its determined effort to force down the role of government by cutting taxes. The series of budget deficits, understandable and desirable in the depressed economic conditions of 1980–82, turned into a persistent factor operating to keep real interest rates relatively high throughout the rest of the decade. The effect on debtor countries was to keep the costs of debt service higher than it would otherwise have been, contributing to pressures for nonpayment in some cases and to severer domestic contraction than would otherwise have been necessary. The poor of Latin America—and much of the middle class as well—were forced to help pay the cost of rising consumption, stimulated by tax reductions, in the United States.

For the world economy as a whole, one of the most important consequences of the budget deficit and associated high interest rates was that international capital began to flow into the United States on a large scale. That had complex effects in many directions, including rapid appreciation of the dollar, swiftly rising imports in response, and intense pressures by U.S. firms to tighten import restrictions.[24] The administration resisted these pressures to some degree but still increased import restrictions through quotas and by exerting pressure on exporting countries to adopt "voluntary export restraints." The controls were aimed mainly at exporters from the Far East but they included tighter restraints on consumer products in which many Latin American countries might have been able to compete, as well as steel for which both Brazil and Mexico were becoming effective competitors. The inescapable effect of blocking some of the key exports otherwise possible for Latin American countries, in conditions of desperate need for foreign exchange earnings, was to exert greater downward pressure on wages in order to become competitive in other products.

U.S. policies on international financial questions gradually turned for the better as the debt crisis wore on. The administration reversed its initial resistance to expansion of lending power by the international institutions, and in the Baker and then the Brady plans began to give at least official support, if little actual money, to the idea that Latin America needed new external credit to resume growth. The more positive thesis became that renewed growth is essential in order to pay for debt service out of rising incomes rather than by grinding down living standards. Although external financing has been extremely modest so far, the change at least suggests recognition that extramarket help for growth is linked to the chances for more sustainable democracies.

In another promising change, the U.S. government quietly toned down its position that exchange rates and interest rates should be left up to private financial markets. Old clichés never die, but the United States began to take an active role in promoting coordination among the major industrial countries to limit conflicts over policies toward exchange rates and monetary conditions, to promote joint consideration of needs for either expansion or restraint of world demand, and to emphasize the needs of the developing countries for greater flows of new credit. The dangers implicit in such coordination by a few of the rich countries, without a voice for the rest of the world, are clear enough to invite debate about how to handle the objective in more participatory ways. But coordination itself, insofar as it reduces the violence of swings in world demand, in the terms of trade of developing countries, and in the conditions of external credit, could in principle do a great deal to lessen the kinds of shocks that have repeatedly upset whatever degree of economic stability Latin American countries have been able to achieve.

Economic Policies to Support Latin American Democracy in the 1990s

The implications of the preceding discussion might be summarized in terms of three groups of questions: first, external debts, conditions of international finance in general, and the ways in which U.S. macroeconomic policies affect those conditions; second, issues of international trade, including protection on both sides and positions toward export subsidies by Latin American countries; and third, the kinds of economic policy changes within Latin America that are encouraged or discouraged by conditions attached to credit either from the United States or from the international institutions in which it plays a major policy-determining role.

Debt and External Finance

Had the Latin American countries been relieved of the burden of external debt in 1982, when the extreme costs of servicing it first became evident, poverty would be less than it is now, employment and output would be higher, greater investment through the 1980s would have provided greater scope for growth in the 1990s, the extremes of inflation sweeping many countries would be much less likely, and democratic governments would probably have stronger public support. On the other side, so to speak, the creditors would have had to find some solution to their loss of financial assets, it is possible that some of the nondemocratic governments that have been replaced in the 1980s might still be holding on, the stimulus to more active opposition parties and possibly more meaningful democracy evident at present in Brazil and Mexico might be weaker, the measures taken under pressure to increase government revenue and reduce inefficiency would have been less likely, and the widespread shift of the region toward development of more diversified exports—and therefore to potentially greater autonomy—would also have been weakened. It is easy to vote in favor of eliminating the debt, but not all its consequences have been negative.

One of the best things that could happen to Latin America would be to learn to live without reliance on external credit. That could force a greater effort to develop domestic sources for capital equipment and inputs into production, encourage the search for domestic technological solutions, and keep up pressure for more diversified exports. Too much and too easy external credit fosters excessive dependence on foreign goods and foreign methods, and lessens pressures for efficiency and for change of any kind. In the words of Alejandro Foxley, the impossibility now of "depending, as in the past, on high levels of external credit would make it possible for Latin America's new leaders to launch an appeal for large-scale nationwide mobilization to solve the debt crisis through domestic savings and internal efforts."[25]

Foxley does not go on to conclude that the present context is optimal in such respects: it is not in fact one of independent growth but instead of near stagnation due in part to the costs of transferring resources to creditors. The intensity of the squeeze on Latin America might be measured by the change from a net resource inflow equal to 3 percent of gross domestic product (GDP) in 1981 to a net resource outflow equal to 6 percent of GDP by 1985.[26] Output per capita, consumption, and investment have all been driven down. Consumption per capita in 1988 was 9 percent lower than in 1980. Investment had averaged 23 percent of GDP for 1970–79, was driven down to 16 percent for 1983–87, and then barely edged back to 17 percent in 1988.[27] The burdens of dealing with the debts in a context of excessive constraint on new credit were clearly too great to allow reactivation of Latin America's capacity for economic growth.

More independent growth requires raising the share of output that can be exported, but to get the extreme inflation rates in Argentina, Brazil, and Peru under control, and to keep inflation from turning up again in Mexico, that objective may need to be made conditional on prior macroeconomic stabilization.[28] Stabilization requires first of all that the countries control their primary fiscal deficits (the deficits for domestic spending as distinct from purchases of foreign exchange to pay service requirements on the debts). But it would be greatly helped by reductions in required debt service to reduce both those domestic financing requirements and the need to generate a trade surplus to earn foreign exchange for external payments.

Negotiations over debt service included for several years a requirement by the IMF that countries continue making interest payments to the commercial banks as a condition of new IMF credit. A key change promoted by the United States, meant only for the special case but still significant, was to come to the rescue of the Bolivian stabilization program by permitting, or inducing, the IMF to stop insisting on this condition. That change made it possible to avoid continuing devaluations aimed at pushing additional exports to get the foreign exchange needed for the interest payments.[29] It allowed Bolivia to concentrate on efforts to stop inflation, uncomplicated by the contrary policy of export promotion. So far at least this approach—coupled with the essential counterpart of restraint on spending in Bolivia itself—has been one of the few instances of success in stopping hyperinflation. How all this will affect democracy remains most uncertain: everyone welcomed the striking success in slowing inflation, but not the accompanying rise in unemployment and fall in real wages. In this case, with poverty levels so extreme and democracy so new, aid that provided net new resources linked to alleviation of poverty might make a great difference.

If inflationary pressures return in the United States, that will rightly call for greater restraint on domestic spending. But the degree to which such a change would hurt debtor countries can be very different according to whether the restraint comes through taxes and reduced government spending or through restrictive monetary policies. To apply restraint on the monetary side alone maximizes the costs to debtor countries. Tax cuts in the United States in the 1980s, not matched by reductions in government spending, increased domestic consumption and had the counterpart effect of reducing living standards and growth in poorer countries. The United States and the international financial institutions are right to insist on the need for more responsible fiscal policy in Latin America; it would be in Latin America's own interest. But the world needs more of a two-way kind of pressure: fiscal irresponsibility by the United States can worsen poverty and destroy macroeconomic balance abroad.

Trade Policies

U.S. policies toward the use of protection and export subsidies by Latin American countries have had increasingly important effects in the 1980s, partly because their heightened need for credit has forced them to pay more attention to conditions established by the international lending institutions, partly because the United States has taken a tougher line within these institutions, and partly because it has adopted more aggressive bilateral negotiating techniques with greater use of retaliatory import restrictions. These pressures respond to real problems of trade restrictions abroad, but the more that the U.S. government gives in to them the more difficult it becomes for Latin American countries to restore growth of income and employment.

To exert strong pressure on Latin American countries to liberalize imports, while deliberalizing them in the United States, is not the kind of policy stance to make one glow with pride. But it is true that past excesses of protection have reduced efficiency and have probably worsened inequality by sheltering monopolistic firms, so reductions in protection clearly could have positive effects. They could be especially significant for actual or potential export industries, if the latter are released from excess costs imposed by being forced to get inputs from protected domestic suppliers. The overall effect would be to drive structures of production closer to the existing pattern of national comparative advantage. If comparative advantage includes a significant share of competitive export industries, as it does in East Asia and now in Brazil as well, the net effect could be to open up better possibilities for growth. Where the underlying pattern of relative costs is on the contrary more favorable to exports of primary products and imports of most industrial goods, then the net result could be to worsen both the distribution of income and the chances of future growth.

A return to comparative advantage could have seriously negative effects because of the structural characteristics explained in the chapter's first section: concentrated ownership of land and other natural resources, combined with growing ratios of labor to land and downward pressure on wages. If increased imports of industrial products act to reduce industrial employment, the most likely consequence is not a rise in more efficient alternative lines of production but a worsening of employment conditions. More positive results would be possible if industrial exports could be promoted through selective incentives, including subsidies. This type of export strategy was a central feature in the dynamic, and relatively egalitarian, styles of postwar economic growth in Japan, Korea, and Taiwan. Export subsidies can have adverse effects when they are given to inappropriate industries, when they are not financed by taxation to offset effects on the budget, or when they reduce the supply of goods because imports are not raised as fast as exports are increased. They need to be kept within a ceiling of maximum stimulus, to be financed by taxation, and to be used for increasing supplies of imports to keep up the growth of supplies for domestic use. Given such conditions, subsidies for industrial exports could be a potent help for any semi-industrialized developing country, including many countries in Latin America.

Relationships between promotion of nontraditional exports and income distribution have two important aspects: (1) if rapid growth of employment can be fostered by promotion of labor-intensive exports, the effects on real wages and income distribution are bound to become positive eventually; but (2), the initial effects on real wages in the formal sector may be negative and, if conditions of excess labor are extremely adverse, these negative effects may continue for a long time. The consequences depend on the degree of initial imbalance, the labor intensity of new exports, and the speed of their growth. Possible conclusion: it would be very much worthwhile to move the structure of production in the right direction for sustained increases in real wages by promoting industrial exports, but negative effects in the first stage point to the need for complementary social expenditure policies to keep up living standards of the poor until market forces become sufficiently positive.

U.S. Pressures on Latin American Economic Strategies

Mutually helpful relationships between the United States and Latin American governments are not likely to be furthered by using a period of intense need for external credit on their part as the time to demand that they remake their economic systems in the U.S. image. Some aspects of liberalization and privatization may be desirable in their interest, and more attention to macroeconomic balance is certainly in their interest, but to insist on detailed internal changes as the price of credit is not in the interest of either side. Negative effects are likely in part because many of the changes that the United States has been trying to sell in recent years would worsen inequality and for that reason could weaken democracy. Negative results are also likely because using a period of extreme financial need to force countries to swallow unwelcome medicine (as distinct from choosing it freely by their own decisions) demeans the governments concerned and sets up a good case for reversal of such policies in the future. Democracies need a minimum of self-confidence and self-value if they are to hold together in the face of strains. To build up such confidence by providing external conditions that help their economic systems function better would be a clear gain. To insist that they change their systems is not.

The central thesis of the chapter's introductory section is that the free operation of market forces acting through private enterprise is in common Latin American conditions systematically adverse to equality and to the minimal levels of personal security necessary for public acceptance of democratic governments. Informed voters will, if given the chance, consistently get rid of governments that follow the main lines of economic policy on which the United States has in the 1980s tried to insist. Our style of economics is not at present favorable for democracy in Latin America.

The other side of the coin is that particular *kinds* of economic strategy frequently practiced by Latin American governments can be just as bad or worse for equality and growth than our free-market themes. Overvalued exchange rates can hurt industrialization and employment by blocking potential industrial exports and by making imports too cheap; fiscal deficits in conditions of supply shortages and inflationary pressure aggravate inflation and turn the public against any democratic government; and high protection for particular firms may worsen inequality at the same time as it wastes resources and takes away the possibility of competition that could help restrain inflation. Changes made from common past practices in these respects, or more generally an increase in attention to the need for both external and internal macroeconomic balance, should be helpful for Latin American economies and strengthen rather than hurt the survival chances of democracies.

The scope for gain by specific changes in economic policies does not mean that it is desirable to insist on reducing the economic role of government in general, either for support to increase economic growth or for efforts to lessen inequality. The case for relying more on market forces is superficially strong because of the multitude of self-inflicted forms of past damage, under both authoritarian and democratic regimes. But the underlying structural context is one in which positive action is essential if growth is to be more equal. The main problem is not government action per se; what counts is the basic set of purposes and the methods that governments actually use. Given a democratic government truly interested in more equitable growth, it can do more to pursue that objective if it has a strong tax base; participates actively in shaping incentives for investment; can keep up its own investment in education, infrastructure, and social programs in general; and can use subsidies when appropriate both for social purposes and for stimulation of new industries and new exports. If by any succession of miracles Latin America is blessed with democratic governments that want to move in directions of more equitable growth, they should be encouraged and helped to act, not discouraged.

Conclusions

Economic conditions do not dictate political outcomes. One of the most promising and in many ways surprising characteristics of both new and established Latin American democracies in the 1980s was the resilience they displayed in the face of severely adverse economic conditions. The strains helped stimulate increased political awareness and activism, but in most cases this has been a positive activism through participation rather than a return toward mutual destruction.[30] That strengthened flexibility may be related to an increase in the value that many Latin Americans place on the survival of democracy.[31] Given greater concern to negotiate solutions acceptable to conflicting interests, response to economic adversity may serve to build up confidence in national ability to handle problems peacefully. But economic strains do not go away just because conflicting groups within societies try to cooperate: it is also essential both that they adopt workable economic strategies and that the outside world does not create intolerably adverse conditions.

The United States can help by providing more resources to alleviate current strains, by promoting greater stability in world economic conditions, by turning back from the trend of the 1980s toward increased protectionism, and by paying more attention to the negative consequences of trying to force on everyone else its own preference for private market solutions. A fundamental change for the better might just possibly be developing now. The United States "may be released from a great fear: the fear of communism that has dominated American society for so long."[32] For relationships with Latin America, that fear has led to persistent reinforcement of the side of their societies opposed to change in the interest of equity. It led to the destruction of reformist democracy in Guatemala, poisoned the Alliance for Progress, and encouraged the right-wing military factions that crushed democracy in the Southern Cone.

The most evident economic constraint holding back growth and aggravating inflation in the majority of these countries throughout the past decade has been tight restriction on external credit combined with the burden of service payments on their debts. Latin America has had to transfer resources to the United States ever since 1982, effectively helping to finance spending in excess of production in the United States at the cost of lower investment and living standards in the region, greater inflation, and slow or no growth in per capita income. If the United States were seriously interested in being helpful, it could provide new external credit and share the costs of writing off most of the debt. How could that be financed when the United States itself has a budget deficit and has been running close to the limits of its productive capacity? It could be done by adopting exactly the same kind of fiscal responsibility recommended for the Latin American countries: raise taxes, restrain consumption, offset any fall in demand by monetary expansion, and raise the share of output that is directed to exports.

It hardly needs saying, but clearly needs changed actions, that import restrictions by the United States go directly contrary to the possibilities for stabilization and growth in Latin America. Domestic pressure for such restrictions could be eased by a more competitive exchange rate for the dollar, and that in turn depends on more responsible fiscal policy.

Coordination of macroeconomic and exchange rate policies among the main industrial countries could reduce the violence of swings in aggregate world demand and monetary conditions, and thereby lessen dramatic changes in the terms of trade of developing countries, in the room for growth of exports, in real interest rates, and in the availability of international credit. Coordination requires that the United States responds to advice of other countries on such sensitive questions as fiscal policy and exchange rates. That may be asking too much: advice is easier to give to others than to hear. But any coordination that might be achieved by the industrialized countries could lessen external shocks and thereby raise the chances of successful economic policies for all developing countries.

The changes that the United States has tried to encourage in the economic policies of the Latin American countries include some features that are almost surely desirable for their own ability to control their economies and resume growth, and a good many that are not. The desirable group includes pressures to keep up exchange rates favorable for exports, to reduce extremes of protection, and to make greater efforts to hold down fiscal deficits. The unhelpful side includes opposition to intervention by governments even when it could foster more equitable growth, to subsidies for new exports, and to the kinds of intervention in the price system that could act to lessen poverty and inequality. To drive governments away from such policies in favor of reliance on private market forces could foster more inequity and more strains for democratic government than can possibly be justified by any gains of efficiency.

Pressures to cut down the role of the public sector can readily be understood in terms of frequent waste and costly actions by governments, but the fact that mistakes are common does not mean that weaker governments are desirable. Democratic governments in Latin America, facing severe constraints on all sides, need a high capacity to carry through decisions, to control the operation of market forces in the interest of lessened inequality without blocking efficiency, to impose taxation effectively, and to act in some degree on behalf of the people in these societies who get left out of the growth process. The U.S. preference for a restricted role of government goes in many respects in the wrong direction for the needs of democratic government in Latin America.

Attempts to induce changes in the economic strategies of Latin American countries by conditions attached to debt relief or new credit involve a contradiction between two important principles. One is that provision of access to valuable resources should not be allowed to serve as a prop allowing governments to continue policies that weaken their economic systems, foster inequality, and compromise the future. The second is that the outside world should not force countries to follow paths contrary to the preferences of their people. Even if the prescribed paths are more productive in economic terms, to be forced into a kind of subservience contrary to national values is bound to weaken confidence that democracies can respond to what their people want, and confidence in the value of the nation itself. Both principles have claims to respect. The conflict between them argues for a difficult balancing act, avoiding ideological prescriptions of the kind of economic institutions and strategy that other countries should adopt, while at the same time trying to help implement the specific kinds of structural change needed for more participatory growth.

Notes

1. The U.S. government has avoided, probably wisely, any detailed official statement of what it would mean to conform fully to the call for liberalization and privatization in the Baker and Brady plans. Statements by the International Monetary Fund (IMF) and the World Bank have been frequent, with a consistent core but varied specifics. For two clear but different statements by IMF economists, see Anthony Lanyi, "World Economic Outlook and Prospects for Latin America," and Vito Tanzi, "Fiscal Policy, Growth, and Design of Stabilization Programs," in Ana Maria Martirena-Mantel, ed., *External Debt, Savings, and Growth in Latin America* (Washington, D.C., and Buenos Aires: International Monetary Fund and Instituto Torcuato di Tella, 1987), pp. 26–50 and 121–41.

2. John Sheahan, *Patterns of Development in Latin America: Poverty, Repression, and Economic Strategy* (Princeton: Princeton University Press, 1987), esp. chap. 12.

3. Alan B. Simmons, "Social Inequality and Demographic Transition," in Archibald Ritter and David Pollock, eds., *Latin American Prospects for the 1980s* (New York: Praeger, 1983).

4. World Bank, *World Tables*, 3d ed. (Washington, D.C.: World Bank, 1983), 2: 158–59.

5. Thomas F. Carroll, "The Land Reform Issue in Latin America," in Albert Hirschman, ed., *Latin American Issues: Essays and Comments* (New York: Twentieth Century Fund, 1961); Solon Barraclough, ed., *Agrarian Structures in Latin America* (Lexington, Mass.: Lexington Books, 1973); Alain de Janvry, *The Agrarian Question and Reformism in Latin America* (Baltimore: Johns Hopkins University Press, 1981).

6. Sheahan, *Patterns,* table 3.1, p. 56.

7. This process is traced through for six Latin American countries in Jeffrey Sachs, "Social Conflict and Populist Policies in Latin America," and Rudiger Dornbusch and Sebastian Edwards, "Macroeconomic Populism in Latin America," National Bureau of Economic Research, Working Papers no. 2897 and 2986 (Cambridge, Mass.: National Bureau of Economic Research, 1989).

8. François Bourguignon and Christian Morrisson, *External Trade and Income Distribution* (Paris: OECD, Development Research Centre, 1989).

9. John Sheahan, "Economic Policies and the Prospects for Successful Transition from Authoritarian Rule in Latin America," in Guillermo O'Donnell, Philippe C. Schmitter, and Laurence Whitehead, eds., *Transitions from Authoritarian Rule* (Baltimore: Johns Hopkins University Press, 1986), pp. 154–64.

10. Marita Garcia and Per Pinstrup-Andersen, *The Pilot Food Subsidy Scheme in the Philippines: Its Impact on Income, Food Consumption and Nutritional Status,* Research Report 61 (Washington, D.C.: International Food Policy Research Institute, August 1987); Harold Alderman, *The Effects of Food Price and Income Changes on the Acquisition of Food by Low-Income Households* (Washington, D.C.: International Food Policy Research Institute, 1986).

11. Robert A. Pollard, *Economic Security and the Origins of the Cold War, 1945–1950* (New York: Columbia University Press, 1985).

12. Robert A. Packenham, *Liberal America and the Third World: Political Development Ideas in Foreign Aid and Social Science* (Princeton: Princeton University Press, 1973).

214 • John Sheahan

13. Thomas Melville and Marjorie Melville, *Guatemala: The Politics of Land Ownership* (New York: Free Press, 1971); Richard H. Immerman, *The CIA in Guatemala: The Foreign Policy of Intervention* (Austin: University of Texas Press, 1982); Stephen C. Schlesinger and Stephen Kinzer, *Bitter Fruit: The Untold Story of the American Coup in Guatemala* (Garden City, N.Y.: Doubleday, 1982).

14. William Paddock and Elizabeth Paddock, *We Don't Know How: An Independent Analysis of What They Call Success in Foreign Assistance* (Ames: Iowa State University Press, 1973).

15. Abraham Lowenthal, *Partners in Conflict: The United States and Latin America* (Baltimore: Johns Hopkins University Press, 1987), p. 30.

16. Alfred Stepan, "Political Leadership and Regime Breakdown," in Juan J. Linz and Alfred Stepan, eds., *The Breakdown of Democratic Regimes: Latin America* (Baltimore: Johns Hopkins University Press, 1978), pp. 110–37; Phyllis R. Parker, *Brazil and the Quiet Intervention* (Austin: University of Texas Press, 1979); Michael Wallerstein, "The Collapse of Democracy in Brazil: Its Economic Determinants," *Latin American Research Review* 15, no. 3 (1980): 3–40.

17. Sheahan, *Patterns,* pp. 207, 211, 242–43.

18. Merilee Grindle, *State and Countryside: Development Policy and Agrarian Politics in Latin America* (Baltimore: Johns Hopkins University Press, 1986).

19. U.S. Senate, Committee on Foreign Relations, Subcommittee on American Republics Affairs, *Survey of the Alliance for Progress,* Document 17, 91st Congress, 1st Session (12844–2) (Washington, D.C.: U.S. Government Printing Office, 1969).

20. Although these changes in economic strategy were favorable for earnings of the rural poor and of unorganized urban workers, they were initially adverse for real wages in formal urban sector employment. If one focuses on wages versus profits of industrial workers, the changes were initially adverse for equity; if one focuses on relative earnings of the poor, they were favorable. By 1975, real wages of workers in the formal urban sector began to go up too, and recent studies suggest that the overall distribution of income has become less unequal: Miguel Urrutia, *Winners and Losers in Colombia's Economic Growth in the 1970s* (Oxford: Oxford University Press, 1985), and Eduardo Sarmiento, "El desarrollo colombiano: un proceso de desequilibrio," monografía presentada al Simposio internaciónal sobre la obra de Hirschman y una nueva estrategia de desarrollo para América Latina, Buenos Aires, noviembre de 1989.

21. Leon Zamosc, *The Agrarian Question and the Peasant Movement in Colombia* (Cambridge: Cambridge University Press, 1986); Bruce Bagley, "The State and the Peasantry in Contemporary Colombia," *Latin American Issues* 6 (1988): 1–86.

22. Sergio Molina, "La pobreza en América Latina: situación, evolución y orientaciones de políticas," in CEPAL-PNUD, *¿Se puede superar la pobreza en América Latina?* (Santiago: Naciones Unidas, 1980), p. 23.

23. Andrés Bianchi, "Adjustment in Latin America, 1981–86," in Vittorio Corbo, Morris Goldstein, and Mohsin Khan, eds., *Growth-Oriented Adjustment Programs* (Washington, D.C.: International Monetary Fund and World Bank, 1987), pp. 179–225; Inter-American Development Bank, *Economic and Social Progress in Latin America, 1985 Report: External Debt: Crisis and Adjustment* (Washington, D.C.: IDB, 1985), and following *Annual Reports.*

24. Rudiger Dornbusch and Jeffrey A. Frankel, "Macroeconomics and Protection," in Robert M. Stern, ed., *United States Trade Policies in a Changing World* (Cambridge: MIT Press, 1987), pp. 77–130.

25. Alejandro Foxley, "The Foreign Debt Problem from a Latin American Viewpoint," in Richard E. Feinberg and Ricardo Ffrench-Davis, eds., *Development and External Debt: Bases for a New Consensus* (Notre Dame, Ind.: University of Notre Dame Press, 1988), quotation from p. 81.

26. Inter-American Development Bank, *Economic and Social Progress in Latin America, 1988 Report,* p. 5. The net outflow of resources stayed close to 5 percent of GDP through 1986 and 1987.

27. IDB, *1988 Report,* p. 22, and *1989 Report,* pp. 1, 11.

28. Jeffrey Sachs, "Trade and Exchange Rate Policies in Growth-Oriented Adjustment Programs," in Corbo, Goldstein, and Kahn, *Growth-Oriented Adjustment Programs,* pp. 303–7.

29. Ibid., pp. 316–17.

30. Paul Drake, "Debt and Democracy in Latin America, 1920s–1980s," and Robert Kaufman and Barbara Stallings, "Debt and Democracy in the 1980s: The Latin American Experience," in Robert Kaufman and Barbara Stallings, eds., *Debt and Democracy in Latin America* (Boulder, Colo.: Westview Press, 1989), pp. 39–58 and 201–23; Karen Remmer, "The Political Impact of the Debt Crisis in Latin America," Paper presented at the conference on "Financing Latin American Growth: Prospects for the 1990s," Bard College, October 1988.

31. James M. Malloy and Mitchell A. Seligson, eds., *Authoritarians and Democrats: Regime Transition in Latin America* (Pittsburgh: Pittsburgh University Press, 1987), especially the chapter by Silvio Duncan Baretta and John Markoff, "Brazil's *Abertura:* From What to What?", pp. 43–65.

32. Anthony Lewis, "Free at Last?" *New York Times,* November 23, 1989, p. 27.

8 | The Imposition of Democracy

Laurence Whitehead

HISTORY indicates that democracy is quite frequently established by undemocratic means. This is especially true of the history of U.S. foreign relations, which have frequently involved the promotion of democracy by force of arms. France, Italy, Japan, and West Germany all acquired or re-acquired democratic institutions under the tutelage of American armed forces. So, the "imposition" of democracy is no contradiction in terms, at least not in the U.S. political tradition. In fact one feature distinguishing the United States from all previously dominant or hegemonic powers is its persistent and self-proclaimed commitment to the promotion of democracy as an integral element of its foreign policy, and its long-standing confidence that "all good things" (U.S. influence and security, economic freedom and prosperity, political liberty and representative government) tend naturally to go together. With such confidence and assertiveness rooted in the American tradition, and with some remarkable successes available as confirmation of their initial intuition, policy makers in Washington are disinclined to believe that "democracy by imposition" is a concept containing any particularly intractable contradictions. On this issue, however, the perceptions of most Latin American policy makers are strikingly different.

For although a democratic regime may originate from an act of external imposition, it will subsequently be necessary to secure the withdrawal of intrusive foreign influences if the democracy is eventually to take root and to secure the trust and acceptance of the national society in question. Unfortunately this intuitively plausible model of the democratization process assumes the prior existence of a well-defined nation-state in which no major problems of national identity remain pending. It also implicitly views the act of imposition as an isolated event, rather than as one episode in a protracted sequence of interactions between a dominant nation and a subordinate one. Neither of these assumptions can be safely made in relation to the United States and Latin America, which is why the imposition of democracy in the region has often proved a problematic and frustrating experience. In fact, as discussed in this chapter, the broad notion of "imposition" may embrace a considerable variety of distinctive forms, each with its own logic and consequences. Three variants are considered here: incorporation, invasion, and intimidation.

For most of the present century, and in particular since the 1940s, the United States has occupied a dominant position in the affairs of the Western Hemisphere. Its ascendancy has been not only economic, demographic, and military but also political, ideological, and to some extent even cultural. In contrast to the position of the majority of dominant ("hegemonic") powers in the course of world history, U.S. ascendancy over its neighbors has been underpinned by a series of shared values, traditions, and assumptions. These were all liberal republics, at least in origin and rhetoric; they were all sheltered by the wide Atlantic from the internecine struggles of Europe, a region from which the dominant elites nevertheless drew much of their inspiration. For the most part these were underpopulated rather than over-populated territories, with corresponding opportunities for geographical and social mobility. Although Latin America contained large areas of poverty, overcrowding, and misery, there were also considerable economic dynamism and modernity. Both private enterprise and public welfare provision, such as that for education, were considerably more advanced than in most of the Third World, and they were well established much earlier.

In short, by world standards this was quite favorable terrain for the implantation of conventional liberal democracy. And indeed democracy *did* flower here—in Uruguay before World War I; in Argentina in the 1920s; in Chile from the 1930s; in Costa Rica after 1948; in Colombia and Venezuela since 1958; and more generally in the 1970s and 1980s. Moreover, throughout this whole period the United States, as the dominant power, proclaimed the promotion of democracy to be one of its enduring regional priorities. So, on the face of it, the subject of this volume should be unproblematic. Both Latin America and North American predispositions favored the generalized establishment of liberal democracy, and that is what we are now witnessing with only a few laggards where extrahemispheric antidemocratic influences are yet to be eradicated (the most important of which is Cuba).

The view just outlined may have some instinctive support (at least within the more conservative circles in the United States); but of course, as the various contributors to this volume make clear, it requires a great deal of qualification and revision. In particular we cannot yet assume a liberal democratic "end of history" for Latin America at the end of the twentieth century. The obstacles to such an outcome remain extremely large and can by no means be encapsulated under the rubric of extrahemispheric subversion.

But if after half a century or more the construction of democracy in Latin America remains incomplete and uncertain, then a critical examination of the limitations of past efforts is required. Why, if the United States has generally favored democracy promotion for so long, and if U.S. influence in the region has been so great, and if the underlying local realities have been relatively favorable—why then have the results been so slow, uneven, and modest? For clarity this chapter concentrates on one aspect of the U.S. record of democracy promotion: its reliance on various methods of imposition, particularly in those countries where the relative power of the United States is most overwhelming.

The point can be put provocatively, but not unfairly, as follows. There is only one place in Latin America where a strong consolidated liberal democracy has been established largely as a result of a sustained U.S. commitment to that end. (The reader unable to identify the place in question may wish to skip a few pages to solve the puzzle.) Apart from this one very clear-cut exception, there is no reason to dissent from the verdict of G. Pope Atkins: "U.S. attempts to extend the practices of representative democracy and protection of human rights have been ambiguous and vacillating. When resources have been committed to the goal of democratic development, it has usually been viewed as an instrumental objective aimed at achieving one or the other of the long-range goals,"[1] namely, the maintenance of political stability and the prevention of foreign control.

The interpretation proposed in this chapter derives from the assumption that not all good things necessarily go together. Where the promotion of democracy reinforces political stability, creates profitable business opportunities, and excludes rival powers from any real influence within a given territory (as in the exceptional case to be discussed), strong and sustained support for democratization may be expected from Washington. But what if democracy promotion might destabilize a key ally (as in Mexico in 1988)? What if the local electorate supports parties or policies hostile to U.S. business interests (Guatemala, 1950; Chile, 1970; almost Brazil, 1989)? What if the "institutionalization of uncertainty" implied by an open democratic contest includes uncertainty over the future international alignment of a strategic neighbor (Jamaica, 1980; or, prospectively, Nicaragua, 1996)? In all such cases both history and theory would suggest that Washington's commitment to the goal of democracy promotion could be expected to waver; and that at least some part of the U.S. policy-making apparatus would be tempted to disregard democratic niceties in pursuit of the more urgent goals of stability, a good business climate, and the preservation of U.S. ascendancy in the region.

In South America during the 1980s the conflict between democracy promotion and other U.S. foreign policy goals was attenuated as the Cold War faded, and as the debt crisis impelled Southern Hemisphere governments of all persuasions to compete in attracting scarce foreign capital.

Even so, many in Washington were reluctant to destabilize friendly authoritarian regimes. In fact, the sharp distinction made in the early 1980s between "authoritarian" and "totalitarian" variants of undemocratic politics had the effect of deflecting pressure against the former. However, the Argentine military regime destabilized itself by precipitating the Falklands/ Malvinas war, and the Uruguayans achieved a similar result by holding and unexpectedly losing a plebiscite. As the decade progressed, the argument about destabilization shifted, for it became increasingly clear that rigid defense of an authoritarian status quo was likely to be more destabilizing than a controlled and gradual liberalization. Even where the eventual outcome of liberalization was likely to be full democratization, with all the risks and uncertainties that that might entail, almost any incoming civilian government would be driven to mend its fences with Washington by the severity of the socioeconomic problems it would inherit, and by the need to circumvent the potential veto power of vested interests left over from authoritarian rule. Thus the United States had less to fear from South American democratization in the 1980s than would have been the case a decade or two earlier. It also had relatively limited influence south of the Caribbean and therefore prudence dictated that if democratization was coming anyway, Washington would be well advised to anticipate and herald the change.

Conditions were different in the Caribbean basin and on the Central American isthmus, however. There America's Cold War reflexes still predominated during the 1980s. Even after fears of Soviet intentions were assuaged by Gorbachev's new policies, Washington policy makers remained affronted by Castro's Cuba, and by the challenges from Havana that they still perceived in El Salvador, Nicaragua, and Panama. Several of America's allies still seemed vulnerable to destabilization if too much was demanded of them in the areas of human rights and respect for political pluralism. Although by the eighties U.S. investments were generally far less important than they had been in earlier periods, this part of Latin America had become quite intimately linked to the U.S. economy via migratory flows, the concessionary trade links encouraged under the Caribbean Basin Initiative, and large-scale illegal transactions concerning narcotics, armaments, and money laundering. In contrast to South America, therefore, the promotion of democracy in the Caribbean Basin still had the potential to clash quite fundamentally with Washington's other more traditional foreign policy priorities. Moreover the inequalities of power between the U.S. and many of the region's mini- and microstates was far greater than in most of South America, and the interventionist tradition was far more strongly entrenched. It is here that the U.S. capacity to "promote democracy" in foreign lands should be at its greatest; and it is here that the U.S. has the longest track record of "teaching good government," including by direct occupation and military imposition.

This chapter therefore examines three selected examples of the imposition of democracy in those parts of the Caribbean Basin where U.S. ascendancy has been longest and greatest. The object is to determine under what conditions (and with what limitations) Washington has succeeded in achieving this proclaimed policy goal; and therefore *what kind* of democracy is likely to be favored by a massive and unilateral deployment of U.S. power in the region. This is an exercise in recent comparative history, but, as noted briefly in the conclusion, it also has implications for the 1990s, particularly in relation to the still-pending issue of Cuba. Three methods of imposition have been selected for comparison: incorporation, invasion, and intimidation. This highlights the contrast between U.S. and European Community approaches to democracy promotion in adjoining territories. Whereas the decision-making processes of the United States tend to favor democracy promotion by imposition, the European treaty structure precludes such an approach.

Democracy Promotion through Incorporation: Puerto Rico

The one Latin American country with a fully consolidated democratic regime where the United States has played a consistent, sustained, and determining role in the democratization process is of course the Commonwealth[2] of Puerto Rico. Yet this spectacular example is overlooked in the literature, perhaps simply because it is so easy to forget that Puerto Rico is indeed a Latin American country, or more seriously perhaps because the political price paid for this U.S. support—namely, the absence of sovereignty—is unwelcomely high. But in fact the Puerto Rican experience cannot be dismissed at all lightly, for although it is such a rare case of "success," it actually dramatizes in an extreme form processes of imposition that can also as we shall see be observed elsewhere.

In the exceptional case of Puerto Rico there is no ambiguity about use of the term *imposition* to describe the first phase of American policy. Whereas in Cuba and in Panama U.S. intervention was at least nominally in support of local forces fighting for national liberation, the U.S. seizure of Puerto Rico from Spain in 1898 was a straightforward act of colonialism. Cuba and Panama were both allowed a degree of semi-independence in the early 1900s, whereas fifty years were to elapse before Puerto Rico's colonial status began to shift. Even now the eventual outcome (labeled here democratization through incorporation) is by no means complete. However, if we take incorporation as the essential pattern, then the U.S. contribution to Puerto Rican democracy can be compared with the experience of Hawaii, or with the French role in Guadeloupe and Martinique, not to mention various British colonies such as Bermuda. In all these instances it seems that the domestic entrenchment of representative institutions has been forcefully promoted by a metropolitan power whose permanent involvement and commitment precludes the possibility of self-determination. In other words, they all appear to involve some kind of trade-off between sovereignty and external support for democracy.

The Puerto Rican experience provides a model case. Here we shall briefly consider the nature and scale of the U.S. contribution to Puerto Rican democracy; the reasons why it was more durable and effective than elsewhere in Latin America; and the consequences for the regime both positive (strong consolidation) and negative (insecurity over political identity, lack of national authenticity). In the light of this discussion some conclusions can be drawn about the *type* of democratization likely to arise from such strong external involvement, and about the applicability or otherwise of this broad approach in other parts of Latin America.

Political parties, representative institutions, and competitive elections existed in colonial Puerto Rico long prior to the landing of U.S. troops in July 1898, although the Spanish imperial authorities retained the right to veto local laws. On the other hand, starting in 1812, Puerto Rican deputies were seated in successive Spanish Cortés and could vote on all legislation (a contrast to the present situation in which the island's commissioner in Washington may vote in committee but has no vote on the floor of Congress). However this system of representation was far too restricted to qualify as a modern democracy. Whether one would have developed in the absence of U.S. intervention is a tantalizing but unanswerable question. (It could also be asked of Cuba, Panama, the Dominican Republic, and other countries.) At any rate, in 1898 the Spanish system of representation appears to have commanded little loyalty, and most Puerto Ricans are said to have welcomed the American troops, accompanied as they were by the promise "to give to the people of your beautiful island the largest measure of liberty consistent with this military occupation . . . to promote your prosperity and bestow upon you the immunities and blessings of the liberal institutions of our government," according to the U.S. military proclamation of July 28, 1898.

From 1900 onward U.S. law guaranteed islanders the right to elect mayors and the lower house of a legislative assembly (on a restricted franchise), but executive power was vested in nominees from Washington. Since 1917 Puerto Ricans have enjoyed American citizenship (including liability to the military draft), and there has been an elected bicameral assembly with some authority over the cabinet. From 1948 onward the governor has been directly elected. However, these American citizens cannot vote in presidential elections, and the island's elected authorities lack various attributes of sovereignty such as the power to set tariffs, to enter into international economic agreements, or to control the immigration of foreign (non-U.S.) citizens. Although the island has its own electoral commission and its own supreme court, the ultimate arbiter of disputed local elections, like that of 1980 (and indeed of all constitutional issues), remains the U.S. Supreme

Court. Other matters of vital concern to the islanders, such as the Internal Revenue Code and the funding of the U.S. welfare system, are also decided in Washington without their participation. It is true that they can vote from time to time in plebiscites to determine possible changes in their constitutional status—for example, in 1967 39 percent voted to apply to Washington for statehood, and more may do so in the next test expected in the early 1990s. But the power of decision on such changes remains vested in the U.S. Congress, and such tests of Puerto Rican public opinion are no more than advisory, albeit of great moral force. This, then, is the current status of Puerto Rican democratic institutionality.

So in what sense does Puerto Rico have a "fully consolidated democracy," and what was the U.S. contribution to the consolidation process? There is as yet no clear consensus on what constitutes the "full consolidation" of a democratic process, but by most criteria Puerto Rico ranks ahead of almost every other Latin American and Caribbean country. The closest rival with full sovereignty is Costa Rica. Elsewhere[3] I have argued that one partial but very revealing test of whether a fragile democracy has become fully consolidated is to ask whether the citizens of a long-established and secure democracy would feel unthreatened by an act of political unification or incorporation. By this standard the European parliament in Strasbourg implicitly judged Portugal, Spain, and Greece to have fully consolidated democracies by the 1980s (but not Turkey). Likewise the U.S. Congress made this judgment about Hawaii in 1959. It seems extremely probable that Puerto Rico would have passed this test in 1967, if the plebiscite of that year had favored statehood, and the same outcome seems even clearer if that situation arises in the 1990s. By this severe test, then, Puerto Rican democracy has long been remarkably "consolidated." This is not a claim that can yet be safely made about, say, the Dominican Republic or Venezuela.

By more conventional criteria Puerto Rico established a modern electoral democracy in successive stages. Female suffrage was obtained in 1932; universal adult suffrage in 1936; the exchange of votes for favors became less common after 1940; promotion by merit began to replace the spoils system of public employment in 1947. The U.S. Congress was of course directly responsible for progress while the island remained a colony. Then with the 1952 constitution the local legislature established a strong legal framework for electoral competition. (It is worth noting that whereas in the British Caribbean democratic structures were created from above by the less-than-democratic method of imperial orders in council, in Puerto Rico this was the work of a popularly constituted constitutional convention.) The organization of a well-structured majority party, the Partido Popular Democrático (PPD), no doubt facilitated this process of institution building. U.S. support was ensured when the PPD politically isolated and neutralized the once-powerful independence movement; thenceforth the best way for

Washington to stabilize the power of its Puerto Rican allies was to back their democratization project.

In due course a second more conservative party, the Partido Nuevo Progresista (PNP), gained sufficient electoral strength to constitute a genuine alternative to the PPD, this time by advocating full statehood. The governorship has alternated between these two parties in successive elections (in 1968, 1972, 1976, and 1984). Control of the legislature has also passed back and forth in a normal manner. Minor parties have also established niches for themselves (in part because Puerto Rican law provides for minority-party representation on local councils), and the political commitment of the electorate is confirmed by the extremely high levels of turnout that characterize most elections, even after the voting age was lowered to eighteen in 1971 (an estimated 88.3 percent in the 1980 governorship election, for example, compared with the 59.2 percent of the U.S. voting age population who reported voting in the presidential election held on the same day).[4] Since 1977 Puerto Ricans have also participated in the primaries organized by the two main U.S. parties to select their presidential nominees. As already noted, the law also provides for the possibility of holding plebiscites, as was done in 1952 and 1967 on the status issue.

In view of this record it is hard to dissent from the conventional judgment that Puerto Rico has established a free and democratic system of political representation. Freedom House, for example, considers that in 1985 Puerto Rico was one of only 10 nonsovereign territories (out of 55) to enjoy full civil liberties (only 20 out of 167 sovereign states met this condition). In the nonsovereign territories of the Caribbean only the Netherlands Antilles and the British Virgin Islands reached the same standard, and in the sovereign states of Latin America and the Caribbean only Belize, Costa Rica, and St. Kitts were rated as highly.[5] For the sake of realism it must also be mentioned, however, that when in 1981 the Puerto Rican supreme court ruled in favor of the PPD and against the PNP in an election dispute, the PNP governor accused it of blatant partiality, arguing that six of the seven judges had been appointed by the PPD. He therefore appealed the case to the U.S. Supreme Court (claiming that the matter was a civil rights rather than an electoral issue and was therefore subject to federal law). Eventually the Washington court upheld the original Puerto Rican court judgment.

As this appeal to the U.S. Supreme Court indicates, the whole process of democratization in Puerto Rico has been continuously stabilized and guaranteed by the institutions of the United States. Certainly the islanders and their political leaders have played leading and for the most part constructive roles in this process, but always within a framework provided from outside. Even the electoral timetable is set by the rhythms of Washington. Indeed one reason why Puerto Rican democracy receives so little international recognition is that gubernatorial election results coincide with and are therefore swamped by simultaneous U.S. presidential results. So this case represents a clear exception to the generalization that in postwar Latin America democratizations are internally driven, with external factors playing only a secondary part.

Why was U.S. support for democracy so much more durable and effective than elsewhere in Latin America? Obviously the 1898 invasion denied external powers access to the island and thus removed a competing foreign policy concern. The key step was the Jones Act of 1917 by which the U.S. Congress conferred citizenship (albeit "passive"—that is, without congressional representation). This was regarded as an irrevocable step. It made young Puerto Rican men liable for U.S. military service and therefore eligible for the benefits conferred on ex-servicemen. Unsurprisingly, then, the island also became an indispensable element in the U.S. naval system. The Jones Act also implied a general right to travel and work on the mainland without fear of deportation. Of course, these political arrangements were linked to an economic settlement. These passive citizens would be exempted from federal taxation as well as from congressional representation. Even prior to the 1952 constitution, therefore, the island possessed a degree of fiscal autonomy (it could raise its own taxes, and grant its own tax exemptions), while at the same time enjoying duty-free access to the huge mainland market for its goods, and relying on the U.S. Federal Reserve to provide its currency and to conduct its monetary policy.

In short, Washington has undertaken a succession of economic, strategic, and political commitments to Puerto Rico that are far more far-reaching and irrevocable than any other obligations it has shouldered in Latin America. U.S. business interests enjoy the full panoply of legal guarantees available on the mainland; so Washington is not cross-pressured between democracy promotion and business promotion. Puerto Rico's small population and peculiar history made it possible for the United States to accept such obligations in this case, precisely because no general precedent would be set. It seems unlikely that American policy makers could seriously have offered similar arrangements to larger or more indigestible Latin republics (such as Cuba). But in the unique case of Puerto Rico, Washington was willing to undertake such massive and durable (if lopsided) commitments that the United States effectively underwrote an American-style democratization of the island.

What, then, were the costs and benefits of this method of democracy promotion for Puerto Rico? The political benefits have already been outlined—a stronger system of civil rights, a securer rule of law, and a more firmly entrenched system of electoral pluralism than almost anywhere else in Latin America. The economic benefits must also be mentioned, for the stability of the political system has been powerfully reinforced by the accompanying experience of considerable relative prosperity. Income levels have risen well above the Latin American norm (and now approach half those of the poorest state in the union, Mississippi): Puerto Rico is sheltered from the inflation, debt crisis, and International Monetary Fund (IMF)-imposed austerity programs of its neighbors (for example, government borrowing benefits from a federal guarantee). Living standards have risen to such a point that by 1982 minimum wages on the island could be raised to the federal level. However, there is a negative side to the economic record. High unemployment is a predictable counterpart to high minimum wages. The federal food stamp program provides a costly safety net for the poor. But the most important cushion has come from the unrestricted right to emigrate to the mainland, where about two-fifths of all islanders now reside. Were it not for some very expensive subsidies to Puerto Rican industry (notably tax breaks for U.S. firms investing on the island), unemployment and/or emigration would be even higher. Federal transfers, welfare payments, and tax concessions account for about a quarter of the island's regional income, and of course the laws governing inflow are written by a legislature in which the islanders have no vote.

The political price of such a democracy is therefore a considerable loss both of sovereignty and of formal representation. Puerto Ricans sent to fight in Vietnam had no voice in America's debate over the war; their rights to abortion may be curtailed or extended by the decision of others; decisive elements of economic policy are fixed by mainlanders without their concurrence; their elected representatives have no voice in international economic forums. From the standpoint of democratic theory these are serious imperfections, signifying that some U.S. citizens have formal rights that are gravely and permanently impaired compared with those of the majority. In place of the ethic of citizen autonomy, with rights and duties conventionally balanced, Puerto Rican democracy rests on a constrained and dependent form of citizenship with special exemptions excused by the provision of unilateral subsidies. In fact this is a democracy based on the acceptance of second-class citizenship. According to theory, such a formula should breed both resentment and irresponsibility. In practice the main result seems to have been to generate a persistent obsession with the status issue, and an associated insecurity over the island's real social identity. Although this chapter has classified the islanders as a Latin American people, in many respects they still find themselves in an international limbo.

What lessons can we draw from this example of strong U.S. involvement in democracy promotion? Above all, the Puerto Rican path to democracy is most unlikely to be repeated. The U.S. Congress will almost certainly not grant citizenship (and the unrestricted right of entry) to any other Latin American people or nation in the foreseeable future. The only wholly democratic outcome consistent with the extension of U.S. citizenship would be full Puerto Rican entry into the union as an additional state. This may eventually come about if the next plebiscite clearly favors statehood, but if so it will only occur after an extremely protracted interregnum. Almost a century has already elapsed since the military proclamation of July 1898, and still opinions remain divided, both within the United States and on the island, about the shape of the eventual constitutional settlement. If Washington is to promote democracy strongly in other parts of Latin America, it will almost certainly seek a shorter route, and one that can be traversed at lower cost to the U.S. taxpayer. For their part Latin American beneficiaries of such strong U.S. support will presumably seek to achieve a greater degree of sovereignty at a lower cost in terms of social identity.

Democracy Promotion through Invasion: Panama

It would be rash to anticipate the unfolding consequences of the December 1989 U.S. invasion of Panama, but some inferences can be drawn from that country's now quite lengthy past. Because of the canal, and because of all the history associated with it, we can be fairly sure that Washington will continue to seek a strong influence over the course of Panamanian politics. If the U.S. commitment to democracy promotion is anything like as strong as declaratory statements suggest, Panama is second only to Puerto Rico (perhaps equal with Nicaragua) as a country where one would expect that priority to materialize.

In November 1903 Panama broke away from Colombia under the protection of U.S. gunboats. The new republic received prompt recognition and financial assistance from Washington, and in return granted the United States extensive concessions over the proposed canal route. In theory U.S. military action responded to Panamanian aspirations and sheltered a sovereign and liberal new regime.

However, on May 16, 1908, Secretary of War Taft wrote to President Theodore Roosevelt about a proposed treaty with Panama:

> We should be given direct control over the elections, so as to permit us, should we desire, to intervene and determine who is fairly elected. This I agree detracts from the independence of the "Republic" but as the Republic has not shown itself competent in this regard, we are justified . . . to protect our own interests.[6]

This American supervision persisted until the Great Depression. But in January 1931 a Panamanian president was surprised to find his appeal for U.S. military assistance against his political rivals unanswered. "The old political hierarchy, which had survived for nearly three decades by periodic threats of American intervention, suddenly found itself discredited. In the ensuing campaign for the Panamanian presidency, no candidate solicited American endorsement."[7]

Under the Good Neighbor Policy of the 1930s Washington to some extent backed away from this degree of external supervision, signing a new canal treaty in 1936 that somewhat increased the Panamanian government's room for maneuver. On the political front, in place of gunboat diplomacy the United States sought to substitute good neighborly abstention from direct involvement in Panama's electoral processes. But this policy proved quite as problematic as the one it displaced, because in Panama as in other former U.S. protectorates the political forces that moved to fill the space created by Roosevelt's self-denying ordinances were less than wholly democratic. By the time of the tense elections of April 1948 Secretary of State Marshall was straining to avoid U.S. intervention.[8]

The 1948 election revealed in the starkest terms the contrast between what Washington could achieve in conditions of direct rule in Puerto Rico and what American policy makers would have to contend with in an ex-protectorate where the national police had been allowed to acquire an identity of its own. At first Colonel Remón of the national police chose to support a fraudulent electoral outcome, and both the electoral tribunal and the supreme court of Panama fell into line with this decision. The United States, following the policy of nonintervention, also accepted this outcome. Within eighteen months, however, Colonel Remón decided that his interests would be better served by a reversal of position. Disregarding Panama's supreme court, in November 1949 he forced the incumbent president to resign and summoned the elections board to recount the 1948 results. "In hours the Board found pro-Arias votes it had been unable to find in weeks after the 1948 ballotting."[9] U.S. Ambassador David was left to fulminate:

> While action [by] Remón and Arias may evidence flattering confidence [in the] reality [of] our non-intervention policy, it shows also a cynical disregard of principles democratic and otherwise, and complete disdain for our oft repeated expressions of policy. It is believed Remón and his gangster associates are incapable of understanding international implications. Apparently it is their idea that they can be brazen about their illegal procedure and yet insist we recognize decisions forced upon their judicial and legislative branches. . . . Since we let it be known we would be guided by action of National Assembly and Supreme Court, it would be logical to do, stating U.S. government therefore recognizes (deposed) Charis as constitutional president and is prepared to proceed with conduct of normal business once illegal interference by force ceases to impede. This course should not, however, be taken unless we are prepared to take a determined stand and see it through.[10]

The ambassador's recommendation was not adopted, however, in part because the internal legality that it invoked was so unreal. Within three days the State Department had concluded that Arias was in control, at which point a very different view of the 1948 election emerged: "There can be no doubt that he won the election last year and was cheated out of the Presidency by the fraudulent actions of the electoral jury."[11] In the absence of full U.S. control over internal political processes, there was no way that even the sincerest and most single-minded Washington supporter of Panamanian democracy could sidestep the reality of competing partisanships and fragmented legitimacy.

In reality, of course, any concern Washington might have felt for democracy in Panama was always overshadowed by the higher priority of preserving the security of the Canal Zone. U.S. policy documents record a close and continuing interest in the internal politics of the republic, but this was always viewed from the standpoint that a friendly and secure pro-American administration would be the best guarantor of Washington's overriding security interests. On the many occasions where that priority conflicted with an even-handed concern for the sovereign democratic order, the issue of democracy took second place. All Panamanian political factions understood that reality and conducted their activities accordingly. Thus, regardless of all the rhetoric in favor of democracy and nonintervention, the objective structure of these power relations was systematically weighted against the consolidation of a democratic order. This goes far to explain why from initially fairly similar points of departure at the turn of the century the Panamanians made virtually no progress in the establishment of democratic institutions, whereas especially since 1950 the Puerto Ricans achieved major cumulative advances.

The Panamanian electoral process of 1948–49 deserves reconstruction because it anticipates so much of the experience of the 1980s. It therefore demonstrates the existence of a systematic pattern of political interaction between the United States and Panama that cannot simply be attributed to the criminality of General Noriega; and since this pattern of political behavior is entrenched, the task of averting future repetitions of the cycle will require far more than just the seizure and imprisonment of one military leader.

In May 1984, as in May 1948, a hard-fought presidential election ended fraudulently. The head of the electoral tribunal resigned rather than certify the results, which were imposed by the National Guard under the direction of General Noriega; international observers described them as rigged, but the U.S. State Department accepted them at face value. The incoming president was more acceptable to Washington than his electorally more successful rival—indeed U.S. policy makers appear to have played an important role in selecting and nominating him. In any case the State Department feared a coup if the progovernment candidate lost the first election held in sixteen years. Even with the benefit of hindsight the chief U.S. policy maker, Elliott Abrams, still defended the endorsement of a fraudulent outcome, which in his view "seemed to help propel Panama into the flow towards democracy that is powerfully moving the hemisphere."[12] In 1985, as in 1984, the illegitimate civilian president attempted to assert his authority against the National Guard that brought him to power. The results were the same, as was the initial U.S. response. Abrams later conceded that the forced resignation of the president was a setback to democracy, but consoled himself with the observation that "constitutional procedures were followed, at least formally, and Panama remained an open society."[13] In the ensuing four years Panama was headed by a succession of nominal presidents while real power was retained elsewhere. As in 1948–51, conflicts of jurisdiction escalated and political institutionality degenerated, until following an even more fraudulent election in May 1989, the United States recognized a government in hiding and finally in December 1989 resorted to armed intervention. The stated grounds for this invasion by twenty-six thousand U.S. troops were, first, to safeguard the lives and property of American citizens; second, to terminate General Noriega's drug trafficking; third, to "restore democracy" in Panama; and fourth, to maintain the normal operations of the canal. It is the contention of this section that the first, second, and fourth goals on this list express the tenor of U.S.-Panamanian relations far more typically than the third; the method they imply is imposition, a method that would be far less appropriate if the principal goal of policy was democracy promotion.

The record of U.S. policy toward Panama in the 1980s culminating with the 1989 invasion leaves plenty of room to argue, with the benefit of hindsight, that some alternative choice of policies would have been more effective, more prudent, more principled, or even more supportive of Panamanian democracy. While that may be so, the critical point is that, despite all the advantages available to Washington policy makers, and despite their strong interest in shaping a favorable political outcome in Panama, their choices were all suboptimal, and their capacity to reshape Panamanian political processes proved once again to be remarkably limited. In the absence of stable and autonomous legal institutions (which might sometimes clash with immediate U.S. security interests), and in the presence of a perverse pattern of reactions established over several generations through which Panamanian leaders learned how to play off what Washington said about their country against what it really meant, the United States was reduced to the starkest and most unattractive of alternatives, either to endure continuing ridicule and defiance from a patently oppressive and corrupt former protégé, or to intervene unilaterally and with massive force in the hope of establishing a fresh beginning.

Although the first eighty-seven years of U.S.-Panamanian relations has not proved very productive from the standpoint of democracy promotion, there are those who regard the December 1989 invasion as the start of a bright new era. Such claims should never be dismissed out of hand. Just as the directly colonial phase of U.S.–Puerto Rican history gave way to a somewhat more equitable relationship in the 1950s, similar possibilities should be considered in Panama. This chapter does not exclude that hypothesis but merely argues that it will take some time before we can judge. Meanwhile the legacy of the past will continue to impede the prospects for authentic and durable democracy promotion in Panama. The security of the canal, although less vital to the United States than in earlier years, will continue to preoccupy Washington policy makers as much as the health of Panamanian democracy. If the two priorities were ever again to conflict the United States would again seek above all else to protect the canal. After all, America's power, its prestige, and even the lives of its soldiers have just been reinvested in that enterprise.

In the wake of *any* invasion, the first priority of the occupying force will naturally be to protect the security of its nationals and to make the outcome of the invasion irreversible. Where the aims of the invasion are temporary, and coincide with the wishes of the local population (as in the Grenada "rescue mission" of 1983), the occupying force may subsequently manage to withdraw leaving a well-functioning democracy behind. But in Panama the situation is not so clear-cut, in part because American nationals are not about to be withdrawn from the Canal Zone; in part because the National Guard or some equivalent military force is likely to retain a degree of local control; and in part because the Panamanian economy will continue to revolve around supplying "services" within this dollar zone and as an adjunct to the entrepôt functions of the canal. Therefore the postinvasion regime will continue to grapple with very similar problems to those that impeded democratization before 1989.

If drug trafficking, money laundering, and arms dealing are no longer to provide the basis of the Panamanian economy, how can an independent democratic government achieve reconstruction and the restoration of confidence after the dislocation caused by the U.S. sanctions and invasion? If the new government (which bases its legitimacy on 1989 election results that were annulled before the count was complete) lacks sufficient authority or resources of its own it will be forced to depend once more on the protection of Washington. But a restoration of the 1903–31 protectorate system is unlikely to work any better at the end of the twentieth century than it did at the beginning. Because Washington has no wish to incorporate Panama (as it incorporated Puerto Rico), the problem of anti–United States nationalism is almost bound to recur in one form or another. It is inherent in the enterprise of promoting the appearance of national sovereignty while intrusively supervising the substance of local politics. Of course the option of nonintervention may eventually return to favor. But unless Panama undergoes a major economic transformation, unless the public administration, the courts, and the military are improbably transformed, and unless the citizens of Panama come to see the legacy of American influence as U.S. opinion makers wish them to see it, then an eventual shift back to nonintervention is unlikely to serve the cause of democracy promotion any better than before.

With the passage of time it could be that these doubts will be dispelled. However, an objective assessment of the effects so far of America's massive presence in Panama offers little encouragement to those who suppose that all good things come readily together. Democracy promotion does not necessarily accompany the projection of U.S. power, least of all when that result is sought on the cheap; without any dilution of Washington's other purposes; and without much understanding of the perverse psychology engendered by a combination of formal sovereignty with real dependency.

Democracy Promotion by Intimidation: Nicaragua

Our third example of democracy promotion in the Caribbean Basin is Nicaragua. Here too the United States has an extremely long track record; again Washington's power in relation to any government in Managua is potentially overwhelming; although in the nineteenth century there was some thought in the United States of incorporating Nicaragua, that notion has had no currency in the twentieth; and since the 1920s the idea of invading Nicaragua has been distinctly out of favor with U.S. military planners. There was a U.S. military presence from 1912 to the Great Depression, and the United States did propose in 1979 that the Organization of American States (OAS) might send a "peacekeeping force" to prevent the Sandinista revolutionaries from seizing full power (along the lines of the successful U.S. intervention with OAS approval in the Dominican Republic in 1965). Throughout all these episodes the defense or promotion of democracy has been repeatedly articulated as a justification of American policy toward Nicaragua. In a similar way it is currently claimed that the February 1990 elections vindicate hotly contested assertions made throughout the Reagan administration concerning the democratic purposes of the "covert" or "contra" war against the Sandinistas, launched in November 1981, and sustained for more than eight years thereafter. So does the recent history of U.S.-Nicaraguan relations demonstrate the efficacy of Washington's strategy of democracy promotion through intimidation, or does it more nearly resemble the pattern just sketched of U.S.-Panamanian interactions?

Once again we are dealing with a long history. Over several generations the United States has exerted its extensive influence in Nicaragua in ways that have not served to generate political consensus or to encourage respect for democratic norms. In the second and third decades of this century, the Marines were used to prop up strongly contested governments in Managua. For example, they supervised and administered the 1928 elections against a substantial military and political challenge from the revolutionary general César Augusto C. Sandino. In American eyes he was a "bandit," but to many Nicaraguans and to a wide swathe of Latin American opinion he was a more authentic political leader than the Nicaraguan party leaders who had consented to elections on Washington's terms. Latin disbelief in Washington's ostensible commitment to democracy in Nicaragua was reinforced by U.S. conduct during the almost half-century of the Somoza dynasty. As in Panama, Washington attempted a stance of nonintervention in Nicaragua's internal affairs, and as in Panama this provided undemocratic armed forces with a license to commit abuses and to pursue personal enrichment with political impunity. Successive American administrations hesitated to criticize such a well-entrenched ally (with good friends in Congress), especially since he could be counted on to endorse Washington's most controversial foreign policy initiatives. To lock in U.S. support the Somozas took care to neutralize the democratic center in Nicaragua, always presenting Washington with the choice between an undemocratic but reliable right, or a radical and potentially "disloyal" left.

The Sandinista revolution of 1979 was a logical outcome of this long history. The many nationalist and radical currents of opinion that had been suppressed by the Somozas resurfaced under the umbrella of the Sandinista Front. Although the bulk of the front's leadership was Marxist-inclined, and although many of the key figures had been Cuba-trained or -influenced, the rigid and repressive nature of the Somoza regime enabled the Sandinistas to build a broad alliance, with centrists attracted by the promise of democratic elections, a mixed economy, and nonalignment. According to the official U.S. view, Washington's policies of "intimidation" during the 1980s were in fact intended to force the Sandinistas to honor these original promises, and that is the result they are said finally to have achieved in the February 1990 elections that displaced the Sandinistas from government.

On closer inspection of the record of U.S. intimidation of Nicaragua during the 1980s the picture is less clear-cut. To avoid misunderstandings it must be stated at the outset that the Sandinista front chose to overplay its hand, attempting to consolidate a far more radical, political, and economic order than that initially promised. Thus it was not only Washington but also Managua that chose the path of continued polarization in the 1980s. Although the Sandinista strategy may seem explicable in view of the long preceding history of U.S.-Nicaraguan relations, it was not entirely forced upon them (certainly not by the Carter administration). They therefore bear considerable responsibility for the ensuing consequences, which included missing the opportunity to promote national reconciliation and democratization.

That said, let us turn to the topic of this chapter, which concerns the U.S. role. Let us consider first the motives, then the methods, then the results of the U.S. response. This policy of intimidation was motivated by a variety of considerations, among which concern over the quality of democratic governance in Nicaragua was not, to put it mildly, always foremost. Initially policy was shaped by the pressures of the Carter–Reagan election campaign in which a dominant theme was the need to reassert American self-confidence and international leadership. In this setting Nicaraguan realities were compressed to fit into the terms of a debate set by the Iranian hostage crisis. After Reagan's victory campaign, perceptions continued to override reality and the "Nicaraguan threat" was inflated to improbable proportions. The genuine issue that underlay mounting U.S. hostility toward Managua was the fear of a second revolution in neighboring El Salvador. It was to cut off supplies to the Salvadoran guerrillas rather than to promote democracy in Nicaragua that the "contras" were initially funded by the National Security Council, in November 1981. (After all, Washington was at that time sheltering a regime in El Salvador whose democratic credentials were at least as dubious as those of the Sandinistas.) As the contra war expanded, U.S. objectives became more complex and difficult to decipher. One possibility was certainly the armed overthrow of the Sandinistas, and it remains extremely questionable whether that would have heralded a new dawn of democracy in Nicaragua. (The precedent of Guatemala in 1954 hardly seems encouraging.) Another was simply to isolate and discredit the Sandinista model, so that no other Central American republic would be tempted to follow that example. (Again, the democratic content of this outcome would seem questionable.)

By 1984, with the Salvadoran regime becoming more stable and respectable, and with the Grenada "rescue mission" accomplished, the theme of democratizing Nicaragua became much more prominent and explicit. To the Reagan administration the promotion of democracy in Nicaragua had one great advantage over all other possible justifications for the "contra" war. With any other war aim, the danger existed that the Sandinistas would accept U.S. demands, and the administration would therefore come under pressure to call off hostilities before the regime in Managua had been toppled. "Democracy," by contrast, could be promoted as an unimpeachable goal that would attract the support of many waverers. Under Reagan the State Department would adhere to a definition of the term designed to ensure that no form of Sandinismo, however toned down, would ever qualify, just as no form of facade democracy in El Salvador would ever be allowed to disqualify.

This may seem a harsh and uncharitable explanation of Washington's motives in the mid-1980s. But we cannot overlook the fact that in November 1984 the Sandinistas did finally honor their 1979 pledge and hold national elections, and that various respectable foreign observers considered these acceptable. If the United States had genuinely sought the strengthening of democracy in Nicaragua, would it have pressured the leading opposition candidate to stand down, and would it have disdained to see any merit in this electoral process? The trouble with these elections from Washington's point of view, was not that they were fraudulent (we have seen that fraudulent elections held in Panama at that very time were praised as a step toward democracy). It was that even under clean elections the United States believed the Sandinistas would probably win.

During the 1980s the Sandinistas were progressively weakened by the long U.S. campaign of harassment against them, but they were never toppled by the contras, and no U.S. invasion ever came. Their response to the demand for democracy was to offer to extend political freedoms if the campaign of harassment abated, but to curtail them if U.S. hostility put Nicaragua's national security at risk. This can be viewed as just a question of tactics, but it also reflected an underlying disagreement about the *kind* of democracy that might be established. The Sandinistas might be willing to move toward democracy-with-sovereignty, but as the very name Sandinista implied they could not contemplate democracy on Puerto Rican terms, or of the post–Panama-invasion variety. The Reagan administration, by contrast, seems to have defined democracy to require congruence with American interests. A sovereignty that clashed with U.S. priorities was unlikely to be regarded as acceptable. Since the end of the Reagan administration the United States has somewhat softened its position on such questions, but it remains to be seen how Washington would react to some future Sandinista electoral victory. Thus it cannot be said that pure democracy promotion motivated U.S. policy toward Nicaragua in the 1980s.

Even if the *motives* for U.S. policy had been straightforwardly democratic, the *methods* chosen were not. As we have seen, there was never any intention to incorporate Nicaragua into the democratic system of the United States, and although invasion may at times have been contemplated this method was also ruled out by the time of the "Irangate" scandal. Therefore Washington resorted to less direct methods of pressure, including covert operations, economic sanctions, and political warfare—"intimidation" for short. But intimidation is inherently a blunt instrument. It does not destroy but merely cows. So the result of a successful act of intimidation is more likely to be purely formal compliance than willing cooperation. In addition, because intimidation stops short of complete destruction of the enemy, it leaves open the option of continuing defiance regardless of cost, so intimidation risks destroying the social prerequisites for democratic compromise and accommodation. Moreover, the Reagan administration's acts of intimidation were also often prima facie undemocratic in domestic U.S. terms (deceiving Congress, misleading public opinion, diverting funds, etc.). Reliance on such methods broadcasts an example that hardly squares with the ostensible goal of democracy promotion. In fact, whereas democracy promotion through incorporation is likely to strengthen the democratic institutions of the metropolitan power (by generalizing and reinforcing them), democracy promotion through intimidation is more likely to damage the qualities of trust, cooperation, and lawfulness in the home democracy, to lower its international reputation, and to breed cynicism and opportunism in the target country.

These are objections in principle to the practice of democracy promotion through intimidation. Nevertheless *in practice,* it may be asserted, the Reagan administration achieved the desired results, and these were unlikely to have been accomplished by any alternative approach. As in the case of Panama, it may be too soon to judge. A great deal will depend upon what is considered to count as a "successful democratization" in Nicaragua—and on who controls the judgment. The foreign observers who authenticated the

1990 election came from many democratic countries—not just from the United States—and it may therefore be that in 1996 the Sandinista electoral opposition will benefit from the same international guarantees that served their opponents in 1990. But the result of the conflict of the past decade has been that many thousands of lives have been lost and the Nicaraguan economy has been ruined. Clearly this does not assist the promotion of democracy, and it seems unlikely that Washington will devote as much resources to reconstruction in the nineties, as it did to destruction in the eighties.

However, defenders of the Reagan administration will argue that there was no other way to "save Nicaragua for democracy." It could be that intimidation was the surest way to break Nicaragua's ties with Moscow and Havana, and with the Salvadoran guerrillas (although the Contadora and Esquipulas initiatives suggest that alternative approaches merited more attention than Washington was willing to concede). But on the question of democracy, the centerpiece of Reagan's strategy was the claim that since the Sandinistas were Marxists-Leninists, by definition *any* political concession they gave was just a stratagem to buy time. This was the argument for seeking to discredit the 1984 election, and for rebuffing all subsequent Sandinista proposals for a political settlement. In view of their scrupulous conduct of the February 1990 election, and of their disciplined acceptance of an unexpectedly adverse result, it remains a serious question whether the Sandinistas were previously as intransigent and antidemocratic as they have been portrayed. The obvious alternative way to promote Nicaraguan democracy would have been to support and reinforce the electoral process of 1984, and to encourage and reward subsequent compliance with the pluralist provisions of the 1987 constitution. Arguably, then, intimidation was not the only possible form of democracy promotion available to the United States in the eighties.

Intimidation was, however, the only form considered, and in the end the Sandinistas were evicted from office by the Nicaraguan electorate. So the policy worked, which on one view is what really matters. As in the discussion of Panama, this chapter does not dismiss that view out of hand but only argues for caution. The legacy of the past will continue to darken the prospects for an authentic and durable democratization of Nicaragua in the nineties. The Sandinistas are likely to remain a major political force, perhaps capable of blocking the reversal of key measures accomplished during their decade of government, perhaps capable of winning a clean election at a later date. Will all their opponents abide by the rules of democratic procedure if this assessment of Sandinista strength and popularity proves correct? After so many years of harassment and political warfare against the Sandinistas, will Washington now become a staunch defender of Nicaraguan democracy, even if their old antagonists stand to gain? One of the greatest dangers of resorting to a policy of intimidation is that it is so difficult to find a clear rationale for stopping. And, as the English discovered when they finally stopped coercing the Irish, it is even more difficult to convince the other side that you really have stopped.

Conclusion

The three instances of democracy imposition reviewed here are extreme, not typical. Other chapters in this volume discuss a much broader range of examples. Here we have selected those cases where the U.S. track record is longest; where the scale of American involvement in shaping the political affairs of its Latin neighbors has been greatest; and where the underlying inequality of power and resources maximizes the likelihood that Washington can have its way. After applying these restrictive criteria, one might expect to find three highly successful cases of democracy promotion, but in fact the results are very mixed. They are also startlingly diverse, with U.S. power being deployed in markedly different ways in each instance. "Incorporation," "invasion," and "intimidation" are quite varied methods for imposing democracy on other countries; when such contrasting methods are used it is perhaps hardly surprising that the outcomes are also various.

The incorporation of Puerto Rico produced the best results. By most normal criteria the islanders live in a well-consolidated political democracy that has received massive and sustained U.S. support over several generations. Even here, however, certain qualifications are called for. Almost a century has elapsed since the United States began reshaping Puerto Rican politics, perhaps half a century since serious democracy promotion began. Yet the process is still incomplete, in that the islanders remain in an international limbo, and viewed from within the U.S. system they are still second-class citizens. Full incorporation, and definitive democratization may well occur in the next few years. But in the meantime Puerto Rico's half-house status requires indefinite transfusions of federal funds, which typically account for around one-quarter of the island's domestic product. Even for those who think that the gain in democracy and prosperity justifies the surrender of sovereignty, the Puerto Rican example hardly constitutes a model, since neither the U.S. government nor the population of any other Latin American nation expect this pattern of democracy promotion through incorporation to be repeated elsewhere.

The invasion of Panama reinstated the authorities chosen in the frustrated election of 1989 and destroyed a tyrannical government. Taken out of context, these two accomplishments can be presented as another major success for democracy promotion. But on a longer view the contribution of the United States to the democratization of Panama is little cause for congratulation. The first eighty-seven years presents a fairly sorry record, and the best that can be claimed is that the invasion could mark a new beginning. The Grenada operation of 1983 offers some encouragement for this view, but the differences should also be kept in mind. In Panama the United States was protecting its long-established vested interests, whereas the population of Grenada viewed the "rescue mission" as an act of altruism by a country with no prior record of intervention there. In Panama the United States acted with the endorsement of neighboring democracies, and against a ruler whose power it had previously built up; its credibility as a disinterested protector of the popular will was accordingly reduced. In Grenada it was possible for the United States to withdraw rapidly and comprehensively leaving a fairly broad-based multiparty democracy to function on its own. Such an outcome is likely to prove far more problematic in Panama. If comparisons are to be made with other instances of democracy imposition through invasion, the Panamanian experience may more realistically be compared with the Dominican intervention of 1965. But in that case twelve years had to elapse before the outcome of the invasion could be subjected to genuine democratic control, and even in 1978 the transition to pluralist democracy remained precarious and unsatisfactory. In view of the continuing U.S. interest in the canal and the nationalist reactions this is still likely to generate, not even the distinctly qualified success of the Dominican democratization-through-invasion can be taken for granted in Panama.

The intimidation of the Sandinistas forced them to accept an unprecedently high degree of international supervision of the 1990 elections due under the constitution they wrote in 1987. For most of the 1980s they had derived political support from their role as defenders of national sovereignty against U.S. provocations, but by 1990 this mechanism no longer worked in their favor. The voters preferred a compromise settlement that would end U.S. harassment, permit national reconciliation, and open the way to economic reconstruction. The Nicaraguan electorate made a democratic choice (albeit constrained from without). Indeed the 1990 result has the potential to trigger a cumulative process of democratization as rival power contenders are forced to recognize that they must work together within an agreed political framework, since none is strong enough to rule alone. However, the election outcome did not signify a general willingness to compromise Nicaraguan sovereignty, nor to abandon all the changes brought in by eleven years of Sandinista government, and the Sandinista army was not defeated by the "contras." The election has given Washington an unexpectedly easy opportunity to reinforce the democratization process in Nicaragua by ceasing all acts of intimidation and by respecting the new political framework. But this requires a clear U.S. understanding of *all* the implications of the 1990 vote. The main test of democracy promotion through intimidation is whether interventionist methods can be convincingly and lastingly foresworn once the democratic transition is underway. In Nicaragua that test has yet to come.

Although the three examples considered here are all extreme, they are unlikely to be unique. Indeed in the 1990s we are likely to witness not only further evidence of the fruits of these three democracy-promotion strategies in the countries studied, but also greater tests of the U.S. capacity for democracy promotion in other parts of the Caribbean Basin. Despite their importance, the difficult cases of El Salvador, Haiti, Guatemala, and even Mexico cannot be considered here but some mention must be made of the largest imponderable, namely Washington's posture toward a prospective post-Castro Cuba.

As is well known, after 1898 the policy of incorporation applied to Puerto Rico was not extended to Cuba, and after the failure of the Bay of Pigs in 1961 Washington also dropped the policy of invasion. Instead for over thirty years Castro's Cuba has been subjected to an unbroken policy of isolation and intimidation, more comprehensive and sustained than that which brought the Sandinista revolution to a halt. Yet Cuba's personalist brand of Communism succeeded in resisting all such pressure, in part because of large-scale Soviet assistance, in part because of Castro's own achievements and determination, and in part because of his success in promoting an anti–United States definition of Cuban nationalism. Following the collapse of Communism throughout Eastern Europe in 1989–90, a widespread impression developed that at long last the U.S. policy of intimidation might be about to pay a massive dividend, in the form of a spectacular collapse of the Castro regime. If this were to occur, it would overshadow all the three cases considered here; indeed, if the outcome were to be the installation of a conventional pluralist democracy in Cuba, then no amount of academic reservations about the past history of U.S. democracy promotion through intervention would dent the surge of American self-confidence. Nevertheless, without foreknowledge of Cuba's route beyond Castroism, an attempt can be made to extend the logic of the preceding analysis to the Cuban case.

The Cuban armed forces have not been, and probably will not be, defeated. Unlike Nicaragua the Cuban people have not been, and probably will not be, offered an internationally supervised electoral forum within which to choose their preferred future. Moscow is probably unable to bring about the downfall of the Cuban leadership (as it appears to have done in several East European cases), even if it wishes to do so. Thus the question is whether a further reinforcement and intensification of Washington's long-standing policy of intimidation is likely to prove an effective instrument of democracy promotion in Cuba. The suggested limitations to this method are that it is too blunt (and may therefore damage rather than build up the social supports for democracy); that it seeks to grind down rather than immediately to destroy (therefore leaving the target regime with a possibility of retaliation, albeit at a disproportionate cost to itself); that it is in its own terms contrary to the spirit of democratic accommodation (therefore potentially harmful to the democratic processes of the country that employs it, and damaging to a nation's democratic credibility); and that great self-control is required to halt practices of intimidation once a democratic transition has begun. These are the reasons for fearing, in advance of the fact, that the long-standing U.S. policy of intimidation may not even now very well serve the cause of democracy promotion in Cuba.

It should not be too readily assumed that the collapse of Communism in Eastern Europe vindicates the U.S. approach to democracy promotion in Cuba. After all, the Federal German constitution of 1949 offered the East Germans the unqualified prospect of reunification whenever they chose to apply for it; this was voluntary incorporation rather than imposition. West Germany also relied heavily on incentives rather than sanctions to win the East Germans round. As for the rest of Eastern Europe (and previously in relation to Southern Europe), the Treaty of Rome offered the permanent incentive of a right to apply for admission to the European Community to any neighboring state that adopted the required standards of political democracy and market liberalization. In contrast to these European incentives to voluntary reform, Washington appears to seek the national prostration of Cuba, an unconditional surrender in return for which the United States offers neither full admission to the union nor any assurance that an independent democratic Cuba would be allowed to exercise its sovereignty.

Thus, however events in Cuba may unfold, this discussion raises an important theoretical issue related to the nature of the democratic outcome being sought or promoted. The traditional view to which most Latin American (and for that matter most European) democrats would probably adhere is that the consolidation of national sovereignty is a precondition for the implantation of a representative democracy. For a government to be securely democratic—answerable to the citizenry through the test of competitive elections—it must establish its authority and policy effectiveness throughout the national territory, and must secure international acceptance of that authority. If extraterritorial authorities not accountable to the local electorate were to exercise decisive power, then according to this view the quality of that particular democracy would be drastically impaired. By this test Puerto Rican democracy falls short, in that San Juan has no say over such critical issues as the waging of war; Panamanian democracy depends on the acquiescence of an occupation force whose first loyalty is to Washington, and whose second priority is the security of the canal; only Nicaraguan democracy appears more or less sovereign. What U.S. efforts at democracy promotion in the Caribbean Basin seem to assume is that democratization can be a *substitute* for what Washington regards as unacceptable or impractical assertions of national sovereignty. Given the overwhelming inequalities of power involved, and the wide range of strategic, economic, and political interests Washington is expected to promote there, such a redefinition of the concept of democracy may be understandable. But from the standpoint of democratic theory it would only be tenable if the relinquishment of sovereignty were to be offset by full incorporation into the American political union. The peculiarity of the form of democracy promotion practiced by the United States in the region where it has the greatest influence is that neither full incorporation nor full democratic sovereignty is consistently envisaged. This peculiarity goes far to explain the apparent paradox presented at the outset of this chapter—why in such favorable conditions such a powerful country, with such a long commitment to democracy promotion, has achieved such modest results. The policy-making process within the United States largely accounts for this peculiarity, in that the American public demands a strong rationale for foreign policy initiatives (democracy promotion), while the Constitution erects formidable barriers against the incorporation of new states, and specific lobbies have frequently induced Washington to exert its power whenever the assertion of sovereignty by small Caribbean states (even the most democratic) seemed likely to clash with their interests.

With the ending of the cold war and the rapid extension of economic and political liberalism, it becomes even more important than before to determine whether (or in what circumstances) democratization involves a trade-off in sovereignty, or whether a new phase of democracy promotion can now begin, with more respect for nonintervention and the formal equality of all democratic states, however large or small.

The three methods of democracy promotion discussed in this chapter (incorporation, invasion, and intimidation) all have one thing in common—they express a radical inequality between the power and rights of the country acting and the country acted upon. They involve unilateral acts of imposition. This radical inequality has deep roots in U.S. history[14] and is a particularly celebrated feature of the U.S. presence in the Caribbean Basin throughout the current century. The U.S. military proclamation of July 1898, already quoted, expresses the central idea common to all forms of democracy promotion by imposition. This is the assumption that one's own domestic political arrangements are secure and beyond reproach. From this starting point, it follows that democracy promotion involves a unilateral transfer that will be best facilitated by maximizing the power and control of the giver, and by minimizing the scope for resistance or modification by the receiver. For this reason the imposition of democracy abroad is likely to prove highly affirming to the status quo at home.

However this is not the only possible model of democracy promotion, as the European Community has recently demonstrated in Southern and Eastern Europe. It is not even the only model of democracy promotion in the Caribbean, as both the decolonization of the British and Dutch West Indies and the incorporation of the French overseas territories in their different ways attest. The broad alternative to democracy promotion by unilateral imposition is democracy promotion by mutual accommodation. In this case the giver may well recognize the imperfection or vulnerability of the home democracy, which may be strengthened by external reinforcement. (This certainly helps explain why the recently restored democracies of Europe engage in democracy promotion.) In this case democracy promotion will involve strengthening the authority of political forces in the receiving democracy (usually this includes enhanced respect for its sovereignty), and may well require some demotion of the agencies of control in the countries engaged in democracy promotion. (For example, European decolonization required a dismantling of imperial institutions, which was often unsettling to the status quo at home but which, once achieved, contributed to the quality of west European democracy.)

Probably the most interesting of these alternatives to the historical U.S. approach is the partial pooling of sovereignty in an enlarged community of democratic nations, as currently envisaged in Europe. This is not an easy alternative for the United States to pursue, in part because the objective inequalities of wealth and power are so much greater than between the European states, in part because it runs counter to strong historical traditions, and in particular because both the U.S. legal system and the policy process would have such difficulty in adapting to any form of supranational constraints. However, recent proposals for a North American Common Market, and eventually even for an America-wide free-trading zone, might seem to imply a new willingness to consider the mutual accommodation of economic policies by agreement with sovereign neighbors. If so, then Washington might also be ready to develop more mutually respectful (more properly *democratic*) methods of democracy promotion than those highlighted in this chapter. As noted at the beginning of this chapter, the republics of the Americas share a number of common liberal features and traditions—more so than the Europeans—that *ought* to facilitate the establishment of a democratic community of nations, provided that nineteenth-century traditions of unilateralism and imposition can be overcome.

Notes

1. G. Pope Atkins, *Latin America in the International Political System,* 2d ed. (Boulder, Colo.: Westview, 1989), pp. 111–12.

2. In Spanish "Estado Libre Asociado," but the literal English translation, "free associated *state*," has connotations unacceptable to U.S. constitutionalists.

3. Laurence Whitehead, "The Consolidation of Fragile Democracies: A Discussion with Illustrations," in Robert A. Pastor, ed., *Democracy in the Americas: Stopping the Pendulum* (New York: Holmes & Meier, 1989), pp. 76–95.

4. For a detailed account, see Fernando Bayrón Toro, *Las Elecciones de 1980* (Mayagüez, Puerto Rico: Editorial Isla, 1982). The statistics on turnout are from p. 33.

5. Raymond D. Gastil, *Freedom in the World, 1985/6* (New York: Freedom House, 1986), pp. 32–40. (By 1989–90, however, twenty-nine sovereign states and thirty-three nonsovereign territories were ranked by the same institution as enjoying full civil liberties.)

6. Quoted in Richard L. Lael, *Arrogant Diplomacy: US Policy Toward Colombia, 1903–22* (Wilmington, Del.: Scholarly Resources, 1987), pp. 18–19.

The following headlines from the *New York Times* give the flavor of the period: "Elections in Panama Must be OK'd by Taft" (May 11, 1906); "Panama Must Make Its

Election Fair" (June 12, 1908); "Want US to Intervene: Panama Parties Would Insure Fair Play at Coming Elections, Says Former President" (May 28, 1916).

7. Lester D. Langley, *The United States and the Caribbean in the Twentieth Century* (Athens: University of Georgia Press, 1980), p. 139.

8. "While we will not permit conditions to reach a stage that could produce another Bogotá, we will not pull anyone's chestnuts out of the fire to maintain a government in power" was how Chargé Hall summarized the conversation with Marshall, in *Foreign Relations of the United States (FRUS) 1948,* vol. 9 (Washington D.C.: U.S. Government Printing Office, 1972), p. 667.

9. Walter LaFeber, *The Panama Canal* (Oxford: Oxford University Press, 1978), p. 111.

10. Ambassador Davis to Secretary of State Marshall, November 25, 1949, printed in *FRUS 1949,* vol. 2 (Washington D.C.: U.S. Government Printing Office, 1975), pp. 725–26.

11. Ibid., p. 729. Subsequently, in May 1951 President Arias dissolved the National Assembly and abolished the 1946 Constitution in an attempt to extend his power. Colonel Remón thereupon overthrew him, and had himself elected president in 1952. Ambassador Wiley wrote to Secretary of State Acheson in December 1951 that "the American eggs all seem to be in one basket, that of Colonel Remón, since he is the sole anti-Communist leader in the entire political panorama. Though the basket, as the Department is well aware, is far from commendable, Colonel Remón still remains an irreplaceable *faut de mieux*"; *FRUS, 1951,* vol. 2 (Washington D.C.: U.S. Government Printing Office, 1979), p. 1567. In January 1955 President Remón was assassinated, apparently in a dispute with the Mafia over control of Panama's narcotics traffic (LaFeber, p. 120).

12. "Panama and the Path to Democracy," a speech by assistant secretary of state, Elliott Abrams, June 30, 1987.

13. Ibid.

14. See, for example, Albert K. Weinberg, *Manifest Destiny: A Study of Nationalist Expansion in American History* (Baltimore: Johns Hopkins University Press, 1935).

9 | The United States and Latin American Democracy: Learning from History

Abraham F. Lowenthal

THIS BOOK tells a cautionary tale. Recurrent efforts by the government of the United States to promote democracy in Latin America have rarely been successful, and then only in a narrow range of circumstances.

From the turn of the century until the 1980s, the overall impact of U.S. policy on Latin America's ability to achieve democratic politics was usually negligible, often counterproductive, and only occasionally positive. Although it is too soon to be sure, this general conclusion may hold true for the 1980s and the 1990s as well. Despite Washington's current bipartisan enthusiasm for exporting democracy, Latin America's experience to date suggests that expectations should be modest.

U.S. officials have tried often to harness the influence of the United States in support of Latin American democracy. The sources and motives of their concern have been mixed, the instruments used have differed widely, and the concepts of "democracy" officials have had in mind vary. But the results of U.S. efforts to promote democracy, with few exceptions, have been equally disappointing.

This chapter, drawing on the others in the volume, summarizes the twentieth-century record of the United States in promoting Latin American democracy, highlights what can be learned from closer looks at a few cases, derives some general conclusions, and offers a few guidelines for U.S. policy. Its aim, like that of the whole symposium, is to gain insights from the past that may illuminate current and future choices. Political leaders and policy makers should reflect upon this sobering history, lest uncritical acceptance of a noble objective once again lead to disillusion and to misguided actions.

Reviewing the Record

From 1913 to 1933, as Paul Drake chronicles, the United States at one time or another promoted democracy in Mexico, Peru, Ecuador, Cuba, the Dominican Republic, Haiti, Nicaragua, Honduras, Costa Rica, and Guatemala. In some cases, U.S. efforts were restricted to rhetorical declarations or halfhearted diplomatic pressure. In others, however, the United States undertook more energetic activities: supervising elections, reorganizing local military forces, pushing for civic and social reforms, favoring those political groups perceived by Washington as most committed to democracy, and offering or withholding financial assistance to Latin American governments on the basis of whether or not they were considered democratic.

U.S. officials sought to nurture democracy in Latin America during this period for various reasons: as a means of pacification to end local civil wars; to help legitimize national regimes in the eyes of the local population, the U.S. public, or international opinion; to permit the extrication of U.S. forces from military interventions that no longer had domestic support in the United States, and thus to counter rising "anti-imperialist" sentiment at home; and to assure that U.S. foreign policy in the border region did not contradict salient U.S. policies elsewhere in the world.

As Drake emphasizes, U.S. officials in the 1920s invariably had in mind a limited and formal institutional notion of "democracy"—that is, constitutional government based on periodic free and fair elections. From time to time, however, individual U.S. officials opined that deeper structural changes might be required in order to assure the preconditions necessary to foster such elections or to permit the elected regimes to govern.

The most strenuous U.S. efforts to promote democracy during this period occurred in the small Caribbean and Central American countries—precisely those nations in which the structural and institutional circumstances for democratic politics were least auspicious. They all lacked political parties, an independent judiciary, an apolitical police and military establishment, broad civic education, and a substantial middle class. Washington concentrated on these countries not from a calculation about where and how democratic politics might likely emerge, but because of U.S. strategic and economic concerns. The promotion of democracy became an end in itself, and was taken seriously as an objective by U.S. officials. But when strategic or economic considerations clashed with the democratic goal, democracy promotion almost invariably got short shrift.

In country after country, from the mid-1920s through the early 1930s, U.S. officials circumscribed and eventually abandoned their direct efforts to promote democracy. U.S. officials faced opposition to their interventionist presence within various Latin American countries and also at home. Often they resented being manipulated by Latin American politicians whose prime motive was not democracy but power. In many cases, they acutely felt the lack of reliable local democratic partners. Aware as well that a strong U.S. presence in the Caribbean Basin was harming U.S. relations elsewhere in Latin America and even in Europe, U.S. officials began to back away from their efforts. They persisted in doing so, indeed, even in the face of evidence that the new local regimes—which were consolidating their holds while the United States was reducing its involvement—were less democratic and more repressive than their predecessors. That was the case in the Dominican Republic, Nicaragua, Cuba, and Haiti.

By the early 1930s, in the absence of any extrahemispheric challenge to U.S. dominance, U.S. officials were ready to embrace the Latin American norm of "nonintervention." After 1934, when President Franklin D. Roosevelt formally pledged the United States to refrain from interference in the domestic affairs of Latin America, the United States gave up the active promotion of democracy in the hemisphere. This recurrent concern of U.S. policy was not to surface again until the end of World War II.

With its triumph in that war, ostensibly fought on behalf of the Four Freedoms, the United States renewed its expressed interest in Latin American democracy. The motives, circumstances, and chosen instruments for this new wave of promoting democracy differed considerably from those of the 1920s, but the results were almost equally meager, as Leslie Bethell points out.

The main impetus for the regionwide move toward political liberalization and at least partial democratization after World War II came from the countries of Latin America themselves. Whereas U.S. efforts to promote Latin American democracy from 1913 through the 1920s concentrated primarily on the Caribbean Basin border nations, after World War II Washington's concern for building democracy extended throughout the hemisphere; indeed, U.S. efforts were especially strong in Argentina, Brazil, and Bolivia, three of the countries farthest from Washington. The prevailing concept of "democracy" was also different; although U.S. policy makers in the 1920s were preoccupied with elections, Washington was more concerned in the 1940s to assure that authoritarian movements—whether profascist or pro-Communist—not come to power in Latin America, through elections or otherwise.

The U.S. desire to promote democracy in Latin America after World War II, again, had mixed sources. The underlying ideological preference for democracy in the United States was strongly reinforced and given broad popular currency as a result of the antifascist wartime campaign. After the difficult and costly antitotalitarian exertion, U.S. citizens no longer felt comfortable about their government's maintaining cordial relations with Latin American dictatorships, and close U.S. ties with such regimes came to be questioned. As Washington began to criticize Soviet policies in Eastern Europe, where undemocratic regimes were being imposed, there was also a natural wish to be sure that the United States could voice such complaints without finding its own record embarrassingly inconsistent with its professed values.

Perhaps most important, the prodemocracy stance of the United States in the years immediately following World War II was a concrete response to the changing internal conditions of Latin America, where strong domestic pressures to open up politics were beginning to build. A generation of urbanization and economic growth was changing the social structure in several Latin American nations. The urban middle class and, to a degree, the working class were now themselves pushing for full political participation.

From 1945 to about 1948, the United States both directly and indirectly reinforced Latin America's democratizing tendency. North American cultural influence became increasingly strong, both because of war-related propaganda efforts and because of the expanding presence of the U.S. media, particularly radio and motion pictures. So did Washington's political influence, especially after the war left the United States unchallenged as the world's greatest economic and military power, with no competitor for hegemonic standing in the hemisphere. The ideological power of the United States and its political system was then at its height.

The strong indirect influence of the United States was reinforced in particular cases by specific U.S. policies—as in Brazil, where Ambassador Adolf Berle pushed for the dismantling of Getúlio Vargas's authoritarian regime; in Mexico, where Ambassador George Messersmith called for competitive elections and briefly promoted the prospective candidacy of Ezequiel Padilla; in Paraguay, where persistent U.S. pressure in 1944–46 led to brief democratizing reforms in 1946; and most strenuously in Argentina, where strong U.S. pressures backfired and the elections held in 1946 were won by strongman Juan Perón.

On the whole, Latin American politics did move in a democratic direction during the immediate postwar years, and the United States seemed generally to support this trend. But by the late 1940s, Latin America's democratic window was closing and the strict limits on Washington's enthusiasm for Latin America's democratic opening became evident. In Argentina, the United States dropped its ideological stand against Perón and instead sought close cooperation with the Argentine caudillo, who was now prepared to cooperate with Washington and with U.S. investors on economic issues. In Peru and Venezuela, where military coups soon overthrew democratically elected regimes, Washington made it clear that it could easily accommodate again authoritarian governments, as long as they respected concrete U.S. interests. And as the wartime antifascist ethos gave way to the emphasis on Europe's reconstruction and to the incipient cold war, the main U.S. concern in Latin America moved from promoting democracy to fostering political stability and economic growth.

The U.S. emphasis on stability and growth was in part a response to the emergence of militant labor unions and strengthened Communist parties in several Latin American countries. Washington's preference for popular democracy did not fully apply when staunch U.S. allies were being challenged, especially by leftists. As U.S. concern grew with the perceived worldwide Marxist threat, Washington's bias for stability strengthened, even when that meant support for nondemocratic or antidemocratic politics. As George Kennan put it, "Where the concepts and traditions of popular government are too weak to absorb successfully the intensity of the Communist attacks, then we must concede that harsh government measures of repression may be the only answer."[1]

It was not much of a leap from this line of reasoning to Washington's orchestration of the successful overthrow of the democratically elected Arbenz government in Guatemala. The covert U.S. intervention in Guatemala in 1954 was possible in part because the U.S. government was no longer according much priority, if any, to promoting Latin American democracy. After 1948, Washington did little to support Latin America's democratizing efforts. The United States attempted to thwart the attempts of the "Caribbean Legion" to overthrow dictatorships in Nicaragua and the Dominican Republic, for example, and took no prodemocracy initiatives of its own.

Promoting democracy was not one of the stated objectives of U.S. policy in the Eisenhower administration's first strategy paper on Latin America, nor was it a major factor in shaping U.S. policy during the first Eisenhower administration.[2] Once again, regional circumstances and U.S. concerns elsewhere in the world combined to overwhelm the impulse to reform Latin America.

During the course of the 1950s, when as many as thirteen out of twenty Latin American states were ruled by dictators, the Eisenhower administration slowly changed its views, however. Authoritarian regimes came to be considered inherently unpopular, thus unstable and perhaps susceptible to subversion by anti-American movements. Pushed by well-informed advice from his brother Milton (who traveled to Latin America several times in the 1950s on behalf of the administration) and from special assistant Nelson A. Rockefeller, President Eisenhower moved during the course of the decade from a policy of indifference toward democracy—and sole reliance on open markets and direct investment as a sufficient foreign economic policy—to a positive interest in promoting both political and economic development in Latin America. This new interest was to be expressed through the transfer of public funds, the establishment of regional economic institutions (especially the Inter-American Development Bank), and the mobilization of U.S. influence in concrete cases in order to promote democratic politics. This policy crystallized in 1957–58 with the crumbling of Fulgencio Batista's long-time dictatorship in Cuba. With some lingering ambivalence, to be sure, the Eisenhower administration pressured Batista to leave office and to make possible a democratic transition. Batista resisted, but the evident withdrawal of U.S. support decisively weakened his hold.

The fall of Batista's regime in Cuba and the coming to power of Fidel Castro, a radical nationalist who was soon to develop close relations with the Soviet Union, precipitated a strong revival of U.S. concern with Latin America. The key preoccupation now was how to assure that the "twilight of the tyrants"—the weakening of a number of personalistic dictatorships—would not revert to another authoritarian night.[3]

The newly inaugurated administration of Pres. John F. Kennedy focused sharply on this challenge, and designed the Alliance for Progress. The idea was to nurture reformist democracies that could steer a middle course between reactionary oligarchs and revolutionaries on the left. The architects of the alliance recognized the revolutionary potential of extreme poverty, inequality, and political repression. Accordingly, Washington undertook to foster economic development, social reform, and democratic politics in Latin America in order to preempt revolution. Based on theories then prevailing in the U.S. academic community, U.S. officials believed that economic growth, the expansion of the middle class, land reform, political democracy, and enhanced stability all went hand in hand, and that the United States could effectively assist these processes from outside.[4]

As initially conceived, the Alliance for Progress called for an infusion of $20 billion in U.S. public and private funds over a ten-year period: to build infrastructure, raise per capita income, reduce illiteracy, improve public health, reform land tenure, and ameliorate income distribution. Because U.S. officials assumed that somehow economic growth and social reform would facilitate democratic politics, they devoted little systematic thought to the actual promotion of democracy. As Tony Smith indicates, the emphasis of policy was on how to nurture economic development; U.S. policy makers believed that democratic opening would follow ineluctably. To the extent that any conscious U.S. effort was made to promote democracy during the early 1960s, it was by not recognizing de facto governments arising from coups, by offering foreign aid as an incentive for democratization, and by providing military assistance and training programs and "public safety" efforts to put down insurgent movements and control instability.[5]

In any case, the Kennedy administration's commitment to democracy was at best conditional. As President Kennedy is reported to have expressed it in considering U.S. policy toward the Trujillo dictatorship in the Dominican Republic: "There are three possibilities, in descending order of preference: a decent democratic regime, a continuation of the Trujillo regime, or a Castro regime. We ought to aim at the first, but we can't really renounce the second until we are sure we can avoid the third."[6] U.S. efforts to promote democracy under Kennedy were often contradicted by programs to strengthen counterinsurgency forces and to shore up the local militaries. Modest efforts to push for land reform in places like northeast Brazil (where land tenure was highly inequitable) gave way quickly when local vested interests opposed the reforms while Communist groups favored them.[7]

Moreover, U.S. attempts to promote democracy during this period were brief and impatient. Disappointed by the lack of multilateral Latin American support for U.S. initiatives to use nonrecognition and political intervention to support democracy, the Kennedy administration backed away from its prodemocracy policy. It remained passive, at best, while Juan Bosch was being overthrown in the Dominican Republic in September 1963, and then edged toward recognition of the Dominican and Honduran de facto governments.

The drift of U.S. policy back toward accepting Latin American governments "as they are," without seeking to reform them, was accelerated and formalized after Kennedy's death, particularly after President Lyndon B. Johnson put career diplomat Thomas C. Mann in charge of Latin American policy. The "Mann Doctrine," a statement of U.S. policy announced by the new assistant secretary in 1964, made it clear that the United States would no longer push for democratic transitions in the hemisphere.

On the contrary, Washington supported the military overthrow of João Goulart's democratically elected government in Brazil in 1964, backed the military coup in Uruguay in 1973, and welcomed General Augusto Pinochet's overthrow of the elected government of Salvador Allende in Chile in 1973. During the late 1960s and early 1970s, Washington seemed comfortable with Latin America's swing toward military rule. Governor Rockefeller, in a report for the Nixon administration, now urged that the United States maintain normal diplomatic and economic relations with military regimes, which he argued could be progressive and reformist, though they were not to be preferred to democratic governments.[8] By the mid-1970s, U.S. relations with the military regimes were so cordial that Washington was widely perceived, indeed, as the champion of authoritarianism in the Americas.

The Vietnam war and its impact on U.S. politics and policy soon reversed this tendency, however. Domestic opposition to U.S. foreign policy, galvanized by the anti-war movement and then by the revulsion against the Watergate political scandal, led to strong criticism of the association of the United States with Latin American dictatorships. A deep current of domestic opinion, crystallized by human rights and religious organizations, pushed during the early and mid-1970s for legislation curbing U.S. economic and military assistance to any country with a record of gross and systematic violations of human rights.

The administration of Jimmy Carter, elected in 1976 after a campaign in which Carter promised to give the United States "a government as good as its people," initially made human rights the cornerstone of its Latin American policy. Convinced that prior U.S. policy toward Latin America and many of the developing countries had been distorted by "an inordinate fear of Communism," the Carter administration initially reduced the prior U.S. preoccupation with stability and anti-Communism in the Western

Hemisphere, and accepted "ideological pluralism" in the region. Its prime concern was with curbing gross violations of human rights—torture, "disappearances," and prolonged incarceration of political opponents—rather than with facilitating general democratic political opening (*abertura*, in Latin American parlance).[9] The administration's efforts were fully consistent with *abertura*, however, and served to reinforce the internal processes in Brazil, Peru, Ecuador, and Uruguay that were impelling those countries back toward democratic politics. In one specific situation, in the Dominican Republic in 1978 (discussed in Jonathan Hartlyn's chapter), the Carter administration pushed effectively to counter electoral fraud and assist a democratic transition. But this was an exceptional case of direct U.S. pressure; in most instances, the Carter administration's support for Latin American democracy was indirect.

Ronald Reagan came to office in 1981 highly critical of the Carter human rights policies, which were said to have destabilized friendly regimes, particularly those of Anastasio Somoza in Nicaragua and of the shah of Iran, without producing democratic (or friendly) governments in their stead.[10] The new administration sought to reverse the perceived mistakes of the Carter period by refurbishing U.S. relations with the "moderately authoritarian" regimes of the Southern Cone, particularly in Argentina, Brazil, and Chile.

The Reagan administration befriended the Argentine military regime, a virtual pariah during the Carter period, and enlisted it as an ally in support of U.S. policy in Central America. Ambassador Jeane Kirkpatrick traveled to Chile to mend fences with General Pinochet. The White House sought, as well, to restore what one National Security Council staff person called a "beautiful relationship" with Brazil. Secretary of State Alexander Haig explained that terrorism from the left would be the new administration's major human rights concern. Indeed, the first Reagan appointee for the post of assistant secretary of state for human rights, Ernest Lefever, was rejected by the Senate because, in keeping with the new administration's thrust, he opposed systematic U.S. efforts to promote human rights in non-Communist autocracies. But despite this initial Reagan approach to Latin America, by the end of the 1980s the U.S. government was once again trumpeting its strong efforts to promote Latin American democracy, and was even taking considerable credit for the region's strides in that direction.

Although promoting democracy was a unifying articulated theme of Reagan pronouncements on Latin America, particularly after 1982, Thomas Carothers points out that in practice there were at least four different subpolicies, each adopted for different reasons and each with diverse effects. At various times and places, the Reagan administration was promoting: "democracy by centrist transition" through the emergence of elected civilian governments in El Salvador, Honduras, and Guatemala; "democracy by force" in Nicaragua and Grenada; "democracy by applause," through limited diplomatic support to the many transitions from authoritarian rule in South America; and "democracy by pressure" to induce the remaining right-wing dictators in Chile, Paraguay, Panama, and Haiti to cede power through elections.

The Reagan administration's first focal point in the Western Hemisphere was Central America, for the new U.S. policy makers believed that the Soviet Union had targeted the region as part of its "master plan" for threatening U.S. interests. The administration's initial aim was simple: to counter leftist gains in Central America by shoring up the governments of El Salvador, Guatemala, Honduras, and Costa Rica—primarily through military and economic assistance as well as by pressuring the Sandinista regime in Nicaragua to cease supporting the left in neighboring countries, if not to give up power themselves. Administration policy makers soon came to understand that it would be easier to obtain congressional approval for these military programs if they were couched in "prodemocracy" terms. The thrust of the administration's policy, however, was not so much to promote democratic openings as to fortify the incumbent regimes, while portraying them in the most favorable light possible.

Late in the Reagan period—after José Napoleon Duarte's regime in El Salvador was safely stabilized and the administration's hard-liners could focus single-mindedly on Nicaragua—the administration concentrated on promoting free and fair elections throughout Central America. Even then, however, the efforts were motivated far more by the aim of mobilizing congressional backing for the anti-Sandinista campaign than by a desire to reshape Central American realities. And whenever a conflict arose among policy objectives in the region, priority went to thwarting the Left.

As part of the effort to isolate Nicaragua, Reagan administration operatives took credit for Central America's democratization during the 1980s, but this tendency merely illustrated the superficiality of that administration's concern with democracy, at least in this context. Washington's efforts certainly did not bring robust democracy to any of the Central American countries, and in most cases the U.S. emphasis on supporting local military establishments arguably reinforced their dominant and ultimately antidemocratic role. Further, the administration's massive economic assistance and its political intervention were so intrusive as almost certainly to reduce the long-term changes for indigenous and autonomous democratic politics.

Although administration officials portrayed the policy toward Nicaragua as intended to induce the Sandinistas to permit free and fair elections, the goal of "democratization" in Nicaragua was actually imposed on U.S. policy by hard-liners within the Reagan coalition who saw it primarily as a way to prevent U.S. accommodation with the Sandinistas by establishing a precondition Managua presumably could not fulfill.[11] Once included in the stated U.S. policy, the objective of democratization in Nicaragua had two effects: to block any negotiated agreement on security issues (just as the

252 · *Abraham F. Lowenthal*

hard-liners intended) and to change the terms of the debate in Congress by enabling the administration to sell military aid to the contras as a means of pressuring a nondemocratic government to open up its politics. But this was largely a ploy to strengthen a policy of hostility toward the Sandinistas based on their ties to the Soviet Union and Cuba, not to their lack of full-fledged pluralist democracy.

As an instrument for actually opening up Nicaragua's politics and fostering the conditions for democracy, the Reagan policy of military aid to the contras was surely counterproductive. It was only when the Congress finally forced the administration to drop the contra war that there was space for the Arias Plan, the diplomatic initiative spearheaded by Costa Rica's president, which eventually opened the way to the democratic elections of February 1990.

The striking transitions toward democracy that took place in South America during the 1980s have been cited by former Assistant Secretary of State Elliott Abrams and others as examples of the efficacy of Reagan's efforts to promote democracy. In fact, however, U.S. verbal support for the first few transitions was no more than an overlay on the basic policy of improving relations with the military governments.[12] The administration had no identifiable positive role in facilitating the transitions to democracy in Argentina, Brazil, and Uruguay. If anything, its policy worked against the democratizing trend, as friendly overtures from the United States and the tone of renewed material and diplomatic support temporarily buoyed the military governments.

When the Reagan administration finally did embrace South America's democratic openings, this was mainly in response to the failure of its first attempts to establish durable warm relations with the Argentine and Chilean military regimes and as a belated reaction to indigenous trends in South America; it was also in part motivated by the desire to have a more consistent prodemocracy image in order to build congressional support for the contra aid. The policy of "democracy by applause," although a shift from the earlier stance, was in any case essentially limited to rhetoric. Washington did not provide the economic support the fragile democracies called for. Such verbal backing as was furnished was ineffective or irrelevant in almost all cases.

It was only in the last years of the second Reagan administration that the United States clearly exerted its influence to nurture democratic transitions from the remaining right-wing authoritarian governments in Haiti, Panama, Paraguay, and Chile.[13] In all four cases, the United States did take specific measures, including diplomatic and economic pressure, to try to persuade long-time dictators to cede power. What is most notable about these cases, in turn, is how spectacularly the administration's efforts at democracy promotion failed in Haiti and Panama, how largely irrelevant they were in Paraguay, and that they were apparently successful only in Chile.

And although U.S. officials often cite Chile as an example of the Reagan administration's Democracy Agenda, U.S. policy was not more than a marginal factor in the Chilean transition. As Heraldo Muñoz shows, Chilean opposition groups largely on their own developed the strategy and tactics that brought an end to the Pinochet dictatorship, and they restored national political institutions and practices that were entirely indigenous. Even the exceptional Chilean case thus provides evidence to prove the rule that the United States did not do much during the 1980s that was important and effective in promoting Latin American democracy.

Getting Down to Cases

From the time of Woodrow Wilson to the present, in sum, there has been a recurrent, sincere, but limited U.S. impulse to promote democracy in Latin America. This U.S. drive to export democracy has only rarely had a positive and lasting impact, however. In most cases, in all periods, the strict limits on Washington's capacity to nurture Latin American democracy, even when it wants to do so, have been plainly evident.

These preliminary conclusions are strongly reinforced by focusing on five countries where the United States has repeatedly tried to foster democratic politics: Argentina, the Dominican Republic, Mexico, Nicaragua, and Chile.

Carlos Escudé's comparison of U.S. policy toward Argentina from 1943 to 1955 and from 1976 to 1983 shows that the United States pursued vacillating, contradictory, and indeed incoherent policies with respect to democratic politics and the related issue of human rights in Argentina. At times, Washington pushed Argentine governments hard to respect human rights and constitutional democratic guarantees. But there were also moments, sometimes hard on the heels of a binge of democracy promotion, when Washington subordinated this concern to other considerations, or seemed to abandon it altogether.

Escudé illuminates the divisions in Washington regarding the ends and means of U.S. policy toward Argentina, demonstrating that struggles among policy makers often determined U.S. actions. He hypothesizes that this tendency has been heightened in the Argentine case by the country's peculiar stature as sufficiently large and visible to have some salience, yet sufficiently distant and marginal to the vital interests of the United States to allow full play in the policy-making process to personal idiosyncrasies and bureaucratic rivalry.

Whatever the reasons for the cycles in U.S. policy, Escudé's main contention, although perhaps exaggerated, is compelling: the activation and deactivation by the United States of its prodemocracy concerns has had the perverse effect, over time, of helping to undermine Argentine political stability, contributing to further polarization of a divided society, and thus diminishing the country's chances for sustainable democratic politics.

A similar point is made in Jonathan Hartlyn's survey of the relationship between U.S. policy and democratic prospects in the Dominican Republic over a seventy-five-year period, from the U.S. military occupation of 1916 through the 1990 presidential elections. Hartlyn analyzes five different times when the United States was deeply engaged, although to varying extents, in the Dominican Republic's political life: during the military occupation until 1924, at the time of the accession to power of long-term dictator Rafael Trujillo in 1930, in the period of democratic ferment immediately following World War II, in the kaleidoscopic years from the last phase of Trujillo's government through the inauguration of Joaquín Balaguer in 1966, and in the 1978 democratic transition, when Balaguer became the first elected president in the country's history to relinquish power to an elected opponent. Hartlyn demonstrates that the United States has long had great influence in Dominican politics, no matter what its policy, but that Washington has not easily or often determined the Dominican Republic's course. He also finds that Dominican actors invariably try to mobilize the United States as a potential ally in their struggles; that democracy promotion has often been on the U.S. agenda in Santo Domingo, but for sharply changing reasons; and that the extent of U.S. involvement in promoting Dominican democracy has usually been more a function of the general international context than of internal Dominican conditions.

Two points stand out in Hartlyn's account. First, the most effective instance of U.S. democracy promotion occurred in 1978 at a time when Washington was relatively unconcerned about the Dominican Republic, when U.S. actions were confined to supporting local institutions and actors, and when Dominican internal processes played the crucial role in facilitating a democratic transition. Second, the net effect of seventy-five years of U.S. involvement in Dominican affairs, the cumulative impact of three generations of episodic democracy promotion, has been to create a pathology of dependence that will have to be overcome eventually if meaningful democracy is ever to be consolidated in the Dominican Republic. Repeated U.S. efforts to foster Dominican democracy—combined with sometimes abrupt shifts in U.S. policy, as priorities and concepts change— have distorted the Dominican Republic's politics in ways ultimately inimical to democracy.[14]

At many points in this century, U.S. policy makers have articulated the goal of promoting democracy in Nicaragua, as Joseph Tulchin and Knut Walter emphasize, but up to now their efforts have been repeatedly and remarkably unsuccessful. Over and over, U.S. officials have underestimated the difficulty of establishing stable democratic conditions in Nicaragua. Time and again, limited U.S. intervention has expanded until its exaggerated extent has led Washington to curtail its involvement, even at the cost of giving up the democratic policy objective—at which point the nondemocratic dynamics of Nicaraguan politics has taken over once again.

The Nicaraguan presidential elections of 1990, widely recognized as the most open and honest national poll in that country's history, took place to a significant extent because of U.S. pressure, and it is therefore commonly cited as an example of Washington's successful promotion of democracy.[15] What is almost universally accepted in Washington, however, was broadly perceived in Nicaragua as but the latest in a long series of blatant U.S. interventions that have had less to do with democracy than with a continuing U.S. desire to control the country's politics. No one who reads Tulchin and Walter's review of eighty years in Nicaragua's history would entirely discount this interpretation. Perhaps decades of previous experience will be reversed now, but it is certainly much too early to assume that Nicaraguan democracy will be consolidated, or even that the United States would unambiguously and effectively support sustained democracy there.

In Argentina, the Dominican Republic, and Nicaragua, U.S. officials have often talked about promoting democracy and have sometimes tried to do so, but with little positive effect and with some contrary results. In Mexico, however, according to Lorenzo Meyer, U.S. concern about the prospects for democracy, even at the level of rhetoric, occurred only for a brief moment. That was in 1913–14, early in the Mexican Revolution, when President Woodrow Wilson, essentially for ideological reasons, pushed hard but only briefly for democratic opening. Within months, the internal Mexican struggles and intrabureaucratic wrangling in Washington combined to frustrate Wilson's impulse to teach Mexicans "to elect good men." From then until the 1980s, Meyer argues, the United States did little or nothing to promote democracy in Mexico, or even to concern itself about whether Mexico was or could ever become democratic. Washington's overriding concern about Mexico, decade after decade, was not democracy but stability.

Even in the 1980s, when Washington's campaign to promote democracy was applied, if very discreetly, to Mexico, Meyer suggests that the U.S. concern with Mexico's prospects for democracy was at best superficial. During the early and mid-1980s, Washington pursued the goal of democracy tactically, as an instrument for strengthening the rightist opposition party, the Partido Acción Nacional (PAN), and thereby pressuring the government of Mexico to adjust to U.S. preferences on Central America, immigration, drugs, and economic policy. Dramatic evidence that the United States was not fundamentally concerned about democracy in Mexico was provided in 1988, Meyer argues, as the previously fragmented U.S. government quickly and unanimously rallied to support President-elect Carlos Salinas de Gortari despite indications that his election in July 1988 had been marred by fraud.

Ironically, as Meyer briefly suggests, the positive influence of the United States on Mexico's democratic prospects has actually been rapidly expanding since the late 1980s, not because of official policy but despite it. The U.S. media, human rights groups, scholars, and labor and business groups have all become increasingly active in Mexico. For different reasons, all are concerned about the rule of law, free expression, and democratic politics, and their interest is likely to be mobilized with increasing effectiveness by those in Mexico who are pushing for democratic change.

Perhaps the best example of a successful U.S. effort to foster democratic politics in Latin America occurred in Chile beginning in the mid-1980s. From the time of Harry G. Barnes's appointment as U.S. ambassador in Santiago in 1985, the government consistently employed its influence to encourage the authoritarian military regime of Gen. Augusto Pinochet to move toward restoring constitutional democracy. At various critical moments in the late 1980s, U.S. pressures or appeals helped nudge Pinochet toward conducting a national plebiscite under conditions that were sufficiently open and fair to permit the dramatic victory of the opposition coalition and the end of the Pinochet dictatorship. The U.S. also provided encouragement, advice, and assistance to the democratic opposition at a number of points and in different ways—indirectly by supporting the plebiscitary process itself and directly by making available funding and technical help. On some issues and at some critical moments, the U.S. role may well have been significant—in insisting that the opposition campaign have access to television as a condition of U.S. recognition of the plebiscite's validity, for example, and in warning the Pinochet government that an eleventh-hour plan to derail the plebiscite would be strongly condemned.

But, as Heraldo Muñoz argues, even the Chilean success story carries a mixed message about the relationship between the United States and Latin American democracy. Muñoz persuasively argues that Washington has never been particularly interested in democracy in Chile, where the emergence of strong democratic traditions and institutions over the past century had nothing to do with the United States. Indeed, the historic U.S. attitude toward Chilean democracy has been generally neutral and occasionally negative. For several decades, the U.S. approach to Chilean politics was to prevent the left from gaining power, even if it could gain office through democratic means, rather than to bolster democracy as such. The U.S. government conspired against and in some sense contributed to the eventual unconstitutional overthrow of the democratically elected and constitutional administration of Salvador Allende in 1970–73.

The sources and motives of U.S. support for Chile's return to democracy in the late 1980s were mixed, as Muñoz shows: the built-in tension between support for Pinochet and underlying American values; the pressures on U.S. policy exerted by human rights groups and other nongovernmental organizations; the skill of Chilean opposition leaders in taking advantage of the pluralism of U.S. society to mobilize U.S. influence; and, above all, the internal evolution of the Chilean situation, which permitted a consensus to emerge against prolonging the dictatorship and allowed very diverse opposition groups eventually to submerge their differences toward this end. An important ingredient, too, as Muñoz underlines, was career diplomat Barnes, who skillfully transformed U.S. policies to support a democratic transition and thus gave encouragement to many in Chilean society who wanted assurance that an end to the dictatorship was both possible and safe.

In contrast to most of the other cases here reviewed, U.S. efforts at promoting democracy in Chile were effective. But even here, the limits of the case emerge plainly from Muñoz's account. External influence, including that of the United States, helped at the margin to restore democracy, but this was in an already fundamentally democratic nation, under conditions of stability and prosperity, with a strong moderate opposition movement and a weak left mostly committed to peaceful and incremental change. Circumstances as favorable as those in Chile for the nurturing of democracy do not often arise.

Key Nongovernmental Actors

The essays reviewed thus far discuss the impact of U.S. government policy on Latin America's prospects for democracy. Some of the most important ways in which the United States affects Latin America, however, derive not from governmental policy but from the acts and omissions of nongovernmental agents with a strong presence in the region. There are many relevant examples, including religious groups, journalists, scholars, and human rights organizations. All merit more treatment than they receive in this volume, but our symposium does include two chapters focusing on key nongovernmental actors: U.S. business and organized labor.

Elizabeth Cobbs argues, contrary to conventional assumptions, that in the period following World War II U.S. business has often shown a stronger commitment to constructive relations with Latin America, and ultimately to reinforcing the region's democratic movement, than has the U.S. government. This is not because business has particularly noble motives or an ideological attachment to democracy, but rather because the self-interested concerns of business leaders have led them over the past few decades to learn that intervention is often counterproductive and that respect for local sovereignty and neutrality toward local political decisions are ultimately more conducive to political stability and to economic growth than cyclical but short-lived direct efforts to promote their interests.

The contrast between U.S. government policy and that of U.S. corporations in the case of Nicaragua illustrates this point. U.S. firms were willing and able to cooperate with the Sandinista regime at a time when the Reagan administration was determined to undermine it. Even in the most famous cases of political intervention by U.S. corporations—by United Fruit Company in Guatemala in the 1950s and by International Telephone and Telegraph in Chile in the 1970s—the firms were implementing U.S. government policy more than driving it, and the corporate policies were largely opposed by other elements of the business community. On the whole, U.S. companies in Latin America, at least during the past fifty years, have been increasingly respectful of national sovereignty, and thus have contributed to one of the prerequisites for genuine and lasting democratic politics.

Throughout most of the century, the organized labor movement of the United States, by contrast, has been more of an obstacle than an ally to Latin America's democratization. From World War I to the 1970s, U.S. labor pushed pro–United States "business unionism" in Latin America—aimed at guaranteeing profitability for U.S. investors and countering the influence in the region of radical, class-based, nationalist, and independent trade unions. For decades, labor's efforts in Latin America had a consistently conservative and often antidemocratic bias, as its interests were tied primarily to U.S.-led capitalist expansion and to Latin American stability, rather than mainly to political pluralism or social change.

But since the 1970s, Paul Buchanan shows, economic and political changes in the United States, Latin America, and elsewhere have combined to induce U.S. labor to take a positive interest in the political liberalization of Latin America. U.S. labor has come to play a significant role in promoting democratic openings in Latin American nations as different as El Salvador and Brazil, not so much out of ideological conviction as for self-interest. U.S. labor today sees the promotion of economic and political democracy around the world as the best way of equalizing the international labor market, and thus pursuing its own material and organizational objectives. Like U.S. business, U.S. labor has thus come to play a role at least compatible with—and perhaps supportive of—strengthening Latin American democracy. In the 1990s, in contrast with the past, U.S. labor, like U.S. business, may well exert a democratizing influence in Latin America.

General Conclusions

Some tentative propositions may now be advanced about when and where the United States has tried to promote Latin American democracy, why, how, and with what results.

1. The United States Government has often adopted policies intended to strengthen Latin America's prospects for democracy, conceived of in political and institutional terms. These efforts have been most salient in the Caribbean Basin nations close to the United States, and in distant nations (such as Argentina and Chile) large enough to be visible politically and internationally but too far away to be closely

connected with the United States or perceived as vital to its security. Washington's attempts to promote democracy have been least evident in such major nations as Mexico and Brazil, where the overriding U.S. objective has been long-term stability.

2. There is an underlying predisposition in the United States to favor democratic politics throughout the Western Hemisphere (and the world, for that matter), and this fundamental tendency makes unstable and ultimately unviable any U.S. alliance with a repressive authoritarian regime. But the U.S. bias for democracy is rarely sufficient to overcome general and specific constraints on the impulse to promote democracy abroad, or to give the promotion of democracy priority over the other goals of U.S. policy. The impulse to promote democracy may be reinforced in particular situations, however, either for instrumental reasons—as a means of coercion, to achieve consistency in order to bolster U.S. efforts elsewhere to dislodge an antagonistic regime, or to facilitate the extrication of the United States from an unwanted involvement—or because of effective pressures from concerned groups within the United States or in the Latin American nation.

3. The United States has been more likely to push actively for democratic opening in a Latin American nation when:

a. An incumbent authoritarian regime is perceived by U.S. officials as anti-American; or,

b. An incumbent authoritarian regime is pursuing specific policies perceived by Washington officials as contrary to U.S. interests; or,

c. A high priority effort to dislodge or pressure one regime qualifying under condition *a* or *b* requires consistent attempts to promote democratic opening in other nations that can easily be portrayed as comparable; or,

d. Democractic opening, or at least a "demonstration election," is needed as a means of legitimizing a significant diminution of the U.S. presence in and influence upon a country where Washington has heretofore been deeply engaged;[16] or,

e. Local democratic forces by themselves are so close to obtaining power that Washington officials conclude that a timely identification of U.S. policies with their fortunes is opportune; or,

f. Local political forces are particularly adept at mobilizing groups within the United States to pressure for the alignment of U.S. policies with their movement; or,

g. No important U.S. economic or security interests are engaged in the particular country, and the underlying U.S. cultural and ideological preference for democratic politics has recently been strongly reinforced in the minds of policy makers in a broader international context; *and,*

h. The left in the specific country is either thought to be insignificant or else understood to be committed to democratic and nonviolent forms of political competition.[17]

4. Specific U.S. efforts to promote democracy in Latin America are motivated more often by domestic U.S. or broader international considerations than by particular trends within the affected country. It is largely for this reason that U.S. prodemocracy efforts so often occur in waves and are played out in a number of very different nations within the same period, regardless of whether these nations are themselves evolving toward or away from democratic politics.

5. The United States has used a wide variety of means to nurture Latin American democracy, ranging from quiet diplomacy through pressures and sanctions to outright occupation. Each of these instruments has been useful in pushing for democratic politics in at least one concrete situation. By and large, however, the more interventionist the United States has been in Latin America—by contravening sovereignty and overwhelming local actors—the less it has been able to foster lasting democratic politics, except in the limiting case of Puerto Rico; that is, of outright and permanent imposition.[18]

6. None of the instruments employed by the United States to promote democracy has ever succeeded in an enduring fashion unless local conditions were propitious. By the same token, U.S. influence has been more effective when it could be exercised in support of local actors and even more so when it could back locally controlled processes and institutions rather than specific participants. Similarly, it is easier for the United States to help protect a democracy under siege than to implant democratic practices where they have not previously been rooted.

7. Recurrent U.S. efforts to promote Latin American democracy have not been long sustained. Enthusiasm for active democracy promotion has ebbed and flowed, and the inconstancy of U.S. policy has tended not only to erode the efficacy of U.S. policy but actually to undermine the conditions for democratic politics.

8. The capacity of the U.S. government to nurture democratic politics in Latin America is greatest in those countries where the United States is sufficiently involved to be influential but not so extensively engaged as to warp the domestic fabric of social and political life. Even in such nations, the United States is only likely to be effective in promoting democracy when U.S. influence is consistently exerted.

9. External factors, including U.S. policy, are usually of secondary or tertiary importance in determining a Latin American nation's prospects for democracy, except in highly unusual, very finely balanced circumstances when foreign influence can tip the scale—or else in the small, nearby nations most penetrated by and vulnerable to the United States.[19] In the latter case, however, the immediate prodemocracy influ-

ence of the United States is often overcome by longer-term obstacles to democracy building that derive precisely from U.S. interventionism.

10. The indirect impact of the United States may well be more important in affecting Latin America's prospects for democratic politics than specifically designed U.S. government policies. Among the important ways that the United States affects Latin America's chances to democratic politics are its role as historic model, its cultural and educational traditions, the effect of free-market economics on political institutions and practices, the impact of broad international economic policies and of human rights concerns, the influence of U.S. military doctrines and training on Latin American officers, and the impact of exile in the United States upon Latin American political actors. Of great significance, too, are the activities undertaken by a wide variety of nongovernmental actors: not only business enterprises and labor unions but churches, journalists, scholars, human rights groups, environmentalists, tourists, and others. The U.S. government can probably do more to promote democracy in Latin America by encouraging nongovernmental policies and processes to support the region's democratization than by direct governmental pressures.

11. When U.S. government officials do undertake directly to promote democracy in Latin America, they are most likely to be effective if:

a. The U.S. foreign-policy-making bureaucracy accords a shared sense of priority to Latin American democracy.

b. The goal of nurturing democracy is broadly supported domestically and is undertaken as a bipartisan commitment.

c. The instruments used by U.S. officials are noncoercive and overt, support local processes and institutions, and are carried out with multilateral participation or approval.

Promoting Latin American Democracy: Guidelines for U.S. Policy

Despite its frequent and fulsome rhetoric, the U.S. government has actively promoted Latin American democracy only on occasion. Even when Washington officials have done so, their efforts have often been ineffective and sometimes counterproductive. The few successful instances of democracy promotion by the United States have only rarely been sustained. In the rare cases when U.S. policies to promote Latin American democracy coincided with sustained democratic consolidation, it is unlikely that U.S. influence was determinative.

These sobering conclusions, amply supported in this volume, should not discourage U.S. officials from supporting democracy in Latin America (and elsewhere, for that matter) as a legitimate and significant long-term goal of U.S. foreign policy. The citizens of the United States have good reasons to want their government to foster open, participatory, and constitutional politics throughout the Western Hemisphere. A region of consolidated democracies would be more humane and peaceful than one in which authoritarian regimes predominate. A democratic hemisphere would also be more stable, for effective democracy is the best insurance against guerrilla movements, terrorism, extremism, or anomic violence. The balanced economic social reforms that Latin America must undertake to develop and eventually to expand commercial exchange with the United States are more likely to be sustained under democratic conditions. Perhaps most important, the core values of the American people—tolerance for diversity, respect for fundamental human rights, and the rule of law—are best, indeed only, protected under democracy.

Promoting democracy is not an unworthy, unimportant, or impossible objective, but it is an extremely difficult task. It should be pursued consistently over many decades, not exuberantly chased in short bursts. Because democracy inherently involves self-determination and autonomy, outside efforts to nurture it must be restrained, respectful, sensitive, and patient. These are not qualities for which U.S. foreign policy is generally noted, but they are needed to promote democracy abroad.

Democracy is not an export commodity; it cannot simply be shipped from one setting to another. By its very nature, democracy must be achieved by each nation, largely on its own. It is an internal process, rooted in a country's history, institutions, and values; in the balance of its social and economic forces; and in the courage, commitment, and skill of its political leaders and of plain citizens.

But there is a good deal the United States can do, especially in concert with like-minded countries, to nurture and reinforce democracy in the Americas.

First, the United States should consistently emphasize its concern with the protection of fundamental human rights, for these rights are at the heart of democracy. Through diplomacy that is discreet, tempered, and professional—but not so quiet as to be unheard—the United States, together with the other democracies of the hemisphere, should invariably criticize regimes that grossly and systematically violate human rights. These regimes should be denied military and economic assistance, and they should not be treated as allies or friends. The specter of international isolation may help turn former supporters of authoritarian regimes into influential opponents at a delicate moment in the transition process. Similarly, in the period of consolidation, individual pressure may or may not dissuade backsliding toward the subversion of democratic institutions. U.S. leaders and their counterparts throughout the Americas can, in turn, positively support and reinforce the democratic network that is growing in the hemisphere, involving parties, trade unions, professional associations, women's groups, religious organizations, student federations, and others.

Second, the United States can cooperate with other nations to help strengthen the governmental institutions and practices that make up the very fiber of democracy. The United States should respond positively to requests from Latin American nations for technical assistance to legislatures on such matters as budget, oversight, and civilian control of the military, as well as support programs to improve the training and reinforce the democratic commitments of judicial and law enforcement officials.

Third, Washington should support inter-American efforts to institutionalize an independent and professional capacity to monitor elections, upon request by sovereign governments, and to help assure that elections are—and are accepted as being—free and fair. Elections by themselves do not make democracies; democracies make elections. But periodic and meaningful competition for political power, with a high level of participation and a level of civil and political liberties sufficient to ensure the integrity and legitimacy of the process, is a crucial element of democracy and external monitoring can help assure the proper conditions.

Fourth, the United States, directly through government actions and indirectly through the activities of private groups, can support the network of nongovernmental organizations—economic, social, educational, and civic—that express and mediate public demands and build the pluralism needed to keep democracy vital. Washington can help provide material and moral support to professional associations, trade unions, research centers, and the media in order to reinforce the democratic fabric.

Fifth, U.S. officials can strengthen Latin America's prospects for democracy by providing unambiguous and consistent signals that the maintenance of democratic politics is a high priority goal of the United States. Through the advice of its military missions and the content of its training programs, for example, the United States can help keep Latin America's armed forces out of politics. Latin America's business leaders, too, are likely to be responsive to clear U.S. signals of the importance of democracy.

In all such efforts, multilateral programs are more likely to be effective over time than bilateral ones, which are too easily perceived as partisan and interventionist. The United States should nurture and support cooperative efforts among the democratic governments of the Americas to strengthen democracy region-wide, not go it alone or insist on a leadership role.

It is also wise for Washington to employ mechanisms—such as the National Endowment for Democracy and the affiliated party, labor, and business institutes—that to some extent separate U.S. programs to support democracy from the immediate priorities of the foreign-policy-making bureaucracy. It is equally important that these institutions keep their focus squarely on supporting democratic processes; they should not identify themselves with particular candidates nor parties, or lend themselves to instrumental efforts to press for a specific political outcome.

Probably the most decisive ways the United States can promote Latin American democracy are indirect.

First, the United States can certainly improve Latin America's prospects for democracy by helping countries of the region cope with their fundamental economic problems. U.S. foreign economic policies should reinforce Latin American efforts to make their economies both more productive and more equitable, and thus help to build the underpinnings of democracy. Of all the means available to the United States to strengthen Latin American democracy in the 1990s, this is no doubt the single most important. Democracy is under seige in Latin America after a "lost decade" of depression, declining investment, decaying social services, and worsening inequalities. It is in the interest of the United States—among other reasons because of its commitment to democracy—to help Latin America resume economic growth and development.

Finally, the United States strengthens the democratic cause throughout the hemisphere and elsewhere when it is true to its political values and protects the vitality of its own democratic institutions. Conversely, whenever U.S. officials flout the rule of law, domestic or international—as they did in the case of Nicaragua in the 1980s—they inevitably make the Americas and the world unsafe for democracy. Clandestine, undemocratic, or illegal means are neither justified nor effective as ways of nurturing democracy. The United States should never pretend that it can promote democracy abroad by trampling upon it at home.

Notes

1. The memorandum from which this quotation is drawn is cited at greater length on pp. 64–65 of Leslie Bethell's chapter in this volume; see his discussion and n. 42.

2. Stephen Rabe, *Eisenhower and Latin America: The Foreign Policy of Anti-Communism* (Chapel Hill: University of North Carolina Press, 1988).

3. Tad Szulc, *Twilight of the Tyrants* (New York: Holt, 1959).

4. See Robert Packenham, *Liberal America and the Third World* (Princeton: Princeton University Press, 1973); and Howard Wiarda, "Did the Alliance 'Lose Its Way,' or Were Its Assumptions All Wrong from the Beginning and Are Those Assumptions Still with Us?" in L. Ronald Scheman, ed., *The Alliance for Progress* (New York: Praeger, 1988), pp. 95–118.

5. See, for example, Abraham F. Lowenthal, "Foreign Aid as a Political Instrument: The Case of the Dominican Republic," *Public Policy* 14 (1965): 141–60.

6. See Arthur M. Schlesinger, Jr., *A Thousand Days: John F. Kennedy in the White House* (Boston: Houghton Mifflin, 1965), p. 769.

7. Riordan Roett, *The Politics of Foreign Aid in Northeast Brazil* (Nashville: Vanderbilt University Press, 1972).

8. See Nelson A. Rockefeller, *The Rockefeller Report on the Americas* (Chicago: Quadrangle Books, 1969). A good doctoral dissertation could no doubt be written on the evolution of Nelson Rockefeller's thinking about Latin American democracy from the 1940s to the 1970s.

9. See Lars Schoultz, *Human Rights and United States Policy toward Latin America* (Princeton: Princeton University Press, 1981). Cf. Joshua Muravchik, *The Uncertain Cru-*

sade: Jimmy Carter and the Dilemmas of Human Rights Policy (Lanham, Md.: Hamilton Press, 1986).

10. The classic statement of this view was Jeane Kirkpatrick's "Dictatorships and Double Standards," published in *Commentary* (November 1979). See also Kirkpatrick's "U.S. Security in Latin America," *Commentary* (January 1981).

11. Cf. Constantine Menges, *Inside the National Security Council* (New York: Simon & Schuster, 1988), and Roy Gutman, *Banana Diplomacy: The Making of American Policy in Nicaragua, 1981–1987* (New York: Simon & Schuster, 1988).

12. See Elliott Abrams, "Latin America in the Time of Reagan," *The New York Times,* July 27, 1988. Cf. Andrew Hurrell, "International Support for Political Democracy in Contemporary Latin America: The Case of Brazil," paper prepared for the Latin America Study Group, Royal Institute of International Affairs (London), May 10, 1989.

13. These cases are more extensively discussed in Thomas Carothers, *In the Name of Democracy: U.S. Policy toward Latin America in the Reagan Years* (Berkeley: University of California Press, forthcoming). Cf. Adam Garfinkle, *Friendly Tyrants* (forthcoming).

14. See Abraham F. Lowenthal, "The Dominican Republic: The Politics of Chaos," in A. von Lazar and R. R. Kaufman, eds., *Reform and Revolution: Readings in Latin American Politics* (Needham Heights, Mass.: Allyn & Bacon, 1969).

15. See Robert A. Pastor, "Nicaragua's Choice: The Making of a Free Election," *Journal of Democracy* (Summer 1990): 13–25.

16. See Edward Herman and Frank Brodhead, eds., *Demonstration Elections: U.S.- Staged Elections in the Dominican Republic, Vietnam, and El Salvador* (Boston: South End Press, 1984).

17. With the waning of the Cold War in the 1990s, it may be that this final condition will be relaxed, for the link between the left and a powerful international competitor of the United States has been broken. See Jorge G. Castañeda, "Latin America and the End of the Cold War: A Mixed Blessing for the Left," *World Policy Journal* (Summer 1990): 471–92.

18. In correspondence with the author, Carlos Escudé has pointed out that it is the incompleteness and inconstancy of U.S. intervention in Latin America (see proposition #7) that makes ineffective U.S. intervention for democracy in the region, rather than the fact of intervention itself. He compares the more profound, single-minded, skillful, and effective U.S. intervention for democracy in Italy in 1948. See E. Miller, "Taking Off the Gloves: The United States and the Italian Elections of 1948," *Diplomatic History* (Winter 1983).

19. On the likelihood that external influence will be most significant when the local political equation is delicately balanced, see Robert A. Pastor, "How to Reinforce Democracy in the Americas: Seven Proposals," in Robert A. Pastor, ed., *Democracy in the Americas: Stopping the Pendulum* (New York: Holmes & Meier, 1989), p. 141.

Note on Contributors

Paul W. Drake is currently chairman of the department of political science at the University of California, San Diego. He is a former president of the Latin American Studies Association.

Leslie Bethell is director of the Institute of Latin American Studies at the University of London and editor of the *Cambridge History of Latin America*.

Tony Smith is professor of political science at Tufts University.

Thomas Carothers is an attorney at Arnold & Porter in Washington, D.C. When he was writing this essay, he was an International Affairs Fellow of the Council on Foreign Relations.

Elizabeth A. Cobbs is assistant professor of history at the University of San Diego.

Paul G. Buchanan is assistant professor of political science at the University of Arizona.

John Sheahan is professor of economics at Williams College.

Laurence Whitehead is official fellow in politics at Nuffield College, Oxford, and an editor of the *Journal of Latin American Studies*.

Abraham F. Lowenthal is professor of international relations at the University of Southern California and executive director of the Inter-American Dialogue.

Index

267